D0054243

AMERICA-WATCHING

GERALD W. JOHNSON

AMERICA-WATCHING

Perspectives in the Course of an Incredible Century

with an introduction by
Henry Steele Commager

1976

STEMMER
HOUSE
PUBLISHERS, INC.

Owings Mills, Maryland 21117

Inquiries are to be directed to
Stemmer House Publishers, Inc.
2627 Caves Road, Owings Mills,
Maryland 21117

A Barbara Holdridge book
Printed and bound in the United States of America
First Edition

Library of Congress Cataloging in Publication Data

Johnson, Gerald White, 1890-
  America-watching.

  Bibliography: p.
  Includes index.
  1. United States—Civilization—20th century—Addresses, essays, lectures. I. Title.

El69.12.J64   973.9   76-12459

ISBN 0-916144-05-4

CONTENTS

Introduction   ix

THE 1920s

Fourteen Equestrian Statues of
   Colonel Simmons   3

The Third Republic—and After:
   Meditations upon Our Plutocratic
   Government   7

Baltimore: a Very Great Lady
   Indeed   14

Southern Image-Breakers   21

The Cadets of New Market:
   a Reminder to the
   Critics of the South   27

How a Lover Celebrated His Lady by
   Saying Nothing
   from *Andrew Jackson:
   An Epic in Homespun*   38

THE 1930s

The Policeman's Bed of Roses   41

Bryan, Thou Shouldst Be Living:
   a Plea for Demagogues   46

For Ignoble Pacifism   53

Since Wilson   58

What an Old Girl Should Know   68

If There Is a Maryland   76

A Piano with Dirty Keys
   from *A Little Night Music:
   Discoveries in the Exploitation
   of an Art*   84

An Excuse for Universities   92

This Terrifying Freedom   100

One for Roosevelt   107

When to Build a Barricade   110

THE 1940s

To Our Thirty-Year-Olds   120

Roosevelt Against Hitler   128

The Changelings
   from *American Heroes
   and Hero-Worship*   140

The Liberal of 1946   155

The Devil Is Dead,
   and What a Loss!   159

THE 1950s

Not to Be Taken for Granted   165

The Villains   171

One Abides: He Has Lived
   from *Incredible Tale: The Odyssey
   of the Average American in the
   Last Half-Century*   180

Romance and Mr. Babbitt   183

Mudslinging as a Fine Art   185

The Stevenson Blade   187

Oppenheimer: The Right to
   Be Wrong   189

Beyond Indo-China   190

L'il Abner Nixon   192

If It Isn't Joe   194

Athens and Sparta and
   Red China   195

Nixon's Indispensable Man   197

Henry L. Mencken
   (1880-1956)   199

The Next Chapter   203

Indorsing a Philosopher, a Pope
   and a Poet
   from *The Lunatic Fringe*   205

A Measure of Doubt   211

The Hangman Cometh   213

The Ears of Midas   215

Personality in Journalism   217

John Foster Dulles   224

Time to Get Up   226

THE 1960s

Come Forth, Dickens! 228
To Live and Die in Dixie 230
I'm for Adlai Stevenson 239
If He Scrapes Off the Barnacles 241
He Will Be Great 243
What Every Man Knows 244
What Is Kennedy? 246
God Was Bored 248
The Cult of the Motor Car 250
Our Need to Know 252
By Hook or Crook 254
Meditation on 1963 256
"Once Touched by Romance" 262
Judgment in Mississippi 264
After Forty Years—Dixi 266
Adlai Stevenson 273
Laugh, Casca, Laugh! 274
The End of Incredulity 278
Program for the
    Mini-Intellectual 285

THE 1970s

Presidential Bowstring 291
Reflections at 80 293
The Turkey-Gobbler Strut:
    A Dangerous Political
    Infection 296
Watergate: One End,
    but Which? 302
Position Paper for the
    American Realist, 1974 308
On Voting Democratic: Confession
    of a Party-Liner 314
The Nothing King 318
Truman Nostalgia 320
The End of the Beginning 325

Bibliography of Longer Works 333

Index 335

Note: Consult the index for full names of persons identified partially in the text.

ACKNOWLEDGMENT

While I wrote the text, this book is mainly the achievement of two women who did the heavy work of assembling, editing and preparing the contents. They are Kathryn Johnson, my wife, and Barbara Holdridge, my publisher, to whom my Scottish grandfather, had he known them, would have awarded his highest encomium: "a lady of quality."

G.W.J.

The publisher is in every way indebted to Kathryn Johnson, who devotedly preserved all the writings of her husband through fifty-five years, for her staunch friendship and aid in bringing this book to fruition; and to Gerald Johnson, always the "parfit, gentil knight."

INTRODUCTION

For more than half a century now, Gerald Johnson has been not only a public figure but an institution. As a writer he is indefatigable: daily editorials, weekly columns in the *Sunpapers* of Baltimore; articles in half the journals of the country—proper journals like the *Atlantic Monthly* and the *American Scholar,* and improper journals like the old *American Mercury* and the *New Republic;* books pouring out from the presses—biographies, histories, even novels—and just to fill in the idle moments, a running commentary on almost everything in lectures and addresses. It is all formidable quantitatively, but it is not the quantity that most impresses us: other journalists and historians have achieved that.

No, what is impressive is the quality—a quality unfailingly Johnsonian. What is impressive is that for fifty years Gerald Johnson has been a most perspicacious reporter of the passing scene, a thoughtful interpreter of politics and morals, a re-creator of the American past, and, for good measure, a prophet of the American future. One of Henry L. Mencken's aptest disciples, he possesses a style unfailingly lively, pungent and witty, and often eloquent; and it has one quality that Mencken conspicuously lacked—at least in his journalistic forays: it is balanced and judicious. Like Mencken, Gerald Johnson has enjoyed deflating pretentiousness, exposing hypocrisy and puncturing vanity, but equally he has enjoyed celebrating honesty and wisdom and virtue. He grew up (who among us did not?) under the shadow of Mencken and in the sunlight of Walter Lippmann. Like Mencken he can pack a punch; like Lippman he can be magisterial: what a combination.

Johnson came out of North Carolina—more particularly out of Baptist Wake Forest College, to which he has always confessed a deep loyalty. He has remained, for all his cosmopolitanism, very much a Southerner, as he has remained, for all his worldliness, very much a moralist. He began on the Greensboro, North Carolina *Daily News,* where he wrote mostly about the Tarheel State, laying about him mightily. He graduated to a professorship at Chapel Hill where his interests turned to the past and to scholarship. He advanced to a post-graduate journalism and commentary on the Sunpapers of Baltimore, then among the very best in the country. There he embraced the whole national scene, and there he began that career of America-watching which he has followed so assiduously ever since.

Professor Johnson's study of America has always been retrospective as well as current and—increasingly in the later years—prospective. He early launched himself on the turbulent seas of biography and history, and his historical writings cover the American scene from Randolph of Roanoke and Andrew Jackson to Woodrow Wilson and F.D.R. Nor has he neglected the ladies—real ladies, like Dolley Madison, and termagants like Carry Nation. His interpretations cover—one is tempted to say—almost everything: formal (he can be formal) essays on literature and music and on education, higher and not so high, all drawing on his rich store of classical and Scriptural learning, and of English poetry.

"The will to know," said the philosopher Karl Jaspers, "is not a harmless business." Mr. Johnson quotes this, as he quotes Horace's *sapere aude*—have the courage to know—with approval. Mr. Johnson has never lacked the courage to know—and to tell the world what he knew and what he thought, too. In all this he has been remarkably consistent, and why not? men's characters are pretty well formed by the time they are twenty, after all, and Mr. Johnson's character and philosophy display an unmarred consistency from youth to age. As a young man he had the courage to denounce the South of the Ku Klux Klan and segregation, the South of Gastonia and Marion, the South of Vardaman and Coley Blease who, if not quite as dangerous as George Wallace, were just as revolting. He had the courage to belabor the vulgar antics of the House UnAmerican Activities Committee which lingered on for over thirty years, proving just how unAmerican Congress could be when it wanted to. He had the courage to mock Senator McCarthy and to denounce the excesses of the Cold War and the wickedness and folly of the Vietnam War, and the usurpation of Richard Nixon which placed the Constitution in mortal peril.

This is one theme which runs through the whole of Mr. Johnson's writing—the necessity of freedom and justice in our society. Another theme —and here he was at one with Mencken—was the idiocy, the vulgarity and the buffoonery of much that passes as politics in America—politics at every level, local, state and national. Johnson's heroes are Washington, Jefferson, and—in his own lifetime—Woodrow Wilson, who, like Johnson himself, was a product of a religion-affiliated college in North Carolina; and he never ceases to inquire what happened to the American genius for statesmanship and political leadership, or to raise the question—ever more importunate— whether we can survive without the kind of statesmanship that the generation of the Founding Fathers provided.

Confronted with excesses—and what America-watcher is not—Mr. Johnson fears the excesses of the Right far more than those of the Left—of a Nixon, let us say, rather than of a McGovern. For he agrees with William Ellery Channing that what we need is radicalism: the conservatives can be counted on to take care of themselves! And he quotes with approval Woodrow Wilson's observation on the exuberance of the young, that it is "an effort of Nature to release the generous energies of our people." For—and here Mr. Johnson differs strikingly from Henry L. Mencken—he believes that Americans are indeed capable of generous energies. Democracy, he confesses, is short-sighted, wrong-headed, ignorant, frivolous and inconstant, but still does better than any other system and, with the leadership of a Wilson or an Adlai Stevenson, can rise to heights of valor and magnanimity. We have crises enough—increasingly Johnson's writing is addressed to these—but not leadership; now, at the close of a long life, Mr. Johnson is no longer confident that we can summon up the virtue and find the leadership that will enable us to solve the problems that crowd upon us.

> *The defeat and death of the Republic* (he writes) *will come not when it loses its armies and fleets, but when it loses its own self-confidence,*

*its certainty that its high destiny is linked with liberty, and in that
faint-hearted moment surrenders, not to the Russians or the Chinese,
but to panic.*

But Mr. Johnson is to the end an America-watcher: more than anything he is determined to be around to see how it all comes out—the American experiment, the human experiment.

*To a newspaperman it is the breath of life to be around when the great
story breaks. In 1789 the national republic plunged into the fog and came
through very well, but that is no guarantee that the imperial republic
will be as lucky. Either course may end in disaster, but if so it will be a
honey, possibly involving the end of civilization.... What is just around
the corner for this nation is certainly no triviality. It may very well be
hellfire and damnation, but it might be a period of greatness beyond
our imagining.*

One of the liveliest essays in this collection is called "Not to be Taken
for Granted." Mr. Johnson has been around now for two generations, and we
tend to take him for granted; indeed we can scarcely imagine the journalistic
landscape without him. We should not take him for granted; we should
thank our lucky stars that we have had him for so long and that we still have
him. Justice Holmes used to say that one of the qualities of greatness was in
being *there*. Gerald Johnson has been *there;* he is still *there;* in his ebullient
person, and in his writings, he will be *there* for a long time.

HENRY STEELE COMMAGER

Amherst, Massachusetts
March 1976

FOURTEEN EQUESTRIAN STATUES OF COLONEL SIMMONS

Colonel William Joseph Simmons, founder of the Ku Klux Klan, probably will go to his grave without receiving from a grateful South that tribute of weeping, honor and song prescribed as the just due of a citizen whose services to the state have been of extraordinary value. Colonel Simmons, it is true, has not gone altogether without reward. He has an imperial title, an imperial palace and, if rumor lieth not, an income rather better than imperial. But these, except the title, are material things and probably dross to a spirit avid not of gain but of glory. Ironic fate has contrived that even the title, doubtless most precious of the Colonel's possessions, is of a style that gives the lie to the Colonel's most important work in the world. He is Emperor of the Invisible Empire, and no association of ideas can connect the word "emperor" (except unfortunately) with the names of Brutus, Kosciusko, Marco Bozzaris, Lincoln and Enver Pasha; yet if history is to classify men according to the net result of their work in the world it is into this list of the great Liberators that the name of Simmons must go. There is a steady increase of the evidence that his work will put him there, willy-nilly, and due acknowledgment of the fact might as well be made before his epitaph is written.

The sober truth is that Colonel Simmons is swiftly winning a just claim to recognition as the Deliverer of the South. Not from negro domination. That was purchased long ago at the inconsiderable price of a Presidency of Rutherford B. Hayes. Nor has he freed us from danger of domination either by the successors of Peter or the seed of Abraham, since no such danger ever existed in the South. It is a menace more subtle and insidious than negro, Jew or Catholic that the knights of the Ku Klux Klan are attacking with every promise of success. It is a spiritual bondage of the South that they are breaking; and if they succeed, who could in justice deny their present Emperor the more illustrious title of Emancipator?

The careless superficiality with which the Ku Klux phenomenon has been examined by most of those who have written on the subject is incredible. Most of the accounts of its origin and increase might have been written by scandalized Catholics, Israelites, or negroes for the light that they throw upon its more profound cause and its less immediate effects. Without exception so far as I know, the writers have assumed that the order owes its existence to a contempt for established authority in the South. The truth is exactly the reverse. Far from proving that Dixie is fierce, haughty and intractable, the Klan is merely the latest demonstration of the amazing docility of the masses of the South.

The evidence is so obvious that it is astonishing that it has been over-looked. The thing that the investigators have ignored unanimously is the fact that, while Colonel Simmons did found the order, its principles were not original with him. He did no more than organize an agency to carry into effect, in due form and order, the prevailing social, political and religious doctrine of the region. White supremacy certainly did not originate with him. Detestation of Jews is still more remote from Atlanta in its beginnings. Admirers of Dr. Martin Luther will hardly concede that Colonel Simmons was the first man ever to hold the church of Rome in slight esteem. And suspicion and dislike of foreigners was a prominent characteristic of the peo-ple with whom history began. Long before William Joseph Simmons became Imperial Wizard, long before he became even a Colonel of Woodmen of the World, long before he practiced as a local preacher of the Methodist per-suasion, in fact, long before he was born, the principles of the Ku Klux were fixed and established among native white gentile Protestants in the South. Press and pulpit harped upon them daily. For scurrilous abuse of the Catholic church, for instance, no kleagle, klud, titan, cyclops or goblin ever could hold a candle to many a backwoods preacher or peripatetic evangelist performing regularly in the South. For vilification of foreigners and surly suspicion of new ideas the propagandists of the Klan found precedents in the campaign speeches of candidates for every elective office in the South for the past thirty years. The Klan's crazy idea of what constitutes Anglo-Saxon civilization was not conceived by William Joseph Simmons in a fit of delirium tremens, but is precisely the conception presented for years by a considerable proportion of the Southern press, and but rarely challenged by those Southern journals that are fairly intelligent.

The vast success of the organizers of the Klan is absolute proof that they went to the masses in the South with no brand-new philosophy. Neither did they propose any startling innovation in procedure. Stepping outside of the law to achieve a laudable end is not regarded as a serious crime in the South. The South discovered nearly sixty years ago what was revealed to the North only when the Eighteenth Amendment gripped it, namely, that the law is an ass. Therefore the proposal of the Ku Klux organizers that enforcement of the current religious, social and political code be removed from the hands of the peace officers and undertaken by a masked secret order was not par-ticularly shocking to the average barber or cotton mill hand. The soundness of Ku Klux doctrine seemed to him to be beyond debate, for had not its essentials been expounded for years by his pastor, his paper and his political boss? The methods of the Klan seemed only slightly irregular, for had they not been winked at in the South ever since Reconstruction? On the other hand, the possibilities of the Klan as a purveyor of pleasurable excitement are obvious even to a moron, and its capability of being used as an instrument of private vengeance is clear to a knave of rudimentary intelligence. It was bound to flourish.

But the greatness of its success has had the effect of rousing the intelligence of the South to a realization of the thralldom under which it has lain. It has revealed to the South that its lack of keen and relentless self-criticism, the only effective social prophylaxis, has laid it open to invasion by any sort of disease. It has shown how an intelligence not vigorously on the alert to resist every attack will eventually be laid by the heels while kleagles and wizards triumph over it.

Many and many an intelligent Southerner has sat somnolently in his pew while his pastor, snorting prodigiously, applied to the Pope all the curses in the Apocalypse. He has read in his newspaper miles of editorial belchings about the immorality, treachery, poltroonery and fantastic wickedness of all the nations of Europe. He has heard reports of the way in which the honorable gentleman from Stinking Quarters, candidate for coroner subject to the action of the Democratic primary, has risen in his campaign speeches to heights of imbecility that Bedlam never dreamed when he paid tribute to the beauty, the chivalry, the godliness and the wisdom of this Our Southland. Yet it has actually never occurred to him that it is his manifest sacred duty as Christian, scholar and patriot, to strive for the unfrocking of the Rev. Andrew Gump on the ground that he is preaching diabolism in the name of Christianity, to cancel his subscription to his newspaper unless and until it discards the custom of seeking its editor among the inmates of a madhouse, and to greet the candidate for coroner with an enthusiastic kick.

But Colonel William Joseph Simmons has revealed to him in startling fashion the imperative nature of that duty. Colonel Simmons has organized those who take seriously the empty gabble of political, religious and journalistic blatherskites, thereby filling that vacuity with possibilities of infinite mischief. The deliverances of the lower orders of Southern divines on Romanism may be, regarded strictly as sermons, as futile as they are ignorant and foolish; but they may be fearfully effective as incitations to the gas-house gang to beat up old Father O'Connor. Editorials on the total depravity of Europe written by Greeleys who have never crossed the State line may be worth slightly less than the ink required to print their final exclamation point if they are valued strictly as editorials; but they may have power to move a platoon of masked barbers to wreck Pete Skalchunes' banana stand while Pete is foregathering with his brother Shriners at his lodge meeting. Even the ultimate imaginable achievement of fatuity, the campaign speech, may so intoxicate the inferior classes with a false sense of their dignity, wisdom and worth as Southerners that they may presume to use their secret organization to censor the morals and manners of their superiors.

These outrages are to be prevented only by removing their cause. This cause, it cannot be asserted too emphatically, is not the Knights of the Ku Klux Klan. Unassisted, they are as incapable of understanding the desirability of pogroms directed against Catholics and negroes as well as Jews as they are incapable of understanding the theory of relativity, or Beethoven's Fifth Symphony, or that two and two make four. If their minds ever worked, except as they are goaded and guided into working, they would almost immediately work out the absurdity of the whole preposterous business. In fact, in most communities the organizers did gather in a few men capable of voluntary cerebration, which explains the wholesale desertions of the Klan that almost invariably have occurred a few months after the organization of a new klavern. The fact that a man remains a knight for any considerable length of time is conclusive proof that that man never thinks. The knight is no peculiar being; his intellectual and spiritual brethren swarm in the ranks of every fraternal order in the republic, including the Knights of Columbus, B'nai B'rith and the Sons and Daughters of I Will Arise.

The cause of the sinister record of the Ku Klux Klan is not to be found in its personnel, which is as harmless as that of the Junior Order of United American Mechanics. It is to be found among those agencies that have pumped the empty skulls of the knights full of hatred and suspicion of other creeds, other races, and other nationalities than their own. The fight of the intelligent South must be made on these agencies. But these agencies include large and influential sections of the Southern press, pulpit and political organizations. To attack these, the Southerner must burst all bonds of conservative tradition, break with the past and defy the present with the bald, unequivocal and conclusive assertion that lying is wrong.

The revolutionary character of such a declaration is derived, of course, from its lack of modification. It is traditionally wrong for the cook to lie about the eggs she stole, or for any salaried employee drawing less than five thousand dollars a year to vary in the least from strict accuracy in his reports. It is only in businessmen known to Bradstreet that lying becomes acumen; only in editors that it becomes the creation of healthy public opinion; only in politicians that it becomes patriotism; and only in holy orders that it rises to the crowning dignity of defense of the faith. It is by revealing to the literate minority in the South that a liar in any of these positions is really more pernicious than a lying cook or clerk that Colonel William Joseph Simmons has wrought his great work of liberation. It required some such work as his to do it; therefore if there is any sense of justice in the South it will in years to come hold his memory in esteem.

Uproarious patriot that he is, Colonel Simmons probably will not share in the regret of others that circumstances apparently are going to confine the liberating influence of his career to his native section. If there were any way of getting rid of the Ku Klux except the arduous and painful way of turning honest the South unquestionably would adopt it. The Southerner is no more than human. In his objection to having his own weaknesses and follies thrust upon his attention he is indistinguishable from a New Englander, and almost as much inclined to overestimate his own virtues.

But Simmons and circumstances have left him no choice. Elsewhere the Knights of Columbus, the tribal orders of Israel, and the National Association for the Advancement of Colored People may be relied upon to define and delimit the activities of the klansmen. Recent history has proved that buckshot may furnish an effective cure when exhortation and admonition fail, and that that remedy is pretty certain to be applied. But the situation in the South is different, for none of the three powers cited above possesses in many communities below the Potomac strength enough to cope with the Invisible

Empire. If she is not to turn entirely imperialist the South must escape by strengthening her republican institutions with practically no assistance from K. of C., B'nai B'rith, or W. E. Burghardt Du Bois. The hard-pressed South is under the necessity of restoring law and order by strictly lawful and orderly means!

In view of the fact that the South is thoroughly American, one might reasonably conclude that it can't be done. But such a conclusion, after all, gives small credit to the celebrated ingenuity of the American; the fact that he has never done anything of that sort before is surely no conclusive proof that he never will do it. Besides, the effort required in this particular instance is not superhuman. To suppress the Ku Klux it is not necessary for the South to achieve and maintain anything remotely approaching absolute intellectual integrity. She has merely to become a little more honest, intelligent and liberal than any section of the country is at present.

Yet this accomplishment, relatively trifling as it may seem, would be of such vast importance that the man through whose agency it came to pass is entitled to the grateful recognition of the section. The least that is due Colonel Simmons is the erection by each Southern State of an equestrian statue of the Emperor-Emancipator as the chief ornament of its capitol grounds. Let no one raise the foolish objection that the Colonel is unaware of what he is doing. What liberator ever foresaw the final result of his efforts? Did Garibaldi expect to raise Mussolini to the throne of the Caesars? Did Lincoln expect to open the way to fame and fortune for John Arthur Johnson?

HARPER'S MAGAZINE, *February 1928*

THE THIRD REPUBLIC — AND AFTER

Meditations upon Our Plutocratic Government

I t has been approximately half a century since Roscoe Conkling informed a Republican National Convention that if asked whence came his candidate he would reply, "He comes from Appomattox." This answer, as the *précieuses* would say, stood the convention on its ear, and the fact affords a certain insight into the psychology of that convention. If Conkling had said, "He comes

from the American Exchange Irving Trust Company, Capital $32,000,000"
he would not have achieved the same effect.

If some mighty orator of 1928 should nominate, say, Machine-Gun
Parker with the remark that he comes from Château Thierry, the convention
would applaud, of course, but in a fatally decorous manner, and some other
candidate would get the votes. For we are no longer living in 1880, and the
spell of military adventure works less mightily upon us than does the logic
of Field Marshal Sir William Robertson, who has discovered that war is a
fool's game.

But it does not follow that we are disillusioned as to all games. The
soldier may be revealed as a puppet, worked by strings held in invisible hands,
but there are still magicians. The captains and the kings depart, but business
goes on at the old stand, and the Ku Klux Klan and finance still produce
wizards. Some of us, indeed, are pretty well convinced that the wizardry of
the Ku Klux is comprised in a bed-sheet, wherein we are probably in error.
But what sound hundred-percenter harbors the shadow of a suspicion that
the great lords of the business world are anything less than great lords? Julius
Rosenwald, indeed, asserted the other day that one of the most important
elements in the making of a vast fortune is blind luck. But Mr. Rosenwald
is relatively a still, small voice as against the thunderous chorus of the country.

I do not mean that we fall down and worship the satraps of our economic empire. On the contrary, many of us are persuaded that they are
altogether evil. But we do believe in them. We think them potent for good
or for ill; and our political activity consists largely in fighting for them or
against them. In short, either as protagonists or as antagonists, they dominate
the scene.

I submit that an America which the Plutocrats dominate openly is not
the America of 1880. To be sure, they were pretty successful in getting what
they wanted during the administration of Grant. But they got it more or less
secretly. They did not appear on the stage in their own proper persons and
monopolize the limelight.

But as the year preceding the present Presidential election wears away
and the time for choosing a nominee comes to be reckoned in months, there
are in the dominant party at least half a dozen men of immense wealth who
are admittedly probable choices. Mr. Mellon is perhaps the second richest
man in the country. Mr. Hoover is said to have made his first million at the
age of twenty-seven. Mr. Lowden married a Pullman. Mr. Dawes, before he
entered politics, was a power among the great bankers. Mr. Longworth's family
owns the heart of Cincinnati's business district. Mr. Hughes is not, indeed, a
multi-millionaire, but the year he withdrew from public life to recoup his
personal fortune he is said to have paid taxes on an income of about fifty
thousand dollars; and a man who regards his fortune at a low ebb when he
draws only fifty thousand dollars a year is not to be numbered among the
paupers.

It is impossible to forecast the situation next June. It is within the realm
of possibility that some impecunious citizen may have captured the imagina-

tion of the Republican Party by that time. But now six months prior to the convention, Republican leaders are so strongly convinced of the possibility of electing a millionaire President of the United States that they are giving scant attention to anyone else.

Does anyone believe that they would have given serious consideration to a millionaire in 1880, or in 1896, or even as late as 1912? In those days a Plutocrat might work from behind the scenes, but as an active candidate for the Presidency he belonged to an ineligible class. Today his class is so far from being ineligible that six months prior to the convention it seems to be the only eligible class, in so far as the party in power is concerned. That is to say, Republican political leaders—on this subject the best-informed persons in the country—are convinced that it is entirely feasible to elect a millionaire President.

This has not been true since the early days of the Republic. George Washington, indeed, was immensely rich, but it is significant that the fact is forgotten. George was so many other things that his status as a Plutocrat didn't count either for him or against him. The thing that did count was his status as a gentleman, as a member of a ruling caste which based its claims to power on aristocratic standards.

For it was an aristocratic republic that the men who overthrew the British autocracy set up in its stead. It was the third profound alteration in our polity. The country, when it became the habitat of white men, really began as a theocracy which gradually merged into an autocracy as the royal power undermined and supplanted the power of the clergy who, in the beginning, ruled as effectively in Virginia as they did in Massachusetts. Even Maryland, traditionally the home of religious tolerance, had its Puritan revolution in the seventeenth century. At one time the clergy were the dominant personalities in every community from Charleston to Boston, and we had, for all practical purposes, a theocratic government.

But, like the Israelites and the frogs, we demanded a king; and George III, like Saul and the stork, proved more than had been bargained for. So down he went, and the First Republic rose under another George who did not claim to be royal, but who was lordly, all the same. A country at war has, of course, a very special form of government, namely, martial law; and after 1783 there were several years when the government of the United States was nondescript. So the First Republic really dates from 1789, when the Constitution was adopted.

It lasted just forty years, but it was a fancy government while it lasted. Gentlemen only were allowed a voice in the settlement of affairs of great importance. Gentlemen manned the American embassies abroad and gentlemen only were eligible candidates for the Presidency. The Virginia Dynasty not only ruled, but ruled with an air. The only exception to its chosen succession, John Adams, strengthened, rather than weakened, the aristocratic tradition. True, one of the giants of the Virginia Dynasty was Jefferson, the Bolshevik, but he was a Bolshevik in the proper English tradition, in alignment with, say, Bertrand Russell or Ramsay Macdonald, rather than with Leon

Trotsky. He was well born, a man of property, and had the cultivated tastes of the upper classes—an eye for architecture, an ear for music, and a keen appreciation of fine wines and fine wits.

So the First Republic set up a standard of conduct which could be, and was, approved by the English gentry. It had its crudities, but it was by long odds the most polished government the country has ever known, and its charm has lingered in memory so long that sentimentalists are prone to believe that it was the Golden Age of America.

But the history of nations is one long reiteration of the axiom that your ruling class, no matter how good, will go down when there appears in some other class a "harder-boiled egg" than the ruling class can produce. George Washington was as hard as they made them in his day, but James Monroe was softer, and John Quincy Adams softer than Monroe. In 1828 the farther west you went the harder the politicians grew, and Andrew Jackson came from the extreme frontier. He took the theories of Thomas Jefferson perfectly seriously. His philosophy was that it matters but little how you played the game, provided you won. He won in 1828, and the following March the First Republic passed away.

Then came the democratic Second Republic, to rule for ninety years. This was incomparably the noisiest regime the country has ever known. The two administrations of Jackson, in which the Second Republic was established, were the most clamorous administrations ever heard in time of peace. In this uproar Democracy captured Washington. Thirty-five years later, to an artillery obbligato, it captured the country, when Lincoln's million bayonets swept away the last formal negation of democratic theory that still lingered in our governmental system. Fifty years after that it grasped at the empery of the world, and in the thunder of the greatest war ever fought the democratic Second Republic blew up.

But noise was not all there was to it. The Second Republic was enormous. Its mistakes were gigantic, but its triumphs were great, also, and its aspirations prodigious. It lacked the grace, the wit, the charm of the First Republic. It could produce a many-sided Roosevelt, but not a man with the innumerable facets of Jefferson. It could produce a Lincoln, who had the greatness of soul, but not the greatness of manner, of Washington. And when it rode to ruin, it rode with a man who seems to have been mistaken, and who may have been quite mad, but who was, in the language of the philologists, certainly no piker. It is far too early to attempt to evaluate the statecraft of Woodrow Wilson, but if we assume the worst, and rate it as a total loss, even then we must admit that the man's fall was attributable to no simple misstep, but to such a fault as Phaëton's, who seized the chariot of the Sun and fell only when he was struck from heaven by the thunderbolt of Jove himself.

There was greatness in the Second Republic. There must have been, or it could not have dreamed such mighty dreams.

But it has passed, and the Third Republic reigns in its stead. As the gentleman was the master of the First Republic, as the man of the people—apparent or real—was the master of the Second, so the Plutocrat is master of the Third. As usual, it began its reign with a momentary triumph of its extremists. At the beginning of the First Republic there were those who wished to call Washington "Majesty" and install him in office for life. At the beginning of the Second, there were men who thought democracy meant permission to stand with muddy boots on damask-covered chairs in the White House and to insult their betters in the streets. So at the beginning of the Third Republic there was the Ohio Gang.

The inevitable result is that Plutocracy begins its reign with a bad name. Arguing from the particular to the general, many people think Plutocrat is synonymous with thief, just as foggy-minded people used to think that aristocrat is synonymous with snob and democrat with boor. But the thieves are really the camp-followers of Plutocracy, not its commanders; and one of its first tasks, once it was really established in Washington, was to put an end to the thieving.

It is foolish to rail at Plutocracy on account of what it does, for it is giving us, and may be expected to continue to give us, what is in many respects the best government we have ever had. If he is the least inspired, the Plutocrat is also the least dizzy of all our rulers, not excluding those in the pre-republican era of theocracy and autocracy. The foundation of his statecraft indeed may be described in two words—No Nonsense. Since the average man has always suffered much more from the nonsense than from the rascality of his rulers, this is, from his standpoint, an excellent foundation for any polity.

The catalogue of the merits of Plutocratic government, as those merits appear to the commoner, must begin with its dislike of first-class wars. Under the Plutocracy, the average man's chance of being dragged out of his home by conscript officers and sent to stop an enemy bullet is extremely remote. The Plutocrats understand too well that in a first-class war everybody loses, including the investment bankers. Therefore, such wars as it will fight will be reasonable wars, small wars with clearly defined and attainable objects. Plutocracy will never sally out in defense of idealism—to make the world safe for any idea, to relieve oppressed nationalities, or to avenge an insult to the national dignity, provided the insulter is really a first-rate fighting power. When it goes to war, it will be to gain something definite, as, for example, the mahogany of Nicaragua, the sugar of Haiti, or to retain the rubber of the Philippines. But there are always volunteers enough to fight these small wars, and no need of conscripting the average workman.

Then if great wars are unlikely under the Plutocracy, so are other scourges of populations, such as pestilence and famine. The Plutocrats are not illiterate in the social sciences, for economics happens to be the first of them and in its broadest aspects includes the others. The intelligent Plutocrat appreciates the necessity of keeping the livestock in prime condition. He does not relish the prospect of having to operate his business with starveling workmen; therefore, he favors a wage scale that will enable his operatives to be always well fed. Nor does he care to risk having his working force decimated by disease, not to mention his own risk of contagion; therefore, he favors maintaining the public health services at a high level of efficiency. Education and recreation are so intimately involved in the problem of public health that they, too, are bound to be supported by any really intelligent Plutocratic government.

Therefore, the chances are at least even that under the plutocratic Third Republic the average American will be better fed, better clothed and better housed than he ever was before.

What, then, is to be urged against it? Nothing, so far as I can see, except the probability that it will pave the way for a frightful catastrophe, namely, the establishment of the Fourth Republic, which is likely to be atavistic.

For the Plutocracy cannot possibly last. With all its merits, it has one defect that is fatal. It is so damnably dull that eventually the people are certain to rise against it and destroy it out of sheer boredom.

Man shall not live by bread alone. He must have circuses, also, and these the Plutocracy is simply incapable of providing. Its motto is No Nonsense, and it is fundamentally the most idiotic motto statesmen can adopt, for where there is no nonsense the government perishes. There is no lack, Heaven knows, of nonsense in America to-day, but the trouble is that it all operates against the ruling caste, rather than in its favor. Plutocracy is, in the very nature of things, as unemotional as compound interest. It regards emotion as nonsense and is, therefore, impotent to capitalize it.

Who was the most powerful individual politician in our history? Andrew Jackson, of course. He captured the government, he put through every important item of his program, he defeated every enemy who rose against him, and at the end of his second term, so far from declining in popular power, he was able to dictate the succession. Who came closest to tying that record? Theodore Roosevelt, without doubt.

As regards their political philosophy, Jackson and Roosevelt were far apart, but one thing they had in common—they were both interesting. During the eight years that Jackson, and the seven that Roosevelt, resided there, not a single dull day was seen at the White House. To borrow a phrase from the theologians, hell popped continually. Is this state of affairs imaginable under a Plutocrat of the first order? If Andrew Mellon, for example, were President of the United States, it is impossible for any sane man to conceive of stories coming out of Washington to the effect that the President was threatening to hang the Vice President, or inviting Chief Justice Taft to go out and enforce the Volstead law himself, since he had sustained it judicially, or bawling out American women for not patronizing the maternity hospitals more extensively, or sending United States marshals to chase the editor of the New York *World* into foreign lands.

No, President Mellon would be correct, soft-spoken, reasonable, and unexciting. He would be admired, but not idolized. And he might be defeated for re-election.

Eventually the Plutocratic candidate for President will be defeated, and what then? Aye, there's the rub! With theocracy, autocracy, aristocracy, democracy and plutocracy all behind us, we shall pretty well have run the gamut. What then?

I advance the suggestion that we may start all over again. To support it, I invite attention to certain phenomena of the last five years, roughly the period since Wilson and the Second Republic blew up together.

What are the great movements that have agitated the public since 1922? I mean the things that have really agitated the great mass of the people, not such playthings of the intellectuals as the World Court, disarmament, and the payment of war debts. Obviously, they are three in number, namely, prohibition, fundamentalism and Ku Kluxism. Each of these has produced fistfights, as well as formal debates. Each is, therefore, a matter that "comes home to men's business and bosoms." Each is a weapon made to the hand of a leader strong enough and clever enough to wield a mighty blade.

Now the characteristic common to the three is the fact that each purports to be divinely inspired and to be, therefore, not an appeal to men's interests, but the embodiment of a moral principle. Their protagonists and, in the main, their anatagonists as well, demand support, not as a matter of policy, but as a matter of righteousness. The basic assumption of prohibitionists, fundamentalists and Ku Klux Klansmen alike is that the most important function of the United States government is not the accommodation of conflicting interests and the establishment of a *modus vivendi* in a necessarily imperfect world, but the establishment and guarding of the rule of righteousness within its jurisdiction. And that assumption, it seems, has power to move more people than any other idea which impinges upon politics.

This is, however, nothing unprecedented. It is simply a revival of the philosophy of theocracy. The drift is plainly toward re-establishment of the most ancient form of government that the English-speaking inhabitants of this continent have known. The indications are that the Fourth Republic will be a theocratic republic.

As the aristocrat was for a while admittedly the most important personage upon the national stage; as the democrat later was the figure that held the limelight; as the plutocrat now commands most of our attention; so, apparently, will the Bluenose stand in the estimation of our children.

Our children? Well, at least let us hope that the next revolution will be postponed so long. For to the remnant of us whose minds hark back sentimentally to the old days of the Second Republic the prospect is sufficiently appalling. We are aware that all human attempts to rule in the name of God have uniformly resulted in a polity that might much more appropriately have been established in the name of Satan.

If theocracy must be re-established, your congenital democrat prefers not to be here to see it. But its inevitability, after all, is predicated on the plausible, but not demonstrable, theory that the youngsters are no better than we are. There remains always the half-doubt that we are really the finest fellows that ever will be created. It is conceivable that this uproarious younger generation may develop a sounder political wisdom than is known to us.

The demand for stimulants apparently is everlasting. Deprived of alcohol and the heady wine of democracy, the present generation tends to adopt vitriolic beverages and still more fiery ideas—the moonshine of theological controversy, for example, or some such antifreezing mixture as Big Bill Thompson's political philosophy. But the stuff is deadly. We know it, but apparently we can do no better.

Let us speak for ourselves. In time youth will discover the deadliness of these things, and perhaps it will know how to do better. The contrary cannot be proved, and the scientific spirit never accepts as truth anything which is unproved. That being the case, let us scientifically bet our shirts on the boys.

THE CENTURY MAGAZINE, *May 1928*

BALTIMORE

A Very Great Lady Indeed

The song is vaguely associated with troop trains crowded with soldiers clad in blue, whose officers had a broad white stripe down the seam of each trouser-leg. It seems now that it must have rung in the ears of a small boy in North Carolina who stood by the railroad tracks wide-eyed, hoping to catch a bit of hard-tack flung from a car window with "Just from Cuba" written upon it. Perhaps the rollicking air postdates the Spanish war, but I hope not. I prefer to believe that I heard it the first time bellowed from the leather lungs of the infantry. It suits them so admirably:

> *I got a gal in Baltimo'*
> *Street-cars run right by her do',*
> *Turkey-red carpet on the flo' . . ."*

That city meant nothing to me then, and not much a few years later when, as a gangling school-boy, I joined with others in issuing impassioned pleas to be carried "Back, back, back to Baltimore." But its name was a sonorous, mouth-filling vocable, and presently as the world began to impinge upon the consciousness of a growing lad, it began to gather other associations. There was a Baltimore boat running out of practically every South Atlantic port. There were consignments from Baltimore to most of the village merchants. There were trips to Baltimore by these same merchants. Presently there was a Baltimore fire of such tremendous magnitude that the old Charlotte *Observer,* driven into a frenzy of excitement, shattered all precedents by printing a two-column head on the front page!

A little later our State went dry in a sort of tentative, cautious fashion. There were no saloons any more, but postal facilities were adequate; and presently some philosopher observed that to judge by shipments through the express-office, North Carolina lived exclusively on fish and whiskey, both shipped from Baltimore. Then a sinister phrase crept into one's consciousness; people, grave-faced, would say of a neighbor, "They have taken him to Baltimore," and the mood induced was precisely that in which The Preacher must have written, "Man goeth to his long home, and the mourners go about the streets." One realized without being told that it was practically all up with the poor fellow, and the family physician, his own resources exhausted, was reduced to conjuring with those magic names, Osler, Halsted, Welch and Kelly.

There was a superior person whom one scorned publicly but admired privately for his ability to squelch all argumentation by quoting something he had read in the Baltimore *Sun,* to which he was the only subscriber in the village. And there was a wicked old man, immensely rich—they said he was worth easily $50,000—of whom it was whispered that he went regularly to Baltimore to go on a spree.

Twenty years ago the Queen of the Chesapeake loomed gigantically in the imaginations of all Southern youngsters. She was a glamorous city, full of wickedness and lust, but shining; full of wine and women, but also full of song, not altogether ribald.

"Avenge the patriotic gore
That flecked the streets of Baltimore, . . ."

filled Uncle Ben, who was crippled by a Minié ball at Sharpsburg, with positively pious fervor. Baltimore might have her stains, but her street-mobs had fallen furiously on the soldiers of the Union in 1861, however much might be forgiven her. Her heart was in the right place.

And then, somehow, Baltimore seemed to get lost. The giant of the North bit by bit absorbed her radiance, and she slid out of the consciousness of the South. People's studiedly casual references began to be to Fifth Avenue and the Waldorf-Astoria, instead of to Charles Street and the Rennert. The railroads throttled the Baltimore boat lines. The Anti-Saloon League throttled the whiskey business. "East side, West side, all about the town" drowned out "Turkey-red carpet on the flo'," and small boys who had stood wide-eyed while the blue-clad soldiers passed, grew up themselves to go swarming in dun-colored garments down to the sea at Hoboken while the bands played "Over There." The very term "Sunpaper" became strange in ears accustomed to "Woild, Hur'ld 'n' Amurrican." Baltimore faded into an old refrain sung by voices already faint and rapidly vanishing in the distance of many years: "I got a gal in Balt—"

Enter, then, along about the year 1913, a professional gentleman, laughing. He held a copy of the Baltimore *Sun* to which he invited attention in a surreptitious and picaresque fashion; for, being a professional gentleman, he was not quite sure he had a right to laugh. The article which he pointed out was a report of a revival meeting lately held by the Rev. Billy Sunday. The story carried a by-line which held no significance until the article had been read; but when he had read it, the reader, utterly bemused, returned to the by-line and stared at it, knowing that a new planet had swum into his ken. It read, "By H. L. Mencken." Shortly thereafter a book appeared containing, among others, an essay entitled "The Sahara of the Bozart." That essay whipped away in a breath the mists of antiquity that were settling around Baltimore in the eyes of the South, and endowed the city again with a startling, but distinct, individuality. Patriots damned Baltimore with damns both loud and long, but they thought about it again, and that before they began to fear they had cancer of the stomach.

So this was Baltimore Unvisited—a cosmopolis from which the ancient glory had departed, but which lately had produced a prodigy; a deserted capital which still faintly echoed of old revelry, and now began to resound to a crescent roar. To our fathers it had been indeed a great and magnificent city, and it was still a good place for sick people and doctors; but why on earth should a healthy man visit Baltimore, when the express would carry him straight through to New York? It had been a good town, but was it not now as dead as Charleston itself? Mr. Mencken, unquestionably, was very much alive, but was he not something in the nature of a sole survivor?

The South, once the great satrapy of Baltimore, would unquestionably answer these questions in the affirmative. Baltimore no longer dominates the South. Her suzerainty has gone north, and as far as the imaginations of Southerners are concerned, there is only one important stop on the line to New York, namely, Washington. Baltimore has become as dim and difficult to descry as Philadelphia, or Wilmington, Delaware, or Newark, New Jersey. One passes through all these places on the road to New York; but who ever thought of getting off at any of them? The Eighth City, and even the Third City, are left darkling in the effulgence shed abroad by the First City.

Yet if size counted for anything the tale would be different. Eighth city in the United States, Baltimore is bigger than Boston, bigger than San Francisco, bigger than Los Angeles in 1920, and far bigger than Washington. It is a great steel-manufacturing town. Its harbor receives from or despatches to a foreign port a ship for almost every hour of the day, not counting coastwise and bay traffic. It is one of the world's greatest coal-exporting ports. In population, in wealth, in industrial power, it is a very much greater city today than it ever was before.

But they don't sing about it below the Potomac any more. Soldiers don't sing about it as they go to war. Turpentine hands and cotton choppers, steel-drivin' men and tobacco curers do not embody its name in their chanteys. Small boys once dreamed of it as Whittington dreamed of London, but not now. New York has swallowed Baltimore as it has swallowed every other city along the Atlantic seaboard. New York has drained it of color, of glamor, of romance. New York has left it dry and dull.

That at least is the impression of most people of my acquaintance who do not know the city. To some extent it is shared by Baltimoreans, also. It grows steadily more difficult for any city in eastern America to retain its individuality against the influence of the monstrous congeries of cities around the mouth of the Hudson. We are in danger of developing a genuine metropolis in the territory east of the Appalachians. Already as regards the arts, the sciences, social intercourse, habits of speech and habits of thought, the other cities are satellites of New York. The danger is that presently they may cease to be planets, with a life of their own, and become unchanging, windless moons.

Yet it cannot truthfully be said that Baltimore has completely gone under. She is a genuine shellback. She is impermeable. The fact that a proposed innovation is New Yorkish makes no appeal to her, while the fact that it is an innovation is the reverse of appealing. Among American cities above the half-million class, Baltimore is unquestionably the greatest harker back. Like the gentleman who was going to Bangor to get drunk, Baltimore is becoming a modern city, but, gosh, how she dreads it! With desperate tenacity she clings to every remaining fragment of antiquity. She still has lamplighters and alley saloons. Both. diminish in number yearly, but Baltimore cherishes the few survivors. The last horse-car disappeared some years ago, but Baltimore still retains the old-fashioned overhead trolley-wires, which make the streets appear as if festooned with cobwebs.

While the "bright, bitter cities down the West" are striving desperately to become spick-and-span and imitating the showiness, if not the magnificence, of Fifth Avenue, Baltimore sets her face steadfastly in the other direction. To say that she is an ugly city is to give altogether a false impression, for ugliness ordinarily is construed as a negative quality, the absence of beauty. The astounding, the incredible, the downright fabulous ugliness of Baltimore, on the other hand, is distinctly a positive quality. The amazed newcomer to the city is almost persuaded that she studied ugliness, practiced it long and toilsomely, made a philosophy of ugliness and raised it to a fine art, so that in the end it has become a work of genius more fascinating than spick-and-span tidiness could ever be.

The center of the town conforms to no sort of standard ever heard of anywhere else. It is typical of America to the extent of having a group of vast office-buildings, but what buildings! Some of them are mere boxes, but several have achieved an architectural dizziness that makes the most eccentric of New York's look commonplace by comparison. Crazy angles, astounding cornices, dadaistic whorls and spirals mount insanely to a mad climax in a mighty tower, reminiscent of the Giralda, but capped by a patent-medicine bottle three stories high!

On the ground level the effect is masterfully carried out. With one exception, the business streets are all narrow and most of them tortuous. Parking is permitted on both sides, thereby limiting the range of vision to right and left. Projecting signs, many of them of unbelievable hideousness, effectually interfere with any possibility of a vista along such streets as are relatively straight.

Within the last twenty years since factories have sprung up all around the harbor, and especially since the building of the enormous steel mills at Sparrows Point, countless smokestacks have been belching soft-coal smoke into Baltimore's atmosphere. Therefore the prevailing tone of the business buildings, originally red, or gray, or buff, or white, is now a uniform black, except for an occasional structure on which the sand-blast men have recently been at work.

Yet the total effect is not, as you might suppose, maddening. It is not even seriously depressing. The dull coloring of the city, its emptiness of stimulation, its lack of sparkle, make for quiet, but not for melancholy. It is a slatternly city, but curiously easy, curiously comfortable. It does not spur one, but neither does it threaten. Nothing aspires in Baltimore, but nothing forbids.

It is perhaps worthwhile to repeat that all this applies to the center of the city only. Baltimore has charming suburbs. Indeed, there is some foundation for the claim that the modern "development" was invented in the Maryland metropolis. Certainly Roland Park was one of the earliest of its type in this country. Now one finds miles of streets laid out according to the best landscape engineering and lined with houses the design of each of which has passed an exacting test. In these suburbs not even the editor of the *Ladies Home Journal* could find a flaw. They are as impeccable as Mr. George F. Babbitt's model home in Zenith. But they are no more native to Baltimore than are their counterparts around every other American city. Overnight they might be detached from their present connection and attached to Cleveland, or Atlanta, or Kansas City, and no one would note anything strange the next morning.

What is typical of Baltimore, architecturally, is the famous red-brick block with white marble steps. The existence of extensive marble quarries just outside the city made such steps relatively cheap a few decades ago; and in the Victorian era the spotlessness of her steps was the basis of a housewife's reputation in the neighborhood. One shudders to think of the backaches those quarries have indirectly caused.

In those days old George Washington, standing on the top of his Doric column in Mount Vernon Place, could look over and beyond the houses of all the rulers of the city. Today the monument is in downtown Baltimore, its simple loveliness an incongruous element there, while the rulers have retired over the hills and far away.

Yet the evacuation is not accomplished with cheers and happy laughter, but with a sort of reluctance. Baltimore becomes modern, but morosely. She clings to her remnants of antiquity, such as, for example, the Camden Street Station of the Baltimore and Ohio and the Charles Street Station of the Pennsylvania. Go-getterism is not to her fancy; she accepts it, but with a certain disdain.

One who will walk in Charles Street at the proper hour on any fine afternoon may behold a marvel—namely, the spirit of Baltimore incarnate. It is a great lady, perhaps eighty years old, but still erect, taking the air as she has taken it in good weather these sixty years. When she began the practice, Charles Street was the promenade of the fashionable, and everybody who was anybody was seen there in the afternoon. Today it is to the ordinary person a clanging, howling, screeching bedlam through which trucks, trolleys, taxis, horse-drawn vehicles and private automobiles fight their way, while along the sidewalks surge mobs drawn from all the four corners of the earth. Hard-driven traffic cops fight valiantly for control, but at that, crossing Charles Street is frequently a hair-raising adventure—to ordinary persons.

But a great lady of Baltimore is not an ordinary person, and you know it the moment she comes in sight. This one, in particular, is unmistakable. She is invariably clad in black silk, yards and yards of it and of the stiffest, with a touch of white at throat and wrists. Her one concession to Time is an ebony cane. It is her sole concession, to man or to nature. She is small of stature, and her countenance is certainly not formidable; but she has The Presence. When that small, black figure moves down Charles Street, it is as if the cathedral had suddenly started out for a stroll. She takes the road, all of it, and Charles Street instantly recognizes its place and gets out of her way. She saunters into the stream of traffic; and policemen, instead of exploding into picturesque blasphemy, whirl upon the charging monsters with white gloves uplifted. Motormen and taxi-drivers slam on the brakes and pray. There is the squealing of tortured steel, the clangor of bumpers suddenly meeting; rubber slides hissing over the asphalt. But the great lady saunters through untouched, and (this is the miracle) nobody swears. For she is so obviously a great lady that all Charles Street knows she has always the right of way.

Baltimore city is in some respects the great lady. She has her habits which she disdains to alter merely to avoid being run over by a deplorably hasty and noisy world. But neither will she enter into vulgar disputation with any one. She simply holds to her course, supremely confident that the lesser breeds will scatter before her. Does the nation adopt an Eighteenth Amendment to the Constitution, contrary to Baltimore's notion of what is fitting and proper? She does not explode into vituperation; she merely shrugs and instructs her police officers to attend strictly to the business of enforcing the laws of the city and of Maryland, letting prohibition severely alone. Does the Ku Klux Klan rise to high tide on all sides of this, the colony founded by Catholic Baron Baltimore as a refuge for his coreligionists? She shrugs again and does nothing beyond seeing to it that nobody throws a brick at a Klan parade.

The rest of the country, noting these peculiarities, arrives at the conclusion that Baltimore is the most tolerant city on the Atlantic seaboard, and begins to accept at face value the *Evening Sun's* designation of the commonwealth as the Maryland Free State. But tolerance is an effect, not a cause. The cause of Baltimore's tolerance is her towering self-sufficiency. She is so supremely confident of her ability to deal effectively with Ku Klux or prohibition enforcement agents that she can afford to be tolerant of them all. Baltimore is mild because she isn't afraid; and she isn't afraid because she has limitless confidence that what Baltimore has always done is right and will continue to be right to the end of the chapter.

I have sedulously avoided employment of the term "complacency" to describe the spirit of Baltimore, because complacency connotes self-confidence not well founded. Baltimore's has at least this foundation: she has worked out a *modus vivendi* under which Dr. Howard A. Kelly and H. L. Mencken can live in the same town very amicably; under which the Johns Hopkins Medical

School and a college of chiropractic have existed for years without either being sacked and burned; under which the police refuse to arrest bootleggers, but fight off a mob which would prevent federal agents from arresting them.

As to whether or not this passionless spirit will ever produce anything great, there is much doubt. Great work is not often done by passionless men. Even great ironists are not unemotional. But Baltimore city is moved to the depths by one thing only, to wit, science. The city's artists are accepted in pretty much the same spirit as are the city's Ku Klux Klansmen—tolerantly, but with no marked enthusiasm. But the professors at the Johns Hopkins— ah, there now are great men. Baltimore never giggles, but she can smile at almost any picture ever painted save one. Show her Sargent's "Four Doctors," and she is instantly on her knees.

Well, what of it? Science is no laughing matter. Some of us, to be sure, think that music is no laughing matter, either, or sculpture, or painting, or drama, or architecture, or even literature. However, a city that can recognize sound work in anything is not without hope; eventually it may come to cherish sound work in everything.

At all events, it is something to have The Presence. The great lady of Charles Street may cause many a chauffeur and traffic cop to die of heart-failure, but there is a touch of the magnificent about her, none the less. She has serenity, and in America in 1928 that is a pearl of great price.

Baltimore is full of excited monuments—generals brandishing weapons, poets singing lustily, soldiers dying uncomfortably, civic dignitaries standing in a high wind, George Washington up a tree with the British Lion baying him—but otherwise it is a serene city. It isn't New York and, wonder of wonders, it really has not the faintest desire to be New York. It is Baltimore, it has always been Baltimore, and it is firmly convinced that being Baltimore is the best of all possible destinies. A very great lady indeed.

And yet there was an imaginary city greater still—a glamorous city, full of wickedness and lust, but shining; full of wine and women, but also full of song, not altogether ribald. The cotton-choppers sang about it, and the turpentine hands, and the steel-drivin' men from the Potomac to the Tombigbee. By comparison with that city, the Baltimore of today is a tank town, after all.

abridged from THE VIRGINIA QUARTERLY REVIEW, *October 1928*

SOUTHERN IMAGE-BREAKERS

Once upon a time I taught, or at least was a professor of, Journalism, and I suppose that for the rest of my life whenever my liver grows sluggish, reviving a latent faith in Predestination and Infant Damnation, I shall reflect miserably upon the terrible accounting I shall have to make at the Last Judgment for the mayhems I then committed upon the minds of quite decent college students. But in such moments of depression a small consolation remains to me. There is one outrage of the kind which I might have committed, and did not. At least I think I did not. I believe that I never told a class that personal journalism is a thing of the past.

Yet this statement has been made so often that it is accepted and repeated quite generally by men otherwise sane and intelligent. Even the South is coming to believe that it is axiomatic that personal journalism is gone forever. Nevertheless, the idea is a false one; it is applesauce, it is hooey, it is the sublime and ineffable baloney. In brief, there's nothing in it.

For we still have journalism, and as long as we have it at all we must have personal journalism, because there is no other kind. That is, there is no other kind that is worthy of the name. The newspaper world is filled with dreadful incompetents, to be sure. So is the world of business; ninety per cent of the men who set up in business for themselves cannot make the grade, and either go into bankruptcy or fail less spectacularly. The mortality in the law may not be as heavy, but it is tremendous. The rigorous training exacted of doctors eliminates most of the hopeless incompetents before they are permitted to begin to practice, but happy is the man who has never in his life seen a physician who is no good. The sacred desk I hurriedly pass by to land with a crash upon the farmers. Farmers, as a class, are so notoriously incompetent that it was once thought that the present Presidential campaign might revolve around the question of whether or not they are to be supported out of the National Treasury, as Messrs. McNary and Haugen demand.

Therefore, if the land is filled with bad newspapers, still it cannot be said that their worthlessness is a characteristic mark of the business. The swarms of bad business men, bad lawyers, bad doctors and bad farmers are sufficiently great to obscure the multiplicity of bad journalists. The point is that there remain numerous good newspapers, and in the South, especially, they tend to multiply. But every good newspaper indicates the existence of at least one good journalist; it is the personality of a competent man that makes a newspaper good—that, and nothing else under heaven.

Early this year a Southern newspaper—the *Enquirer-Sun,* published at Columbus, Georgia—celebrated its hundredth anniversary, and not only the Georgia press, but half the metropolitan newspapers of America, as well, seized the occasion to fling editorial bouquets in that direction. Yet for ninety-two years the country had hardly heard of the place. I know five men who have been in Vladivostok, and three who have been in Tsinan-Fu, and two who have been in Bangkok, but I have never, to my knowledge, seen but one man who had ever been in Columbus, Georgia, and he is the editor of the *Enquirer-Sun.*

Why, then, did American newspaperdom get so excited over the birthday of this journal published in a remote Southern town? The answer is contained in two words—personal journalism. Eight years ago the editorship of the *Enquirer-Sun* was assumed by Julian Harris, a journalist who had learned his work thoroughly and who has the great courage which is as much the foundation of really fine newspaper work as a sense of rhythm is the foundation of good musicianship. Incidentally, he had prudently married Julia Collier, who is a good newspaper woman, and thereby doubled his effectiveness.

Julian Harris is not a "fine writer." His English is graceful enough to make pleasant reading, but he carefully eschews the ornamentation that obscures and weakens. His writing, however, depends for its effect on the matter, not the manner. Yet what he says is not bizarre, not unheard-of, not a plunge into unexplored realms of thought. Ordinarily it is just what any honest man of sense would say, under the same circumstances. But unfortunately what any honest man of sense would say in private conversation is but rarely what the same man would write for publication in a newspaper. Therefore the effect was sensational when Harris began to print in the *Enquirer-Sun* just the sort of thing that intelligent men all over Georgia were saying in private about such developments as Ku Kluxism, and the pernicious activity of preachers in politics, and the ghastliness of Georgia penology. Not only was Georgia stirred, but newspaper men throughout the country took notice of the fact that here was a newspaper speaking sensibly, honestly, and candidly.

Most newspaper men desire to speak like that, but not all of them have the guts to do so. Harris has, and the fact has made the Columbus *Enquirer-Sun* one of the notable newspapers of the country. If this isn't personal journalism, what is it?

This story might be applied almost without changing a word to a newspaper man just across the State line from Harris. This man is Grover Hall, editor of the *Advertiser,* of Montgomery, Alabama. Hall is apparently a more excitable type than Harris. He loves to put the language through its evolutions; he knows how to make it march, wheel, about-face, stand at attention and salute. He loves to make an editorial surge and thunder. When he gets in a weaving way on such as subject as, for example, the menace of Ku Klux government in Alabama his sentences, crowded, hurrying, almost leaping over one another, come crashing in like breakers with a Gulf hurricane behind them. But his rhetoric is effective because it is based on common sense. He has no preconceived notions which he is determined to sustain, even if he has to warp the facts all out of proportion to do it.

Both Harris and Hall have gathered able assistants around them, but they have none the less made their papers stand for the things in which they, personally, believe. Each paper represents a definitely individual point of view. And if this isn't personal journalism, I repeat, what is it?

The same thing is true of Charlton Wright, the South Carolina image-breaker of the *Columbia Record.* Wright has laid violent hands on taboos that no South Carolinian had dared touch for generations. He does not, like Jurgen, content himself with doing what seems to be expected. He prefers, rather, to do always what seems to be unexpected, at least in South Carolina. It is journalism as personal as a toothbrush.

On the other hand, personality need not necessarily be injected into a newspaper directly. Sometimes it is as well, or better, inculcated more subtly. A case in point is that of the Greensboro, North Carolina *News,* one of the sanest, steadiest, and withal most enlightened newspapers to be found in the South. Its editor, Earle Godbey, is one of those who hug the delusion that good journalism may be impersonal. He lays great stress on the impersonal character of his editorial page. His paper recognizes no pet enemies who must always be denounced, and no friends who must always be praised—in the language of the craft, no son-of-a-[Here the Editor used his blue pencil] list and no Sacred Cow. He lays no explicit inhibitions upon his men. He is the one editor of my acquaintance who has no assistants, but only associates.

But he has the knack of asking two questions in fifty-seven different ways, and they are perfectly appalling questions to a man who has just handed in an article which he knows is more ingenious than sound. One question is, "Are you certain of this?" The second, and even more destructive one is, "Is it fair?" These two queries inevitably force the *Greensboro News* into a certain, definite mould, which is the mould chosen by Earle Godbey, although others may actually fit the paper into it. Thus he stamps his personality not merely on his paper, but also on his men, which is surely carrying personal journalism to its ultimate extreme.

As for North Carolina's most celebrated editor, Josephus Daniels, of the *Raleigh News and Observer,* and President Wilson's Secretary of the Navy, nobody ever hinted that there is anything impersonal about his journalism. Mr. Daniels is full of romantic notions about the Democratic Party and the *ante-bellum* South which sometimes lead him to support what seem to me to be dubious men and more than dubious measures. But his newspaper is unquestionably a power, and what has made it powerful is the personality of its editor. He can't be bought and he can't be scared. Those two traits are the assets of the *News and Observer,* and all the world knows it.

These modern Southern newspapers differ somewhat in their economic theories, but there is nothing resembling true radicalism among them. They startle the conservatives often enough, but that is because the Southern conservative is the most easily startled man on earth. The Southern conservative has been on the defensive ever since 1831, when William Lloyd Garrison first began to hit his stride; and ninety-seven years of incessant defending and explaining have developed in the Southern conservative an inferiority complex so gigantic that it colors and flavors his whole life. He has established defense mechanisms which operate so perfectly that not only is he unaware of them, but it is next to impossible for him to be persuaded that they exist.

One of these defense mechanisms is the belief that the South is set apart from the rest of humanity so completely that the very laws of nature, not to mention statute law, do not operate in the region below the Potomac as they do elsewhere. Therefore the assertion that two and two make four in the South exactly as they do in darkest Yankeedom is enough to startle the true Southern conservative.

But the new Southern press seems to be completely devoid of the inferiority complex, hence under no compulsion to believe and to teach that the South is super-human lest the common enemy establish his doctrine that it is sub-human. Accepting the theory that the twelve Southern States are simply twelve States and not necessarily a peculiar spot set apart as the dwelling place of God's chosen people, the better Southern newspaper comments on events in the South precisely as it would comment on similar events in other regions.

The rise of the Ku Klux Klan therefore was regarded by this section of the press precisely as it regarded the activities of the Black Hundreds under the Russian czars, and the activities of the Mafia in Italy. A secret society which undertook to regulate the lives of non-members seemed to these newspapers as evil in the South as it would be anywhere else.

A Pogrom in Georgia or Mississippi was deplored by these newspapers precisely as they deplored race-riots in Kiev or Odessa.

Duels à l'outrance between Southern gentlemen have been regarded by these newspapers exactly as they regard fights between Chicago gunmen.

Peonage in the South they have seen as just the sort of disgrace to this country that peonage used to be to Mexico.

But in all this there is nothing even faintly reminiscent of red radicalism. It is merely the reaction to be expected of any intelligent man, decently educated, and candid enough to speak what he really believes. It is exactly the reaction that intelligent, educated Southerners exhibit in private conversation.

The new element that these newspapers have injected into Southern journalism is, in the last analysis, nothing but candor. But candor does not exist suspended in mid-air. It cannot exist except where it is based on a foundation of very solid courage. Now courage is an intensely personal quality. No corporation was ever per se courageous. No group was ever more courageous than its leader. And no newspaper ever possessed courage except as it was endowed with the personal courage of its directing executive. Therefore the new journalism that is reconstructing the South intellectually is primarily personal journalism.

To be sure, it is quite different from the personal journalism of the past. There is no Henry Watterson in the modern South, no Horace Greeley, no Charles A. Dana. There is not even a Henry Grady, nor an Edward W. Carmack.

But who was Henry Watterson? Why, he was first and foremost the archetype of the Kentucky Colonel. He fought in the Confederate Army, he presided over Democratic National Conventions, he served upon commissions, he advised Presidents, he made after-dinner speeches, he charmed the high-born and fascinated the lowly. Incidentally, he edited a newspaper. But if from his multitudinous activities he had omitted editing altogether, he would still have been a celebrated man.

To a lesser, but still important degree, this was true of Greeley, and it was conspicuously true of Grady and Carmack. All the old stars, except Dana, were not so much men who became great editors, as great men who became editors incidentally. Dana, alone, was an editor primarily and a great man incidentally. The rest found in their newspapers only one of many expressions of their personalities, and in some cases not the most important one. Their newspapers were appendages, not their whole lives. They wore their newspapers as a man wears a *boutonnière*. Men respected the papers on account of the editors, instead of respecting the editors on account of the papers.

But was this really personal journalism, or the reverse? Did it not, in fact, strip the journal of personality and convert it into a purely impersonal stage property, a mere background for the editor? It might be argued very plausibly that the great protagonist of real personal journalism is not Greeley nor Watterson, but the elder Joseph Pulitzer, who buried his personality in the *New York World* and thereby made it the greatest personal journal of his day. It is argued that this is impossible, because the *World* survived Pulitzer; but the most astonishing achievement of Pulitzer's career was his picking an editor as big as himself. Frank I. Cobb, indeed, made the paper glitter as it never did under J. P. himself. And Ralph Pulitzer inherited something of his father's genius, as well as his father's fortune. If the *World* survives Ralph, then the theory will begin to wabble.

The London *Times* remained the Thunderer under generation after generation of the Walter family; in the course of a century it had gained enough prestige to carry it forward for years after Northcliffe bought it. But it was plainly going to pieces when Northcliffe died, and the method adopted recently to restore it was to return it to the control of another Walter. This is stretching the theory of personality pretty far, but not too far. There are plenty of examples of an art being handed down from father to son through several generations. The violin makers of Cremona come to mind at once, as do certain painters, goldsmiths, potters and other artists. These families gave a distinctive stamp to all their work, and what shall we call it, if not personality?

The confusion of ideas that had led to the assumption that personal journalism is out has grown up since newspapers have become immensely profitable. When newspaper proprietors die leaving scores of millions—and this has come to be nothing at all uncommon—the public assumes that such men must have been engaged in a business, or a profession, with a sound scientific basis. Not only do laymen make this assumption, but newspaper men themselves do the same thing. Within the craft for years there has been a persistent and vigorous effort to persuade journalists that they are professional men.

This is arrant nonsense. The professions are, in theory at least, born of the sciences. The case of the medicos is obvious, but lawyers maintain that jurisprudence is a science, and some day it may become true. So do clerics claim that theology is a science, while economists advance the same claim for economics, and historians for history. These claims may be pretty shadowy, but they exist, and on them is erected the claim of professors of these branches of knowledge to the status of professional men.

Newspaper men have no such claim, for their work is as unscientific as any activity in which men engage. There are rules, to be sure, but a man may observe every rule with scrupulous care and produce a bad newspaper, just as a man may observe all known rules of play-writing and produce a rotten play.

Newspaper work is not a science, but a craft, and its practitioners are craftsmen, that is to say, artisans or artificers. They fall naturally into the three grades of apprentice, journeyman and master-craftsman; and when one adds a touch of genius to superb competence, he is not a professional man, but an artist.

This concept is difficult because the world cannot be persuaded that art produces colossal fortunes. Yet what is so strange about that? After all, even in newspaper work it is not the artist who gets the fortune, but the impresario. Why should it be strange that a publisher should die a multi-millionaire, when it is well known that a theater-manager who knows an actor when he sees one can do the same thing? Yet no one seriously regards actors, or singers, or pianists as professional men.

Nor is producing plays, or operas, or managing concerts regarded as the same type of occupation as practicing medicine or law or preaching. The impresario may be something of an artist himself, but he is not a member of a learned profession. No more is a newspaper publisher.

There is, indeed, a sort of journalism that is almost completely impersonal, just as there is a sort of acting that is impersonal. There are scores and hundreds of newspapers as mechanical as the presses they are printed on, as mechanical as a performance by a troupe of ham actors. But which of the arts is not full of dull fellows who ought to be swinging a pick or carrying a hod? Which of the learned professions has no ignorant members? Which of the sciences is free of quacks?

It is not by the dull, machine-minded, uninspired hacks that journalism deserves to be judged, but by the best it can produce. And the best newspapers are being produced today, at least in the South, not by a corporation and not by a committee, but by individual men who stamp their personalities upon their papers. I do not mean that every good newspaper is a solo performance. On the contrary, no big newspaper can be anything of the sort. It is necessarily more in the nature of a symphony. But no symphony was ever played creditably without a conductor who made a personal matter of it.

Most competent newspaper editors seek advice constantly, but none worth his salt accepts dictation. An able staff, ably commanded, makes a great newspaper; but under incompetent command the abler the staff the more certain it is to fly to pieces, and probably to explode the newspaper too. A really fine newspaper never existed without the presence on its staff of at least one journalist who is better than a master-craftsman and approaches the rank of an artist.

Now the most curious fact about the intellectual life of the modern South is its sudden fecundity in literary artists. The last ten years have brought into national fame Paul Green, DuBose Heyward, Julia Peterkin, Frances Newman, James Boyd, Clement Wood, T. E. Stribling, Laurence Stallings and I know not how many more. What obscure forces are responsible for this sudden flowering I have no idea; but I do believe that the same forces that are responsible for these acknowledged artists are responsible for such men as Julian Harris, Grover Hall, Charlton Wright, Robert Latham, Earle Godbey and Louis Jaffé. They are part of the renaissance. Their contribution to the life of the South affects its economics, its science, its mechanics; but in itself it is no more economic, scientific or mechanical than is the "Perseus" which Benvenuto Cellini contributed to the Florence of Lorenzo de' Medici.

HARPER'S MAGAZINE, *December 1929*

THE CADETS OF NEW MARKET

A Reminder to the Critics of the South

I was born," said O. Henry, "in a somnolent little Southern town . . ."

This statement is almost unique, because in it William Sydney Porter wasted no less than two words—a record for him. He was born in 1867, therefore "Southern" was the only adjective he needed; for in 1867 Southern towns were all little and all somnolent.

The town to which O. Henry referred is Greensboro, North Carolina, and it was still little and still somnolent when he left it, about the time its population was increased by the birth of the child who was to be his successor in the favor of the story-reading public; for Wilbur Daniel Steele also first saw the light in the same village.

But neither man wrote anything memorable in Greensboro. Steele was taken away by his parents when he was still a child; and in O. Henry's time

Greensboro had no more use for a short-story writer than a hog has for a hip pocket. Will Porter was a drug clerk and a drug clerk he remained until he went, first to Texas, then to jail, and finally to New York, where he became famous.

His most vivid memory of his birthplace, thirty years after he had left it, was of summer evenings spent on somebody's front porch with a crowd of boys and girls. Someone always had a guitar, and the group sang old ballads behind a lattice heavy with honeysuckle. So it happened that the name of the town was always associated in O. Henry's mind with soft summer nights whose air was drenched with the scent of honeysuckle and disturbed by no noise harsher than young voices singing "Ben Bolt" or the "Spanish Cavalier" to the twanging of a guitar.

The charm of this picture is due, of course, to the haze of memory; for in the years between, say, 1870 and 1900 Greensboro was desperately poor as well as small and quiet. The struggle for a bare existence was so stern that its citizens had no time to hearken to a spinner of yarns, even though he were gifted with the magic of an O. Henry. So he had to go away to obtain a hearing.

Today this same town still calls its principal business thoroughfare Elm Street, although there has been no elm there for a generation; but that is almost the only feature of the place that fits O. Henry's description. There are half a dozen skyscrapers on Elm Street. There are traffic bells that jangle, and trolley cars whose wheels screech on curves. There are policemen's whistles, and thousands and thousands of automobile horns. There is, in short, the same devilish uproar that characterizes every lively American town. Somnolence is no more possible there than it is in the interior of a boiler factory.

Universal poverty has disappeared along with tranquility. There are now a platoon of millionaires and a battalion of bootleggers in the town's sixty thousand population. The largest denim mill in the world and half a dozen giant insurance companies testify to the vigor and acumen of the business men; and a garland of colleges does credit to the intellectual activity of the place.

This transformation has occurred since the turn of the century. It is merely a sample of what has taken place all over the South since the year 1900. It is the work of the new generation, whose youth was not poisoned by the aftermath of the Civil War. Within these latter years North Carolina cotton mills have acquired more spindles than those of Massachusetts. Southern tobacco has produced a group of millionaires with fortunes great enough to impress even Wall Street. Birmingham has become a gigantic steel manufacturing city. Norfolk threatens to dominate the shipbuilding industry. New Orleans claims the rank of the second greatest American port.

Nor is the new activity below the Potomac wholly, or most impressively, industrial. Broadway has blossomed with the names of Southerners, picked out in electric lights—DuBose Heyward, Laurence Stallings, Paul Green, others. Pulitzer prizes for writing folk stream South—to Green, to Julia Peterkin, to Robert Latham, Julian Harris, Grover Hall, Louis Jaffé, Lamar Stringfield. A South Carolinian takes the Prix de Rome in sculpture. With

Heyward, Mrs. Peterkin, and James Boyd at work in the Carolinas, Ellen Glasgow no longer represents the farthest south of the fine novel. Poets, as distinguished from poetasters, pop up like crocuses in the spring; Addison Hibbard compiles an anthology including thirty who have published each a volume of verse which is better than respectable. The Universities of Virginia and North Carolina publish in the *Virginia Quarterly Review* and *Social Forces* a literary quarterly and a learned journal which are viewed respect-fully throughout the country.

Small wonder, then, that the world has decided the South at last is wak-ing up, and is inclined to give young Southerners enormous credit for having shaken off the intellectual and moral drowsiness that afflicted their fathers.

The South has its glamorous traditions, to be sure, but they come down only as far as 1865. George Washington, Thomas Jefferson, John Marshall, James Madison were giants, as everyone admits; and the South in their day dominated the nation. Andrew Jackson, John C. Calhoun, and Henry Clay were no weaklings, either; such men do not spring from a degenerate race. In moral stature and military genius Robert E. Lee overtops George Wash-ington himself, although Lee had not the statesmanship that secures Wash-ington his primacy. And Stonewall Jackson, the two Johnstons, Longstreet, Beauregard, Stuart, Early, and Forrest were such soldiers as delight the heart of the romancer and flutter the maiden pride of any nation. Tardy justice now begins to admit that Jefferson Davis and Alexander Stephens also were men of genius.

Who was the next Southerner to fire the imagination of the nation in a way comparable to the least of these? Woodrow Wilson—but you have leaped a generation to come to him. Furthermore, his notable work was done outside of the South. What happened to the Southern boys just a little older than Wilson, who remained in the South? Were they really unworthy of the tradition of the South, incapable of greatness?

At New Market, in the Valley of Virginia, when the Confederates were hard pressed on one occasion they threw into the line of battle the cadets from the Virginia Military Institute. They were largely striplings of sixteen or so, too small to handle a heavy army rifle except by straining, far too young to have anything to do with the business of organized butchery. As they marched into battle the band of a veteran regiment played "Rock-a-bye Baby." But they held their position and actually captured a Federal battery. When the fight was over they buried their dead, gathered up their wounded, and the heroic, pitiful survivors marched back to their schoolbooks. What became of the New Market cadets after the war?

Theirs is the lost generation of the South. Remarque has lately won the applause of the world with his eloquent threnody of the generation that Europe lost in the war of 1914-18; but no man has had a good word for the generation represented by the New Market cadets. It was during their matur-ity that the South lay as in a coma. Economically, intellectually, morally, Dixie, as the world believes, drowsed those years away; and now that the sons of that generation are bestirring themselves enough to make a noise in the world, men congratulate the South on the passing of the Rip Van Winkles—

Walter H. Page called them Mummies. Of this generation the consensus of mankind seems to be that nothing in its life was so becoming as the quitting of it.

There is no arguing away a popular superstition, and it is much too late to attempt to retrieve the reputation of this generation if it were possible. The men and women who composed it are already in the graveyard, or so nearly there that another injustice, more or less, affects them but little. The world will doubtless go on believing that the new activity in the South, intellectual and industrial, was generated in a vacuum and that the young Southerners who are now commanding the admiration of the nation sprang from the head of Jove, or anywhere rather than from the loins of their putative forebears. Can the intellectually dead generate intelligence? Can mummies give birth to living offspring? Can any good thing come out of Nazareth?

But while this theory may be well enough for outsiders, to credit it would be shameful in a Southerner of the twentieth century. We cannot forget the pit whence we were digged, nor the crushing toil that went into the digging. What went on in the South between 1870 and 1900 was too completely tragic to furnish material for theatrical tragedy, far too high in spirit for written romance which crawls along the beaten paths of life, too stark for poetry. The New Market cadets went back to their schoolbooks for a little while after the battle; but a few years later they were flung into the line again, and this time they were never relieved, for the battle never ended. They went home from school to find the old civilization wrecked; and they spent the rest of their lives fighting hand to hand with intangible foes far more ruthless and far more dangerous than Federal infantrymen.

It is all but impossible now to present an adequate picture of the odds these men faced. The material destruction in the Southern states is relatively easy to compute. Most of us are under the impression that the United States fought quite a war ten years ago; but to survivors of the Confederacy it was a mere skirmish. The war ten years ago cost the country something like an eighth of its total wealth, and called into military service about one-sixth of the men of military age, that is, 4,000,000 out of 23,000,000 available. Suppose the war had taken all the money and all the men? Suppose we had put into the field 25,000,000 men? At that, we should have failed to equal the record of the Confederate State of North Carolina, which supplied 120,000 soldiers to the Confederacy when the State had only 105,000 voters, including all those too old and too infirm for military service.

This part of the situation can be put into figures. We are also able to construct a statistical representation of the damage caused by a policy of reconstruction of which one is at a loss to say whether its stupidity or its viciousness was the more conspicuous. For instance, this same State of North Carolina, already so completely bankrupt that Serbia, in 1919, was by comparison in a flourishing condition, was loaded with an additional debt of $32,000,000, nearly all of which was stolen outright by officials put in power, not by the votes of the people, but by the bayonets of the Federal army of occupation. Much the same sort of thing happened to all the other conquered States.

All this, also, can be represented to a certain extent to the modern world. What cannot be represented is not the outward difficulties under which this Southern generation labored, but its own inadequacy to the task which it had to perform. One can imagine the bombardment to which the cadets were subjected at New Market. One can find out the number of troops flung against them. One might calculate the intensity of the rifle-fire along their front. But there is still a factor in the equation not taken into account, and it is the most important factor of all. That is the weakness of the cadets themselves, due to their youth. Everyone who has been a soldier knows how a grown man's arms ache, how his shoulders turn to water, how his back bends and his head droops after he has handled a heavy army rifle in rapid fire for even a short while; but who can imagine the fatigue of a small boy subjected to the same inhuman strain for hour after hour. The sheer weariness of that child-regiment makes the heart ache, even after seventy years.

II

But the generation which had to fight its way out of the chaos that followed the Civil War in the South was hardly better prepared for the task than were the cadets for theirs. The great crime of the Old South was its neglect to exercise a larger measure of intelligence in its economic organization. The fact that it was involuntary, that it involved no malevolence, has no relation to the magnitude of the offense. The really great crimes are nearly always committed by stupid people rather than by bad people.

When the old order was overthrown by the Civil War, the rising generation found itself without either the equipment or the training to establish a new order in conformity with the altered environment. The lack of equipment was a handicap, but the lack of training was a well-nigh fatal handicap. France, after 1870, and Germany, after 1918, proved that lack of equipment cannot long keep a nation submerged if it has been bred to commerce and industrialism. But the economic system of the Old South was already falling into ruin before the war struck it; the war itself might be described as the last desperate expedient of a people exasperated beyond endurance by its own inability to devise any better economic order than a one-crop system and slave labor. But it was a suicidal expedient, for no such moribund system could possibly stand the strain of war. As a matter of historic fact, it collapsed so completely that not even the amazing military genius exhibited by Southern commanders could stave off ruin. The world is still unable to comprehend, not their defeat, but how they managed to last so long.

And there was no resilience in it, no rebound after the war. It was the deadest system ever killed by a disastrous campaign.

So the New Market cadets and all their generation were faced with a worse than Israelites' task. Not only were they required to make bricks without straw, but also without any adequate knowledge of how bricks are made even with straw. The old system was demolished, and, far from being trained in another, they were hardly aware of the existence of any other. Yet they were required to build a new civilization.

And in forty years they had built it. It is no Periclean Athens, or Augustan Rome, but it serves to produce scholars and artists. It begins to bring forth romancers, scientists, poets, playwrights, philosophers. It begins to excite the admiration of its contemporaries, who say that at last the South is undergoing an intellectual and moral regeneration.

But those of us whose memories are long enough to reach back twenty years have a different point of view. These members of the new generation are very fine fellows, but they did not draw their vigor, their stamina, their intellectual power out of the air. They got it from the hard-bitten old boys who sired them; and for my part, I cherish serious doubts that, with all their admitted brilliance, they are quite the men their fathers were. That is to say, if they were suddenly stripped, not merely of all they possess, but of all their traditions, all their habits of thought, all their manner of living, and compelled to build anew and in a different order of societal architecture, I doubt that they would build in forty years as high a civilization as the Southern States enjoyed in 1900.

As I write I recall the achievement of a certain Southerner who shall be nameless here for reasons which will presently appear. He was a schoolman. He was shockingly ill-educated, judged by modern standards and, to adopt the phrase of John Kendrick Bangs, if his mind had been a slot you couldn't have inserted a nickel in it. He was fat, oleaginous, and tawdry. He was never addicted to pineapple, or any other sort of rum, but otherwise he was a replica of the Reverend Anthony Humm encountered by the elder Mr. Weller at the Brick Lane Branch of the United Grand Junction Ebenezer Temperance Association. And his school was like him. In the light of 1929 it seems to have been everything connoted by the Southern word "tacky." It was a starveling institution in which famished professors half-educated gawky country girls. It was enormously long on piety, and short on good manners and good sense.

Nevertheless, this squat, dull, semi-illiterate almost single-handed pounded into the head of a bankrupt, starving, and distracted State the notion that it must educate its women at any cost. To this accomplishment he gave his whole life. For it he planned, he spoke, he intrigued, he toiled like a convict in a chain gang. To secure his scanty appropriations from the Legislature he had to resort to every known political device, from eloquence to blackmail. Again and again when the cause seemed lost he wept openly and unashamed on the floor of the House. He was laughed at, reviled, slandered, and kicked, but he stuck to it, and before he died, in his early fifties, he had committed the commonwealth to the principle of unlimited educational opportunity for every girl.

With a little less intensity, with a little more easeful living, he might have lasted another twenty or thirty years; but it is my profound conviction that he would have regarded the shortening of his own life by twenty years a small price to pay for the success of his idea.

But in this is no pettiness. Here is no smallness of soul, no cheapness, "nothing but good and fair." What, then, is the true measure of this man—the oddities, provincialisms, asininities so conspicuous in the eyes of outsiders?

They are attributable, largely if not entirely, to the accidents of his environment. What education he had he scrambled for in the chaotic days immediately following the Civil War; no wonder it was a thing of shreds and patches. His experience of the world was that of a man desperately put to it to find enough to eat; no wonder it was narrow and acidulous. But the keen vision with which he pierced the future and saw the future need, and the intense, terrific devotion which made him pour his whole life into one purpose—these were no accidents. Perhaps he was a fool. Perhaps any martyr is a fool. In any case, he was worth more to his State than five gross of assorted cottonmill barons, plus three dozen Grade A poets, novelists, and dramatists, and a million run-of-the-mine statesmen. His State today spawns shoals of pedagogues who are better educated, handsomer, and far more gentlemanly fellows; but if it can find among them just one who is half as much of a man as was this pot-bellied little ignoramus, then well indeed may it thank God and take courage.

I have seen a farmer come in, dripping with sweat, from the fodder-field. He wore half a shirt, trousers tattered from the knee down, broken shoes without socks, and the ruin of a hat. He plunged his head into a basin of water, splashed vigorously for a moment, and then, looking at me quizzically over the towel as he dried his hands, recited in tones too mellifluous for sincerity, *"O fortunatos nimium, sua si bona norint, agricolas!"*

In 1859 they taught the classics thoroughly at the University of North Carolina, and as a freshman there he had learned his Georgics by heart; but before he could obtain a degree the curse fell upon the land, and he rode away from the campus to follow J. E. B. Stuart, instead of Virgil. "My heart was with the Oxford men who went abroad to die" reflects pretty faithfully the attitude of all England; but who ever gave a damn for the Carolina men who did the same thing? The Oxford men won, and the Carolina men lost, which makes all the difference. This man, for instance, when the fighting was over, came home to find the University looted and closed, and women and children of his own blood starving. He fed them by the labor of his hands; and in the sweat of his face did he and they eat bread for the rest of his life.

> *God rest you, happy gentlemen,*
> *Who laid your good lives down;*
> *Who took the khaki and the gun*
> *Instead of cap and gown—*
> *God bring you to a fairer place*
> *Than even Oxford town!*

It brings tears to the eyes of Englishmen, but all it gives North Carolinians is a horse-laugh. "A fairer place than even Oxford town"—to wit, a fodder-field, where back-breaking labor is performed in a temperature of 115 degrees. "O too happy husbandmen, if only they knew their good fortune"—do you wonder at the sarcasm in his voice? The marvel is not that he was sarcastic, but that he was gaily sarcastic. The man was designed by nature to wear the academician's robe. He was meant to be a citizen of the gentle and fair republic of letters, where he might have won renown; but the fortune of war made him a field-hand, and he could smile ironically over the ruin of his own aspirations. And to do this, surely, one must be a manful man.

I knew a doctor of brilliant attainments who died in the gutter, died like a dog. Liquor, said the neighbors, dolefully shaking their heads. But nobody ever thought to seek for any reason other than original sin for his drinking too much. He had come out of the Confederate army still a stripling, and how he contrived to get his medical education God only knows. But for forty years he carried on a practice so immense and so widely scattered that it would drive three modern medicos into nervous prostration in six months. The horses the man drove to death would have remounted a regiment of cavalry; and in the vast, poverty-smitten region over which he ranged, not one patient in five could ever pay him a cent. He could hardly buy a decent coat, not to mention expensive surgical equipment; yet I doubt that he slept a single night through for half a lifetime. Through sleet and snow on many a bitter night alcohol carried him through when he must otherwise have failed some suffering pauper in the remote wilderness. Alcohol got him at last. It was foolish of him to rely on it, of course. He should have guarded his own health and let the poor devils die in the backwoods. Then he might have had time to study, and to become famous in his own profession. Yet I am inconsistent enough to believe that the old doctor, drunk, was a more valuable citizen than is the soberest prohibition enforcement agent ever heard of.

I knew an editor whose paper, judged by every standard of modern journalism, was a lousy one, but who was, nevertheless, a great journalist—greater, I almost suspect, than the Lathams, the Harrises, the Jaffés, and the Halls, although these have won Pulitzer prizes, and the old fellow was hardly heard of across his own State line. He lacked the brilliance of a Watterson, and the technical training, as well as the mechanical equipment, which fortifies modern Southern newspapers. But in the late eighties and early nineties, when the South touched its nadir, when passion was most venomous and obscurantism loudest, this man was truthful and fair. Financially, socially, and politically, it was a disastrous policy; for truth and fairness in journalism, so far from being in demand, were regarded as damnable heresy; political office, prestige, and such money as was available were all reserved for the kept press. Yet, against every conceivable outside obstacle, and against the more formidable inner handicaps of poor education and narrow experience, he maintained his standard of decency and intelligence so well that his spirit slowly infected the press of his State and hauled it up from barbarism. He made no stir in the outside world, but he was decent when it was harder to be decent than it is now to be great. Yet he was of the generation which we are accustomed to regard as intellectually and morally sterile.

Even the textile industry, which now threatens conversion of the South into a region of brassy, loud, and curiously brutal go-getters, had, in its early days, its magnificent men. In the beginning many a man toiled at the business with no real liking for it, and not much hope of financial profit, because the creation of industry promised to drag his native land from the morass. These, indeed, had their reward, since climate, proximity to the raw material, and an almost limitless supply of pauper labor combined to make cotton manu-facturing vastly profitable. None the less, the first venturers into this field were far-seeing, bold and vigorous—certainly no slothful generation.

Any Southerner thirty-five years of age or over can remember, if he will turn his mind to the past, such feats of valor, endurance, and resourcefulness as amaze him in retrospect. Money, of course, is a highly deceptive standard of value; probably most Americans would find it difficult to live on the sums which represented their fathers' total earnings. But in the South the disparity between this generation and its predecessor is greater than elsewhere. A dollar was bigger thirty years ago than it is now; but even then a man who supported and educated half a dozen on a salary of seventy-five dollars a month was a financial wizard who need not stand abashed in the presence of Henry Ford or Andrew Mellon. Yet the South was full of them.

Nevertheless, the impression persists that this was a lethargic, drowsy, dull generation. The truth is, of course, that only those who were vibrantly alive, incredibly keen, superlatively wide-awake survived. The others went to Texas. In the South from the seventies to the end of the century one dared not go to sleep, on penalty of his life. Perhaps he might not actually be carried to the graveyard, but he found himself promptly a charge on the charity of his neighbors, and his children definitely went under—the boys usually departing for the West, and the girls winding up in the cotton-mill.

Art did not flourish, it is true, but when did art ever flourish on the frontier? The South after the Civil War was to all intents and purposes a frontier, except for the fact that its fields had been cleared. But this was an advantage more than compensated by the fact that if the fields had been cleared, they had also been sterilized by a ruinous cropping system. For the rest, the old order had been completely wrecked, and the inhabitants were compelled to build anew. Since their training, such as it was, had all been designed for the old order, they were compelled to proceed by the slow and expensive method of trial and error. They were surrounded by an economic and moral wilderness, much more difficult to subdue than the physical wilderness their forebears had entered.

In such circumstances, mere living is a triumph, and art would be a miracle. The Muses, indeed, are and have always been kept women. Artists may be poor, but art is for the rich, and it flourishes only in rich countries. A nation, like a man, may be crass as well as rich and, therefore, devoid of art; but art cannot survive except where the country is rich enough to maintain a certain number of dreamers. In the years immediately following the Civil War to dream, in the South, was death. Every able-bodied man was desperately needed for the task of rebuilding material civilization, and he who abandoned that task, even if he survived physically, suffered the moral death of betraying his people. The least he could do was to take himself away, to do his dreaming in some region where the surplus was sufficient to enable some men to refrain from materially productive labor without inflicting appreciable injury upon society.

Perhaps the most tragic figures in the South are the men who might have been artists had not their obvious duty compelled them to throttle their

dreams and turn their hands to material labor. Every Southerner knows them
—wistful figures, a little apart from their fellows, even in old age, dimly
aware that they have somehow lost, but not sure what, or why, or when. In his
latest novel DuBose Heyward sketched one of them lightly; it is a pity he did
not do a full-length study, for they are worthy of justification.

But the necessity for that sort of sacrifice is passing, if it has not altogether passed. Heyward himself, with nothing to offer the world but poems
and plays and stories, not only survives in Charleston but is acclaimed as a
great man there. Julia Peterkin was born late enough to be able, after long
years devoted to the affairs of her house, to lay aside the broom and pick up
the pen; and the State of South Carolina recognizes her as one of its orna-
ments. William Alexander Percy can sing in Mississippi, and John Crowe
Ransom in Tennessee. Paul Green and James Boyd are honored in North
Carolina. Indeed, the most ill-rewarded of all the arts begins to raise its head
in Dixie; Lamar Stringfield, a Tar Heel composer, won the Pulitzer prize in
1928 for an orchestral suite based on folk music of the North Carolina moun-
taineers, and last summer he conducted a symphony orchestra in his home
town, Asheville.

In all this Southerners can take legitimate pride. In so far as the individual artists are concerned, it is in every respect creditable. But I submit that
as regards the whole generation which rules the South at this moment, it
proves only the existence of money below the Potomac. That is to say, it
substantiates what the existence of the cotton mills, the hydroelectric lines,
the steel plants, the furniture and tobacco factories had first asserted, namely,
that the material losses of the Civil War have been made good. The South
now has leisure, therefore it can give some attention to other things than the
struggle for existence.

III

But who gave it the money, and so the leisure to appreciate and encourage art? Who but the lost generation, which had no time to search after
learning, or abstract beauty, or anything but the bare necessities of life? Who
but the Rip Van Winkles, the Mummies, regarded by the world as having
drowsed their lives away?

A life may be hard and bare and bitter without necessarily being degraded. Indeed, it is rare that true degradation sets in until some degree of
softness, of fatness, has been attained. Consider the worst offenses charged
against the generation in the South that has just passed, and compare them
with the corresponding charges brought against the present generation. There
was a Ku Klux Klan in the South immediately after the Civil War. But it was
no preposterous group of addlepates striving to give themselves dignity by
mysterious trappings. It was an organization of desperate men committed to
desperate deeds. When the old Ku Klux Klan donned its robes and sallied
out, it was not for child's play. Before it returned it was more than likely that
somebody had died—far more often than is generally realized, one or more of
the Klansmen. Harried by private detectives, Secret Service agents, organized

bands of negroes, and the United States Army, the member of the old Klan rode with death on his crupper. How does that compare with the Klan which the modern generation has produced?

Far worse than the Klan, the older generation evolved tolerance of Judge Lynch. For this there are many reasons, but no adequate excuse, so let the reasons go. The modern generation has to its credit the reduction of lynchings from 255 in 1892 to 16 in 1927. But if we are to believe Walter White, who has made a meticulous investigation of the subject, as the lynchings have decreased in number, they have increased in bestiality. The older generation hanged or shot its victims; it remained for the younger to invent and apply tortures that might appall a Chinese executioner. In the olden time there was no suspicion that there existed in the South a race of connoisseurs of lynchings—men who would race across country a hundred miles to attend an event of the kind, to offer their expert aid in dispatching the victim with the utmost possible cruelty.

The older generation, as most frontiersmen have done, developed a religious faith as hard, as gnarled and knotty, as were their own lives. Puritanism flourished then in its sternest and stiffest form. But Puritanism in Jonathan Edwards' day had dignity, at least. The Puritanism of the South's lost generation had dignity, and more. It was a bleak faith, if you please, but it was a powerful faith, with which nobody trifled. Its priests were frequently austere men, and not seldom terrible men, but they believed themselves to be servants of the Most High God. Nobody suspected them of selling their religion to cotton mill owners as a convenient narcotic with which to keep the wage-slaves quiescent. Nobody found them denouncing the carnalities of the poor white trash and discreetly glozing over the faults of the rich and influential. They did not convert their pulpits into sounding-boards of partisan politics. Their bishops did not invade Wall Street. They may have served God in ways sometimes not to His liking, but they served Mammon in no way whatsoever.

The South remains perhaps the most religious section of the country, but it finds it more and more necessary to rely on the strong arm of the police to sustain the faith. Comment is unnecessary.

The South may be waking up, as the optimists assert; but it might be plausibly argued that the reverse is the truth—that it is just now beginning to drowse, because only now has it dared sleep. At any rate, as it develops the graces of a rich civilization, it begins to develop the vices also; and it should take heed to these things before it congratulates itself on having produced a finer generation than those who, as children, fought at New Market, and, as men, cleared the way to greatness for their sons.

HOW A LOVER CELEBRATED HIS LADY
BY SAYING NOTHING

Down to New Orleans, when the shooting was over, came Rachel, with Andrew, Jr., then seven years old. The Creole ladies received a shock. Rachel was the backwoods incarnate. When the famous General Jackson first appeared in their city, they had half expected to see something resembling the Wild Man of Borneo in a circus sideshow. Instead, they had seen merely a grizzled, leathery, hard-bitten man who had little to say and said it in few words; whose manners, as Fanny Kemble remarked years afterward, were "perfectly simple and quiet, and, therefore, very good"; but who also possessed, on occasion, a certain grace that enchanted women. When he first met Cora Livingston, wife of the aide-de-camp, she was in a group of Creole belles, and his simple, but perfectly correct, greeting, his grave, unostentatious politeness and his calm but unassuming manner captivated that thorough woman of the world and her cortege as well. From that moment Jackson was a success among the ladies of New Orleans.

But with Rachel it was different. Society, indulgent to an able man, is relentless toward his wife. Everyone realized that a man who had spent his life fighting the wilderness, the Indians, the Spanish and the British, had had no opportunity, if he had the desire, to learn the manners of a courtier. Too much courtliness in such a man would, indeed, have been regarded with disfavor. It would have spoiled him.

In justice the same reasoning ought to apply to that man's wife, but it is seldom so applied. The scars that the same battles have inflicted upon them both in him are regarded as honorable, in her as ridiculous. Jackson's coarse homespun was dignified garb for the frontiersman; Rachel's appeared unseemly. The tan that Jackson had acquired in his campaigns excited admiration. The tan that Rachel had acquired struggling with his deserted plantation, in order that the soldier might go to the wars with a quiet mind, excited mirth. Jackson's mistakes in orthography drew forth the reflection that, after all, he spelled better than George Washington did. Rachel's failure to acquire in a frontier town all the graces of Paris was apparently held inexcusable. The fact that Jackson was a true man got him honor and praise all over the world. The fact that his wife was a true woman got her nothing.

That is, it got her nothing from what is, for some inscrutable reason, known as society. Parton reprints two comments upon her written by society people, one a man, the other a woman. These are not the putrescence later vomited upon her name by ordinary political buzzards of the newspaper press. They are of a different order—comments presumably realistic by people of education professing friendship for her. There is nothing obscene about them. They are merely hateful. They do not slander. They only sneer. Through every paragraph there runs, under the main theme as a sort of contrapuntal melody, the spitting of the cat. Every line is the mark of feline claws.

But Cora Livingston was not a society woman of that type. She was not allied to the clan of Livingston for nothing. She really knew the world, not merely the society of New York and New Orleans, but men and women in the large. Her polish was based upon her own fine grain, not upon a thin veneer; and she held her leadership of society because her personal charm was reinforced by keen intelligence.

Therefore when Rachel went to her quite simply and asked her aid and advice in the new and strange situation, Cora Livingston was captivated again. She could not, it is true, convert the dumpy, hopelessly countrified Rachel into a *grande dame;* but she could, and she did, devote herself exclusively to the visitor's service, she could advise and assist her in innumerable ways, she could summon the *élite* of the city to her house and present Rachel to them in a setting that gave the ladies of New Orleans a chance to see and to appreciate the splendid qualities of the woman. In consequence, regardless of the sneers of the cads and climbers, with the real aristocracy of the ancient town the queer little woman from Tennessee was also a success.

But the magnificent part of Rachel's visit to New Orleans is the fact that the General marched through the midst of this feminine campaign serenely unaware that anything was going on! He noted, of course, that Mrs. Livingston was gracious to Rachel and that Rachel liked her; and, no doubt, in his eyes that raised the value of Mrs. Livingston's husband in later years when offices and honors were to be distributed. But that Mrs. Livingston had done anything in particular for Rachel he apparently never guessed.

Why should she do anything? There was nothing the matter with Rachel that the General could see. Even the spiteful screeds that Parton quotes bear testimony to this. Both remark with amusement upon the obvious blindness of the General to any defect in his wife. But such laughter is the inevitable cackle of fools in the presence of anything fine. Here was a tribute that Guinevere never won, a compliment never paid to Iseult, a prize finer than the golden apple that fell at Helen's feet. Rachel had made a man love her so well that nothing could release him from her power, not even the ravages that time had worked upon her beauty.

Superficially, it seems preposterous to mention Rachel of Nashville in the same breath with the glamorous women of legend and history. The years had dealt spitefully with her, as they do with a soldier's wife; while her man was away at the wars her days had been filled with toil and her nights with anxiety. Not merely the house and the dairy knew her, but the cotton fields, the corn fields, the byres and stables and paddocks knew her well. The winds buffeted her. The sun scorched her. But that which her man had intrusted to her, she kept well. Her skin was roughened and tanned, her hands grew calloused, her once lissome figure gradually slumped into shapelessness. But her household prospered. Her husband suffered nothing by reason of waste or indolence.

He had been suffering hardships, but also gaining glory in the world. She must have been more—or less—than woman if she had no moments of trepidation when news came back from him. He had smashed the Indians. He had smashed the Spaniards. He had smashed the British army. He had saved New Orleans and that rich and splendid city lay at his feet. Famous men crowded to salute him. Beautiful women contended for the honor of paying him their intoxicating homage. Once he had loved Rachel, but Rachel once had been graceful and gay and young. Now she was old and dowdy and fat. Would she shame him, when she appeared in that glittering capital and he saw her among the lovely women who were its pride?

Well, she came. She appeared with him at the grand ball at the Exchange, when the delivered city paid its farewell tribute to its defender and all its wealth, beauty and distinction crowded the place; and it was perfectly clear that he saw her nothing less beautiful than the most beautiful woman there.

What a triumph for Rachel! And what eloquence in her lover was his obliviousness! Songs can be sung with the lips only. Poems can be written from the head and with a heart untouched. But when a woman's lover is blind to her flaws, she is loved indeed.

Andrew Jackson doubtless never saw a ballade and didn't know a sonnet from a sight draft. His taste in music ran to appalling hymns, full of hell and damnation, and he knew no more of the language of flowers than he did of Sanskrit. But where is the troubadour who has paid his lady a compliment more tremendous than his simple inability to comprehend that there might be lovelier ladies than the one by his side? Rachel knew it. Any woman would know it. And his blank obliviousness must have been, to her, delicate and lovely verse, must have sung in her heart music that made the best efforts of the orchestra at the ball seem harsh and discordant by comparison, must have blossomed in her memory like flowers rarer than any grown on earth.

The dancers smiled, doubtless not without reason. But what of it? Rachel could afford to smile, too.

THE POLICEMAN'S BED OF ROSES

One of the high spots of that curious play *The Green Pastures* comes when the Lord, troubled by an unusual display of perverseness and forwardness on the part of the children of men, remarks to the archangel Gabriel, "Being God ain't no bed of roses, Gabe."

The observation is irresistibly brought to mind by an interview given out early in the year by the Police Commissioner of New York City, Mr. Edward P. Mulrooney. Mr. Mulrooney, it should be borne in mind, is what is known in the State Department as "a career man." He did not come to the Commissionership by making himself serviceable and agreeable to some mayor. He came up through the ranks. He has pounded the pavement on a patrolman's beat, he has been sergeant, lieutenant, police captain, inspector. He is a professional policeman, not a successful business man, or engineer, or lawyer drafted into the service at the top. Hence it is but natural that he should feel matters affecting the honor of the force more keenly than might be expected of one who has not spent his whole life in it.

But Mr. Mulrooney had hardly had time to warm his office chair when the force under his command found itself the target of accusations so horrible that they shocked the country. The vice squad was accused, not merely of preying upon prostitutes, but of bringing false charges against innocent women in order to extort money from them. When the reporters called on the Commissioner the interview he gave out was, in the most literal sense, pitiable. He was too upset even to be wrathful. All he could think of was that twenty thousand men, most of whom he knew were honest and decent, would have to bear the burden of this slimy charge. To be sure, only the vice squad was under attack, but Mulrooney knew the public would not discriminate. A cop is a cop, in the mind of the average man; and if one goes wrong, all come under suspicion.

And that is what Mr. Mulrooney gets for trying to do what God has never undertaken, namely, to make people continent, not by persuasion, but by compulsion.

If New York alone were concerned the melancholy case of Mr. Mulrooney would perhaps be worth no more than the tribute of a sigh. But the conception of police work which is responsible for his discomfort is not typical of New York, but of America. The vice squad, or its equivalent, is known to every city in the land. Everywhere we insist that the police be God, to the extent of seeing that sinful men be hampered as much as possible in their sinfulness; and everywhere the police find it no bed of roses. Efforts against prostitution, liquor, and gambling are the three pitfalls into which most of our errant policemen stumble. Who ever heard of the police selling protection to forgers, counterfeiters, embezzlers, or bank bandits, unless these criminals were in some way connected with one of the great overlords of gambling, bootlegging, or commercialized vice? Yet all the crimes mentioned are crimes against property, and it is quite conceivable that the criminals could pay well for protection—as well, perhaps, as those who get it.

On the other hand, what city of any considerable size in the forty-eight States and the District of Columbia has not had, at one time or another, a police scandal in which liquor, prostitution, or gambling featured? Indeed, in the larger cities such scandals are endemic, and the best police departments are those in which they are exposed and dealt with before they have involved more than a patrolman or two. There are none in which they never occur at all.

Americans are acutely conscious of the fact that the reputation of American police in the world at large has come close to being a hissing and a by-word; but Americans usually refrain, at least for publication purposes, from connecting the low estate of the police with the fact that the major police scandals start, with monotonous regularity, in the vice squads, the prohibition squads, or the gambling squads. Police Lieutenant Becker of New York went to the electric chair for the murder of a gambler. The bad police record of Chicago is intimately connected with racketeering, which started with the beer-running racket. Pittsburgh, Cleveland, Detroit—all have seen police scandals based on bootlegging. Now comes the latest New York affair, which started with the work of the vice squad.

However, if one draws the obvious inference, namely, that employing the police against prostitution, liquor, and gambling is much more dangerous to the police than it is to the evils attacked, one is immediately written down as a suspicious character. Such an attitude is promptly explained as a mask covering secret sympathy with liquor, prostitution, and gambling; and few Americans can bear even to be suspected of harboring such sympathies. I am very well aware that this article is likely to be regarded by some people as in the nature of aid and comfort to prostitutes, policy-players, and bootleggers; and I am enough of an American not to like that prospect. But if it be so, so be it. I hereby formally advance the theory that there are worse things in the world than any of these three, and that one of those worse things is the American method of dealing with them.

That method, furthermore, is bad not on account of any defect in the organization of our police departments, numerous and serious as those defects are; or on account of the political control of police departments, although this contributes to the evils of the situation; or on account of the stupidity of police authorities, although they are not seldom idiotic. It is bad because the whole theory of police control, as it is now practiced, is a false one. It is bad because it employs a coarse, blunt instrument to perform an operation requiring the highest degree of keenness and skill. The removal of these ancient evils from the body politic is a matter of social surgery; and a surgeon who made a practice of removing vermiform appendices with a pair of pliers and a butcher knife would be a worse menace to his patients than is appendicitis. To protest against such surgery is surely not to write oneself down as in favor of appendicitis; but if it were, still the risk would be worth while.

For generations America has been the happy hunting ground of every type of quack, medical, religious, social, and political. Only the medical profession has made any consistently vigorous effort to eliminate them, and yet there is some reason to believe that the medical quacks, on the whole, do less damage than those of any other type. After all, as Mr. H. L. Mencken has frequently pointed out, a system of therapeutics kills only those who adopt it, and may conceivably be, in the long run, a social asset, in that it tends to eliminate the feeble-minded. But quacks who practice on the social structure are an active menace to everybody.

Of these the most dangerous, by long odds, are the quack reformers. These are the only ones who do not bring down swift retribution upon themselves and their followers. Patients of the medical quacks soon die and disappear. Political quacks usually end by growing so absurd that even their followers have to laugh, and that ends them. Economic quacks invariably wind up by doing something like passing a Smoot-Hawley tariff bill and are buried under the ruins of the subsequent collapse. But quack reformers merely poison and pervert morality, which is a process so slow that its evil effects may not show up for generations.

One of the most vicious follies which quack reformers have foisted upon America is the notion that the police are a proper instrumentality to be employed for the advancement of public morals. This idea is accepted almost without question, almost everywhere; yet it cannot survive even a superficial examination. What is a policeman? Essentially, he is a club and a revolver. Whatever may be effected by a club and a revolver he can accomplish, and no more. Clubs and revolvers can dissuade malefactors from overt acts against the peace and dignity of the state, but they cannot reform any man, still less any woman. Clubs and revolvers can maintain order, but the belief that they can promote morality is fantastic.

But the employment of the police power to advance morality is worse than merely ineffectual. The very existence of the police power, although it is a necessity, is an unfortunate necessity which should be restricted within the narrowest possible limits. It is regrettable that we have to delegate to any man authority to molest or interfere with his fellows; and those to whom such authority must be delegated should be subject at all times to the most careful scrutiny. Above all things they should never be allowed to operate in such ways and under such circumstances as to prevent a complete check upon their activities; for police power irresponsibly exercised constitutes the most abominable form of tyranny.

This, however, sets very definite bounds to the capacity of the police to deal with commercialized vice. Certain things they can do. For example, they may safely be required to prevent open solicitation on the streets, because it is possible to check this activity. That was proved in this New York investigation. Some years ago a woman of notorious reputation complained that she was being arrested whenever she appeared on the streets, whether she committed any offense or not. Her story could be checked and was checked. All that was necessary was to detail a pair of reputable witnesses to trail the woman through the streets and watch what occurred. Sure enough, she was arrested without rhyme or reason, and the evidence of the two witnesses was enough to secure her release.

Similarly, it is possible for the police to suppress open brothels, for in such cases there are always enough reputable witnesses to prove that the police acted upon good and sufficient reasons. But when we go a step farther, authorizing and requiring the police to prevent prostitutes from plying their trade anywhere and under any circumstances, the business immediately gets out of control. For in the nature of the case there can be no adequate check upon their operations.

This, also, was brilliantly illustrated in the New York scandals. What jury of honest men would like to send anybody to jail on the testimony of such witnesses as the State was able to present? But what other witnesses could the State hope to secure? Reputable men are not likely to have any first-hand knowledge of what goes on inside a bordello; and any man or woman who does have such knowledge is hardly likely to be able to withstand a skillful cross-examination. The very character of the State's witnesses is an almost perfect guarantee that in dealing with such people the police may do anything, and get away with it. In New York there is a great deal more than mere suspicion that they even brought false charges against innocent women and got away with that. Why not? The very fact that a woman is innocent is a guarantee that she will have no witnesses to prove what happened in her bedroom when the police broke in.

Yet Sodom itself was a safer place of residence than a city in which the police are capable of "framing" any woman, innocent or guilty. In Sodom, as Lot's experience when he stood at the door and argued with the mob proves, one could at least hope for a measure of safety while he remained indoors; but in New York, if the stories are true, a woman is in more danger from the police while she is indoors than while she is outside, where she may at least hope to have witnesses of any outrage.

To such lengths has American tolerance of police tyranny proceeded that the idea prevails, in many places, that mere arrest is not, in itself, a wrong. So rarely are the police penalized for false arrest that at the moment I cannot recall a single conspicuous instance. If the victim is released within a day or two, with or without an apology, he is considered to have no real reason for complaint. The notion prevails that it is infinitely more important to apprehend malefactors than it is to protect the rights of the unoffending. That is to say, the policeman is justified in harrying the whole population if, by so doing, he captures more evil-doers than he would otherwise capture. It is not hard to trace the basis of this belief back to the naïve theory that jailing criminals somehow promotes morality. The fallacy of the theory is glaringly demonstrated in the crime statistics for this country, where every city of over half a million has more homicides annually than all England. Yet in England a false arrest, unless made in very exceptional circumstances, means the end of the policeman who made it.

The older countries of Europe have long since outgrown the childish notion that morality can be beaten into people's heads with a policeman's club. They know what the police are good for, and employ them for that, namely, to maintain order in public places, so that decent-minded people may go about their legitimate affairs without having crime or vice flaunted in their faces. And the curious part of it—curious, that is, to an American—is that in attending strictly to this business the police of most European cities have proved themselves far more efficient in suppressing crime than have the police of American cities of the same size. In our anxiety to make the police promoters of morality we seem to have damaged their efficiency as suppressors of crime.

And then, when scandals break out, we rise in righteous indignation and hurl at the police every hard name we can lay tongue to. When the operation turns out to be worse than the disease, the surgeon who used a butcher knife blames the blade!

It takes no Freudian to discern in this peculiar American psychology an inferiority complex of startling proportions. To assert that we insist on burdening the police with the impossible task of supervising our morals because we dare not be free men is a hard saying, but what other explanation covers the facts? Doubtless it is but one aspect of materialism, which is of all philosophies the most slavish. Material things are moved by material force; and if our morality is purely material doubtless nothing but force will sustain it. This doctrine assumes that unless we be clubbed out of them we shall immediately begin swarming into brothels, gambling-halls, and saloons; it is a cardinal doctrine of that dismal form of religion which offers its adherents no solace, inspiration, or reward save the feat of escaping hell. That is to say, it is a morality of terror, affiliated with a religion of terror.

This religion can adopt the outward form of Catholicism, of Protestantism, of Judaism, or anything else, but it is essentially none of them. It is the religion of fear. And he who would indignantly deny that it is the dominant faith of America today is hard put to it to explain many phenomena of our national life. The proceedings of the Fish investigating committee, for example, are eloquent of a nation frightened half to death. Our countless "patriotic" societies seem to do nothing else but people the very air with terrors the least of which, we are stridently assured, is formidable enough to overcome and destroy the nation. The Scopes trial grew out of the effort to prop up the very Ark of the Covenant with a policeman's club. Every session of Congress is flooded with bills designed to save the terrified nation from perils of every imaginable description. So faintly and from so far away as to be unheard in the din of the stampede comes the word of the Lord to Zerubbabel, saying, "Not by might, nor by power, but by my Spirit, saith the Lord of hosts."

We don't believe it. Not for one fleeting moment do we believe it. It takes courage to swallow that doctrine, even to the extent of believing that the best defense of religion is "to do justly and to love mercy and to walk humbly with thy God"; that the best defense of the nation is to deal fairly with all other nations; that the best defense against prostitution, gambling, and liquor is to persuade men, one by one, to be decent, honest, and temperate. "By my spirit, saith the Lord"—but that was said to Zerubbabel long, long ago. Today the phrase is "By the Senate and House of Representatives of the State of Tennessee be it enacted" that men shall not believe heresy. "To do justly and to love mercy" may have been all very well in olden times, but the proper thing now is to bar out Russian goods and deport Communists. No still, small voice can reassure us against fire and storm and earthquake now; what we require is a policeman's whistle.

And having changed God into a policeman, is it not natural that we strive to erect the policeman into God? If he must enforce the moral law, instead of being content with protecting the peace and dignity of the state by driving vice out of sight and hearing of decent people, he is acting in a capacity which was of old reserved to Deity. And "it must follow as the night the day" that when the police attempt to act in any such capacity they get into trouble.

"Being God ain't no bed of roses, Gabe." After all, one must feel a twinge of sympathy with Commissioner Mulrooney. He really has too much to do.

HARPER'S MAGAZINE, *September 1931*

BRYAN, THOU SHOULDST BE LIVING

A Plea For Demagogues

Bryan should be living at this hour. Or if not Bryan, then Lord George Gordon, or Cagliostro, or John Brown of Ossawatomie—some first-class faker who believes in his own bunk.

It has been advanced that the decay of liberalism and the lack of a great liberal leader are to be attributed less to the apathy than to the bewilderment of this generation. With the increasing complexity of civilization, men of liberal mind are so hard put to it to know what to believe that they end by being afraid to put too much trust in anything. But the fallacy in this argument lies in the assumption that great liberal leaders think! Go back up the line—Wilson, Lloyd George, Briand, Gladstone, Jackson, Jefferson, Fox—

and you will find only Wilson and Jefferson who are entitled to be rated as first-rate thinkers, and only Jefferson who might set up a fairly good claim to be rated as the greatest thinker of his day.

Nevertheless, each of the others named was responsible for some tremendous thinking. The point is that he didn't do it. It was done by the men who found themselves under the necessity of putting him down. This much is true even of William Jennings Bryan, the quality of whose own cerebration is illustrated by the fact that he stated on oath that man is not a mammal. But he made Mark Hanna think. He made Roosevelt, Aldrich, Tom Reed, E. H. Harriman, the elder Morgan, Judge Gary, Whitelaw Reid, Henry Watterson, John Hay, William Allen White, Lodge, Penrose, Platt, Quay, and William H. Taft think. Later, after he had turned from politics to religion, he made such men as Harry Emerson Fosdick, Rabbi Wise, and Henry Fairfield Osborn think. Indeed, he drew from Walter Lippmann at least one essay, re-examining the principle of the rule of the majority, which was indubitably a contribution to the theory of democracy.

I hold this truth to be self-evident—that the quality of leadership is ability to lead. He who is able to enlist vast numbers of followers and to carry them in any direction he chooses is a great leader though he be mad as a March hare. And this quality has no necessary connection with a keenly analytical or highly original mind. If Gandhi is a thinker, so was Simple Simon; but if Gandhi is not a leader, there is no such thing.

I venture to suggest that what the liberals—and likewise the reds, the conservatives, and the tories—have reason to bewail today is not the lack of a great liberal leader, but the lack of a leader of any sort. A first-class reactionary would help immensely. A really able bolshevist would do us no end of good. For what the country needs most are the by-products of leadership, which are frequently more important than the work of the leader himself.

It is curious that so little attention has been paid to this factor in our political history, since the United States has provided what is perhaps the most perfect illustration of it. Only once have we elected a really ignorant man to the Presidency. Even Grant had had a West Point education. Andrew Jackson, however, was almost completely innocent of book-learning when he came to the White House. Furthermore, he was the most violent of all the Presidents and the least inclined to submit his prejudices to intellectual analysis.

Nevertheless, the fact remains that it was while this unmistakable non-intellectual reigned in the Executive Mansion that our political life attained and maintained a brilliance it had not reached before, and has not approached since. It was Jackson's peculiar virtue that he could heat the opposition to such a point that it burst into incandescence.

Granting that the Jacksonians were great politicians rather than great statesmen, the fact remains that they were superbly effective. The point is that such abilities as the Jacksonians possessed found full scope for their development under the banner of a man who, although glaringly defective as an intellectual was, nevertheless, perhaps the greatest popular leader we have ever produced.

However, the really startling effect of the appearance of this leader was on the men who opposed him. One has only to call the roll of their names to realize something of the brilliance of that period—John Quincy Adams, Daniel Webster, Henry Clay, John C. Calhoun, John Randolph of Roanoke, John Tyler, Rufus Choate, Edward Everett. It would be preposterous to insinuate that Jackson dowered these men with any part of their ability; but it is only sober truth to assert that in the enterprise of saving the country—as they saw it—from Jackson, they attained heights which they might never have reached except under the sting of a sharp and roweling spur.

Even to hold his own, much less to make headway, against such a force as Andrew Jackson, a man had to be good. It may be true that Jackson thought little; but in order to stand up against him at all, other men had to think furiously; and in the course of their efforts to cope with him they developed every latent power within them. The sudden efflorescence of genius in Congress at this period was not altogether an accident. Under the grueling discipline to which members were subjected, it is entirely reasonable to believe that not a few mediocre men grew strong, and that strong men grew great.

II

All this, however, affords no answer to the question of what is the matter with our own times. The lack of leadership is apparent enough. Al Smith aroused a certain amount of enthusiasm in 1928, but nothing comparable to the hysteria which used to attend Roosevelt, and which attended Bryan in 1896; and, barring Al, where is the leader in either party whose mere appearance is enough to set the street crowds to throwing their hats in the air? He is not in sight. Our most popular President since the War was Coolidge; but I have never yet heard anybody yell for Coolidge even as much as they yelled for Al Smith. Mr. Hoover received more votes for President than any man of any party ever received before; but it is plain to the dullest observer that vast numbers of them were not pro-Hoover votes at all. They were anti-Smith votes or, rather, anti-Pope and anti-liquor votes.

Even as late as 1907 there were a few men who were able to grip the imaginations of the people. When the Knickerbocker Trust Company blew up, Theodore Roosevelt was in the White House, and John Pierpont Morgan, the elder, was in Wall Street. When the condition of affairs became critical, it was announced in the press that Morgan had taken charge with the approval of the President; and immediately everybody, including the Democrats, felt better. For even the Democrats (perhaps I should say, especially the Democrats) believed that both of these were potent men. If they were really sound Democrats, such congenital Democrats as are produced in the South, they admired neither man, but they believed in them both. They believed that—to paraphrase a famous line—when either of these men put his foot down, something had to squush. Therefore, when word went around that Morgan had taken charge with Roosevelt's approval, everybody drew a long breath and felt better; and by feeling better, they were better.

In 1929 there was still a Pierpont Morgan in Wall Street; but in what a different light he was viewed by the country! We do not have the same sublime faith in his power, either for evil or for good. The House of Morgan has greater resources, and probably greater power, now than it had in 1907; but neither it nor any other potentate or dynasty of Wall Street any longer commands the imagination of the country.

In 1929 there was still a President in the White House, but not a Theodore Roosevelt. The present President knows more economics, in all probability, than T. R. ever guessed; but he knows less about Americans. Mr. Hoover unquestionably did everything he knew how to do in the terrific days of that terrible autumn, and he knew how to do a great deal. But he didn't know how to gesticulate.

Serious-minded people, who are always incurably romantic, will make the comment that that was of all times the worst time for gesticulations; but ribald realists know better. The world is not ruled by reason and logic. If it were, Mr. Hoover would have saved the situation, for the measures he took were pre-eminently reasonable and logical, as well as energetic. He immediately took counsel with the best business brains in the country. He had a number of sensible, practical suggestions to make and he urged them upon the people who were best able to understand them and carry them out. He labored diligently and intelligently and, doubtless, prevented a number of evils that without his efforts might have befallen the country. But at that, the thing got away from him. Instead of riding the avalanche, he was caught under it and buried deep in popular odium.

Does any man who views objectively the political history of the last thirty years believe that Theodore Roosevelt would have done any more toward reestablishing the economic balance? I, for one, do not believe that he would have done, or could have done, half as much. But I, for one, do not believe that Teddy ever would have been caught as Mr. Hoover has been caught. He might not have done as much as Mr. Hoover, but he would have seemed to be doing ten times more. He knew how to gesticulate. He could dance and yell. The roars emanating from the White House in the closing days of 1929 had Roosevelt been there would have been so loud they would almost have drowned the incessant banging by exploding banks, and so blood-curdling they would have distracted attention from the atrocities being perpetrated on the Stock Market.

Nor am I prepared to assert that they would have been all sound and fury, signifying nothing, or nothing save the preservation of the Rooseveltian hide. No economist doubts that the present depression has been prolonged and intensified by the fathomless pessimism which it has induced in the American people. The energy of the country has suffered a strange paralysis. We are in the doldrums, waiting not even hopefully for the wind which never comes. Roosevelt would have supplied wind. Whatever he did, the country would have been so vastly entertained that it would have forgotten a large part of its pessimism. It would have been amused in part, scandalized in part, infuriated in part; but each emotion would have stimulated it to some sort of action. The psychological part of the depression he could have managed.

This is assuming, of course, that we have not become so sophisticated that it is no longer possible for a Roosevelt, or a Bryan, or an Andrew Jackson to stir us. I think it a reasonable assumption. Of course, none of these men could repeat his former triumphs in precisely the same form. History never repeats itself exactly. But there is plenty of ground for suspicion that all this sophistication about which we are forever talking is in large measure what the incomparable Al calls baloney. It is true that the physicists and mathematicians have resolved the whole material universe into nothing more substantial than "the nominative case of the verb *to undulate*." But who knows it? Mr. Einstein, Sir James Jeans, and Mr. Millikan, along with the fraction of one per cent of the population who have read their books. It is equally true that the psychologists have analyzed Yale, country, and God into conditioned reflexes. But who knows that? Mr. John B. Watson, and he has his doubts. It is true that the novelists, the biographers, and the historians have joined hands to convert history and literature into an endless stentorian reiteration of "Ichabod, Ichabod for the glory hath departed!" But who knows that? Only the all but imperceptible minority which does not read the confession magazines.

Grant that the intellectuals, as a class, are fairly crushed into immobility under the weight of facts which science has heaped upon their somewhat thin shoulders—does it follow that the country is paralyzed? Not unless the country is dependent upon the intellectuals for leadership, which is an assumption not many of us would care to make. When did a genuine intellectual ever lead it? Wilson? He led, all right, but was he really an intellectual? Gamaliel Bradford remarks that, "Even in the fields which might be thought peculiarly his own his information was singularly limited," and at the time of the fight over the Peace Treaty it was intimated in the public prints that he had never read the Constitution of the United States. But, for the sake of argument, allow that Wilson was an intellectual as well as a leader. Does one swallow make a summer?

The spectacularly successful leader has always been not the intellectual, but the histrionic genius. Even Lenin is no real exception, while Mussolini is a museum piece. It is hard to believe that Americans have been so thoroughly imbued with the spirit of modern education that they have really subverted their emotional to their intellectual natures; but until a nation does so it will always remain more amenable to the man on horseback than to the man on the rostrum. Perhaps popular education has made us require a different technic of the men who would mold us to their will. But to assume that we are, therefore, proof against mountebanks is to assume far too much. We require suaver and smoother mountebanks, that is all.

Furthermore, it is hard to believe that the present tremendous sweating through which the nation is being put will fail to produce at least one. The stage is too perfectly set, the time is too ripe, for us to escape the irruption of a Mad Mullah of some variety. The fabrication of a sufficiently crazy program always takes a little time after a great crash. Populism, distilled from the witches' broth of 1893, did not attain its full strength until the very close of the century. Greenbackism, engendered in 1873, made its strongest bid in 1876. The panic of 1837—perhaps the worst of them all—gave rise to a long series of marvelous psychoses culminating in Know-Nothingism, which flourished a dozen years after the crash. Reasoning by analogy, we should hardly expect to see earlier than 1932 whatever apparition the panic of 1929 may eventually call out of the vasty deep. It is not within the bounds of credibility, however, that nothing in the way of governmental extravaganza will be born of the present stresses and strains. Upheavals so profound are not accomplished without loosing uneasy spirits which will haunt us for many days.

But if my argument is sound, this prospect is not one to dismay honest and liberal-minded men. The Mad Mullah always loses in the long run for the simple reason that when he trumpets to the feeble-witted he rouses the intelligent; and even as the former flock to his standard, the latter take arms against him. I hold no brief for Bryanism, but it is evident to the dullest that Bryanism compelled some of the hardest and keenest political thinking of the last generation; and out of the welter stirred up by Bryan emerged both Roosevelt and Wilson, each of whom helped himself liberally to Bryan's ideas, stripped most of the lunacy from them, and employed them to excellent advantage.

III

And when all is said and done, could any madman arise with a program madder than the present polity of the United States of America has turned out to be? The proof of the pudding is the chewing of the bag. The proof of the sanity, or the reverse, of any polity is not its logical perfection but the pass to which it brings the country which adopts it. Never mind how reasonable our program for the past ten years may seem to be. Let us consider the pass to which it has brought this country.

Our present condition is deplorable on account of a terrific burden of unemployment caused by over-production. That is to say, people are going hungry because there is too much wheat, too much corn, too many swine and cattle; people are going barefoot because there are too many shoes, ragged because there are too many textiles, being evicted from their homes because there are too many houses; charitable agencies are being overwhelmed with pleas for alms because there is too much real wealth in the country.

But this is preposterous, this is insanity, this is the very essence of Bedlam. Nevertheless, this is true, and its truth constitutes the incontrovertible proof that we have been following a polity as crazy as the wildest ever preached by any crack-brained fanatic from the Middle West. Our intellectuals have known for years that it was a crazy polity; but unfortunately what the intellectual knows is as completely removed from the experience of average men and women as what the Martian engineers may know is removed from the experience of earthly engineers. That which enters into the experience of the masses of the people is not what the intellectual knows, but what the popular leader feels.

But let a popular leader of a very powerful type enter the field and he arouses passions, even in intellectuals. The only passions he may arouse in their breasts may be aversion and disgust, but to that extent, at least, they begin to feel, as well as think, and as they begin to feel they begin to grow effective. There is much talk these days of the "tired liberal." I doubt that the animal exists. It seems more probable that what we have are emotionally starved liberals. Since Wilson passed off the stage they haven't had a single man whom it was worthwhile to hate; and a liberal without hatred is like a fish without a tail—he moves incessantly, but aimlessly, without direction. Your hate must have a target visible to the naked eye, or it degenerates into mere disdain, which does not nourish action.

Yet action is the final, indispensable test of ideas. The truth is that the human mind is so imperfect an instrument that no sage ever lived who was capable of deciding infallibly, without the test of action, which of our ideas are lunatic and which are sane. Your leader applies this test, but he is able to apply it because he knows, not how to make men think, but how to make them feel; which means that he first feels intensely himself. If he is also capable of thinking, so much the better; in that case we have a statesman of a high order. But it is not absolutely essential that he think. If he can act, and does act, others will do whatever thinking is necessary.

It is perfectly true that the menace of a demagogic leader is very great. One such might easily wreck the country. But if it comes to that, take a look at the country now. Some statistician with a grisly mind recently checked up on the mortality rate of a businessmen's club in my city. He found that the normal death rate among members for the last ten years has been about 15 annually; but in the year 1930 that club lost 57 members by death, of whom 10 were suicides. In the county where I was born—not in Arkansas, either—no less than 500 mules starved to death last year. If it had been 500 tenant farmers who had starved, there might be some excuse to hope that things are not quite desperate; but when landlords let their mules starve, there is no escaping the fact that the situation is serious. When farmers are letting their mules starve and businessmen are blowing their brains out, both in unprecedented numbers, the country is in a fix about as bad as any demagogue is likely to put it in.

At any rate, after observing the results of turning the country over to be run by the magnates of big business and the high priests of prosperity, there are not a few Americans who have decided that if these are the sane men, it might be well to try putting the lunatics in charge for awhile. They could hardly do worse, and they would do differently, so it is within the realm of possibility that they might do better.

At any rate, the country will follow a man who feels intensely, unless human nature has undergone a greater change in the last ten years than it ever underwent in a comparable time before. When a political leader stands up, and instead of saying, "This is logical" or "this is scientific" or "this is businesslike," says "this is right," I think he will strike a popular chord. It is by no means certain that he will actually be right. On the contrary, he may merely be an idiot. But if he thinks he is right, and thinks it with such

burning, passionate intensity that the heat of his conviction is felt by everyone who comes within a hundred feet of him, he will be effective. "Our Federal union—it must be preserved!" Why? There was no very logical reason, but there was one most powerful reason, which was that Andrew Jackson willed that it should be preserved; and preserved it was. "You shall not press down upon the brow of labor this crown of thorns; you shall not crucify mankind upon a cross of gold." Fustian? Without a doubt, but—my sacred aunt—how it got action! "We fight to make the world safe for democracy!" Well, we seem to have failed to make it safe, but you can inform the strabismic world we fought!

Phrase-making is perhaps no contribution to the intellectual heritage of the race, but phrase-makers do snap us out of lethargy, and frequently out of ingrowing pessimism, which may be worse than frenzy. How we could use one at the moment! Bryan, thou shouldst be living at this hour!

HARPER'S MAGAZINE, *November 1931*

FOR IGNOBLE PACIFISM

When the late unpleasantness broke out in Europe, seventeen years ago—Lord, how time does fly!—my native State of North Carolina was still full of Confederate veterans; and as a very young man, I was astonished, and a little shocked, to find as America grew steadily more uproarious, that the old boys, almost to a man, were snorting pacifists. I could not understand it then. But a little later, when we took a hand, I toured France as a member of Sir John Pershing's personally-conducted party; and now I know what the graybeards were talking about.

At that, I admit I didn't win the War. I merely attended it. As we say in North Carolina, nary a German soldier did I kill. I never even shot at one. I was one of the lucky dogs who were detailed to duty around the edges of the disputation; so I have no conception of what was endured by the men who won Cantigny, and Kemmel Hill, and Soissons, and the Argonne. All that I saw was the lighter side of war.

Still, I have a fairly intimate knowledge of the humorous incidents that characterize an active campaign. I have experienced the delights of sleeping in the mud and waking up with hoarfrost an eighth of an inch long on my shoes; and of marching under a full pack with flu shaking my bones and my temperature running one hundred three and a half, and thanking God for the privilege of finding a bunk in a cow-stable. I know what a merry jest it is to have your fingers frostbitten until the flesh comes sloughing off, and how it feels to go three months without a bath, while *pediculus vestimenti* thrives and increases marvelously. I know how laughable it is to have shells land close enough to jar the ground under your feet, and to dive headfirst for cover at the drone of an airplane motor, and to have your village machine-gunned by an enemy aviator. I have known the pleasure of serving under brutal and incompetent officers, and of having to be servile, because he wore eagles on his shoulders, to a man whom I would kick down the steps if he tried to enter my house in time of peace. I have seen burial parties, and hospital trains coming back from the front.

Therefore, although my failure to engage in any of the big fights leaves me little more than a pseudo-veteran, I do know something about war. And I do not like it. Indeed, when the next one comes along it will take a corporal and seven strong men to get me into a uniform.

For what did we, who served in the ranks, get out of this last one? What have we, thirteen years after the Armistice, that we, the common people, who are not statesmen and not international bankers, but who fought the War—what have we now that we won by our efforts in 1917-18? "Count your many blessings, name them one by one." The second biggest navy in the world, with the biggest appropriation to keep it up. Income taxes. Taxes on theater tickets. Taxes on tobacco. The American Legion and other Red-hunters. The espionage act. Criminal syndicalism laws. Communists. Prohibition. Hoover.

Mind you, I have no objection to fighting. I know by experience that a first-class fist-and-skull argument frequently can

> *Cleanse the stuff'd bosom of that perilous stuff*
> *Which weights upon the heart,*

and my opinion of the man who has come to voting age without ever having given battle is but small. But what has modern war to do with fighting? Although I know hundreds of veterans, I have never yet encountered one who had stood up to a German, man to man, and whipped him. A few aviators are the only men I know who can say with certainty that they have brought down a German, even by the aid of chemically propelled leaden pellets. Pumping the bolt of a Springfield rifle with nothing for a target but some distant whiffs of dust, or feeding shells into a 75, hour after hour, with only a set of co-ordinates for guidance is not the sort of fighting that is good for a man. A warm appreciation of the value of belligerence is not at all inconsistent with pacifism, as regards organized warfare.

It is on high moral principles that all wars are fought. At least it is on these principles that all the silly wars are fought. When Brigadier-General Fries, then chief of the Chemical Warfare Service, roundly declared a few years ago, "America has always been right in wars it has been forced to fight," he received many gibes; but he can prove his case by any textbook of history used in the common schools. The only trouble is, the enemy was right, too, as he can prove by his textbooks, written by historians as eminent as our own. As regards the late War, it is pretty generally understood now that everybody was right except Portugal; and all that is needed now to close the incident is for a new Pish-Tush to skip off the stage singing,

> *And we are right, I think you'll say,*
> *To argue in this kind of way.*
> *And I am right,*
> *And you are right,*
> *And all is right—too-looral-lay!*

Yet the dead men insist on remaining dead, my fingers ache again at every cold snap, prohibition remains with us, and Hoover is still President. The fact that the War was fought on the highest moral principles all around doesn't alter the fact that it was a silly business, costing enormously more than it was worth. Therefore, when I am invited to join a pacifist organization on the ground that it is based upon the highest moral principles, I seem to get a whiff of the stenches of the Western Front and hurriedly decline.

II

Yet somehow I believe my objection to war is deeper rooted than that of most of the bishops and most of the ladies. After all, ignoble principles are not easily convertible. A man's tender consideration for his own hide is not to be dissipated, even by bugle calls; and I sometimes think a pacifist organization based upon that principle would be a lasting one. The answer to that is, of course, that the men whose hides are endangered are not the men who make the decisions involving peace and war. If they had been, it is pretty safe to say that America's one hundred and three wars would have numbered, probably, not over fifty or sixty, and these would have been Indian campaigns, which paid. It is significant that not even our most ardent patriots today attempt to argue that the Indian campaigns were all based on high moral principles; yet it is obvious that these were our only wars that brought in more than they cost and, therefore, were a paying investment.

Your typical pacifist, however, lumps these wars in with all others and condemns war *in toto*. In that he goes too far. His moral principles get the better of his respect for facts, which is frequently the way moral principles work, and one reason why they are productive of so many wars.

Suppose governments threw moral principle overboard altogether and never waged a war save upon plainly ignoble motives—what would happen? Why, it is clear that nobody would ever fight anybody else who could fight back; for if you pick an opponent who can fight, under modern conditions no one can hope to win a tithe of what the fight will cost him. In that case defensive armament would really defend, and we should have lasting peace among the great powers.

Members of the Army and Navy—notoriously ingenuous men—have a vague idea that this is what really happens. They are continually assuring us that if our battalions and men-o'-war are numerous and strong, no one will think of attacking us. That would be true if the decisions for war or peace were always made upon ignoble principles, that is to say, upon a cool-headed estimate of the probable gain to be hoped from victory balanced against the probable cost to be incurred in fighting. If that were the process we should never think of attacking, for instance, Japan, in spite of the fact that the ratio of our naval strength to hers is as ten to six; for the business of whipping a nation with even that much strength would inevitably cost far more than could possibly be gained by it.

What Army and Navy officers constantly overlook is the fact that when the crisis arrives statesmen invariably abandon common sense and act on high moral principle, to the ruin of their countries. To illustrate, let us suppose that we fell into an argument with Japan over the possession of some such scrap of the earth's surface as the Island of Yap. As long as statesmen were governed by the ignoble sentiment of Safety First there could be no question of war. Everyone would have in mind the fact that the price of a couple of broadsides from the battle fleet would be more than the whole place is worth. But who can imagine that they would be so guided? As soon as the crisis became acute the question of relative values would be abandoned to give place to the high moral principle of protection of the nation's dignity, which cannot, of course, be measured in money. And we should be betrayed into the imbecility of fighting a war over Yap.

So pacifism, thoroughly sound and sensible if based upon ignoble sentiments, becomes a flat denial of plain facts, that is, a negation of sense, once it becomes involved with high moral principles. To repudiate wars against strong enemies on the ground that it is idiotic to fight a strong nation is thoroughly sensible, if unromantic. But to repudiate war in general on the ground that it is always stupid and wasteful is simply silly. In all the world there exists no great nation that has not been built up by wars. The United States, to be specific, has fought one hundred and three, not counting the present war in Nicaragua. The vast majority of these, so far from being silly and wasteful, were highly profitable, since they secured our continental domain, which is worth infinitely more than all they cost. But if all war is to be repudiated, then we must repudiate wars against people who can't fight much, as well as those against people who can fight. We must repudiate the campaigns against the Indians as well as the campaign against the Germans. We must repudiate the process by which the nation was built.

It is not pleasant to remember that Columbia's throne is a pyramid of skulls, but there are the one hundred and three wars to prove it. In this respect we are no worse than any other nation, and better than some; but to deny that we, like the other world powers, have profited exceedingly by war is to deny the plain fact. It is only when we fight a strong opponent that both sides lose.

But pacifism, as it is now organized in this country, does deny the facts. It prefers high moral principle to facts, and therein it falls into the identical trap in which war-making statesmen are taken. Why should a plain man, whose sole objection to war is its character as the summation and crown of all nuisances, regard the pacifists with any more enthusiasm than he has for the statesmen? They are both full of gassy nonsense which makes them equally unsafe guides.

I like to toy with the idea of a pacifist organization got up by no lady and by no chevalier, but by a lewd fellow of the baser sort. It would have for its first objective the absolute prohibition of war under any circumstances against people who can fight. It would oppose such wars, not on the ground that they are murderous, or on the ground that they are unjust, but on the one point that they are supremely idiotic. It would have for its second objective the absolute prohibition of conscription. This would compel the government to offer soldiers in the ranks a reward somewhat commensurate with the risk they run. It would not prevent wars but it would make them more expensive and less profitable, and it would confine warmaking to the warlike. If the Government planned a campaign against Mexico—as it is pretty sure to do some day—it could undoubtedly raise half a million men by offering every survivor one hundred acres of Mexican land after the conquest. To fulfill this promise would take a little over a tenth of the area of the country, leaving nine-tenths to defray the other costs of the war; but nobody should be compelled to take part in the conquest unless he felt like gambling his life against the stakes offered. Finally, this organization would strive to fix the penalty of death for any statesman who, whether by error or by design, entered into a war which after five years from the date of the beginning of hostilities was still unprofitable.

This scheme, I assert without fear of successful contradiction, is ignoble in every detail. There is not a moral principle in it anywhere. But the way it would head off wars cannot, in my opinion, be approached by any of the existing pacifist organizations. Among our major conflicts it would have obviated the possibility of the War of 1812, the Civil War, the Spanish War, and the War of 1917-18. Only the Revolution and the Mexican War, both of which paid handsomely, would have been permissible under it. Yet it would have prevented none of the campaigns by means of which we obliterated the Noble Red Man and expropriated his territory. Nor would it prevent us in the future from taking over as many banana republics as we think we may require. It would merely tend to restrain us from taking them over too soon and from taking over any of which we cannot make good use. That is to say, it would tend to restrain conquest based on megalomania, while only slightly hampering conquest based on sound economic considerations.

Conquest based on sound economic considerations never has been restrained. When the time came when we could really use Texas, we took it; and when the time came when we could use Panama we took it. When and if the time comes when we can use Mexico to real advantage there is not the slightest doubt that we shall move down in force. Perhaps that time may never come. Under a reasonable economic and social order in the world it probably would not come, for under such an organization Mexico might be made more profitable to us under control of her present population than under our control; but the establishment of reasonable and just trade relations, the elimination of juridical anachronisms, and the extirpation of racial and national prejudices are matters of practical statecraft not undertaken in any pacifist progam with which I am acquainted. Could we eliminate tariffs, chauvinists, fanatics, and plain crooks there would be little or nothing for pacifists to do; but we must just take the world as it is, not as it should be, and the real reason our battalions remain north of the Rio Grande is that relatively few of us can see, as yet, how we could use Mexico profitably enough to compensate us for the expense of the conquest.

If the time ever comes when it is plainly apparent to a large percentage of our business leaders that Mexico could be used to really great advantage, the political independence of the Mexicans will not be worth a plugged nickel. Ignoble pacifism would not, in that case, prevent the conquest; but it would postpone it, because it would run up the expense of the war by insisting that the invading army be adequately paid for its services. Furthermore, it would send us into the country frankly as conquerors who are after the money, and not as agents of the higher civilization intent on inculcating high moral principles in a backward people with the aid of shrapnel, poison gas, and machine guns. Doubtless it is a quaint and old-fashioned prejudice that makes the ignoble pacifists object to their country's lying like Munchausen whenever it goes forth to war; but the fact remains that they do object.

The present opposition to all wars whatever is not getting very far; but I believe that immense numbers of people, including a considerable proportion of Sir John's tourists, could be interested in a pacifism that set some limits to its nobility. No war at all may be the ideal. But as a practical program why should we not, to begin with, demand fewer wars and franker ones, smaller and sounder wars, murder for profit, not for pleasure? For surely it is better to be a hijacker than a sadist.

VIRGINIA QUARTERLY REVIEW, *July 1932*

SINCE WILSON

Thirteen years ago, the thirtieth day of last May, I attended Memorial Day exercises in a military cemetery and saw a man there. In that gathering there were, according to my hasty estimate at the time, a thousand civilians, three thousand Red Cross nurses, nine thousand Y.M.C.A. secretaries, and fourteen soldiers. But as I look back on it now I remember seeing only one man; the rest were doubtless well enough, but they are not worth remembering after thirteen years.

With a comrade I arrived a bit late, and in order to see over the heads of the people who were standing on the level ground we climbed up a steep bank. The soft earth slipped under our hobnailed boots, and we secured ourselves by gripping saplings. When we were finally able to turn and look down on the scene, the exercises were already under way. A coagulation of people in the midst of the field of white crosses showed the center of interest. There were hordes of French generals, the sunlight gleaming on the golden oak-leaves embroidered around their caps. One of them—someone said he was Pétain—took a great sheaf of flowers and, stooping, laid them on a nearby grave. Then they all turned, by common consent, toward the center of the group. Presently an old man's head projected itself above the crowd, evidently because he had stepped upon a box or something. We were much too far away to hear a sound, and the old man's back was toward us, but he seemed to be speaking, for the group around him was attentive. Idly, we speculated upon his identity. His hair was snow-white; at the base of his skull it curled up as Bryan's used to do, like a drake's tail-feather. He was obviously feeble. His neck projected forward a little, and his shoulders hunched wearily. Whoever he was, it was clear that the old boy was about all in. We put him down as some ancient exhumed in the Faubourg St. Germain because he had seen the Commune, and brought out here to perform an introduction and add a touch of the dignity of the past to the present proceedings.

He spoke for three or four minutes before he remembered the people behind him, and turned in our direction. But at last he did turn, and as his face swung into view, what a jolt we had! All suggestion of 1871, of feebleness and age, dissolved and vanished as we caught sight of that grim and arrogant countenance with its narrow steadfast eyes, its dominant nose, its powerful, belligerent jaw. We faced the Conqueror, who had the world at his feet. We were looking at Woodrow Wilson.

Well, I have looked at various dignitaries since that day. To paraphrase Browning's remark to the peasant, I once saw Harding plain, and Coolidge also. On March 4, 1928, I saw Herbert Hoover, although not plainly. Long lines of drenched soldiery, many thousands of people, and a veil of dismal, cold rain were between us, and his face was but a white blob in the distance. At the Jackson Day dinner in Washington last January I saw sitting all in a row, James Middleton Cox, John William Davis, and Alfred Emanuel Smith, who contested three elections with the three Presidents. In the last thirteen years I have seen thousands of people. But I know that when I sit doddering in the chimney corner many years hence and wish to make my grandchildren sit up with a jerk, and regard the old man curiously, instead of mentioning these, I shall say that in 1919 I saw Woodrow Wilson at Suresnes.

II

Probably those same grandchildren will still be squabbling over the place of Wilson in history. Certainly there is as yet no sign of an end to the disputes over whether he triumphed or was defeated, whether he was the herald of a new dawn, or a fatuous chaser of the will-o'-the-wisp, whether he is a new and shining addition to the hagiology, or the Abou ben Adhem of the Book of the Damned. I shall not presume to express a judgment on such high matters. I shall confine myself to an observation which will not be denied by friend or foe: that Woodrow Wilson was the last man in our public life who was capable of inspiring maudlin hatred.

Within the last dozen years various other persons have inspired more or less powerful hates. Tom Mooney, Sacco and Vanzetti, Clarence Darrow, Gaston B. Means, Dion O'Bannion, Bishop Cannon, H. L. Mencken, J. Thomas Heflin, John J. Raskob, Nan Britton, William E. Borah, and Rupert Hughes, among others, have been denounced by various people for various reasons; but all the hatred aroused by all of them put together is, by comparison with the hatred aroused by Woodrow Wilson, as an electric fan is to a Kansas cyclone. Those that hated Wilson most, hated him with an intensity that energized their lives, molded their characters, and sometimes—for example, in the cases of Senators Lodge, Johnson, and Reed—almost made great men of them; or else broke them down completely, and set them to jittering. Nay, more—certain philosophers, notably H. L. Mencken, are of the opinion that hatred of Wilson was occasionally fatal, hastening, if not solely causing, the end of the elder Theodore Roosevelt, and perhaps others.

In any case, it was a big thing. As a measure of the man, I prefer it to the admiration Wilson aroused, because admiration can be blown up to gigantic dimensions by skillful press-agentry, but genuine, thoroughgoing, virulent, and lasting hatred is invariably an achievement of the hero himself, not of clever fellows in his entourage. And, measured by the detestation he aroused, a detestation which has not subsided and perhaps has increased in the eight years since his death, Wilson looms gigantically over the field of history.

No President since has accomplished anything remotely resembling it. Not until after death had removed Harding from Washington did we discover that he had marched into town at the head of a Falstaff's army, recruited by robbing every gibbet in the kingdom; and even then the general feeling was that the poor old fellow had swindled himself worse than all his thieves had swindled the country. Nobody ever hated Harding. What was the use? As for Mr. Coolidge, one still invites a coat of tar and feathers by speaking of him in any but hushed and reverential tones. He is as sacred as Saint Andrew, whom he seems in a fair way to oust as the patron of all Scotchmen. Some people do not greatly admire the present President; but the most rabid anti-Hooverite is as gentle as any sucking dove by comparison with a really rabid anti-Wilsonian.

Hatred is an emotion not well spoken of by respectable persons. It is violent, blind, and destructive, therefore certainly is not to be commended as a national ideal. Yet it is an undeniable fact that a small man cannot be hated in a big way, and some of us would be content to risk seeing the nation corrode in a bath of hatred if only it had a man big enough to arouse such an emotion. . . .

Well, the storms and violences of the Wilsonian age are over, and since he quit the White House we have had eleven years of uninterrupted peace.

Wilson was a war President, which is to say, he was an autocrat, as war Presidents always are. When he appealed to "force to the uttermost, force without stint or limit" he went the whole hog; and not only the Germans, but those Americans who were not nimble enough to catch step with the big parade, felt the impact of that force without stint or limit. The jails swiftly filled with people charged with offenses which in time of peace would have been no crimes at all, and the myrmidons of the Department of Justice frequently filed away luckless individuals whose acts were hardly crimes even by the peculiar standards of war time.

It was a hard, ruthless era, for no country is ever careful of the rights of man when an armed enemy is in the field against it. We may well rejoice that we have had no similar disturbance for a third of a generation. Released from the pressure of war, the country should have made, since Wilson, great progress toward restoration of the respect of the Government for the rights of the citizen. Since Wilson, no armed enemy has risen against us, and we have had eleven years to develop the friendship of other nations. Since Wilson, there has been no occasion to regard homicide as a noble and patriotic occupation, and brute force ought to be much less in favor as a method of settling difficulties. Since Wilson, there has been no weight of fear to drive us into accepting lies as history, hatred as patriotic piety, belligerence as the mark of a manful man; so there should have been a notable elevation of the tone of our public life.

Even after three years of extreme industrial depression, we remain by long odds the wealthiest and most powerful nation on the globe. No enemy threatens our frontiers, and the garrison in our remotest outpost can sleep soundly at night. No rebellion or insurrection threatens our internal peace. No monarchist, or fascist, or communist party exists in this country in strength enough to give the faintest quiver of alarm to any heart stouter than those of the perpetually quaking Daughters of the American Revolution. Our harvests have been only too abundant, we have all too much goods, laid up for all too many days. Pestilence has not smitten us, nor have earthquakes, floods, and fires carried off vast numbers of our people. Tranquillity, wealth, and health have been ours, as a nation, these eleven years; judged by every standard mankind has been accustomed to apply we should have been, since Wilson, the happiest people in all the earth.

Consider how vastly different it was in Wilson's time. For the first year and a half, indeed, we were busily at work building anew our system of social control; but for the next two years we were engaged in scrambling frantically to keep out of the vortex of the whirlpool, losing ground all the time; then for a year and a half our money and our blood streamed away in a horrible flood; and the rest of the time we grappled with the hopeless task of rebuilding a wrecked world. Storm and stress were our portion through it all. We suffered dreadful fears; we knew pain, and hope deferred that maketh the heart sick; we performed Herculean labors and accepted gigantic losses. Without rest, without surcease, we endured and we strove. Well, indeed, may we thank God and take courage that such a time of trial is eleven years behind us.

III

And yet I doubt that the most resolute optimist will assert that all that might have been expected of these years of peace has actually come to pass. Let us consider, *seriatim,* what has been accomplished since Wilson toward the restoration and strengthening of, first, liberty; second, international comity; third, domestic civilization; and fourth, intelligent statecraft. Wilson, his critics aver, attacked all these things; he did it under the plea of military necessity, to be sure, but, they insist, he attacked them, nevertheless. Now Wilson's opponents have been in power ever since, and they have not been driven by any military necessity. Their success in restoring what he attacked should be a fair measure of their ability as statesmen.

First on the list and most important is the matter of individual liberty, for, as Lincoln pointed out, this country was "conceived in liberty" and it has no other excuse for being. Wilson's most conspicuous and least excusable assault on liberty was what he did to Eugene Debs. This was an honest man —silly, no doubt, but conscientious and incapable of deliberate treason, yet Wilson sent him to jail for opposing the war. It was pretty bad, and I have no intention of defending it. Yet I venture to point out that jailing Debs did require a certain amount of nerve, for he was the most prominent Socialist in the country and the idol of hundreds of people, many of them highly vocal and some of them highly intelligent.

It took less nerve for California to jail Tom Mooney, for Mooney had few friends of any consequence. Furthermore, Debs got twenty years for something he unquestionably did do, but served only five. Mooney got life for something he probably didn't do, and has served sixteen years. At that Mooney would unquestionably have been hanged had it not been for the intervention of one man, and he the same man who sent Debs to jail, to wit, Woodrow Wilson. It is true that he intervened in the Mooney case solely on account of international pressure, but was it not also on account of international pressure that he sent Debs to jail?

However, the justification of Wilson is no part of this discussion, which is simply an effort to measure the revival of respect for individual liberty since Wilson. During the course of the war with Germany there is one thing this government, with all its brutality, did not do—it sent no man actually to death for cherishing radical opinions. Even Debs was never in real danger of hanging, and Mooney, as noted above, was saved from the noose by Federal intervention. But Sacco and Vanzetti were not disposed of by the hard-pressed, grim, and ruthless government of Wilson's time—and they went to the electric chair.

The interpretation put upon the law by such jurisconsults as Albert S. Burleson and A. Mitchell Palmer in Wilson's administration was certainly not such as to reassure libertarians. They carried to lengths hitherto unheard-of in America the doctrine of the supremacy of the State. They were accused then, and have been accused constantly since, of attempting to embed in American law one of the most objectionable concepts of Prussianism, namely, the doctrine that the State has a life of its own not merely more extensive, but superior to that of the individual, and may exercise a sort of right of eminent domain in the field of men's loyalties and devotions, as well as in the field of their acts.

This is a serious accusation, for if it is true, it indicates that in Wilson's time there were men in high office to whom that phrase in the Declaration of Independence about "unalienable rights" made small appeal. Naturally, one hopes that in the succeeding years of peace the Government has been purged of such blatantly un-American doctrine. One hopes? Well, hardly that. For it was since Wilson that Douglas Clyde Macintosh, a professor in the Yale Divinity School, applied for naturalization as an American citizen. The applicant's character was unimpeachable, his brain an able one, his record distinguished. But he was a clergyman, and when he was questioned he took the position that most people would expect a man in holy orders to take— he stated that he placed his allegiance to God above his allegiance to any earthly Government whatever. And *on that specific point* the Supreme Court of the United States held Dr. Macintosh unfit to be a citizen of the United States. When the State asserts its right to precedence over the Almighty, even in the matter of the allegiance of its citizens, the doctrine of the supremacy of the State has been carried to lengths to which Palmer and Burleson never dared go.

If Wilson sent men to jail for holding radical opinions, since Wilson we have sent men to burn in the electric chair under circumstances that have led thousands to believe that we have burned them for being political heretics. This equals the record of the Spanish Inquisition. But we have given yet another turn to the screw. Since Wilson we have called upon clergymen to renounce the First Commandment as the price of citizenship. For a Baptist— Dr. Macintosh's denomination—this is equivalent to a sentence to burn, not in the electric chair, but in hell's fire. And this tops the Inquisition.

IV

It is fairly plain, then, that in the matter of individual liberty our progress since Wilson has not been in the direction of its reestablishment as the mudsill of the government. Let us therefore proceed to consider the next item, international comity.

In Wilson's time we assisted in battering to their knees two great empires, one lesser empire, and a kingdom. So it stands to reason that in at least four nations we were regarded with anything but brotherly affection. One could not expect nations which our armies had just been beating into a bloody pulp to love us. But one could hope that in the succeeding eleven years of peace we might accomplish something toward reestablishing amicable relations with all the world.

The best measure of our success in this line is to be found in the foreign press. Diplomats customarily converse in honeyed words up to the very moment when the first shell comes screeching over the lines. The official correspondence of no nation gives any hint of its real opinion of the United States; but its newspapers do.

It is by reading foreign newspapers that some careful observers have been led to the pessimistic belief that the United States today is the most cordially

hated nation on earth. The horror of all Europe is the danger of Americanization, and "Uncle Shylock" is its name for the most dreaded international bully
now extant.

This hatred may be based upon dread of our military and economic
power, but it rises far beyond that. There is hardly an intellectual leader in
Europe who has not sometime within the last decade solemnly warned his
countrymen against becoming infected with the American spirit. It may be
that they do not know what the American spirit is; but they think they
know, and what they conceive to be the American spirit seems to them
dreadful.

If they are deceived, is it not evident that we have somehow failed to
impress upon them the excellence of our intentions and the amiability of our
disposition? In 1917 if we incurred the hatred of the Central Powers, we had
the Allies solidly at our backs. In this respect, peace has been more disastrous
than war; for the circle of nations that dislike and distrust us has steadily
widened.

I do not believe that this hatred is entirely deserved; but as for the
suspicion that accompanies it, I am not so sure. The vacillation and uncertainty
of our foreign policy have been enough to breed distrust. When the average
American has not the remotest idea of what his country's foreign policy
is from one week to another, how shall he expect the foreigner to be other
than puzzled, and being puzzled, distrustful? We search our own hearts for the
peaceableness of our intentions, but the foreigner has nothing to go by but
Haiti, Nicaragua, and the size of our naval budget. However, regardless of
the reason, the fact is that international comity has fared little better than
individual liberty in the last eleven years. Since Wilson, international comity,
also, has gone from bad to worse.

IV

But few of us, after all, are directly affected in our daily lives by the
international relations of the United States. Our first concern must be with
the development of civilization within our borders. And here, again, it is
surely not unreasonable to hope to discover a notable improvement in the
direction of peace and security over the conditions that prevailed in war
time.

For war is by its very nature an enthronement of the brute. When an
armed enemy is in the field, it is the first duty of the country to put him
down by violence; and this necessity inevitably gives violence a respected
place in the routine of our daily lives. Not its men-at-arms only, but the
whole nation is driven to what Norman Thomas calls "the acceptance of
violence"; and this acceptance, however necessary it may be, is a retrogression
in civilization.

It is not surprising, therefore, to find that in the second administration of
Wilson riots were not infrequent. Conscientious objectors were set upon and
beaten; radical meetings were raided by mobs and broken up, not without
bloodshed; there were a few race riots, and some battles between police and
strikers. These were part of the evil products of war psychology, and their

appearance was another strong reason for desiring the return of peace; for only in time of peace is there much hope of rooting out the acceptance of violence from our mental make-up.

But to assert that the eleven years since Wilson have seen a great recession in the popular acceptance of violence is to fly in the face of the common knowledge of all men. It was more than a year after Wilson had retired from office that Herrin, Illinois, suddenly achieved horrible fame; more than two years after he had retired that the fiasco of the murder trials there formally accepted massacre as a means of conducting labor disputes. Since Wilson we have learned that there is a place called Mer Rouge, in Louisiana; and one called Cicero, near Chicago; and one called Gastonia, in North Carolina; and one called Salisbury, in Maryland; and one called Pineville, in Kentucky. Each of these items has come to us because in each it has been demonstrated anew that violence is accepted by the people of that community as an excusable incident of existence in time of peace as well as in time of war.

It was since Wilson that the House of Representatives of the Congress of the United States broke into cheers when it was announced that a boy of twenty-one had been shot to death in the streets because he was suspected of having violated the liquor law which Wilson vetoed; and an American bishop of a Protestant church praised the House for cheering the news of death by violence. It is since Wilson that Al Capone, Dion O'Bannion, Gerald Chapman, Legs Diamond, and other gentry of that ilk have achieved their meteoric and lurid careers. It was eleven years after Wilson that civilization in the United States reached such a pass that it was regarded as good sense for a famous American whose child had been kidnapped to turn in despair from the police and appeal to the underworld to avenge his wrong.

When one thinks of the speakeasy, the racketeer, the hijacker, the bank bandit, the kidnapper, and the gangster, it is hard to believe that civilization is not nearer to collapse in America today than it ever was in Wilson's time.

V

Woodrow Wilson was human, and man that is born of woman is prone to utter folly. He did not escape the common fate, and those who served with him also sometimes said and did foolish things. It has always been so, and doubtless so it will be as long as the race survives and governments are instituted among men.

Nevertheless, while all rulers sometimes speak unwisely, intelligence in its statecraft is one of the marks of a civilized nation, and an increase in that intelligence unquestionably is a good augury for its civilization.

To attempt to make comparisons between the brains of individuals is certainly an ungracious, usually an unfair, and almost always an unsuccessful undertaking. Brain for brain, it may be that the members of the administrations of the last eleven years have been equal, or superior, to those of the Wilson administrations. At any rate, let us eschew such invidious comparisons here.

There are, however, certain standards of measurement of the composite intelligence of the government as an entity, and these, perhaps, we may seek to apply without violating decorum. The government, as distinguished from the individuals who composed it, had at the end of Wilson's time very definite policies, all of which tended to thrust the country in a particular direction. The domestic policy of that government was overwhelmed and reduced to utter confusion by the exigencies of warfare, but it had been pretty clearly outlined between March 4, 1913, and August 1, 1914, the date on which it had to be subverted to the necessities of the foreign situation. These sixteen months showed beyond doubt that the government intended to pursue a clearly liberal policy. The Underwood Tariff, the Federal Reserve System, the original income-tax legislation, the woman suffrage amendment, and a great mass of less conspicuous legislation all testify to the definiteness of the liberal tendency of the government as regards internal affairs. I do not assert that it was a good policy, or a bad policy, but merely that it was a definite policy.

As touching foreign affairs, the attitude of the government in Wilson's time was even more distinct. Its policy was one of vigorous promotion of international organization, culminating in the League of Nations. There was no doubt about it, there was no hesitation or confusion in it. It was proceeding along a well-plotted line toward a definite goal. Again, I do not assert that this was a good policy or a bad one, but only that it was definite.

At the same time, the mere process of outlining and vigorously prosecuting a definite and consistent policy of state-craft involves a certain amount of cerebration. Definiteness and consistency are attainable only by the exercise of intelligence, even though the policy they qualify may be a bad one. The mere fact that the government, in the time of Wilson, chose a mark and pressed steadily toward that mark is proof positive that there was intelligence in the statecraft of that government, regardless of the end toward which that intelligence moved.

In fields other than that of statecraft it is quite commonly believed that the choice of any definite, clear-cut policy and the consistent prosecution of that policy argues a higher degree of intelligence than the choice of no policy whatever. But this reasoning quite obviously does not apply to the field of statecraft because action there is frequently conditioned by the exigencies of politics, and in politics opportunism is frequently the most intelligent of all policies. To argue otherwise would be to argue that the Honorable Calvin Coolidge is something of a fool, whereas the truth is that few more astute politicians have ever occupied the White House. Out of the whole list, only Jefferson, Monroe, Van Buren, Lincoln, and Roosevelt stand out clearly as his superiors in this department, with Madison, Tyler, and Polk contesting with him for sixth place.

Everything depends upon what the administration hopes to accomplish. If its endeavor is limited to the retention of office, then lack of a policy may be proof of intelligence, not evidence of its absence. But if its aspiration includes any of the objectives commonly ascribed to statecraft, that is, the establishment of a better social order, the increase of the national prestige and power, the extension of the national boundaries, or the strengthening of the national defenses, then certainly lack of a policy suggests lack of intelligence.

Since Wilson, however, the man who could define the policy of the United States, either foreign or domestic, must be a master of definition indeed. The Underwood Tariff has been abolished, but most of the other Wilsonian legislation stands unaltered. Nevertheless, no sane man will argue that the domestic policy of the last eleven years has been distinctly liberal. The League of Nations has been repudiated, yet no administration since Wilson has come out flatly against international organization. On the contrary, Mr. Harding, Mr. Coolidge, and Mr. Hoover all have spoken in favor of it. The truth is, we have no definite, consistent policy, internal or external; and this, while it may be no conclusive proof of a decrease of intelligence, can by no sort of sophistry be twisted into evidence of an increase of intelligence in statecraft since Wilson.

VI

Woodrow Wilson's exact place in history must be decided by some future, perhaps far distant, generation. But he was a great man. That this is true is evident from the admissions of his enemies. Reject altogether the testimony of his friends, and consider only that of those who hate his memory. With what do they charge him? With nothing less than wrecking the world.

Assume, for the purpose of argument, that it is true—what then? Do barbers and street-car conductors wreck the world? Do soda-jerkers shake down empires, and plumbers' assistants reduce civilization to the verge of chaos? Do weaklings upset the hegemony of giant kingdoms, or puny hands pull down the temple of the established order? A weakling thrust into a throne may wreck his own country, but Wilson left his own country the most powerful on the globe; if we grant that he strode through all the rest of the world "spreading ruin and scattering ban," we have simply listed him in the category of Attila, Tamerlane, and Genghis Khan, who certainly were not feeble.

The truth is, since Wilson we have had no political leader strong enough to wreck a pig-pen, not to mention the world. Such leadership as we have had has been vested in committees and commissions, and it has been impossible to fix upon any personality as responsible for anything.

For the first eight years this seemed to be an excellent thing for business, at any rate; but recent events have given us reason to believe that it was not good even for business. Certainly it was not good for anything else. Perhaps it was Woodrow Wilson's ambition to vault into the empery of the world. I doubt it, but suppose it was—at least it was a lordly ambition. It compares very favorably with Harding's ambition to be a good fellow, with Coolidge's ambition to get by without a fuss, even with the proclaimed ambition of the present administration to put a chicken in every pot.

As long as Woodrow Wilson dominated the political scene the American people thought constantly of things that have hardly crossed their minds since Wilson—of national honor and national dignity, of the historical past and the far future, of danger and of duty. Whether they were friends of Wilson, or his enemies, they thought of these things. Whether they thought he embodied all noble ideals, or was the opponent of them, they thought of ideals. And in the furious struggle to put him up or pull him down, they were all engaged in a fight that swirled around another focal point than a trading post in the stock exchange. There were then, as there are always, a few astute gentlemen who knew what they wanted; but the great masses of men, in Wilson's time, whether they supported or opposed him, fought for their beliefs, not primarily for their pocketbooks.

It was a great era, and this is a small one. And that is why I know that when I am eighty-five, and palsied and half blind, I shall still be able to fire the imaginations of the rising generation. The youngsters of that day will pay no attention whatever when I gabble about having lived through the great panic of 1929; and when I say that I once saw Henry Ford, they will rack their brains in vain and finally decide that I must be trying to say Millard Fillmore. But one of my grandsons, when he wishes to explain to a college friend why the family continues to treat the doddering old wreck with a certain consideration, will draw him aside and whisper, confidentially, "You would never think it to look at the old man now, but it's the God's truth—he once served under Woodrow Wilson."

HARPER'S MAGAZINE, *April 1934*

WHAT AN OLD GIRL SHOULD KNOW

From the ranks of those who are always saying suavely that the Younger Generation is basically all right, I have definitely withdrawn. I am tired of lying about it to prove how broadminded I am. To the Younger Generation I could address, in all sincerity, the words Mr. Peter Arno put into the mouth of the ham actor denouncing the manager: "Sir, I consider your conduct unethical and lousy!"

But if we are going in for Naked Truth, let's have her naked indeed. When the last shred of illusion is stripped away it becomes plain that, while there is plenty wrong with the Younger Generation, many, if not most, of its rotten spots are attributable to a single cause, to wit, a bad ancestry. So henceforth whenever anyone says the Younger Generation is all right I intend to dissent in a loud voice; but if the declaration is confined to an assertion that, after all, the young hellions are really no worse than their parents, I shall probably be constrained to take time out to consider. To deny that statement would necessarily be to attribute to the Younger Generation a capacity for hellishness astounding in its extent; and I am reluctant to admit that it possesses any astounding capacity.

Specifically, I doubt its capacity to absorb much of the good advice being thrust upon it through many agencies, among them the columns of *Harper's*. There, for example, in the December number is set forth a list of things which a girl of seventeen ought to know. It includes twenty-one items, all based on common sense and shrewd worldly wisdom. Not a suggestion in the lot is without merit and most of them clearly are of high importance.

But, after all, why should any young girl learn the twenty-one things which the writer says—and I admit—she should know? I know that the right answer is because knowledge of these things will improve her physical, mental, and moral health. But I am on the wrong side of forty and have, therefore, developed that appreciation of the value of health characteristic of the senescent. A young girl hasn't begun to worry about her nerves and viscera, so my answer has no validity for her. Now you think up one that will seem valid for youth. The obvious thing to say to the girl would be, "You must learn, in order to be as wise as your mother when you reach your mother's present age." But if that is to be effective in making a flapper learn what she ought to know, then it is obvious that the old girl must know what *she* ought to know. Which brings on more talk.

It is curious that in all the clamor about the Younger Generation so little consideration has been given to what an old girl ought to know. It is basic in any intelligent discussion of what to do with the youngsters, and yet it is almost always ignored. Foreigners who come to examine Americans in their native habitat occasionally comment on the astonishing lack of knowledge of their own business that American women display; but I am not aware that any foreigner has analyzed the situation successfully, while most citizens of the United States let it severely alone. This is without doubt due to prudence rather than to stupidity; for the old boy knows all too well what he is up against in handling the old girl—but he knows, too, what he will catch if he ventilates his knowledge.

However, let the angels quake in their sandals—here is one who is going to rush in where it is too hot for them.

Probably what the American old girl needs most to know is that there is absolutely no *a priori* reason why she should live. If she once gained a clear comprehension of this fact, all the other requisite items of information might follow naturally and inevitably. This goes for the old boy too, but in the average case someone is pretty sure to hammer it into his head before he reaches the age of forty. This salutary drubbing is much less likely to be inflicted upon the old girl, and in countless cases she arrives at middle age with no inkling of the fact that she owes society some reasonable excuse for cluttering up the world and occupying space that might better be devoted to some object of value—a petunia plant, say, or a jimson weed.

The most useless thing in the world, notwithstanding Mr. Clemenceau's opinion that the choice lay between the vermiform appendix and Poincaré, is a woman who is just a woman and nothing more. She is worse than a worthless man, for the same reason that a wounded soldier is a worse handicap than a dead soldier—the wounded soldier and the worthless woman require the attention of others who are really effective. A young girl may be completely worthless *in esse* and yet possess some value as a gambling chance. But a woman past forty is of value only for what she has done, what she is doing, or what she is. If she has done nothing, is doing nothing, and is nothing, then all she is entitled to in this world is enough chloroform to put her out of it with the least possible fuss and bother.

Before going farther, let me insert for the record an emphatic statement of the obvious. Many of the most valuable women in the world are so old that their activities ceased long ago; but out of what they have done and what they have been they have distilled a wisdom that is the very elixir of life to the middle-aged and balm of Gilead to the young. To suggest that such women are worth nothing because they no longer go rushing around would be incomparable asininity. God forbid that I should be thought to identify value with noise and bustle.

These remarks have nothing to do with wise old women. They refer exclusively to females who are still physically vigorous, but too old to be classified any longer as young girls. If one of this class once manages to get it through her head that the question the world asks of her is not, "Fair lady, why do you condescend to honor us with your presence?" but something much more like, "What the hell are *you* doing on earth anyhow?", and if she brings herself to admit—oh, no, not publicly, but to herself—that the world has a right to ask that question, then she has a chance to escape that fate which is worse than death, the dreadful doom of becoming a typical American Woman. To be sure, no one suffers that fate in its entirety, for the American Woman, like the purple cow and the Economic Man, possesses the one merit of not existing in real life. But she is approximated by thousands, perhaps millions, closely enough to make the United States notoriously the saddest nation in the civilized world. If you doubt it, spend an hour in any big department store in any American city when the Christmas holidays are approaching. You will be lucky indeed if you come away without having seen a dozen examples of that compound of arrogance, dishonesty, boorishness, and yellowness that many foreign observers have held up as the typical American Woman. If a crowd of men at a burlesque theater, a prize fight, or a baseball game found distributed through it a tenth as many swine as are in every department-store crowd, the police patrols and the ambulances would be run to exhaustion. That is, of course, the reason why the old boy is more virtuous, in this respect, than the old girl—he knows that if he deliberately rams the person ahead at an elevator door or attempts to elbow someone else out of place, the chances are that presently he will find himself spitting out his own teeth. So he is polite.

The thing penetrates far below mere manners, however. The most completely objectionable types of womanhood are not to be found on the lower economic levels. An ignorant, slatternly, drunken housewife in the city slums or in a tenant farmer's house is unmannerly and unlovely; but she is not valueless, for she does plenty of labor to pay for her board and keep. She is driven to it by sharp necessity, to be sure, but for all that she does furnish a reason why she should be allowed to remain on the earth.

But necessity, to many women as to many men, is economic necessity and nothing more. Let that be removed, and they feel no other urge to justify their existence. This accounts for the curious phenomenon observable everywhere in America of wives who become more and more worthless as their husbands become more and more worth while. The old boy gains a foothold in the economic world and then a handhold. Little by little, he heaves himself up out of the ruck, until presently he arrives at the place where there is no more need to worry over how the family shall be fed or wherewithal it shall be clothed. A house is bought and paid for, or at any rate financed so that it is carried easily. The cook is supplemented by a maid, and then by a gardener-chauffeur. And right there the old girl quits, although frequently the old boy is just hitting his stride and goes on doing better and better work for twenty years or so.

There may be some justification for her quitting if the woman is already past fifty and her children are pretty well grown. Even so, to quit is foolish, but at any rate, there is some color of reason for saying she has done a fair life's work. But when the old boy's success is swift the old girl frequently lies down on the job while she is still in her thirties; and in such cases she isn't much good.

Among these are recruited the vast armies of incessant bridge-players, tea-drinkers, and gabblers of the suburbs, the people who devote themselves to the vapid, empty existence to which they have the effrontery to apply the great name of "society." Here are the most worthless women in the world. The prostitutes, the female crooks, the professional gold-diggers are not half so destructive socially, because they are universally held in fear and contempt as soon as their true characters are known; while these other lives, although equally empty of any sort of value, are rated among the admirable, and the young are permitted to believe they should be imitated.

I do not cherish the delusion that every woman can become a Madame de Sévigné. Nor do I think that many women can assist their husbands by meddling with their work. But I do believe that any woman whose mental age is above that of a ten-year-old, if she realizes that she owes the world an excuse for being in it, can contrive to furnish that excuse. If she once abandons the notion that she graces life merely by existing (some rare women do just that, but not enough to invalidate the generalization) and looks at the facts from that point of view, I do not believe she will have much trouble in finding means to effect the end.

If an old girl once learns that she ought to furnish some reasonable excuse for her presence among us she will soon learn—or recollect—many, if not all, of the other, lesser things that an old girl ought to know. Most of them are not only obvious, but have been obvious for several thousands of years; honesty, sportsmanship, tolerance, and thrift I forbear to discuss. But there are a few that do not arise from the basic conditions of human existence, being necessitated rather by modern ways of living and modern ways of thinking. Some talk of these may not be altogether hackneyed.

For example, the old girl—and by that I mean anyone above thirty, perhaps above twenty-five—ought to know at least one of two things: either how to drink or how to refuse a drink gracefully. This isn't a matter of setting an example to the younger generation but of looking after them. Unhappily we have spent fourteen years carefully forgetting the principles of civilized drinking. Having made it impossible for any but the most barbarously explosive compounds to be sold, we have of necessity let down the bars to barbarous conduct; and we have brought up a generation inured to such conduct and incapable of being shocked by it. We have to contend with youngsters whose idea of drinking is to send rockets, Roman candles, pin-wheels, and Very lights whizzing and roaring through their innards. Naturally, when you speak to such people of a mellow glow they think of a conflagration; and when you speak to them of temperance they think you mean sour fanaticism.

That old girl is a valuable citizen who can do something toward combing and currying these shaggy wild colts. But she cannot do it by pursing her lips, and she cannot do it if the critical moment finds her, in the language of the Academicians, plastered. The experience of men through many generations has taught them that he who puts a souse to bed at night with neatness and dispatch gains a psychological dominance that enables him to do effective preaching the next morning. It is an item of information that women will be wise to acquire quickly.

A second thing the old girl in this country ought to try to learn is that Apollo is a very great god, not a Pekingese pup. He may be served, and he may be worshipped, but he really ought not to be patted on the head.

One of the most appalling effects that useless old girls have had upon American life is their success in gelding the arts, music in particular. If the rise of an American family on the economic scale meant releasing the energies of the woman so that she might apply them to study of the arts, the beneficial effect to the country could hardly be overestimated. But instead of releasing her energies, it more frequently extinguishes them, and she doesn't study; she plays art as she plays bridge, merely to kill time. Her husband, in consequence, lacking leisure to give to the matter himself, acquires the notion that the arts are pretty much like bridge—very well as a pastime for women, but hardly worth the serious attention of a man.

In thousands of American cities concert halls in the afternoons are filled with women. In the smaller cities evening concerts as well are largely populated by women. Whenever a celebrated artist comes to town silly old girls make a clatter over him that is unendurable to masculine ears. As a result it is very hard, even for a man who likes music, to endure the atmosphere in which it is played. The small-town American must have a really great passion for music if his interest in it is to survive. The old boy may not know anything about music but he knows the old girl. He knows what a fraud and faker she is, and his natural assumption is that anything she grows enthusiastic over is a fraud and a fake as well.

As soon as they attain a certain economic level the old girls swarm to the concerts; but how many of them ever think of employing a competent musician to teach them something about music? To how many does it occur that there is anything to learn about music except how to play it? If you said to the old boy that the distribution of the stresses in Hell Gate Bridge is no more ingenious and at the same time severely logical than the distribution of the stresses in one of Sibelius' symphonic works, he would probably think you were lying, but he would admit that it was a comprehensible lie. But tell it to the old girl and you might as well be repeating *Mene, mene, tekel upharsin* to her. It isn't music she likes. It is concerts and gabble and meeting people whose names are always appearing in the newspapers and who are received by the local squirarchy. But by swarming round musicians and other artists she makes the old boy feel that he risks his manhood if he goes anywhere near them; and as for taking up one of the arts as an avocation, devoting to it as intense, concentrated study as he gives to golf, fly-casting, or stud poker, he cannot endure the thought. He would as soon take up embroidery.

At first blush it may seem that by inducing Mr. Babbitt to keep his paws off the *beaux arts* the old girl has done them no small service. But it is true, whether artists like to admit it or not, that just when Mr. Babbitt has butted in, art has flowered into its most brilliant periods. Let us not forget that Pericles was the Greek equivalent of a Tammany politician, that Augustus Cæsar was remarkably like the late Wayne B. Wheeler, both in his political technic and in his outlook on life, that Pope Alexander VI was fundamentally a gang leader, and that Lorenzo the Magnificent was—God save the mark!— an investment banker. Phidias and Praxiteles were told what to carve, Leonardo was told what to paint, Mozart, in his formative years, was told what to write by men who were not themselves artists, but who understood art well enough to know when a job was well done and were resolute enough to fire promptly an artist who couldn't handle his medium.

Art in America greatly needs the masculinity of Mr. Babbitt, not to assist the real artists, but to give the bum's rush to the hordes of pseudo-artists. For these fellows, clumsy though they may be with brush or burin or chisel, are marvelously adept psychologists; and they can take the old girl for a ride with a deftness far beyond the capacity of their betters, who have never learned to be tame cats. But Babbitt, unfortunately, is too unsure of his own judgment to give them the boot. He exhibits marvelous skill and precision in bouncing off the job an incompetent salesman or engineer or plant manager; wherefore good salesmen, good engineers, and good plant managers flourish prodigiously in the republic. But the elimination of bad artists he has left to the old girl; and she, unfortunately, doesn't know her business. She ought to learn it.

Another field in which the old girl ought to know a great deal more than she does is that of sex education. Perhaps it would be more accurate to say that what she needs is not more information but different information—less Freud and more Rabelais. I am not denying the importance of Freud any more than I am denying the importance of liquor. But I would apply the same rule—the old girl should be able to carry her Freud like a gentleman or never touch it at all. But she can carry it if she has a sufficient ballast of Rabelais or his equivalent.

The point is that the old girl should know that, while sex may be a ritual informed with beauty, it ought to be, at the same time, a lot of fun. Perhaps it may be, in the words of Dr. Logan Clendening, "the master joke of the universe. It is so magnificent a joke that the very stars rock with laughter which it arouses." If this information is once acquired then it becomes immediately apparent that, whatever else it is, sex cannot possibly be either a creed or a commodity. The commodity idea is as old as the oldest profession, and it is still going strong. Owen Meredith might have described spring in London in 1934 as characterized by

> Strawberries on sale under all the house eaves,
> And young ladies on sale for the strawberry leaves,

without doing violence to the truth; for plenty of the old girls, not in London only but everywhere, are still consummating monstrous transactions in their own flesh and blood, aided and abetted by archbishops and governors. Sales of youth for fortune and position are still everyday occurrences. They should, of course, be stopped by the morals police; for prostitution is prostitution whether the bargain be made on the sidewalk with the roar of traffic as an accompaniment or in a cathedral to the strains of "The Voice That Breath'd O'er Eden."

However, if the commodity view is old, the creedal idea of sex is relatively new. It is due largely to the Viennese psychologist, with the able assistance of Havelock Ellis and others. To be sure, the last thing these scientists would have dreamed of was establishing a new religion; but their doctrines are peculiarly subject to misinterpretation. They have served to dissipate a number of old superstitions and to snap many ancient bonds—just the things its believers expect from every new religious creed. Perhaps it was inevitable that we should presently find numbers of women of mature years subscribing to the doctrine of salvation by sex. They give it a great deal of attention, but they do not so much talk about it as chant about it; and when they encounter anyone who is frankly bored by discussions of the *libido,* its use and abuse, they are as shocked as is a Fundamentalist at encountering an atheist.

Yet where is the essential difference between a group of old girls, mothers and grandmothers, discussing sex *sotto voce* in a drawing-room, and a group of small boys discussing it *sotto voce* in the alley behind the garage? I fail to see any unless indeed there is more chance of some useful information being distributed by the small boys. They do at least regard the subject as a practical matter rather than as dogma, and sometimes they are capable of laughing at it. Now if there is anything the old girl ought to know about sex, it is when to giggle over it. For laughter and lust are two complete incompatibles; like oil and water, they never really mix but always tend to displace each other. Modern psychology has shown that the old idea that we must sometimes act and always talk as if we were sexless beings is not only silly but positively dangerous to mental health. But it is not much sillier, and perhaps it is no more dangerous, than the new idea of trying to pretend that sex is not really sex at all but a group of axioms and principles embodied in the gospel according to Freud and to be discussed only as an older generation discussed theology. There is a difference, of course, between laughing and leering. The leering attitude toward sex is nauseating; but at that I doubt that leering is any worse than kneeling. The virtue of the great comedians is that they have accepted sex jovially; and if Aristophanes, Rabelais, and Cervantes were alive today, and instructed in all the modern learning, they would accept it, if anything, more jovially than ever.

Finally, the old girl ought to know that feminism has not emancipated women any more successfully than Lincoln's proclamation emancipated negroes. When the negro's chains were struck off the first thing that fell from him was his happy certainty of three meals a day, sufficient clothing, and a place to sleep. The first effect of the emancipation of women has been to compel them, as it compelled the negroes, to take up the white man's burden. But some of the old girls seem to cherish the notion that they can effect a merger of slavery and freedom, retaining the best features of each. Their aspiration is to be men at the pay-window and women everywhere else. They insist on having a man's salary and a woman's deference and consideration from the men with whom they compete.

The result of this effort is that they get neither. A woman frequently gets a man's job but rarely a man's pay. The reason is that there is no conceivable form of daily labor that cannot be done better by some man than by any woman. The greatest dressmakers and milliners are men, or were until yesterday. The greatest cooks are invariably men. The dangerous cases in the psychiatric wards are usually nursed by men and the job is as well done as it is in other wards where nursing is monopolized by women, with the addition that the male nurse can restrain the patient. The greatest interior decorators are men, and there is, of course, no comparison in the other arts.

This may be due to the relatively short time women have had to work at the outside jobs. The time may come when they will surpass men in some, perhaps in many, occupations. But right here and now it is a fact than any employer is willing to give a man more money than he gives a woman for the same work because he has reason to believe that the man will do it better. It isn't any conspiracy against women, as some feminists apparently believe. It is due to the plain teaching of experience that the old girl is worth less than the old boy. But when she takes a man's job and does it badly it does not behoove her to demand exemption from the roughness of life to which men are subjected.

These are some things that theoretically the old girl ought to know; but as a practical matter and, speaking as a man, I am not at all certain that I really want her to know everything she ought to know. After all, some of them do know it, and they are formidable people. To encounter a woman who knows that she must justify her existence and who, therefore, justifies it by making herself economically, morally or intellectually—not merely emotionally—of value to someone other than herself; one who can turn down her glass graciously, or empty it and remain graceful; one whom fig-leaves amuse but neither enthrall nor dismay; one who can enter the business world demanding nothing that she is not willing to accord to all her fellow-workers, male and female—to encounter such a woman is a privilege indeed but not pure delight, by a long shot. For no man who ever walked in shoeleather can cope successfully with a woman like that, because her sex's long slavery has developed in her a finesse and subtlety that men seldom attain. Before a man has time to deploy his forces he finds himself cut off, surrounded, and subjected to enfilading fire from a dozen heights commanding his position.

Only one course of action is possible to an intelligent man in such an encounter. Combat is madness. Flight is ignominious. The thing to do is to apply that greatest and most comprehensive of all the maxims of strategy: "Ef you can't beat 'em, j'ine 'em." That is to say, the obvious recourse in such circumstances is to marry the first one met and leave it to her to take care of any others encountered subsequently. But even this is useless advice; for whenever an old girl who knows what she ought to know decides that a man should marry her, advising him to do so is as futile as advising a seasick man to do what *he* ought to do. He'll do it all right whether anyone tells him to or not.

abridged from HARPER'S MAGAZINE, *July 1934*

IF THERE IS A MARYLAND

The commonwealth lying between Pennsylvania and the Potomac is a small one, but not the smallest, an old one, but not the oldest, a rich one, but not the richest, and a populous one, but not the most crowded among the forty-eight components of this Union. Obviously a median State, yet once she touches the superlative. I firmly believe that Maryland is the most improbable State in the Union.

Officially, her existence has been recognized for so long that she is now celebrating her tercentenary; but we all know what official records are. The fact that the Post Office Department is getting out a three-cent stamp on which a philatelist with a strong magnifying glass can read "Maryland Tercentenary"; and that countless banquets and speeches and water-pageants and fireworks displays were scheduled for the month of June—all these things may impress the historians of the future as indisputable evidence; but they really have little bearing on the question of whether or not there actually is a Maryland.

II

For to establish beyond controversy the actual existence of a cultural and spiritual entity corresponding to the name of any State is quite impossible. I am convinced that there are by no means forty-eight real States in this Union. Among the vast rectangles in the West are some, I am sure, that differ in no detail of their mental and spiritual lives from their neighbors on one side or the other. Their inhabitants are Americans, and Middle Westerners, but otherwise undifferentiated; and the State names that they bear are mere matters of reference, like the numbers on automobile license plates—no more descriptive of the person who bears it than is the number borne by a convict descriptive of him.

Furthermore, in some ways it seems increasingly plain that if there are now less than forty-eight States, the time is swiftly approaching when there may be none at all. One of the most lamentable effects of the New Deal is its rapid erasure of State lines. If this erasure is necessary, it is still lamentable, perhaps even more so, since this dread necessity would indicate that Americans are incapable of enduring that diversity in unity which is characteristic of a rich civilization. When the labor and the reward therefor of Marylanders are fixed by code authorities in Washington; when the right to build a highway or a distillery in Maryland must be sought in Washington; when a Marylander's authority over his children is fixed and limited by Washington; and when a Marylander's right to raise wheat or pigs is subject to the pleasure of Washington, then it is difficult to say offhand where one may find proof that there is a Maryland—or a Massachusetts, or a North Carolina, or a New York, for that matter. Perhaps all these once great names are now become no more than repositories of gracious traditions, like Provence and Aragon and Bohemia.

Nevertheless, one may adopt a doubtful proposition as a working hypothesis, provided its tentative nature is clearly understood. Let me then set up the qualified assertion that if there is a Maryland, it is not to be found where the chambers of commerce and business associations tell you to look for it. There are wide fields on the Eastern Shore capable of producing incredible quantities of tomatoes; but they are not Maryland. On the northern shore of the Patapsco River, just below Baltimore City, is an incredible forest of smokestacks, lying by day under a black pall of fumes, and illuminated by night by the lurid glow of hell itself, constituting the greatest steel manufacturing district on tidewater; but that is not Maryland—God forbid! In Baltimore itself are tall, stately office buildings, full of tall, stately executives, and these are firmly convinced that they are Maryland; but they are fooling themselves, for their replicas are to be found in every city. Among the hills that begin to rise a hundred yards west of the docks and that go rolling back a hundred miles and to a height of three thousand five hundred feet are countless beautiful, smiling valleys, starred with gracious farmsteads and pleasant villages; but these are real estate, not Maryland. Hacked out of the middle of the State is a space of seventy square miles containing the city of Washington, and smeared over the Maryland hills around it is a smudge of suburbs, appendices of the national capital; and these are far more alien to Maryland than anything else between the Potomac and the Mason and Dixon line.

If I were a native son of the State I should probably fall into the delusion of believing that there is one particular spot to which I could take you and say, "There is Maryland!" But as an immigrant from another State, I know better; my own birthplace being elsewhere, my eyes are clear. Sometimes indeed I fall victim to the witchery of Maryland names and am half persuaded that romance must stand out visibly and tangibly on the banks of a river named Tred Avon, or on a plantation called End of Controversy or My Lady's Manor. But it isn't so. It is merely that some special grace seems to have been granted Maryland when her place-names were being bestowed, so that her atlas is made to resound with echoes of the court of Charles the Martyr and those of savage kings—Prince George's County, Queen Anne's County, Wicomico, Anne Arundel, Charles, Cecil, St. Mary's. And the roster of her little towns is a singing list—Conowingo, Nanticoke, Havre-de-Grace, Golden Ring, Point of Rocks, Admiral, Sang Run, Girdletree, Keeptryst, Lonaconing, Seat Pleasant, Arundel-on-the-Bay, Dames Quarter, Wetipquin, Bishops Head, Conococheague. Of course, there are Funkstown, Bozman, Lime Kiln, Oella, Pomonkey, and Woodensburg too; but a dissonance, if it be swiftly resolved, merely emphasizes harmony. However, you may visit Charlotte Hall without seeing Maryland, or even Four Locks, or Ilchester. For if there is a Maryland it is not exposed for observation in houses or streets or factories or landscape even, or seascape. It is an elusive, fleeting thing, which you may stumble on anywhere, but of which you never catch much more than a momentary glimpse.

Some people think to find it in what is merely old or picturesque—the fine, Georgian houses of Annapolis, for example, with their rooms so magically proportioned that four plain walls, a ceiling, and a floor combine into an effect of astonishing lightness and grace; with stairways that seem to have been inspired by the flight of a swallow; with kitchens equipped with wide-throated chimneys and fireplaces in which an ox might be roasted, kitchens built to serve banquet halls. And there are, on a less grandiose scale, the streets of little houses built by sea-captains near the foot of Federal Hill, in Baltimore. Their builders were the men who commanded the Baltimore clippers in the great days of sail; and their houses are somewhat as they were —square and sturdy and spotless. Their red brick is painted as carefully as the woodwork of the vessels, the white marble steps are scrubbed like decks, their brass door-handles shine like a ship's metal work. Here the captains, home from the sea, took their ease; and on quiet summer evenings these streets have been filled with a drone of talk about all strange, romantic spots —of Canton and Bombay, of Cape Comorin, of the Barrier Reef, of Java Head, of Mozambique Channel, of typhoons in the China Sea and of blizzards howling around the Horn. Even today, although the clippers have long since sailed away over the world's edge, and Federal Hill lies under a pall of smoke belched from the stacks of tugs and tankers, and dirty, wallowing tramps, one seems to breathe, in these streets, a whiff of the stinging gales that whip the spray off plunging seas round the Orkneys, or the strong trade winds on the Middle Passage.

And some find the true Maryland in those countless places on her soil that great men and great events have made memorable—in Crooked Lane, that sinuous alley in downtown Baltimore which cannot be insignificant, because down its tortuous length a column of troops once moved under the command of Washington and Lafayette, bound for Yorktown; or on the narrow point in the harbor where Fort McHenry, ancient and toothless now, still frowns across the water as it did in the dawn's early light when the battle smoke, drifting away, revealed that the flag was still there; or away up in the hills where, between Sharpsburg and Antietam, McClellan for once moved swiftly and, therefore, Lee's brilliance and daring went for naught; or in the ruins of the old Fifth Regiment Armory, where Bryan cursed Tammany to its face, cursed it with bell, book and candle, tauntingly, and made the nomination of Woodrow Wilson inevitable.

III

But all these things, Annapolis and the seamen's houses, the forts and battlefields and places made distinguished by the passage of great men, are of the Maryland that was. Granting that they prove there was once a Maryland with an individuality and a character distinctly its own, it does not necessarily follow that such a place still exists. There was once "a grandeur that was Rome" too, but Mussolini is not it. On Mt. Vernon Place George Peabody sits in bronze, and to his left rises the marble façade of the first endowed conservatory of music in America; two of Baltimore's innumerable hills are crowned with forests of buildings, bearing the name of another Maryland merchant, and constituting the first modern university in America—Johns Hopkins. Here is proof enough that energy and imagination once abounded in Maryland, but no proof whatever that they still exist. In fact, neither the Peabody Conservatory of Music nor the Johns Hopkins University has received any notable gift from a native Marylander in many years.

The town of Baltimore is full of beautiful old men—courtly, dignified, charming in manner and impressive in appearance, white-haired, but clear-eyed, serene, and confident. Their only trouble is that many of them have no sense. It would be rash indeed to assume that there is another George Peabody or another Johns Hopkins among them. The town regards them with a curious mixture of affection and humor; there is a ribald theory that those who sit behind the broad windows of the Maryland Club are not living members at all, but former members stuffed and mounted there to maintain the prestige of the place; and a counter-theory that they are living members indeed, but not mere idlers gazing at the traffic in Charles Street for no purpose, being, in fact, paid a monthly salary of a certain number of terrapin dinners for sitting there. Be that as it may, they are members of all known boards of trustees and their names appear on all committees of a civic character; which accounts in large measure for the difficulty of getting anything done in Baltimore. However, as much might be said of practically every old city. The parade of the stuffed shirts is nothing peculiar to Baltimore. Certainly it does not distinguish Maryland from other States.

It would be pleasant to record that the virtue and intelligence of its citizenry set Maryland apart from and above all the forty-seven others; but if it were so recorded, some skeptic would instantly cite certain recent events on the Eastern Shore and make the record look silly. The Eastern Shore is the peninsula lying between the Chesapeake Bay and the Atlantic Ocean. It includes the State of Delaware, nine counties of Maryland, and two of Virginia. With the last three years it has been the scene of two lynchings that for brazen cynicism have hardly been equalled, even in the Deep South; nor have the sadistic details of the orgies often been matched north of Arkansas. The peculiarly appalling feature of the Maryland lynchings is that they were not passionate outbursts of a brutish population inflamed by extraordinary crimes. They were in fact not protests against crime at all, but, on the contrary, protests against civilization. It is generally agreed, not on the Eastern Shore only, but everywhere in Maryland, that the mob murders were precipitated by the Euel Lee case, in which the Maryland Court of Appeals had intervened to halt an effort to railroad a man to the gallows.

There is hardly a reasonable doubt that Euel Lee was guilty of an appalling multiple murder on the Eastern Shore; but there is no doubt at all that to try the man anywhere on the Shore would have been to make a mockery of the processes of the law. The Court of Appeals so decided and ordered the case removed; and when it appeared that in the county on the Western Shore where he was then tried the names of negroes had been excluded from the ballot box, the Court intervened a second time and ordered a new trial. The net result was that it took more than two years to get the man hanged in lawful and orderly fashion. In the meantime two other negroes, accused of later murders on the Shore, were defiantly lynched. This was the reply of the Eastern Shore to the insistence of the Court of Appeals on a fair trial for every man, even one accused of an atrocious crime.

Nor can it be successfully maintained that the Eastern Shore is alone in its detestation of one of the bases of civilization. No other part of Maryland has recently indulged in lynching, it is true, but there was plenty of sympathy for the Shoremen elsewhere in Maryland; and the sincere, if futile, efforts of the Governor and the Attorney General to bring some of the lynchers to justice met with widespread execration, not only on the peninsula, but in Baltimore and on the rest of the Western Shore as well. No, Maryland is none too thoroughly civilized.

But does this constitute a distinction setting her apart from the rest of the States? Well, on the very day that the Governor of Maryland sent a battalion of National Guardsmen to the Eastern Shore to arrest some of the lynchers, the sheriff having failed to apprehend them, the Governor of California issued a statement heartily indorsing a lynching in *his* State. And the highest court of Maryland twice intervened to assure a fair trial for Euel Lee, although his guilt was far better established than that of Sacco and Vanzetti, who had no similar help from the highest court of Massachusetts. Her moments of semi-barbarism indeed seem to indicate that Maryland is precisely like her sisters, rather than different from them.

Moreover, there is no anti-syndicalism law on the statute books of Maryland, and when the Communists stage a parade the cops turn out to protect them, not to harry them. There is no life-for-a-pint law, no sedition law, no law establishing a censorship of books or newspapers; yet when a scandal sheet was started in Baltimore a year or so ago, the people responsible were promptly sent to jail under the ordinary police regulations against obscenity. In these matters Maryland is more, not less, civilized than many of her neighbors.

If there is a Maryland that is something more than a mere subsection of the continent, that is something individual and unique, it is obviously not to be found in measurable and provable facts. Perhaps then it is to be found just in those things that are not historically true. The traditional Cradle of Religious Freedom, for example, is hardly to be described as a historical fact. The fact is that in 1634 Maryland was made safe for Catholics, and that is all. The first Baron Baltimore belonged to what was then a minority sect, bitterly persecuted in England; and it occurred to him that it would be a fine thing to establish in the wilderness a sanctuary for his coreligionists. But for the King of England to have set up anywhere in his dominions a refuge for Catholics under that name would have stung his Protestant subjects into a revolutionary fury, which he dared not risk. The best he could do, and all that he did, was to make Lord Baltimore's colony a sort of religious No Man's Land, where no Christian could legally slit another Christian's throat to the glory of God. Of course it never entered the mind either of the King or of the Baron to grant religious freedom to Jews, atheists, and pagans. For that matter, they have not been granted complete religious freedom to this day. If a Buddhist or a Mohammedan wishes to marry in Maryland in 1934 he must have it done by a Christian minister using a Christian rite, or by a Jewish rabbi with the Jewish rite. He cannot have it done by a civil officer employing a purely legalistic formula, much less by a priest of his own religion. Atheists to this day are debarred from jury service in Maryland, and there is some doubt that their testimony is competent in lawsuits.

Nevertheless, in 1634 the grant of identical legal status to Catholics and Protestants was a tremendous advance over current practice—so great an advance that it inspired G. K. Chesterton, three centuries later, to describe Maryland as the spot

> *where the bonds were riven,*
> *And a hundred faiths set free,*
> *Where a wandering Cavalier had given*
> *Her hundredth name to the Queen of Heaven,*
> *And made oblation of feuds forgiven*
> *To Our Lady of Liberty;*

and by setting up the tradition of freedom it has laid upon the Marylander of 1934 a feeling, vague perhaps but nevertheless existent, that it is a little *infra dig.* for him to get too hot and bothered over religious rows.

Equally dubious, from the standpoint of the historian, is the story of Barbara Frietchie. Nevertheless,

Up from the meadows, rich with corn,
Clear in the cool September morn,
The clustered spires of Frederick stand,
Green-walled by the hills of Maryland,

and while Frederick exists and Whittier is remembered, the legend of Barbara will be a living thing in the lives of inhabitants of Maryland. Barbara's immortality rests upon her stout refusal to permit inconvenient facts to interfere with her beautiful theories. That this spirit is cherished by many inhabitants of Barbara's State to this day is plainly evident. It is a fact, for example, that the Declaration of Rights in the State Constitution asserts,

That a long continuance in the Executive Departments of power, or
trust, is dangerous to liberty; a rotation, therefore, in these Departments
is one of the best securities of permanent freedom,

in the face of which fact the Hon. Albert Cabell Ritchie has been elected Governor for four consecutive terms of four years each; and in the spring his election to a fifth term seemed to depend entirely on his willingness to run again. The Maryland attitude seems to be that since Bert is a pretty good Governor, it is sensible to keep him in the office; and as for the Constitution, what is the Constitution among friends? Shall the State of Barbara Frietchie be deterred from doing what it wants to do by a scrap of paper?

Constitutions, in fact, worry Maryland but little. Certainly the Eighteenth Amendment to the Constitution of the United States never bothered her appreciably. Just at the moment when Great Britain was permitting the Irish to set up their own government, Maryland's bland indifference to Volsteadism stung the Hon. William D. ("Earnest Willie") Upshaw, a great paladin of prohibition, to make a speech in which he formally read her out of the Union. The only permanent effect of the speech was to inspire someone to write a letter to the editor of the Baltimore *Evening Sun,* suggesting that, as Maryland was now expelled from the empire, she should imitate the Irish by setting up the Maryland Free State; which suggestion was so heartily approved by the citizens that as the Free State she has been known far and wide ever since.

IV

But all this, plainly, is not matter subject to statistical analysis nor capable of establishment in open court by the rules of evidence. It leaves always open to doubt the very existence of the State of Maryland. Have three hundred years of rich and varied history really stamped themselves upon the minds and characters of the inhabitants of the State? I think they have, but I don't know how to prove it. I think you can find Maryland all up and down the social scale, but I don't believe anyone can point it out to you. I think I have heard something that was not Virginia, nor Pennsylvania, still less Delaware or Ohio, in the drawling utterance of an ancient waterman on Sinepuxent Bay, entertaining his customers with tales of storm and shipwreck on that treacherous, sandy coast. He sailed for anyone who would hire his boat, but he talked only to those customers who were polite to him. A free man he was and yet, if you spoke him fair, he felt under bond to entertain you; for politeness establishes a claim on any Marylander of any social grade.

I have heard it in the chatter of a well-dressed crowd sitting on the grass of a steep hillside watching red-coated riders flashing over the fearful jumps on the floor of the Worthington Valley in the Maryland Hunt Cup Steeplechase. There is no admission fee to this race, no professional betting, no hawkers of hot dogs. The officials are gentlemen who volunteer for the duty. The riders are not referred to as amateurs—they are "gentlemen jockeys." And the reward for the winner of a race so gruelling that frequently the Rider of the Pale Horse has entered uninvited is twelve months' fame among the members of the Hunt. But to a Maryland horseman this is compensation enough for dicing with Death twenty-two times in eight minutes as he tops the rails in that four-mile course.

I have heard it—heard the same elusive intonation—in the voice of a negro peddler, wailing through an East Baltimore street his wordless chant announcing oysters for sale, and in the voices of a group of gentlemen gathered on the lawn of a vast suburban estate, watching the twilight die while a butler moved among them with a tray of tall, heavily frosted glasses crowned with a spray of mint leaves. Negro peddler, millionaire banker, and savant with a name known to the learned in far countries, all spoke with a certain blandness that is not the music of old Cambridge nor yet the similar, but more languid music of the best Charlestonese, yet akin to both. It is that serenity that informs the speech of people who have dwelt long in an old, established society. In Marylanders of poor quality it degenerates into a revolting smugness; but among the better specimens it is very attractive indeed.

And if there is a Maryland, here it is. The sense that three hundred years of history not without honor lie behind them has given these people the assurance that their position in the world is fixed and firm. It has established within them a profound conviction that Maryland, which has been here so long, will remain a long time yet; so why fret and fume? And it is this core of tranquillity at the center of their minds that enables Marylanders to be tolerant, to wait on wisdom, to regard panaceas and messiahs skeptically, to greet the lather and fury into which mercurial reformers work themselves with quiet chuckles.

It is a maddening place for zealots and fanatics and young idealists. Because it is incapable of divine madness, perhaps it is incapable of greatness; but it is incapable too of certain types of sliminess, of certain types of charlatanry, of the Bœotian brutishness all too frequently encountered in America. It's not so bad.

from A LITTLE NIGHT MUSIC: DISCOVERIES IN THE
EXPLOITATION OF AN ART, *1934*

A PIANO WITH DIRTY KEYS

The 'Cellist, as a housekeeper, does not rank with those fabulous New England women who not only carry out the ashes and clean the hearth, but scrub the fireback after each use of the fireplace. Nevertheless, she has some pride, and for many years it was flicked on the raw every time she glanced at the piano; for the keyboard was, indeed, a dreadful sight to be seen in any household pretending to be civilized. The ivories were not merely smeared, they were grimy; and grimy they remained no matter how many times they were cleaned.

Indeed, they couldn't be cleaned a dozen times a day because our establishment boasts but a single bondwoman, and in these parlous times bondwomen have to be given their due meed of respect or they will walk out on you. Call yours out of the kitchen a dozen, or even half a dozen, times a day to clean the piano keys and see what happens.

So the piano keys went dirty, and the 'Cellist winced, but said nothing. Daily, indeed, she would suggest to the two small Nuisances to whom she and I belong that it is an excellent idea to wash one's hands before sitting down at the piano, but she never made it an iron-clad rule; for, rightly or wrongly, she wanted them to sit down at the piano much more than she wanted an immaculate house.

This was in accordance with a policy deliberately adopted when the Nuisances were very small indeed. The 'Cellist and I are unenlightened parents, reactionary parents, very Bourbons among parents. We are stoutly opposed to allowing the child to express its individuality except, of course, when the expression takes civilized form. We had observed the end results of a policy of enlightenment whereunder the child is permitted to develop his own personality without let or hindrance, and had decided that before we would permit the Nuisances to become such monsters we would take them out and decently drown them. So we have civilized them, sometimes by violence and oppression, but we have civilized them; if we have crushed budding genius by teaching them the difference between *meum* and *tuum*, that is too bad; but we still incline to the belief that what we have really done is keep them from landing in the penitentiary.

However, from the very beginning we made two exceptions to the general rule that the Nuisances had to learn what was theirs and what wasn't. These two were books and the piano. They have been free to have any book in the house to which they took a fancy from the time when they grew big enough to hold it; and they have been free to pound on the piano to their hearts' content.

As regards the books, this was an exception of no great moment, for our library runs heavily to Everyman and not at all to Elzevir. There are few volumes on the shelves to which grimy hands could do much damage, little that is irreplaceable. But the piano is different. The piano is a really good instrument, much better than any we could afford to buy today. Therefore the sight of its once shining keyboard all streaked and smudged filled the 'Cellist with anxiety, as well as mortification. The more honor to her that she continued to hold her tongue and to keep the piano dissociated, in the minds of the Nuisances, from the inflexible principles of law and order that hedge in life so narrowly.

Those years, however, are gone. The Nuisances are older now, getting into high school age, much too old to go about with grubby paws, and the keys of the piano are relatively clean again. Moreover, its frame is still solid and stout and its strings can be tuned, so the menace of imminent catastrophe no longer hangs over the house. It is, however, much too early to know definitely whether the 'Cellist and I were wise or foolish. Certain it is that the family includes no young Mozart; probable it is that it has no professional talent; but it has two young people with the groundwork of a musical education.

This has been and continues to be expensive. Music-teachers are among the worst-paid workers in America, but at that they don't work for nothing. A good many hard-earned dollars have gone into the business and a good many more must go into it if it is carried through. The money cost, though, is one of the smallest items in the whole account. What the 'Cellist has put into it in time, physical energy, and nervous strain is beyond all computation. In merely beating time and shouting, "One! Two. Three. Four!" while pudgy fingers fumbled over the keys, I estimate that she has expended enough footpounds of energy to lift the heaviest locomotive on the Baltimore and Ohio Railroad to a height roughly equivalent to the altitude of Mount Washington. In conferences with music-teachers I am sure she has spoken words enough to fill Webster's Unabridged Dictionary three times, while the number of miles she has driven transporting the Nuisances to and from music lessons and concerts is too great even to be guessed.

Nor is that all. The contribution made by the Nuisances themselves is formidable. Even though they have never been chained to the galley, even though they have always known that it was their privilege to quit if that was their deliberate choice, yet many a golden hour have they spent in the music-room when a smiling world was inviting them outside and all sorts of possibilities of delightful play were clamoring for their attention. Many a time, when exercises were too hard and chords and phrases just wouldn't come right, the keys have been further smeared with childish tears. As I grow older, I see more and more clearly that anything purchased at the price of children's tears is a horribly expensive thing. Sometimes the purchase justifies its price, but to do so God knows it must be good!

How good, then, is this thing that the whole family has combined to purchase at such cost? I do not know. Possibly I shall never know. All human calculations are fallible and I am bound to admit the possibility that this one may have been wholly wrong. Still, one can but do one's best with the light that is vouchsafed at the moment, and I understand very clearly the reasoning that has led the 'Cellist and me into this course and that keeps us following it steadfastly.

In the first place, we have no ambition whatever to turn out a pair of professional musicians. This is in part worldly wisdom. Music is both one of the most exacting and one of the worst-paid professions on earth, nor does our observation lead us to believe that professional musicians are conspicuously happier than other people. Let the Nuisances follow what course they will. In the world of the next generation, pretty nearly all paths will be open to women as to men. Let them become astronomers, or gold-beaters, or neurologists, or corporation lawyers; no matter—we are giving them a musical education, anyhow.

In one sense it is the ancient racial obligation that lies upon us. The man who has stood upon his father's shoulders is a poor specimen indeed if he is not willing to bend his back to the weight of his son. Both the 'Cellist and I were given better educations than our fathers had; can we do less than give the Nuisances something better than ours, if it lies within our power to do so? My own schooling, however, included no music, and the 'Cellist's but little; here, then, is an obvious chance to better the record.

But why music? Why not Esperanto, or thermodynamics, or any of a thousand subjects that neither of us has ever studied?

Well, as we used to say down in North Carolina when a difficult question was posed, that brings on more talk. We have a desire, doubtless sentimental, grounded on folly, perhaps, but none the less strong, to bequeath to our children some legacy of lasting value. Obviously, it will not be money. As for the kind of education that will equip them to fend for themselves in the world, that is less a gift from us to them than the discharge of an obligation laid on us by our fathers, who did as much for us.

What is there, in this chaotic modern world, that a father can leave to his child with a reasonable assurance that it will retain some value always? Certainly not securities—not after 1929. Not material wealth in any form, for our generation has had an almost uniquely impressive lesson in the evanescent nature of the solidly material. Why gold itself, the immemorial wealth of the ages, is now good for nothing except to put into a hole in Kentucky. I would not give the impression that I am scornful of money. On the contrary, I respect it highly, and I wish I could leave some to my children. But no rational man thinks money is the sort of legacy that can never get away from them.

Dismiss the material, then, and consider what intangible values we possess that are worth passing on to the next generation. There is, of course, the inheritance that we are told to prize above rubies, the inestimable treasure of a good name. It is a fine legacy, without doubt, but there is certainly nothing necessarily permanent about it; on the contrary, the child can lose it even faster than he can lose money.

There is religious faith; but he would be bold beyond the point of blasphemy who would arrogate to himself the right to bestow or to withhold this gift.

Beyond that, what is there in the flux of modern life that our generation grips surely enough to be serenely confident of its lasting value? In the economic field, for example, my father held it to be incontestably true, and true without reservation, that thrift is a virtue. I am not so sure. He believed in a system of free competition relieved as far as humanly possible of all artificial restraints, governmental or other. I agree with him in general, but I do not believe that "free" in this connection means what he thought it meant. He believed that *The Wealth of Nations* revealed certain laws of economics comparable, in their universality, to the laws of mathematics; I think that it revealed no more than certain conditional premises, some of which have since been invalidated by changes in the conditions. At all events, I am not prepared to try to instill in the Nuisances any sort of economic faith, confident that it will still hold good fifty years hence.

The uncertainty that has invaded economics is even more pronounced in the realm of politics. I am as yet a stout believer in democratic dogma, but I am bound to admit that it is being sharply and ably challenged. It is no longer inconceivable that the next generation in the United States may have to make a shift to survive under some form of totalitarian state. In so far as I have the power, I propose to transmit to my children my own belief in unrestricted liberty wherever it is consistent with social safety, and in the rule of the majority wherever individual liberty is plainly impracticable; but I am far from certain that if I can give them this gift it will retain its value throughout their lives. On the contrary, it may be just the thing that will eventually lead them to end on the barricades or before some *Fuehrer's* firing-squads.

The lesser intangibles that we inherited from the last generation are even more hopelessly confused. Imagine, for example, trying to transmit to the youngsters of today the code of etiquette rigidly maintained by their grand-mammas! Imagine wanting to transmit it! Even the foundation of etiquette, the moral code, seems considerably less substantial than it did thirty years ago. Sometime during the long reign of Victoria Regina it appears that decency somehow became separated from honesty and remained apart so long that now when efforts are made to reunite them, one frequently fails to recognize the other, to the confusion of moralists. Nor is it our conception of abstractions only that must be regarded with suspicion; the very cosmos itself has been shaken to pieces. Most certainly I dare not set up any kind of notion of the physical world as beyond debate, when every day some physicist goes a step further toward resolving the whole thing into the shadow of a shade.

Yet there is upon me a strong impulse to find and present to the youngsters something relatively fixed and stable, if only by way of amends for having brought them into a world so fluid and confusing.

It is one of the heavy penalties of parenthood that from time to time one must stand appalled by what one has done in engendering children. I suppose, in reality, our generation is no worse off in this respect than any other. Perhaps Cro-Magnon Man frequently gazed at Cro-Magnon children with a desperate sense that he had done them wrong in injecting them into a world wherein all the ancient verities were crumbling to a collapse that could not be many years delayed. Perhaps Buck Rogers in the twenty-fifth century will scratch his head over the same problem. Be these things as they may, unquestionably the present generation is face to face with formidable difficulties in this situation.

No thoughtful man escapes it. Heaven knows, my own life has not been the stuff of which high tragedy is made. As I look back over it, I realize that I have been pretty lucky. If fame and fortune have somehow eluded me, Scottish forebears handed down to me an excellent power of adhesion to some kind of pay-roll through fair weather and foul. Even the three great scourges of the race, disease and poverty and war, when they fell upon me, held their hands and whipped but lightly. It is not within reason to suppose that the Nuisances will have an appreciably easier time of it in this world than their father had.

Yet when I look back over that relatively smooth and pleasant path and remember how many thorns and stones were in it, how many laborious ascents under a blazing and pitiless sun, how many dark passages through bitter cold, how many bogs and quagmires, how much pain and fatigue, the thought that the small feet of the Nuisances are destined to tread a path as hard, and perhaps harder, is one on which I do not care to dwell. But it is reason enough for searching high and low, if perchance I may find and put into their hands something that will serve as a staff, however frail, through the long days, or something that in the inevitable gloom of night will be as a lamp unto their feet and a light unto their path.

Will music serve this purpose? I do not know, but I think it may. At any rate, whatever value it has it will retain for a long time unless history alters its course completely. Of course, music, too, has its changes; the old gods go and the new gods arrive in this as in all other arts. Rubinstein fades as Sibelius emerges; and Stravinsky has hardly challenged Sibelius' leadership before Hindemith is challenging his. But behind the route of household gods there are certain ancient idols, colossi as immovable as Memnon among the shifting sands, and these, I think, will still be colossal when the Nuisances are ancient and gray.

"Put not your trust in princes"—most emphatically not in princes of the present day. Stalin, Mussolini, and Hitler may be great men. There are millions who have staked their very lives on the belief. Yet in the perspective of fifty years they may be as difficult to descry as General Boulanger and Dr. Jameson are today—that is, instead of being regarded as the leaders of immense movements, they may have sunk to the status of slight interruptions of the flow of history. But even if, after half a century, they still occupy each a full page in the encyclopedia, I think that Johann Sebastian Bach will remain a greater personage than all of them put together. Already the Eroica means more in the lives of men than Napoleon the Great does and "Tristan und Isolde" vastly more than Napoleon the Little. In fifty years essentially small men who now loom over the scene because they are close will have sunk out of sight, but I have never a doubt that Händel and Haydn will still be great, that Mozart and Schubert will still have power to stir the hearts of men and that intimate acquaintance with these giants will still be a solace and a boon.

In this I may be wrong for, as these pages bear abundant evidence, I do not understand music, and the years passed long ago when I was capable of attaining real understanding. For me, therefore, it is and must ever remain primarily a charming pastime. Yet ears as dull as mine are capable of catching hints and intimations, if not the full meaning of the masters. I know that for one who goes darkling and alone, hag-ridden by

> *Ghoulies and ghosties and long leggitit beasties,*
> *And things that go Whoosh! in the dark,*

the thunder of Beethoven is oftentimes a strong exorcism, hurling back phantoms and scattering werewolves; I know that for one forspent with the dust and heat of a weary road there is in the clear, simple music of old Papa Haydn the sound of cool water and the shadow of green trees; I know that on desolate days upon which

> *The gray rain beats*
> *And wraps the wet world in its flying sheets,*
> *And at my eaves*
> *A slow wind, ghostlike, comes and grieves and grieves,*

there is in the work of Richard Wagner fire and gold and trumpets, and that lift of the spirit that raises mortal man to challenge the immortal gods; and I suspect that even in some of these uncouth moderns there is a sinewy strength that can help steady the steps of a traveler dizzied by the whirling confusion of this century. Perceiving these things dimly and vaguely, I am persuaded that with an ear trained to hear them clearly and a mind trained to comprehend them fully, life would have been soothed and softened and rendered more pleasant in a thousand ways.

But this is only half of it, and probably the less important half. Even a half-educated amateur is capable of feeling a response to the stimulus of music, but that is his limit; it is beyond his capacity to evoke that response, because to do that one must play very well indeed. Yet we have it on the highest authority that it is more blessed to give than to receive, and I believe it is as true with regard to music as anything else in life. It doesn't follow that a professional's every appearance is a deep emotional experience, for it is not said that it is more blessed to sell than to receive; but unquestionably a fine musician carries the potential ability to sway others in a fashion beyond the power of the rest of us.

If it would be fine to give to the Nuisances something that will be of value to them, always, would it not be finer yet if it were something that will make them of value to others? I have known selfish musicians; but I have known selfish stockbrokers, too. I do not think the power of music ever developed its possessor into the horseleech's daughter, crying, "Give, Give!" My observation leads me to believe that the tendency is the other way and that the musician who is selfish would have been even more selfish without his training in the art.

At any rate, we like to think, the 'Cellist and I, that the piano with dirty keys has started something that will do more than merely assist the Nuisances themselves along a long weary road. For they will not travel alone, nor will their own adventures be all that will interest them. Even if they escape the misfortune themselves, inevitably they will come upon those who have fallen among thieves and who have been beaten and wounded and left half dead.

Perhaps the day will come when they will find one who is close to them spiritually broken and bleeding. Indeed, in this world, who can doubt that such a day will come? God forbid that they should then act the Priest and the Levite, passing by on the other side. But when all has been done that can be done, and all has been said that can be said, perhaps our gift will furnish them with yet one more resource; perhaps hands once grubby and weak, but strong and sensitive now, will touch a keyboard all white and shining and summon from the realm beyond word and act a spirit to touch the wounds with the touch of oil and wine.

If it should so happen, then I know it will be with the victim as it was with the wounded man in the old story—from that time forth, he will be Neighbor unto them.

And so the 'Cellist looking at the smudged keys has compressed her lips and said nothing. And so I, ruefully looking over canceled checks returned by the bank—those creased and ink-stained evidences of so much folly, so much stupidity, so much misfortune, such impotence in the clutch of circumstance—find nothing for which to blame myself when I look at those that went to the music-teachers, to the piano-tuners, to the sellers of sheet music and the sellers of concert tickets. And so we sally out together and do fierce and incessant warfare with the schools and acquire the reputation of cranky and probably anti-social parents.

For to accomplish anything worth while in music one must rescue for one's children a minimum of one hour a day for practice; and who can rescue a whole hour of his own child's time from the clutch of the modern school? Even when classes are over, there are athletics and extracurricular activities; and the parent who dared stand up and declare roundly, "To hell with athletics and all that!" might find himself committed to the lunatic asylum. These things are essential, we are informed with lordly scorn, to developing in the child a social sense, the spirit of give-and-take, the idea of team work.

Then we parents, poor worms that we are, stand and take this rubbish. Granting that outdoor exercise is essential to proper growth, the child doesn't have to take it on a playing-field under the constant instruction and admonition of a hired play-leader. As for social sense, the spirit of give-and-take and the idea of team work, I'll back one hour's playing in a quartet to give the child more of all these than he will get from twenty-four hours' playing on the hockey team.

At any rate, right or wrong, we have done battle ferociously for that hour and propose to carry on. Perhaps this is the last, final proof that we are true amateurs—this determination that our children shall have an opportunity to become something more than rank amateurs, if they have the capacity and the wish to do so.

For the musical amateur is not one to rejoice in his limitations. If he is a wise man, he recognizes them, keeps them ever in mind and makes his course conform to them; that is to say, he accepts them philosophically, which is far from saying that he likes them. If he sees a chance, however, to thrust some one else above his own level of musical competence, he is likely to develop a warm, even fanatical, enthusiasm for the enterprise.

This may be illusion. The supposition is supported by the fact that I have known more than one musician whose high attainments in music command my respect no more than his good sense in other matters, but who exhibits a marked lack of interest in making musicians of his children. Perhaps if I knew more music, I should be less certain of its value. It is the green grass on the other side of the fence.

Yet if the amateur's conception of what it means to be really competent as a musician is illusory, what of it? Life without any illusions at all would be so bleak as probably to be beyond human endurance, and this is one that softens existence without any appreciable enervation of the possessor. At that, it is as likely to be true as any other ideal.

Heaven forfend that I should attempt to set up the thesis that the amateur musician is clear of the foibles and weaknesses that beset the rest of the race. On the contrary, it is just his humanity, his reinforced and emphasized humanity, that makes him a charming fellow. He is too wise to believe that complete disillusionment is either possible or desirable, too realistic to be wholly cynical.

Hence, while he sees with utter clarity the limits of his own ability, and dismisses hope of transcending them, or even of enlarging them to any important extent, he can, and usually does, preserve a childlike faith in the magic of music. His own performance is merely sport, but music is not sport. He may be capable, even at best, of nothing more than sleight-of-hand, but he is confident that, beyond his reach but perceptible, there is a realm of genuine necromancy, inhabited by strong magicians with spells that work.

It is a comforting faith to carry along the road. It means that for the True Believer the road can never come to a dead end, never peter out among sands and cacti. "Man that is born of a woman is of few days, and full of trouble; he cometh forth like a flower, and is cut down." Down, then, we must go; and is it of any marked advantage to go down without a mirage? Is he wise and fortunate who ends in the consciousness only of dust and glare?

I venture to doubt it. I dare to think it is a gracious gift that enables the musician, in the midst of drab confusion, yet to believe in a magic that can bring order and beauty into the world. I count him fortunate, not afflicted, in that he can come to the termination of his journey in the desert, yet with the conviction that although he may go no farther, this is not the end of the road, that though he may never work it, yet there is magic. Deluded your amateur musician may be, but happy he certainly is, because for him the road always goes on, for him, still ahead but in plain sight, there are water and green trees and the mountains of all delight.

HARPER'S MAGAZINE, *February 1935*

AN EXCUSE FOR UNIVERSITIES

It seems to be unanimously agreed that an American doctorate of philosophy isn't worth what it costs—that is to say, it isn't worth so much to the recipient. At least half the cost of manufacturing a Ph.D. is borne by society, either through direct taxation or through endowments. Is this a sufficiently large proportion or should a still greater share be borne by society? Upon the answer to this question perhaps hangs the fate of the privately endowed institutions of learning in this country.

That they are in a bad way is perfectly evident. When such institutions as the University of Pennsylvania, Penn State, and Temple University all apply for State aid practically simultaneously; when Princeton cuts salaries; when Johns Hopkins throws overboard its Institute of Law; when even plethoric Harvard begins to wonder audibly if income from endowment is going to be sufficient to cover expenses, it is obvious that evil days have overtaken the institutions. The explanation is that it's smart to be thrifty now, and the smart boys who go shopping for Ph.D.'s seek them in the cheapest market, which is not the privately endowed universities. In a number of these the student is charged something like half as much as it costs to educate him, whereas in most publicly supported schools the proportion paid by the student is nowhere near half.

If this seems to indicate that the modern graduate student is an appallingly cheap skate, let it be taken into consideration that when he gets his degree he hasn't anything of much monetary value. There are exceptions of course; but it is true as a general rule that a doctorate of philosophy is of value only to a man who proposes to become a teacher or a research worker. There has never been much money in teaching, and there has rarely been any at all in research work; but until recent years there has been a modest

living in both. Today that is no longer true. It is hard for the Ph.D. to find
any sort of job as teacher or scientific investigator—so hard, that in 1934 at
least one university president advised a class of newly created doctors of
philosophy to seek jobs with the Civilian Conservation Corps. From the
strictly business point of view, therefore, it is sensible for the student to get
his degree with the smallest possible expenditure, which means that he should
get it from a publicly supported institution, where the public will pay the
larger part of the bill.

And why not? If the economic value of a scientist accrues rather to
society than to the individual scientist, is it any more than fair that society
should pay the larger part of the cost of making a scientist? At any rate this
is just what is happening. The graduate schools of all universities have been
somewhat thinned since the beginning of the depression, but those of the
privately endowed institutions have been decimated to such an extent that
in many cases the income of the university is seriously impaired. Public institutions have been hit too, but their damage is usually less serious because
they never leaned so heavily upon student fees for their support.

Furthermore, as regards the future, public institutions may always hope
for relief through the taxing power. No such prospect opens before the privately endowed schools. If higher education is to become to an even larger
extent a charge upon the public, the one way in which the private institutions
may hope to remain in the competition at all is by increasing their endowments. One university president stated recently that in order to maintain his
institution at its present level without student fees, he would have to increase
his endowment by twenty million dollars. Five years ago this would have
been a large, but by no means a hopeless undertaking; because five years ago
few rich men really believed that the end of their particular world was at
hand. Today few of them believe anything else. Five years ago, parting with
a million or two was not unthinkable to a man who had five or ten, because
he then held to the comforting doctrine that there was plenty more where
his came from. Today there is much evidence that the era of great accumula-
tions is definitely closed so far as this country is concerned. The obvious deduc-
tion is that the wise man will hang on to what he has since his chances of
replacing it are dwindling; so the very wealthy are clutching their pursestrings
frantically, not because they have suddenly turned stingy, but because they
are terrified. He is an optimist indeed who thinks that the privately endowed
universities have much to hope from the immensely wealthy in the immediate future.

There is one other source from which endowments, theoretically, might
come. This is the man of moderate means, the man who hasn't a million to
give, but who might put up from ten to a hundred thousand. These people,
as a general rule, are not nearly so panicky as the very rich. Not having so
far to fall, they are not so much affected by giddiness—perhaps too they can
see more clearly what is actually happening on the ground and, therefore, are
less impressed by the undermining operations.

However, if they are to put up enough money to maintain the privately
endowed universities as we have known them, enormous numbers of them

must take part. If the university president mentioned above is to get his endowment from the ten-thousand-dollar boys, he must discover no less than two thousand of them. That is to say, any adequate effort in the universities' behalf must take on the semblance of a popular movement of considerable proportions, a movement that demands sacrifices of large numbers of people.

And this inevitably raises the question, are the universities worth any such effort? Of course they have been worth it in the past, but that isn't the question. Are they worth strong popular support now, and are they likely to continue to be worth it in the predictable future?

There is not a doubt that Mark Hopkins was a valuable man, but he's dead. So are Witherspoon, Gilman, Woodrow Wilson, Eliot. Granting that John Harvard, Elihu Yale, Thomas Jefferson, Ezra Cornell, Johns Hopkins served their generations magnificently, it does not necessarily follow that a similar service now would be a similar boon to this generation. For today the State is interested in higher education. When Harvard and Yale made their gifts it was private education or none in this country. Even as late as 1876, when the Johns Hopkins University was founded, although there were many excellent American colleges, there was no American university in the sense in which that term is understood in Europe—that is, there was no institution devoted primarily to original investigation and the training of investigators.

Today the situation is altogether different. There are many graduate schools doing this sort of work with a high degree of competence. Some excellent ones are connected with State universities. In addition, there are several institutes devoted exclusively to the extension of knowledge and not concerning themselves with teaching, in the formal sense, at all. If, then, the State is in position to carry on the pedagogical part of the work at small expense to the student, and the institutes are capable of carrying forward research work, where is there room for the privately endowed university? Especially, what is the excuse for increasing its endowment to the point at which it can offer training to the student at approximately the rates made by the State institutions? Would it not be the part of wisdom to have the existing institutions taken over by the State?

They are, in point of fact, already public property. The endowments which constitute their wealth cannot legally be converted to the use of any individual. The money derived from their stocks and bonds, their lands and houses, is in the form of rent and interest, which is to say, a claim on the income derived from the use of property and the employment of labor. Well, taxes likewise are a claim on the income derived from the use of property and the employment of labor. Whether an institution is supported by the income from an endowment or by an appropriation from the State treasury it is supported by society. Organized society, under the name of the State, is already managing some; why not let it take over the rest and cease from worrying philanthropists for further endowments?

This is a question that those who believe in the privately endowed university cannot ignore forever. A blatant assertion that the endowed university is better than the State-supported one is simply idiotic. In what way is it better? To what extent is it better? Who says it is better? In one way at least it is clearly inferior to the State school. This is in the extent of its direct influence on the population. Graduate schools supported in whole or in part by taxation accommodate far more students today than do the privately endowed ones. The larger part of the job is now being done by the State schools, and the assertion that it is also the worse part would take a great deal of proving.

There is no financial argument whatever in favor of the private institution. It is true that political control has resulted in scandalous mismanagement of the funds of some State universities; but for every such instance it would be easy to cite a case in which the funds of endowed schools have been equally mismanaged.

As for the ability of the State in the field of pedagogy, that was established long years ago in the elementary schools. The American public school is, Heaven knows, a long way from the ideal; but does, in tolerable fashion, a job which private schools never atttempted and which no rational man believes they could possibly perform. Even the Catholic parochial school system, the only considerable rival of the public schools, is frankly designed to serve the needs of one communion including about fifteen percent of the population.

As to the capacity of the State to further research work, one need not mention State universities at all. The case could be abundantly proved in them, but it is proved beforehand by a moment's consideration of the investigations made in Washington by such organizations as the Bureau of Standards, the Coast and Geodetic Survey, the National Museum, the Smithsonian Institution, and the Library of Congress. There isn't a university in the world, endowed or tax-supported, in which the work of United States government scientists is not accepted and used.

As for the contention that political control is, and of necessity must be, ruinous to the best work of a university, that must be accepted. Any doubts on the subject may be resolved by consideration of the state of Princeton when the quarrels of Wilson and Dean West were rending it asunder, of the narrowness of Harvard's escape when she at first rejected the appointment to the faculty of a young professor named Charles W. Eliot, of Vanderbilt's condition during the long battle between the trustees and the bishops. But it happens that none of these is a tax-supported university. Politics is, indeed, poisonous to an institution of higher learning, but politics is not confined to the Democratic and Republican parties—not by a great deal. And politics in an endowed university is frequently of a sort that would scandalize Tammany. On the other hand, more than one State university has pursued its way for years without the slightest interference from professional politicians.

There is, however, one argument in favor of the endowed university which supporters of the State system have never yet answered; but, unfortunately, it is an argument which embarrasses some of the private institutions more than it does their opponents. This is the argument that the privately endowed university is the natural haven of refuge for the born hell-raiser.

To put it in more decorous terms, the State school, like the church school, suffers one irremediable handicap which may be negligible on the lower levels of education, but becomes serious in the extreme in the higher branches. This is irrevocable committal to a particular point of view.

The State university may be free in every other direction, but by the very conditions of its existence it is pledged to support the State. In practice this means not support of a theoretical State, but support of the political institutions then and there existing, and of the communal *mores* that have produced the institutions. The rule may be proved by the exception. In 1925 Dr. Harry Woodburn Chase, then President of the University of North Carolina, shot suddenly into national fame because, although president of a tax-supported institution, he had the nerve to go before the Legislature and denounce a bill favored by a large number of members. In fact, he not only denounced but defeated it. The bill in question was one of the imbecile "monkey laws" which raged like a pestilence through the country at that time, forbidding the teaching of the hypothesis of organic evolution in tax-supported schools. It was such a statute that brought about, a few months later, the incredible farce of the Scopes trial in Tennessee. President Chase managed to save his institution from the affliction; but the feat, and especially the fact that he was daring enough to attempt it, aroused country-wide astonishment at the time.

But were the State university never subjected to the impact of mass hysteria, it would still be committed to support of the State. Even as bold an official as President Chase might well hesitate to tolerate forthright, frontal assaults on the organization that pays the university's bills and that holds power of life and death over it. Any President who did so would be risking the very existence of the institution in his charge; and a man may be indifferent to his own fate and yet loath to subject his university to bombardment by maintaining in office a professor whose views outrage the voters.

One has only to glance about the world, though, to realize that men of the very first rank intellectually are frequently, indeed commonly, unconventional in their views about some phase of life in this republic. The communism of Albert Einstein, for example, has nothing to do with his ability as a mathematician, but it would certainly make him *persona non grata* in the average State University simply because as soon as he appeared as a member of the faculty, the air, in the elegant and expressive phrase of General Johnson, would be filled with dead cats. The feline missiles might or might not hit the professor; but they would certainly hit the university. The taxpayers of New Jersey, however, do not support the Institute for Advanced Study at Princeton; hence they have no very obvious ground for complaining of the political views of any member of its faculty.

To be sure, boards of trustees of privately endowed universities have been known to rise in a fury matching the worst hysteria of the populace. The history of higher education in America records the names of many professors sacrificed to the prejudices of a board of stuffed shirts. But it is self-evident that the chances of placating half a dozen infuriated board members and inducing them to see reason are better than the chances of doing as much with half a million infuriated voters.

I do not confess to any sympathy with the communistic views of Professor Einstein. I do not share the radical views of Prof. Scott Nearing or the moralistic views of Prof. Bertrand Russell or the sociological implications drawn from his psychological observations by Prof. John B. Watson. I cherish some doubt even as to the juridical philosophy of Prof. Felix Frankfurter. But whether these men are right or wrong is beside the point. Each of them is possessed of a powerful, restless, and inquisitive mind. Each of them works habitually on the outer confines of knowledge, seeking constantly to discover a path through the all-surrounding darkness. Each of them, in one way or another, has, at one time or another, pushed back the shadows a little. Hence it is to the interest of civilization that each of them continue to work.

What passes the comprehension of the ordinary layman is the fact that the greatest investigators in the world are now, and always have been, generally wrong, even in their own fields. Such a man as Pavlov, for example, is right only occasionally and at long intervals. The percentage of his experiments that have worked out as he expected is extremely small; the vast bulk of all his life's labor has gone for nothing except to prove that he started in the wrong direction. But what of it? In exploring it is of the utmost importance to learn what path not to take. When a series of Pavlov's experiments has proved definitely and conclusively that one of his theories is wrong, that may be just as important as another series proving that another theory is right.

More than that, common experience supports the belief that one of the rarest things in the world is a first-rate intelligence that is equally great in all fields.

The usual impression, based on observation, is that prodigious effort in one direction—the sort of effort requisite to great achievement—frequently seems to sap the intellectual energies until in other directions intelligence hardly operates at all. The absent-minded professor of the comic papers is not altogether a fantasy. But if a man is a really great bio-chemist, what does it matter if he is a rotten economist? If a man is a swell archaeologist, who except his wife need care if he cherishes dizzy ideas about sexual morality? If a man has learned and recorded more than any other human being ever learned about Mayan civilization, surely we can forgive him for being unaware that the Democratic party

> *is the true embodiment*
> *Of everything that's excellent*

and even tolerate his expression of a contrary opinion—unless indeed the Democratic party has been the champion of his university, in which case a caucus is indicated.

But, it may be asked, granting that these odd fish serve a certain purpose in extending the bounds of knowledge, why is it necessary or desirable to incorporate them in university faculties? Why not segregate them in institutes devoted to research exclusively?

A great many are so incarcerated in America. But this scheme leaves out of account the hereditary nature of the Republic of Letters. It is only a conventionality that dubs it a republic, for it is in reality dynastic in its nature. There are some scholars who have never had a great teacher; but they are rare indeed. Ordinarily, every new Giotto is the pupil of a Cimabue, every new Paul has sat at the feet of a Gamaliel, every new Plato derives directly from a Socrates. It may be argued plausibly that what we need to instruct an undergraduate is a safe and sound man; but what it takes to inspire a graduate student to do original work is a highly original teacher, which usually means a very unsafe and unsound man.

The function of a university—the function in which it differs from an institute—is not merely to make original investigations, but to train new investigators to take over the work and carry it on, perhaps in a research institute. The most strikingly original scientist on earth is really original only in a tiny fraction of his mental activities. The graphic arts, music, literature, even architecture in the degree to which it is an art rather than a science, were never, any of them, half so dependent on the work done in the past as, say, mathematical physics, which seems at this moment to be the most daringly original of all the sciences. W. F. G. Swann's *The Architecture of the Universe,* for example, seems to be a long way from Euclid, but it is easier to trace the later from the earlier scholar than it is to trace Hindemith from Bach or Brancusi from Praxiteles. Thus if it were thinkable that the line of scholarship could be broken, even for a generation, the result to science would be disastrous. The distinctive feature of the university, as compared to the research institute or the research laboratories maintained by many great commercial houses is that it preserves this line.

The question is whether men whose long training in scientific skepticism leads them into skepticism about our political institutions and our social code are to be debarred from participation in the work of stimulating the rising generation of scientists. Their presence in a State university is of doubtful propriety, even in theory, and in practice leads continually to uproars that embarrass all concerned. But the endowed school, being less directly exposed to popular resentment, can use them with relative safety.

Incidentally, while the question now turns on professorial radicalism, the argument holds good in either direction. The time may be not far distant when the privately endowed university may become the one sanctuary in which we shall be able to preserve some of our grandest old reactionaries. Anyone who is familiar with the *genus* in its native habitat must smile at the prevailing notion that the typical professor is a radical. The only thing reasonably sure about a man with an alert and powerful intelligence trained in the scientific method is that he will not be a conformist; but the direction that his nonconformity will take is far from sure. For every Socialist in the academic shades it would probably be easy to find two men who denounce universal suffrage, even manhood suffrage, with great heartiness; and for every Communist professor it would probably be possible to produce at least one who is a monarchist at heart. If the present socialistic trend in popular feeling continues, who dare say positively that the State universities may not ere long be ejecting men caught teaching the doctrines of the Republican party? And then where shall they go if there are no endowed schools left? Yet no man who has been honored by the acquaintance of a really fine specimen can doubt that the influence of these barnacled old crustaceans may be very good for ebullient youth.

In brief, the endowed university, by the very fact of its being privately endowed, is in position to enrich our intellectual life by harboring men whose ideas are valuable but a little too hot for the publicly supported institution to handle safely and comfortably. This enrichment is unquestionably of great value to society, perhaps valuable enough to justify doubling the present endowment of such institutions to enable them to continue their work, even if students continue to be few.

But if the privately endowed schools fail to offer this enrichment, is there any particular reason why they should be maintained? If such a university cannot offer as an excuse for existence a strong belief in and a rigid adherence to academic freedom, what other excuse is there for it to offer? If its faculty does not include some men of originality—which necessarily means some very odd fish—it is nothing but an expensive, and to that extent inefficient, competitor of the state schools. Academic freedom is not merely a theory to which the privately endowed universities should give assent; since the creation of the great State universities it has become the principal, if not the only, excuse for their continued existence.

Some of them have been canny enough to see the point. Although Frankfurter was roundly denounced for defending Sacco and Vanzetti he was not kicked out of Harvard for it. Mitchell has not been fired from Johns Hopkins for running for Governor of Maryland on the Socialist ticket. Columbia declined to bounce Nicholas Murray Butler for raving against prohibition even while it was the law of the land. I have heard of universities that turned a deaf ear to tales of how, after a particularly cheery party, some learned doctor had been put to bed much the worse for wear; and there is credible authority for the story that one institution refused to dismiss an able man although, maddened by a long series of petty irritations, he gave his wife a shellacking that woke the whole neighborhood. In fact I have been told that he was later promoted from assistant to associate professor.

However, it is not the moral, but the intellectual eccentricities of professors that start the trouble. It is hard to recall a single instance of legislative assault on a State university because one of its professors was discovered to be drunken; but anyone can recall many instances of such assaults because one of the professors was discovered to be socialistic. One incautious remark by a professor in a State school may result in a drastic reduction of the maintenance appropriation; but such a lapse cannot reduce the income from endowment of the private school.

Yet who has not heard alumni, and even trustees, of endowed universities lamenting the presence in the faculty of men who profess unpopular opinions? The fact that the maintenance of such men is the principal excuse for preserving the privately endowed schools is completely incomprehensible as far as the true conformist is concerned.

But it is an excuse and until the day when we accept the Hitlerian ideal of the completely regimented nation it will continue to be an adequate excuse.

HARPER'S MAGAZINE, *November 1935*

THIS TERRIFYING FREEDOM

The flight from liberty is assuredly not originally, nor primarily, an American movement. Bolshevism, Fascism, Nazism were all invented abroad, and the number of Americans who have embraced them is statistically negligible. Excited left-wing publicists are continually writing editorials, essays, pamphlets, and books to expose our steady drift into Fascism; Republican campaign speakers almost every day are proving to their own satisfaction that this is practically a Soviet republic now. The great majority of Americans, however, are not greatly impressed by these alarmists of the right or of the left. Most of us are still persuaded that this is "a nation conceived in liberty" and, without thinking much about it, we assume that it will remain so.

Nevertheless, while those who would convict us either of Fascism or of Communism ought not to be taken too seriously, it is certainly not wise to assume that the United States, alone among the great nations, has been unaffected by the world's frenzied rush away from the perils of freedom. It is, in fact, more than unwise—it is virtually impossible. The Red-hunts of the past twenty years have made such a terrific noise that it is hard to believe an anchorite in the midst of Death Valley could have failed to hear some rumors of them; and while a great many were instigated and conducted by publicity seekers, usually journalistic or political, not infrequently they have been joined by grave citizens of weight in the community. Indeed, during the summer the Senate of the United States passed, without a record vote and almost without discussion, a bill that made a frontal assault on the first article of the Bill of Rights, the guarantee of freedom of speech and of the press. And this bill was introduced—by request of the War and Navy Departments, it is true, but introduced—by one of the most conspicuous

Democratic defenders of the Constitution, Senator Millard E. Tydings, of Maryland, by its own citizens yclept "the Free State."

The McCormack-Tydings bill was ostensibly aimed at disaffection in the armed forces. It made punishable by a fine of one thousand dollars or imprisonment for two years, or both, the act of putting into the hands of a soldier or sailor any printed or written document that might incite him to disobey the laws and regulations governing the army and navy. But it did more. It made illegal the possession of such literature and empowered the police to search for and seize it whenever and wherever it might be found. Apparently the police, under this bill as it was originally drafted, might have raided the Harvard University Library to seize any book there which a general or an admiral might regard as tending to incite disaffection. Without doubt a newspaper containing an article denouncing military law might have been seized in the press-room before ever a soldier or sailor had set eyes on it.

The constitutionality of this measure was promptly attacked in the House, and it died with the expiring Congress, but for the moment let that pass and consider the significance of its course through the Senate. There the constitutional question was not even raised, which certainly indicates no avidity for defense of freedom of speech in the Senate. Indeed, the sponsor of the bill was a Senator who has broken with his own party again and again within the last two years and voted against Administration measures strictly on constitutional grounds. Tydings is one of that little group of Democrats, including Glass, Bailey, Dill, and one or two more who have become known as anti-New Deal because they think the New Deal attacks the Constitution. If such a man can introduce such a bill, and if the Senate can pass it merely as a matter of routine, the attack on the First Amendment is not to be dismissed with a shrug. Exactly what is this guarantee? How strong is it? How well is it able to weather continued assaults? Finally, is there any reason why the public should hold it in slight esteem?

For my own part, I had assumed until recently that the guarantee of free speech was among the strongest in the Constitution. "Congress shall make no law . . . abridging freedom of speech or of the press." That seems flat enough. Here is a liberty that Congress is specifically and unequivocally forbidden to reduce. There is no doubt about that, no room for argument.

The catch in it is that this freedom is not defined, and ever since 1787 courts, legislators, and commentators have been struggling to frame a definition that shall be inclusive, exclusive, and conclusive. That it is not absolute everyone agrees. No rational man has ever contended that the First Amendment guarantees the press the right to publish with impunity libel, obscenity, or information dangerous to the state, such as vital military information in time of war; nor have the courts ever admitted that this guarantee has any bearing on their power to punish a contempt. Cooley, in his *Constitutional Limitations,* utters the cautious dictum that

> *Commentators seem agreed in the opinion that the term itself means only that liberty of publication without the previous permission of the government, which was obtained by the abolition of the censorship.*

This is certainly no radical opinion. It is merely a guarantee that if you wish to print a newspaper story asserting that your neighbor is a horse-thief, no policeman has authority to stop you; but it doesn't mean that he lacks authority to put you in jail after you have published it. In other words, the original meaning of freedom of the press was that the editor was guaranteed full freedom to get himself locked up.

The definition usually applied by the courts, however, is somewhat more liberal. It was framed by Chancellor Kent in *People vs. Croswell,* and reads,

> *The liberty of the press consists in the right to publish with impunity truth with good motives and for justifiable ends, whether it respects the government, magistracies, or individuals.*

That is to say, if your neighbor actually is a horse-thief, as you can prove, you may publish the fact and still escape the dungeon, even though he be a Justice of the Peace also. All you have to do is convince the court that you exposed him more in sorrow than in anger and that your purpose was to replace, in the next election, a Democratic official with a Republican, or *vice versa,* according to which the court will consider the justifiable end. This is the rule today. This is the freedom that Congress may not abridge.

Obviously, it is much narrower than many people, including a great many newspaper men, have assumed. It is much narrower, indeed, than current practice would indicate; for when the truth of allegations is proved the courts rarely evince an inclination to inquire very closely into the nature of motives and ends. Nevertheless, the rule still stands and it may be invoked at any time. It is a gun behind the door.

If Kent's definition were applied rigorously it would, of course, end freedom of the press as we now understand it, because it makes no reference whatever to opinion. When Theodore Roosevelt declared recently that Franklin D. Roosevelt regards him (Theodore) as Public Enemy Number One, he assumed a right of free speech which Chancellor Kent certainly did not grant; for that, obviously, is a matter, not of fact, but of opinion, the truth or falsity of which would be equally difficult to prove under the rules of evidence. It occurred to no one, however, to doubt that the Colonel has a right to express his free and frank opinion of his cousin so long as he restricts his language to the ordinary decencies of conversation. For in this matter public opinion has run far ahead of the law. In his famous dissent in *Abrams vs. United States* the late Mr. Justice Holmes expressed a widely prevalent belief when he declared that the Constitution

> *is an experiment, as all life is an experiment. Every year, if not every day, we have to wager our salvation upon some prophecy based upon imperfect knowledge. While that experiment is a part of our system, I think that we should be eternally vigilant against attempts to check the expression of opinions that we loathe and believe fraught with death, unless they so imminently threaten immediate interference with the lawful and pressing purposes of the law that an immediate check is required to save the country. . . . Only the emergency that makes it*

immediately dangerous to leave the correction of evil counsel to time
warrants making any exception to the sweeping command, "Congress
shall make no law abridging the freedom of speech."

But this, although it was the opinion of a very distinguished American, remains merely an opinion, expressed in a dissent. Not a court in the land is bound by it, except in so far as judges may feel a moral obligation to take into consideration the prevailing opinion among intelligent and upright men. In other words, while Kent's definition may serve to protect the publication of facts—always with the limitation as to the motives and object of the publication—the right to publish one's opinions is protected by public sentiment, rather than by the Constitution of the United States.

The States, in some cases, have been more specific, but probably a typical guarantee of that sort is Article 40, of the Constitution of Maryland:

Every citizen of the State ought to be allowed to speak, write and
publish his sentiments on all subjects, being responsible for the abuse of
that privilege.

The value of that guarantee depends absolutely on the definition of the word "abuse" and, since judges and juries do not work in a vacuum, the definition will depend largely on public sentiment.

The point of interest here is that freedom of the press as it is understood in modern America really rests on a fairly widespread public belief that Holmes was right, even though he was overruled in the particular case that brought forth his opinion. If that belief is ever abandoned by a majority of Americans, then any semi-competent lawyer will be able to drive a horse and wagon right through the Constitutional guarantee. The press will remain free as long as the public wishes it to remain free, and it will not remain free any longer, Constitution or no Constitution.

Nor is the possibility that eventually its freedom will be lost merely speculative. The success of the McCormack-Tydings bill in the Senate is enough to prove that; but long before the bill was introduced there was plenty of evidence that Holmes's opinion is far from being shared universally. It was all very well for Thomas Jefferson to declare, "Were it left to me to decide whether we should have a government without newspapers or newspapers without governments, I should not hesitate a moment to prefer the latter." Jefferson was no mystic and such a concept as the Totalitarian State would have been completely incomprehensible to him. A monarch he could understand, and a God as Monarch of monarchs he could understand; but a metaphysical entity which is neither a king nor a deity, yet claiming the allegiance yielded to both, would probably have puzzled him as profoundly as it puzzles his followers today.

None the less the idea is accepted by hundreds of millions of Europeans in Germany, Italy, and Russia and has to some extent infected American thinking. "Congress shall make no law respecting an establishment of religion," but without the assistance of Congress we are developing more and more of the outward forms, and apparently adopting more and more of the inner spirit, of a religion in which the state is the object of worship. Witness the solemnity with which millions of school children every morning are required to celebrate a rite called a salute to the flag, but which tends more and more to become, not a salute, but a sacrament. Witness the increasing demand for the repetition of liturgies which we do not hesitate to call creeds, but which express faith, not in any recognized deity, but in the state. Witness the increasing vindictiveness with which non-participants are pursued, and mark its increasing resemblance to the fury of heresy-hunters. These things leave little doubt that a considerable section of the American population is imitating the Italians, Russians, and Germans in erecting chauvinism into a form of theology.

If this thing becomes predominant in the country there must be, of course, an end to freedom of speech and of the press; for, as Holmes remarked in that same opinion,

> *Persecution for the expression of opinions seems to me perfectly logical. If you have no doubt of your premises or your power and want a certain result with all your heart you naturally express your wishes in law and sweep away all opposition.*

There was a time when Uncle Sam was regarded merely as an elderly gentleman, humorous, kindly, and lovable, but quite capable of error and occasionally a little ridiculous. He was a stout upholder of liberty, largely because he had to have liberty in order to retrieve his own mistakes. But when he is erected into a god, all this must disappear. The chauvinism that now masquerades as patriotism throughout this country is the bitter foe of every item in the Bill of Rights; and as chauvinism goes up, old-fashioned Americanism must inevitably go down.

However, the religion of the state has made relatively slow progress on this continent because it has not behind it the driving power that has propelled it triumphantly through a large part of Europe, the irresistible power of fear. No thoroughly frightened country can be free, because fear and liberty are incompatible. No terrified man is a freeman. Oliver Wendell Holmes could live and die a freeman, because he was master of his fears; but men of that stripe are rare. Old Ben Franklin's contemptuous remark applies to the millions:

> *They that can give up essential liberty to obtain a little temporary safety, deserve neither liberty nor safety—*

nor, as developments in Europe show, are they likely to get either. If Hitler's destruction of liberty has increased the safety of Germany, or Mussolini's that of Italy, then Kelly is a Chinaman.

Americans in the mass are not yet frightened enough to think seriously of surrendering freedom of speech, but countless efforts are being made to terrorize them. Some are directed by astute gentry who know exactly what they want, but the vast majority of them arise from that great American heresy, the theory that whenever and wherever anything unpleasant exists something can be done about it. The first class can be dismissed briefly, not because they are unimportant, but because they are easy to understand. Any individual whose enterprises are of a character that will not bear public inspection naturally is an opponent of free speech. They are to be found in every walk of life, not among politicians only; there are business men, doctors, lawyers, and even clergymen who, at certain periods in their lives, are filled with a great and well-justified yearning for the shades of obscurity, and who, therefore, find free speech and a free press noxious in a high degree. However, once their true motive has been discovered, their influence is small.

It is not so with the honest, but stupid. They have discovered or, to put it more exactly, they have rediscovered, a danger that is not chimerical. Say what you will, freedom of speech and of the press is perilous. The stupidity is not in observing the danger, but in assuming that something should be done about it.

The theory that America is a land of boundless opportunity is a pretty good theory as long as it is kept within the bounds of reason; as regards material advantage it is still true. As regards certain educational and cultural advantages it is still relatively true. But America does not and never did offer an opportunity to reverse the basic conditions of human existence, one of which is the acceptance of tremendous risks. The dullest among us grasp this in part. The most rabid hundred percenter has never claimed that Americans are excepted from the rule that "to every man upon this earth death cometh, soon or late." But the idea that intellectual and spiritual adventure entails risk just as does an active and adventurous physical life is one that is exceedingly hard for us to grasp.

In the quotation cited above Mr. Justice Holmes referred specifically to opinions that he considers "fraught with death." Now when the average American encounters anything that he considers fraught with death, the hardest of all possible courses for him to pursue is to do nothing. Inactivity is contrary to our traditions of thinking and living. The prime condition of our national existence, the subduing of a savage continent, required activity, the putting forth of effort. In the beginning, the very ideal of freedom of speech involved the ideal of activity. Evils were to be denounced, a new system of government was to be built up, a new society was to be created, energy was to be released. Most Americans had, or felt that they had, a larger stake in change than in stability.

The conditions are now reversed. This freedom that was essential in 1787 is now perceived to be dangerous. It was just as dangerous, of course, in 1787, but the counter-balancing dangers of suppression were at that time much more plainly in view. The revolutionary spirit burns low, because most of us have nothing much to revolt against. Hence it is apparent that to guard the freedom of speech of those who are endeavoring to fan the flames of revolt is to incur a risk to all that we have built up since Yorktown.

This is undeniably true. Where we are stupid is in not perceiving that it is also an unalterable condition of liberty, just as the risk of death is an unalterable condition of life. It takes courage to be free—not merely passive courage against theoretical dangers, but active boldness in the presence of definite threats. Danger is always unpleasant. The thrill that an alpinist, for example, gets out of a perilous climb comes from his spiritual exaltation in ignoring the danger and triumphing over it; the risk itself is unpleasant even to the man who seeks it out. Yet there seems to be a growing tendency among Americans to assume that because the risk involved in freedom of speech is unpleasant, therefore it should be removed.

The stupidity of this lies in the failure to understand that this risk can be removed in one way only, which involves the acceptance of vastly greater risks. Oliver Wendell Holmes, demanding freedom of expression for opinions that he loathed and believed fraught with death, was inviting danger, and he knew it; but does any rational man believe that Holmes was inviting a tithe of the danger that hangs over Adolf Hitler's head every day? Consider the nations that have eliminated the dangers of free speech and a free press— how safe are they? Russia, with the mightiest standing army ever supported by a nation in time of peace, is dismally certain that eventually, probably soon, she is going to be assailed on every side. Italy, pouring hundreds of thousands of her young men into Africa, has achieved little safety by making it impossible for the Italian press to oppose Mussolini's imperialistic adventures. Germany—phew!

France, on the other hand, although a horribly frightened nation, has clung desperately to some measure of freedom of speech and the press; and it is precisely in France today that a man who proposes to attend strictly to his own business and leave other people to theirs has the best chance to live in peace and die in his bed.

On an occasion that has become famous Upton Sinclair was arrested for attempting to read the Constitution of the United States in public in the city of Los Angeles. That was a proceeding so idiotic that the whole country has laughed at its stupidity for years. Yet, there is no manner of doubt that when the Los Angeles police seized Sinclair they were eliminating a risk. The crowd that gathered around him might have blocked traffic. There was real, definite danger of that; and in order to eliminate it, the police made their city the target for scorn throughout the civilized world, created thousands of friends for Sinclair, and persuaded thousands of Californians that there was something rotten in their system of government. Thus to eliminate a trifling risk they created others a thousand times as bad.

The same thing is true of other activities that are not so plainly absurd. If soldiers and sailors are permitted to hear the arguments of Communists, some of them may turn Bolshevist. That is as definite a risk as was Sinclair's possible obstruction of traffic; but to eliminate it by throttling free speech is to roast the pig by burning the house. It is possible that some school children, if they are let alone, may develop indifference to the flag and to the country it represents; but to eliminate that by teaching them that the country is too sacred for criticism, a sort of god, and the flag something like its altar, would be to raise up a generation incapable of the sharp criticism and ready, vigorous protest that alone can keep a government of politicians relatively decent. These things, in short, are undermining America. They are subversive activities in the worst sense, because they are infinitely more effective than Communist propaganda. Chauvinism, not Communism, does the boring from within that really may scuttle the Ship of State.

"They that can give up essential liberty for a little temporary safety"—how remarkably right old Ben is, even after a century and a half!—"deserve neither liberty nor safety." And assuredly, they shall have neither.

THE EVENING SUN, *September 14, 1936*

ONE FOR ROOSEVELT

H. L. Mencken has yielded his place today to allow Dr. Johnson to voice his dissent with the editorial position of the Sunpapers.

I am for Roosevelt.

The Sun has declared that it cannot support him, and has stated its reasons. They seem to me wholly inadequate, because they omit all reference to the greatest service that Roosevelt has rendered to the country, to wit, the introduction of intelligence into the conduct of the country's affairs.

I am not against Landon, I am for Roosevelt.

The Governor of Kansas seems to be a very decent citizen. Doubtless he is a good administrator. Certainly he has exhibited a certain appreciation of some things the Roosevelt Administration has done and has intimated that he will continue them if he is elected. But he has uttered no word that evidences an understanding of Roosevelt's great achievement, which is the establishment of contact between statecraft and reality.

I am not for Roosevelt the man, I am for Roosevelt the statesman.

I wouldn't give the traditional whoop in Hades for the famous smile, the golden voice, the charming manners. If he grinned like a gargoyle, croaked like a rain-crow and had the manners of a Hoover chasing veterans out of Washington, I would still be for him—in fact, I am not sure that I wouldn't like him better. All this talk about his charm gets a little wearisome.

I am for Roosevelt precisely because I, like *The Sun,* believe in a free competitive system under capitalism governed democratically. I believe that Roosevelt is the great bulwark of capitalism, conservation and democracy.

Incidentally, for this opportunity to set forth in their columns my reasons for this belief, I can do no less than make a bow to the Sunpapers and to

H. L. Mencken, who has ceded to me for once his customary place in the *Evening Sun*. They may be against Roosevelt, but they are still for free speech.

The most dreadful failure of which any form of government can be guilty is simply to lose touch with reality, because out of this failure all imaginable forms of evil grow. Every empire that has crashed has come down primarily because its rulers didn't know what was going on in the world and were incapable of learning.

This was the catastrophic failure of the Harding-Coolidge-Hoover regime. Have we forgotten how Coolidge and his man Mellon repeatedly assured us that all was well at the very moment when we were plunging toward the edge of the abyss? They were probably sincere enough; they simply didn't know what was going on.

Then, when the crash came, they were incapable of learning. We had to sweat through four years of depression under Hoover, although every single thing that Roosevelt has done might just as well have been done years earlier. The banking situation might have been cleaned up in 1930 or 1931 just as well as in 1933. The public works program might have been started years earlier. The problem of social security might have been tackled long ago. Something intelligent might have been done about the tariff while Cordell Hull was still merely a Congressman.

I say that these things might have been done, but in truth they couldn't have been done, because Washington at that time had not the brains and the courage necessary to do them. The politicians then in power could not think, or act, or even feel otherwise than in the old traditional, political way.

I am for Roosevelt because he, alone, demonstrated that he knew what it was all about.

Any man not an utter fool knows that new conditions demand new methods; but a great many men who are far from being fools are not aware that the conditions are new. With all respect, I am bound to say that *The Sun* itself is guilty of ignoring this factor. It says,

> *Let us restore and preserve the system which produces in abundance the wealth with which we support the fortunate and unfortunate alike.*

Nobody can quarrel with that, but that isn't the question at all. The very system which produces wealth has failed calamitously to distribute wealth. The New Deal, far from interfering with the system which produces, apparently has stimulated it; at any rate, production for the month of July was 108% of the average for the same month in 1924-26. Since it had dropped, under the old regime, to about 55, it is pretty clear that the New Deal has not prevented the resumption of production.

Has it, then, facilitated distribution, except by the violent means of distributing through taxation? I do not know. I doubt that anybody knows, as yet. But I do know that it has brought all its energies to bear on the problem; and I do know that none of the old, purely political-minded regimes had made any effective effort to solve this problem. Yet I am convinced that this, and not the problem of production, is the one that we must solve, or suffer disruption of our economic life indefinitely.

I do not believe that this question is susceptible of solution by any of the old formulae because it contains some entirely new factors. Yet I do not believe that the sort of politicians who were in power from 1921 to 1933 are capable of applying any but the old formulas. It isn't a question of honesty. They are just too set in their ways.

Roosevelt has brought into Washington a set of men who may, or may not, be statesmen, but who are unquestionably alert mentally, unquestionably capable of harboring a new idea, even though it may be non-political. That they have made mistakes is obvious. That many of their methods may be wrong is highly probable; but about one thing they are everlastingly right, and that is their realization that they can't get by simply by relying on precept, precedent and tradition. It seems to me, therefore, that, wild as some of them may be, they are safer than men who know nothing except what bitter experience has shown to be wrong. Ickes, Morgenthau, Wallace and Tugwell do not seem to me ideal, but they do seem to be intelligent; and I like them better than I liked Walter Brown, Deak, the ancient Mellon and the Wilbur boys.

Will Mr. Landon, if he is elected, surround himself with men who are as sharply aware of what is going on in the world and as little trammeled by political traditionalism as these are? Why expect it? A President, no matter how honest, cannot utterly ignore his debts to the men who supported him, and Landon is supported by every political traditionalist in the country, Democratic as well as Republican. He is bound to bring back into Washington at least a few of the Fess-Doak type. He will be lucky if he escapes bringing in one or two of the Fall-Denby type. Why take the risk?

I am for Roosevelt because he is not extravagant.

Extravagance is spending money without getting anything worth while for it. Hoover's Farm Board was gross extravagance, because it spent money on a hopeless project. The RFC was extravagant, because it spent money attacking the depression without making a dent in it.

During the war the country spent $30,000,000,000 in a year and a half, and all it got in return was 350,000 corpses and a lot of bad notes. Since 1933 —that is to say in twice the time—the New Deal has spent a third as much and for it we have thousands of miles of roads and streets, countless schoolhouses, bridges, dams, canals, power plants, forests, sewer and water mains, transmission lines and other things. But, above all we avoided getting a lot of corpses. Troops are not fighting milk farmers in the Middle West as they were just before Hoover went out. That fire, instead of spreading, has been quenched, and quenching it was worth the money if we had received none of the public works that have been built.

The man's administration has been alert, honest and amazingly successful. More than that, it has been libertarian. It is ridiculous to describe as a dictator the man under whom we have seen the abolition of prohibition; the abolition of the more idiotic censorship of books, periodicals and plays; the abolition of great, national Red hunts and the elimination of all suggestion of an underground connection between the Government and the Ku Klux Klan.

I am sorry that *The Sun* cannot support him, for I believe that he represents, better than any other statesman of recent years, the great liberal tradition that the paper has supported for years and still believes in with all its heart.

THE VIRGINIA QUARTERLY REVIEW, *Spring 1938*

WHEN TO BUILD A BARRICADE

Time was when the ordinary, middle-class American contemplated no other end than to die quietly in his bed, attended by his physician and, presumably, by his parson or his priest as well.

Today that is no longer true. Not only do all of us now envisage the high possibility, amounting almost to probability, of ending our lives on the highway in an automobile wreck, but great numbers of Americans seem to be cherishing an increasing expectancy of dying on a street barricade, defending, or opposing, some political theory they had never heard of twenty years ago. Fascism is a creation of the last fifteen years; and while Communism is older, the average American who is now fifty-five probably was thirty-five years old before the word meant anything at all to him, for it was only in 1917 that this theory began to count in our national life. Still, an astonishing number of us are convinced that the world is destined to be divided between these two forces and that the time is near when the United States must choose between them. It is assumed, and the logic of events supports the assumption, that the choice will not be peaceful—that it must involve barricades and spectacular death upon them.

True it is that most of the talking seems to be done by men of my generation, now at an age when we are much more concerned with paunches and bald heads than with romance and high adventure. Even if hell should break loose, not many of us would do any dying on barricades, and to a per-haps too-cynical mind it seems that the loudest talkers would probably die under the bed rather than in it. Yet this gabble about barricades may not be altogether as the crackling of thorns under a pot; if it is improbable that the shiny-pated, bay-windowed members of golf clubs will participate in any armed rebellions, it is possible that their talk may accustom the minds of other men to accept easily the idea of revolution and counter-revolution in America. Among these may be a certain number of simple-minded but muscular and courageous youth, such as those who thrust Adolf Hitler and Benito Mussolini into power. These are entirely capable of manning the barri-cades and of dying there, if the opposition shoots straight.

It is for this reason that the current heresy—the theory that the world is being divided between Fascism and Communism—should not be dismissed with a shrug by thoughtful men. The chance of revolution in America may be, and I think, is, barely within the realm of possibility; but the chance of heavy rioting is much nearer. In fact, we have had some rioting, both Fascist and Communist, and it probably would be no difficult feat to instigate more and much more serious riots. This is why the gabble around directors' tables, in faculty clubs, and in the cafés haunted by the "intelligentsia" is more of a nuisance than the numerical strength of the gabblers would indicate. For the normal young man is a bit of a fool. He is also the strength and hope of the nation, to be sure. He is frequently a better man, morally and physically, than an old man; but he has less sense—if he is normal. He is likely to accept the notion that this country is really confronted with a choice between Fascism and Communism and, having made his individual choice, try to put it through in the only way in which either Fascism or Communism can be established—by revolution.

Then, when the barricades are already built and manned, the discovery will come that this country still musters a third party of considerable strength, namely, the democrats. Both Reds and Whites are incessantly bawling about the failure of democracy, and a man must have either experience or a subtlety of mind not characteristic of youth to realize that as long as any man can stand up in this country and shout, with impunity, "Democracy has failed!" democracy hasn't failed. One of the most important functions of democracy is to make it possible, and safe, for men to shout, "Democracy has failed!" While they can do so, the system is still working, and the best proof that our political philosophy retains some validity is the very fact that it is permissible for men to denounce it as a failure.

Democracy, however, is neither capitalism nor socialism, and democrats are neither Fascists nor Communists. (Surely, it is not necessary to point out to the intelligent reader that democracy is spelled with a lower-case "d," and that under this orthography Mr. Alfred M. Landon, Mr. Herbert Hoover, and perhaps even Mr. Alfred E. Smith may be classified as democrats.) It is true that, from the standpoint of a good many of the moderns, especially of the younger generation, the statement that they are neither Fascist nor Communist completely excludes democrats from reality and reduces them to the status of figments of the imagination. The Hitlerites and Leninites are agreed on one fundamental proposition, which is the universal validity of the theory of economic determinism. They are proclaiming with the voice of Stentor not only that politics is based on economics, but that there is no thinking, in philosophy, in the arts, in ethics, or in anything else that is not economic thinking. True, neither puts it in those words; the Russians call it social and the Germans racial, rather than economic, thinking. But these terms, if they have any validity at all, refer to the remote objectives of the existing polity, which is immediately concerned with the national economy, and this concern is all-embracing. In Moscow literature, drama, even music must be "proletarian," and in Berlin they must be "Aryan"; but both these misapplied terms mean that they must tend to serve the economy under which the nation concerned is operating. If all phases of life are absorbed in this service, then obviously anything that is not must be outside human experience, which is to say, non-existent. Hence, under the totalitarian philosophy, it is as imperative to be either Fascist or Communist as it is to be either man or woman.

Democracy, however, serves no particular economy; or rather, it can serve any economy indifferently. If I were as fond of misapplying terms as Moscow and Berlin seem to be, I might allege that democracy cannot be either Fascist or Communist because it is essentially Methodist; but that word has connotations which might perturb Mr. Joseph Patrick Kennedy, ornament of the Democratic party and faithful son of the Roman Church. I will merely say, therefore, that democracy, being a method and not a program, cannot be cabin'd, cribb'd, confined by any program. Nor can a thoroughgoing, consistent democrat ever be committed irrevocably to any program, not even that of the Democratic party. Only if, and only as long as, the program is consistent with the method can it be accepted by democrats.

At the same time, there is no earthly reason why a democrat should be compelled to choose between Fascism and Communism. There is nothing in the world to prevent him from choosing both, or at least choosing those elements in each which are consonant with the democratic method. I am a non-admirer of both Fascism and Communism. It seems to me that life would be almost intolerable for an intelligent man under either. Yet at the same time I can perceive in both merits that, applied by the democratic method, might ameliorate the condition of mankind appreciably; and I can perceive no reason why democrats should not cull them and apply them.

II

Of all the dictators now flourishing on earth the one that I find least to my own taste is Hitler. His rule is probably no more tyrannous than Mussolini's and is palpably less murderous than Stalin's; but he is more ridiculous than either, and, immoral though it may be, absurdity in a ruler alienates more people than blood-thirst. Burning books, cutting off women's heads, casting Mendelssohn's statue into the melting-furnace because he was a Jew, and rewriting "Stille Nacht" to eliminate all references to mildness and peace —such acts are downright silly, and a tyranny that is both ruthless and silly is twice as bad as one that is ruthless only.

Yet even in the Nazi régime there is at least one element that unquestionably would improve the social polity of the American people if it could be introduced here by a democratic method. This is the social discipline that the Germans are exhibiting.

There has been endless talk in the United States in recent years about the need of a more sensitive social conscience in this country. The need is great enough, heaven knows; but it is about time to do a little talking about another aspect of the same thing, to wit, the need of social discipline. Hitler has carried it to the length of erecting the state into a mythological monster, proprietor of the lives and fortunes of citizens, rather than their servant; but that is another exhibition of his talent for being absurd. Held within the bounds of reason the idea is admirable; and it is one with which Americans are not as familiar as they ought to be.

Consider, for example, the way in which we have had to back into any sort of control of a wild and ruinous agricultural overproduction in certain crops. When it became apparent that cotton, wheat, and corn were being produced in quantities far beyond the maximum that the market could absorb, the only way in which we could approach any sort of control was by paying the farmer either to let his land lie idle, or to plant it to another crop. There was in existence neither the legal mechanism nor, what is more important, the habit of mind that would have made it possible for organized society to say to the wheat, the cotton, or the corn grower, "This year you will grow a different crop, or else——." Instead, we had to disburse sums that threw the budget hopelessly out of balance, swelled still more the already bloated national debt, gave the opponents of Mr. James A. Farley an excuse to wound his sensibilities by accusing him of buying the farmer vote, and filled all the Economic Royalists with an immovable conviction that Doomsday is just around the corner.

Consider, again, the terrific battle for power that has been going on in the ranks of organized labor. The social costs of this civil war are by no means all borne by labor. There is no reasonable doubt that the disturbances attending it contributed materially to the general slackening of business in the latter half of 1937. More than that, the revelation of labor's lack of competence to assume responsibility as one party to a contract hardened the opposition of employers who never liked labor unions anyhow, and thereby made the future development of labor organization slower and more difficult. Labor racketeering and strikes arising from jurisdictional disputes are further examples of a lack of social discipline that threatens the well-being, not of labor only, but of every man who works for money, from Henry Ford to the lowest-paid W. P. A. pick-and-shovel gang.

I have deliberately and carefully confined this discussion to the need of social discipline among workers, because I cannot believe that any rational man needs to have pointed out the glaring need of social discipline among employers, who now hire private armies to bring their workers under subjection.

But if I am convinced that Hitler is the dictator under whom I, as an individual, should live most miserably, I am equally certain that Stalin is the dictator under whom I should die soonest. If the Nazi régime seems to make life worthless, the Soviet régime tends to make it quite impossible.

Yet there is merit in Communism. Russia, apparently, is at this moment rather less Communistic than New Jersey, just as Franklin D. Roosevelt, in his economic policy—but not in his social policy—is distinctly less Jeffersonian than Alfred M. Landon. At the same time, Russia, like Mr. Roosevelt, pays lip-service to a doctrine that circumstances have made it impossible to apply in practice, and in this doctrine there is merit.

This merit is the Communist theory that the state is the servant of the citizen, the term citizen, in this connection, meaning every adult inhabitant of the country. For emphasis I repeat the assertion that Russia, in this respect, is not at this time Communist; perhaps eventually she will become so, although her present trend seems to be all in the opposite direction. But this doesn't affect the theory, and the theory is that the state has no excuse for existence save as it serves the people—not Alexander Hamilton's "rich and well-born," but all the people.

To judge by the language of the preamble of the Constitution of the United States, the founders of the American republic seem to have adhered to the same theory: "We, the people . . . in order to . . . establish justice . . . promote the general welfare and secure the blessings of liberty to ourselves and our posterity, do ordain and establish this Constitution." Plain enough; the government was created by the Constitution, and the Constitution was created, ordained, and established by the people to serve certain purposes that they chose to have served. The Constitution had no other function than to serve the people; therefore the government established under it could have no other purpose.

But language is tricky. The word "people" has borne many different connotations at different times and to different men. There is plenty of evidence to show that "We, the people" meant to the group of country gentlemen who framed the Constitution something very different from what it meant to Vladimir Lenin. For one thing, to the Founding Fathers it obviously did not include negroes, nor did it include women, idiots, and imbeciles; in Maryland it included neither Catholics nor Jews; only recently had it begun to include non-church-members in Massachusetts; in most of the States it included nobody who was unable to give evidence of possessing property to a certain value; for all these classes were excluded from participation in government and therefore had no part in ordaining and establishing the Constitution. In the minds of the framers of the Constitution, the people of the United States included few persons except the landowners of the United States; and it would be no gross misinterpretation of their idea to make that opening phrase read, "We, the gentlemen . . . do ordain."

To this day the idea of a selective definition of the word "people" has not been entirely eradicated from this country. If they had the power, the

Ku Klux would certainly exclude Catholics, Jews, and negroes from consideration as part of the people. Half the Chambers of Commerce in the country, if they had the power, would exclude Communists, and a great many would exclude trade-union organizers, or, as they are usually termed, "agitators." There are those who would deny the right of suffrage to persons on relief and to all officeholders who live upon salaries paid by the government. I am myself opposed to extending that right to any more idiots and imbeciles than now exercise it. On the other hand, the Communists themselves deny that "the people" ought to mean any element of the population other than the proletariat.

But one need not accept the Communist restriction of the definition of the word "people" in order to accept the Communist idea that the government is, or ought to be, the servant of every inhabitant of the country, regardless of his social, economic, or racial status, and that it has no other excuse for being than to promote the general welfare. Most Americans, indeed, do accept this in theory; but many of them are very violently opposed to putting it into practice. Among the most violent, strange to say, are some who deem themselves radical. These are they who have been so enchanted by Communist practice that they are unable to observe how widely it has departed from Communist theory. They cannot see that in making the citizen the servant of the state, Communism is repudiating its own birthright.

But there is no apparent reason why a democrat should not cherish both the Fascist ideal of social discipline and the Communist ideal of the servant state. They are not in the least incompatible. Indeed, the Communists themselves have imposed an exceedingly severe social discipline for the ostensible purpose of assuring a state that will serve the citizen. One may cherish a certain skepticism as to whether or not that is the real objective; but it might be.

As for their compatibility with democracy, that is self-evident, since democracy is not in itself a program, but merely a method that may be applied to the furtherance of any program. It might be used indifferently to establish either Fascism or Communism. It is habitually used by the American people to establish autocracy at every great crisis in the affairs of the republic. Stalin himself possesses no more effective authority in Russia than was readily granted to—nay, thrust upon—Jackson in 1833, Lincoln in 1861, Wilson in 1917, and Roosevelt in 1933.

Democracy is the method of governing by the consent of the governed— their consent, not a reluctant acquiescence wrung from them by force. It is, obviously, not a method universally applicable. If a population will not consent to good government, then democracy necessarily must produce bad government. If a population will not consent even to tolerable government, then democracy must result in a régime that is ruinous. History affords little evidence to support the belief—ostensibly accepted in the early days of the republic, though not by its wisest men—that political competence is innate. It seems, rather, to be a national acquisition, usually attained only after long experimentation by the method of trial and error, involving incalculable loss and suffering.

But once a nation has attained a measurable degree of political competence, that is to say, once it has learned to consent freely to government which, while far from ideal is yet within the boundaries of sanity, then the democratic method is plainly the one best designed to further the permanent maintenance of order. Its first tenet, accepted by all, is that whatever happens nobody is going to shoot. The proximate cause of all revolutions, including the bloodiest, is never a mass mania for slaying, which is incomprehensible, but a simple and easily understood desire to shoot first. The revolutionists cherish a firm belief, usually, but not necessarily, justified by experience, that the party in power will shoot rather than surrender its power; so the revolutionists, if they can, shoot first.

Democrats, to the extent that they are firmly established, have conventionalized the business of revolution and reduced its bloodier and more distasteful features to symbolism. Through the waste of innumerable wars, we have come to realize at last that the only good Indian is *not* a dead Indian; that a dead Indian, on the contrary, is the only one who can never be any good to anybody. So if you have the drop on him, and can easily keep him covered, why drill him? If you do so, you simply lose a cartridge and gain the necessity of burying a corpse, neither of which improves the situation. In 1932 the country, being displeased by the Administration in power, might have effected its purpose by Franco's method in Spain, to wit, butchering the Republicans. But it would have been slow, extremely expensive, and highly dangerous, as Franco discovered. Our democratic method was neater, cheaper, and quicker. We symbolized bullets with ballots; and after the election the Republicans, scrupulously abiding by the rules, considered themselves dead, and that was that.

It has been pointed out repeatedly that the whole thing hinges on everyone's abiding by the rules, and that people will not abide by the rules except in matters of relatively small importance, things that can be reduced to the triviality of a game. The success of our democratic experiment in the United States has been explained on the theory that we are not really at odds on anything of importance; and as proof the explainers frequently cite the difficulty of demonstrating to a foreigner the essential differences of the Democratic and Republican parties. This explanation is profoundly true, but not in the way that many people understand it to be true. There is one fundamental on which we are all agreed. It is the principle that governments derive their just powers from the consent of the governed. Beyond that, though, the assertion of basic agreement among all Americans has little to support it. If Mr. Franklin D. Roosevelt and Mr. Carter Glass are agreed on all matters of importance, then Kelly is a Chinaman; yet they are both members of the same party. They are, however, in agreement on the doctrine that Americans can be governed justly only by their own consent; and they are doubtless in agreement that, this being granted, nothing is left for which it is worthwhile to draw a gun.

Moreover, the argument that if people are agreed on fundamentals, they can then get along together, is an argument that ignores one of the most embarrassing facts in human history—that fact that the greatest and fiercest wars that have ravaged mankind have been fought between people who were agreed on fundamentals. It is unnecessary to point out that Crusader and

Saracen both believed in God; consider only the wars that have arrayed Christian against Christian, Moslem against Moslem, and in 1861 American against American. Consider that one of the innumerable revolutions in Mexico was a fight of the York Rite Masons against the Scottish Rite Masons. Consider the War of Jenkins' Ear.

In spite of such agreement on fundamentals as exists among Americans, they could have found a multitude of excuses for a multitude of civil wars had it not been for the general belief that whatever happens, nobody will shoot.

This is a highly civilized attitude. I know that to speak of Americans in the mass as highly civilized will shock many people, including not merely the intelligentsia, but also the intelligent. Our crudity, our bumptiousness, our arrogance, and our ignorance are all too evident. We have produced no great art and but little gracious living. We have carried the methods of mass production not only into the making of automobiles, but also into the making of citizens, turning out millions of dreary Babbitts with interchangeable mentalities. I know there are areas of the country in which even religion is brought down to the level of voodooism and other areas where it is brought to the level of vaudeville. I know that pretty far up the American social scale Edison is regarded as the prince of scientists and Eddie Guest as the prince of poets. All this is indubitable, and it is all evidence of a pretty shoddy civilization.

Nevertheless, the fact remains that in our political development we have run far ahead of our artistic, social, ethical, and general intellectual development. One of the most highly civilized men on earth today is the American defeated candidate; for he has grasped one of the most difficult of all concepts, the truth that ideas are not successfully propagated by force. It does not necessarily follow that he has the rare intelligence to realize that it is possible for him to be wrong; but he does realize that it is possible for him to be out-numbered. When he is out-numbered, his proposals for government have not the consent of the governed and in that sense are wrong; for in a democracy any government lacking that consent is wrong by definition.

As long as this condition obtains, justifiable revolution in this country is a logical impossibility. The people cannot rise against their oppressors when they are their own oppressors. There might conceivably be a *coup d'état* in which a well-organized minority group would seize the government and bring the rest of us under subjection. But that is not revolution; it is counter-revolution. It is, furthermore, a retrogression in political development, a return to an earlier and a less highly civilized form of political organization. The German "principle of leadership," the Italian "corporative state," the Russian "dictatorship of the proletariat," whatever they may be—if, indeed, they are anything but the rodomontade of politicians—certainly are not new principles of government. One and all, they are based on the oldest of all governmental principles, the principle of tyranny.

It does not necessarily follow, however, that they are completely nonsensical as, and where, they are applied. Belief in panaceas is a characteristically American heresy. We cannot rid ourselves of the notion that the democracy which experience has shown to be excellent for us would necessarily be good for Cubans and Filipinos and Russians and Germans. But there is no proof of this and a good deal of evidence against it. Democracy is possible only in the presence of a strong and almost universally held belief in the consent of the governed as an indispensable condition of just government; and it is useless to expect it to work even tolerably except in the presence of an informed public opinion. In most of the world these conditions are not present. Tyranny in some form may be the only possible government for Germans and Russians because, although both nations may be further advanced than we are in many of the phases of civilization, in the one matter of political method we are far more highly developed than they are.

Does the United States, then, enjoy good government? Oh, no. We have very bad government, but at that it is the best in the world. The proof is obvious. That government is best which kills fewest of the governed. What with Chicago police, fast-shooting G-men, and prosecuting attorneys who want to be Governor, our democratic government slaughters an appalling number of its taxpayers every year; but even so, our annual governmental production of corpses is trifling compared with what the government I believe to be the next best, the British, produced last year on the northwest frontier of India, where it has 35,000 troops engaged in an unadvertised war, not to mention its activities in the rest of the globe. Even our starvation rate compares favorably with that of the Welsh coal districts and the slums of Glasgow.

Yet this same democratic method, when it was tried briefly in Italy, culminated in Fascism, and when it was tried a little longer in Germany, it ended in Nazism. The answer is that in neither country were the necessary conditions present. Neither the Germans nor the Italians had any deep-rooted belief in the consent of the governed as a requisite of just government, nor any long experience of uncensored information in the development of public opinion. To adopt the language of an earlier day, they were little acquainted with either political liberty or free speech. They were not prepared for the democratic method and it did not work.

But there are all too many Americans who are not prepared for it, either. In the highest civilization, there is always a proportion of relatively uncivilized people. There were tone-deaf Germans when Beethoven lived, and color-blind Italians in the days of Raphael. Athens ostracized Aristides, and this country is full of apoplectic clubmen who regard the undistributed surplus tax as the damnation of democracy, and reformers in a hurry who regard the rejection of the Child Labor Amendment in the same light. These are they who talk of barricades and irrepressible conflict.

The time to erect a barricade, though, is the time when someone, conservative or liberal, Tory or Red, comes along with a proposal that the consent of the governed is no longer the essential basis of just government. Of course, no one is going to make the proposal in those words. That would be too crude, too blatant. It is advanced, rather, by indirection, usually not shrewd at all, but curiously ingenuous. The most popular gambit, at the moment, is the perfectly sound assertion that the people cannot be expected to make intelligent decisions if they act on false information; after that comes the poisonous part—the suggestion that something ought to be done to stamp out inflammatory propaganda.

What this really means is the suppression of free speech. It is probably true that most of the people who propose it do not know that. They quite honestly regard it as the suppression of free lying, which, of course, it may be; but lying is a form of speech, and it is impossible to suppress one form alone. The people, indeed, gain their information about all governmental matters very largely by the process that Wilson said he used to get at the truth about Mexico—by balancing lies.

There is no principle of law better established than that a consent obtained by fraud is no consent; and the supplying of false, or the withholding of true, information material to the case constitutes fraud. The consent of the people, obtained by such fraud, is a negation of the entire democratic method; which is to say, it renders void and of no effect the highest development of American civilization, its political organization. Human ingenuity has never yet devised an effective process to prevent lying. Sunrise is no more certain than that the American people—and any other people, for that matter —are going to have lies told them whenever politics is discussed. Hence the only possible guard against the granting of a fraudulent consent is to make certain that they are also told the truth; for the experience of a century and a half demonstrates that, while they cannot always tell which is truth and which lies, they do so sufficiently frequently to keep the government going— wabbling, to be sure, but never quite crashing into complete ruin.

When it is proposed to suppress propaganda—that is the moment to erect a barricade. Propaganda is a word of evil repute. It is a word that is bitter on the tongues of many honest men. Nevertheless, the right to spread propaganda must be defended to the death by all men who love liberty, for it is a two-sided word, and what is your propaganda is my free speech. It may be a sad fact, to many it seems to be an almost intolerable fact, but it is fact that we cannot guarantee the freedom of Alfred M. Landon without guaranteeing that of Earl Browder, too; and in a country which puts the Communist candidate in jail for trying to make a political speech, it is always possible that the Republican, or any other candidate, might some day be jailed for the same offense. The moment any candidate, however idiotic, is suppressed, that moment we make it theoretically possible to gain an apparent consent of the governed by fraud, and the foundation of our system is no longer safe; but as long as we defend resolutely the right of every silly ass to spread nonsense, we make doubly secure our own right to speak words of wisdom, beauty, and truth.

HARPER'S MAGAZINE, *November 1940*

TO OUR THIRTY-YEAR-OLDS

Homespun philosophers have had much to say of the difficulties confronting Commencement speakers in the spring of 1940. It was, indeed, difficult to think of anything cheerful and reassuring to say to this year's graduates; but there was always the negative consolation open to them that most of them, being now around twenty, are not likely to be charged with any great measure of responsibility within the next ten years. Their lives, it is true, may be extinguished on the battlefield; but their minds and consciences are less likely to suffer a blackout than those of older men, who must make the decisions involving not peace and war only, but the reconstruction that is plainly inevitable of the economic and political systems.

Worse than addressing the class of 1940 would be the task of speaking consolatory words to the survivors of the class of 1930. These are the gentry who are on an excessively hot spot. If they graduated at twenty they are now about thirty, well within the age of active military service, yet old enough to be assuming heavy responsibilities. Members of the class of 1920 share the responsibilities, but they are now approaching the upper limit of military age; and earlier classes are beyond it. The Army knows that men of forty do not make troops that are absolutely first-class, so as long as possible it will avoid filling the ranks with men of that age; but the soldier of thirty may be a fine man-at-arms, and he is of the ideal age for command in any rank from major down—that is to say, he is excellent for the ranks of commissioned officers that run the greatest risk of getting killed.

It is obviously advantageous for a male American to be ten years old in 1940, for that means that it will be several years yet before he has to face the realities of the national situation. It is equally obvious that there is an advantage in being ninety, for in the ordinary course of nature the nonagenarian will not have to wade through much of what lies ahead. But is there anything in the world to be said in favor of being thirty to-day? In particular, is there any advantage that a man of thirty holds over his fellows of forty, fifty, and sixty?

Well, there is this much—he stands a better chance of seeing how it all comes out. His life expectancy is thirty-seven years, and it will take a full generation in all probability to obtain anything like an adequate idea of the answers that will be made to the questions confronting us now. There are those, of course, who see this in reverse, not as an advantage, but as an additional handicap laid upon the man of thirty; for they are certain that the answers will be intolerable. These are the truly old, whatever the number of years they may have lived; for when a man is so wedded to the past that he cannot see it disintegrating without the certainty that irretrievable disaster is ahead he is already an old man although he may hardly have begun to shave.

Of course any man, young or old, who cannot perceive that there is trouble ahead ought to be in an institution for the mentally disabled. The difference between the young and old is not a matter of years but the fact that the young can imagine that, even if the inevitable trouble amounts to disaster, it will not necessarily be irretrievable, and are therefore more interested in methods of cushioning the inevitable shock than in either lamenting it or in making futile efforts to dodge it. For a young man of thirty there is a personal stake in it, since he has an excellent chance of observing how his methods will work out; but for a young man of sixty it is rather academic. He *might* live to be ninety-five of course. John D. Rockefeller did. But it is not wise to count on it.

The man of thirty has a double advantage—over the old, because he has a chance to see what really is ahead; and over children, because he passed through childhood and adolescence before the end of the picnic that lasted a hundred and fifty years. There is now hardly an American of voting age who doesn't realize that the picnic really is over—that it ended definitely, as a matter of fact, in October, 1929. We are getting our American history retaught, and after eleven years of constant hammering the idea begins to percolate through our heads that the first century and a half of the republic was not all glorious, and not even altogether sane. It is apparent, now, that what we were taught in school was the conquest of a continent was, in fact, altogether too much like the looting of a continent. No doubt some of the pioneers were impelled by high and heroic motives; but vast numbers of them were merely running away from the results of their own incompetence. They moved simply because within a few years their agricultural methods had worn out the land, some of it to be classed with the finest land in the world until the blight of American stupidity fell upon it. But the pioneers now have skinned the whole continent, and we, their successors, must contrive to live on what they have left.

No, the record lacks much of being as great as the schoolbooks have taught us. In 1776—or, if you choose to exclude the war years, in 1783—we started with two supreme advantages: first, a political and economic system not imposed upon us by superior force, but devised by ourselves to suit our own fancy, and, second, with a continental domain so inconceivably rich in natural resources that no nation of Europe held anything remotely comparable to it. Within a hundred and fifty years we had wasted and destroyed an appallingly large proportion of those national resources, yet our economic system was working so badly that a third of our people were "ill clothed, ill fed, and ill housed," and our political system was working so badly that troops were fighting milk farmers in the Middle West and the regular Army was driving out of the national capital an irregular army of discontented war veterans. The American achievement was wonderful indeed; but a cynic might say that the wonder of it is how a people so richly endowed to begin with could have made such a mess of things in so short a period.

True, when we were slapped in the face we managed to take the hint. When mobs began to drag judges off the bench, when the entire banking system went down in one terrific crash, and when the people facing actual starvation numbered millions, we began to perceive that something was wrong, and for the past eight years we have been trying frantically to patch things up. To a certain extent we have succeeded. Troops no longer are fighting either farmers or veterans; famine has been averted; the banks are open, and industrial production is running higher than ever. But Mr. Roosevelt himself doesn't claim that our patching has been altogether successful. For one thing, it has involved subjecting the fiscal system to an appalling strain. The national debt may be, in a sense, a mere bookkeeping operation, but bad bookkeeping operations can give rise to plenty of trouble. More than that, and worse than that, far too many people are living on what they themselves regard as public charity—and that isn't any bookkeeping operation.

Finally, events in the rest of the world have demonstrated pretty conclusively that even if we had the wit to patch up the old system to the point where it might be made to work again as far as this country is concerned, we should not be permitted to continue in the old, happy-go-lucky style. "You never miss the water till the well goes dry" runs the old song. Vast numbers of us never missed the protection of the British fleet until its power was sternly challenged; but how we began to miss it then! Skyrocketing Federal taxes are reminding us every day that for ninety years we had no occasion to spend our money and energy guarding the Atlantic highway to our shores because that highway was already competently guarded. Roughly half our defense problem was solved for us, and millions of us never knew it; but now that the solution has been largely canceled we know it.

But another of our walls of defense has crashed, and it may prove to be more important than the fighting power of the British fleet. Psychologically, as well as racially, we are of European origin, and our confidence in our own institutions has been buttressed more strongly than many of us suppose by the fact that roughly similar institutions seemed to be working well in Europe. The great democracies of France and England bestrode that continent; and that fact powerfully reinforced American confidence in American democracy. The collapse of the French army was the first great blow to that confidence; yet, if we are doomed to stand as the last defender of democracy among the great powers we shall need all the confidence in ourselves that we can muster.

As the war proceeds there is an accumulation of evidence that it has taken its present course not on account of the strength of the totalitarian powers, but on account of the weakness of the democracies. Regarding France, in particular, the world is full of foul rumors. France was cursed with wooden-headed generals. Beyond a doubt she was cursed with shifty politicians too. But there is more and more reason to believe that part of the secret of the French defeat was, if not active treason, at least a fatal apathy. More and more Americans are coming to suspect that the ultimate reason for that defeat was a conviction on the part of too many Frenchmen that modern France wasn't worth defending. In England that spirit apparently had not spread so far; but England has its Oswald Mosleys. At this moment we have no precise information on how many Englishmen of more or less prominence have gone to the Tower; but we know that some have gone.

In short, we are faced with the fact that a modern population simply will not fight effectively for a government that has not solved its own problems. You may call it what you please, democracy or anything else; but if it has not contrived a politico-economic system that affords content to the great majority of its people, those people will flatly refuse to support it in a crisis. We are at the same time faced with the fact that we have not solved our own problems, especially with regard to the ten millions who are still unemployed. The conjunction is enough to give us a first class case of the jitters.

One of the stock phrases of every American campaign orator is, "We have achieved the highest standard of living ever attained in human history." It sounds well but it is open to at least one question. That question is, Who are "we"? If the orator refers to the luckier two-thirds of the American population he is right. But are two-thirds enough? Imperial Germany under the Kaiser did better than that. The Joads and the Jeeter Lesters in Imperial Germany constituted far less than one-third of the population; and the Germans fought magnificently for four years in defense of the Kaiser. Will an America, of which one-third is "ill clothed, ill fed, and ill housed" fight equally well in defense of the republic? The question is all too likely to become something more than academic within the near future—how near that future may be, one shudders to think.

We are then confronted, as Grover Cleveland remarked, with a condition and not a theory—two conditions, in fact, each disturbing in its kind. In the first place, the seventy-five steel tubes on which we had, consciously or unconsciously, counted—the heavy guns of the British fleet—are obviously no longer to be relied on for our defense on the Eastern side; in the second place, the ancient shibboleth of "democracy" obviously can no longer be relied on to make European peoples fight, and therefore may not be a sure reliance to make Americans fight. Taken together, these are a pretty solid guarantee of trouble ahead.

There is, however, a third guarantee that to many people is more disturbing than both the others. It is the fact that free enterprise, under capitalism, is definitely sunk. It no longer exists in any other great nation than the United States, and even here it exists only fragmentarily. You can no longer build a railroad, set up a bank, or plant cotton in this country without official permission; and in no other world power can you conduct any sort of enterprise without official permission. Nor is there more than a remote chance that free capitalistic enterprise will be reëstablished at any time soon. Even if England wins her war against a totalitarian Europe, it is beyond belief that she will soon restore the conduct of foreign trade to private hands. Therefore American exporters will be competing, not with foreign exporters, but with foreign governments. Obviously that can't be done. The American government will have to back the American exporter if he is to have a chance. But the moment the government backs the exporter, free, capitalistic enterprise is done for in that field. Moreover, if the American government is to back the export trade effectively, it must exercise a considerable degree of control over domestic production; which means that free, capitalistic enterprise must be subjected to even more complete regulation within the country.

This is a condition with which we had nothing whatever to do. As far as foreign trade is concerned, the choice does not lie, and never lay, with us. Governmentally regulated trade is state socialism—or, if you prefer, state capitalism. But we have not been asked whether or not we choose to adopt it. The condition has been created without our advice or consent; we have to accept it or get out of the field.

It is as plain as a pikestaff, therefore, that we must alter our ideas of physical defense, that we must alter our ideas of psychological defense, and that we must modify our economic system if we are to survive as an independent power. This means trouble. It means big trouble. There is no getting away from that ugly fact. But does it mean disaster? I venture to doubt it, and that is why I believe there are advantages in being thirty years old.

The encouraging fact is this—our present troubles are not due to the fact that the government devised in 1787 failed to solve reasonably well the problems it was intended to solve. The political troubles, including the revolt of the milk farmers, the revolt of the mortgagors, the marches of the bonus army and the army of the unemployed, are all directly traceable to economic pressure; and that pressure is being applied by a national economy that did not exist at the time of the Constitutional Convention. The Founding Fathers did not take into account the Industrial Revolution for the sufficient reason that the Industrial Revolution did not begin in Europe until about 1750, hardly touched this country at all until it was forced by the Embargo Act in 1808, and did not attain its full stature in America until about the time of the Civil War.

Hence the fact that our organic law is plainly failing to meet our needs means only that we have developed new and quite unpredictable needs, not that the political genius of the men who framed the Constitution was feeble. The early Americans solved the problems that they faced. New problems have arisen, not even touched by the Constitution. What of it? It means only that new Americans must arise to solve them. It is a nuisance to be thrown out of our old, comfortable complacency. It is a nuisance to discover that our governmental arrangements are no longer adequate. But such nuisances are no proof whatever that the men of 1787 were wholly wrong; it is proof only that they were not prophets.

After all, when you come right down to brass tacks, is it certain that we have lost anything that wasn't phony to begin with? Take the military situation—no doubt it was comfortable and thrifty to rest secure behind the British fleet, but was it quite decent, or was it quite sane? For ninety years it has suited British policy to have the United States free of any threat of European domination; therefore the British fleet has seen to it that no threat came toward us from that side. This saved us a lot of money, but it is doubtful, to say the least, that it was good for us morally. Then, again, it stood to reason that the British Empire couldn't last forever; and the moment it should collapse it was evident that we should be thrown upon our own resources. Would it not have been the part of sanity to develop those resources well in advance of any possible collapse?

The existing generation of Americans accepted a political and economic system devised for it long ago. We have had no occasion, until quite recently, to do any sharp and difficult thinking about fundamentals. Not for a long time, certainly not since 1863, have Americans been compelled to face even the possibility that American institutions may have only a matter of months to survive. We do face that possibility now. The problems facing us are not susceptible of solution by appeals to precedent, for the precedents have created the domestic problems, and there is no precedent for the international problems. We can't think our way through with the thoughts of George Washington and Thomas Jefferson; we must think for ourselves or collapse. The spirit of Washington and Jefferson is, indeed, still valuable; but that is another thing.

This is certainly not an inviting prospect, but does it hold nothing except the menace of disaster? After all, isn't it a pretty cynical view to hold that if America is at last compelled to stand on her own feet she must face inevitable ruin?

Our ingrained respect for the Founding Fathers, a valuable trait in most circumstances, is something of a handicap now. To suggest to Americans that the only hope of the nation's survival is for it to produce new statesmen as great as the fifty-five who met in Philadelphia in 1787 is rather a paralyzing suggestion. Washington presided over that convention, and its members included Franklin, Hamilton, Madison, John Adams, Edmund Randolph, Roger Sherman and Rufus King, among others whose names are still potent. Jefferson, George Mason and Patrick Henry were anxiously looking on and advising. To produce a group of men comparable to that group in ability, originality, and daring is indubitably a large order.

Nevertheless, something of that sort we must achieve, for we are facing a situation that is, in certain important respects, similar to the one they faced. Circumstances, to be sure, are entirely different, but our dilemma is like theirs at least in that there are no more precedents to guide us than there were to guide them. The widespread belief today that our economic choice is capitalism or communism was matched in 1787 by an even more widespread belief that the political choice was monarchy or anarchy. The triumph of American genius then was its success in rejecting both alternatives. That triumph must be repeated; for as monarchy and anarchy alike were impossible to that generation, so are the alternatives now presented impossible. A return to the capitalism of Coolidge and Hoover, when all the rest of the world has forsaken it, is flatly out of the question; and even if it could be restored, the pass to which it brought us in 1929 ought to be a sufficiently persuasive argument against trying to restore it. A turn toward the sort of régime that prevails in the totalitarian states would be an abandonment not only of American institutions but of the faith in the essential reasonableness of mankind on which those institutions are based. The institutions, after all, we might replace, perhaps with better ones; but it is the faith that makes us American, and if we lose that, although we may continue to inhabit the North American continent, we shall no longer be Americans—not if Washington, Franklin, and Jefferson were Americans. Yes, the alternatives—old-style capitalism and

European-style collectivism, whether you call it Communism, Nazism, or Fascism—are both as impossible of adoption by Americans in 1940 as both monarchy and anarchy were in 1787.

But what of it? Is it a lamentable thing for the sons to be called on to repeat the achievement of their sires? It is harsh, it is hard, but is it really injurious to be commanded to be great? The world has not so regarded it in the past. The rule of *noblesse oblige* has always been recognized as a stern one, but dubious, indeed, is the quality of the man who objects to it on that account. To be American and to remain American during the next quarter of a century will be no job for weak men and a weak nation; but what is there about that to appall the heirs of the Convention of 1787?

At this moment, to be sure, it seems all too probable that the task of statesmanship may have to be postponed until the task of the man-at-arms is finished; and if the man-at-arms should fail there would be no point in discussing statecraft. It is possible too that this task may last a long time. It is fairly plain now that we are enduring not the second but the twenty-seventh year of the war. The fighting that began in 1914 was only partially suspended in 1918; there has hardly been a day in twenty-six years on which some part of the world has not seen a continuance of the struggle against the intolerable strains of modern civilization. Surely, no literate American believes any longer that the war was actually caused by the assassination of a forgotten prince in an obscure Balkan town. It was caused by the same thing that set the milk farmers to fighting troops, and the mobs to dragging judges off the bench in this country eight years ago—the failure of statecraft, economic as well as political, to operate the machinery of the new industrial civilization in such a way as to make the lives of the masses of the people at least endurable.

Nevertheless, the fighting continues, and when war is abroad the physical safety of the country takes precedence over every other consideration. Not much enduring statecraft is to be expected from an armed camp; yet wise men, even in the midst of war's alarms, will not forget that peace is inevitable —it may be the peace of a cemetery, but peace of some sort cannot be prevented. The lamentable part of it is that we may come at last to grapple with the formidable problems of peace exhausted and exacerbated by a long war; but so, as far as that is concerned, did George Washington.

Today's man of thirty may, therefore, be a man of forty before he gets a chance to erect new institutions for a prosperous and peaceful nation. Unfortunately he may arrive at the conference minus an arm or a leg left on the field of some new Château Thierry—God forbid that it should be a new Antietam, fought on American soil. But, soon or late, to the conference he will inevitably come, there to face problems as difficult as any presented to military men.

But why concentrate exclusively on the problems? It is equally true that he will face opportunities as great as those men faced who came to the conference of 1787. Whatever else the blasting of the past ten years has done, it has at least shaken Americans out of their long lethargy. Nobody whose opinion commands respect dreams any longer of a return to Coolidge. Coolidge's own political party has this year nominated a man whose chief claim to consideration is his alert awareness that the old shibboleths are completely outworn. Our share of the other qualities of the men of 1787 may be scant, but we have at least something of their realization that all the old paths are blocked and that if America is to continue to exist at all she must hew out a new path toward the old goal.

Since the future is impenetrable, it seems to me as reasonable to assume the best as to assume the worst; or, perhaps I should say, no more unreasonable. The best assumption is that the Americans of the next twenty-five years will come through as handsomely as their ancestors did a hundred and fifty years ago. I cannot prove that they will do so, but neither can you prove that they will not. Yet if they do, how pointless are our current visits to the Wailing Wall, how badly misplaced our sympathy!

"History," observed Kitty Foyle, "always was temperamental when it was happening." Without doubt it was an extremely trying experience to be George Washington. I can conceive the possibility that George hardly thought it was worthwhile; but the rest of us don't see it that way. What really humane man would condemn another to a great career if he had the power to do so? Yet we certainly do not mourn when we suspect that a young man is destined to be great. It is plain to the dullest that the world at present is passing through a period sure to occupy a great deal of space in the history books of the future. Whatever else it may be, it is not a period of trifling events and small men; to look upon the dark side only, when have such crimes been committed, when have such titanic mistakes been made, when have such catastrophes occurred, when have such gigantic villains towered over the world? But there is a law of compensation in history: when the evil is immense, so is the good that rises to challenge it. This age has already produced a numbing array of monstrous men; it will not pass without producing some great ones.

Therefore, the man who lives through it, as the man of thirty has an excellent chance to do, and who has been a part of it, will come to the evening of life with giant memories. Among them, if he is an American, I believe will be the memory of having taken part in the working out of a better order, in the devising of a social and political system that, casting aside the wreckage of old, false ideas, and hewing out new ones, will have carried the republic farther toward the objective chosen long ago: "equal rights for all, special privileges for none."

Those of us who are beyond thirty may not live to see it; but there are probably among us today many who, a generation hence, may look back upon these troubled times and justly paraphrase the words of the ancient Washington: "We have erected a standard to which the wise and honest may repair: the event is in the hand of God."

THE ATLANTIC MONTHLY, *October 1941*

ROOSEVELT AGAINST HITLER

There was a period of approximately twenty-four hours in the year 1933 more fateful for the destiny of mankind than any other one day in the century.

A little after noon on March 4, 1933, Franklin D. Roosevelt was inaugurated as President of the United States. Before midnight on March 5, 1933, the German Reichstag had passed the Enabling Act, putting absolute power into the hands of Chancellor Adolf Hitler.

Eight years later these two men faced each other as the champions of two ways of life so antagonistic that the world is not wide enough for them to exist together in peace. In 1933 not many people were able to perceive any relation whatever between them; but in 1941 not many doubt that one of these men is destined to destroy the other, and it is not beyond the bounds of credibility that they may destroy each other. Hitler has said that the outcome of the duel between the systems they represent will fix the destiny of mankind for a thousand years, and it is by no means certain that his assertion is extravagant.

If Mr. Roosevelt is described as the chief protagonist of the way of life preferred by the democracies it is not by his own choice, nor by reason of his personal superiority to other democratic leaders. The man who saved Britain in her desperate hour, for example, has attributes of mind and character that make it preposterous to rate him as inferior to any man alive; Mr. Roosevelt's resources, not Mr. Roosevelt himself, give him the central position in the present situation. Mr. Churchill does not have available 25 million men of military age, nor a national income of 70 billion dollars, nor the incomparable industrial plant of the United States, nor 359 million acres under the plough. The last reserves of the free peoples are the forces commanded by the President of the United States.

But there is another reason why the President, rather than the Prime Minister, is the central figure on his side. The President shares the quality that has made Hitler strong; he is associated in the minds of the masses with the dynamic, rather than with the static, theory of government. Churchill is a conservative. That doesn't mean that he is a less ardent believer in human freedom than Roosevelt; but it does mean that his first care has always been to preserve what is best out of the past. But it was revolt against the abuses of the past that heaved both Roosevelt and Hitler into power—and has demolished a dozen other governments. The people who revolted do not associate a victory of Roosevelt with a return to the old conditions. As a matter of fact, neither would a victory of Churchill involve such a return, because the old conditions are demolished, and there is no possibility of returning to them. But Roosevelt has no desire to return to them, and all the world knows it; hence a movement led by him cannot possibly be branded as counter-revolutionary.

If there is anything certain in human affairs, it is certain that he did not envisage the present situation on March 4, 1933. He had plans, indeed, that were wide-spreading and far-reaching; but peace is the first prerequisite to the development and perfection of that sort of plan. 'Adapting existing economic organizations to the service of the people' is work that cannot be performed with artillery, tanks, and bombing planes. This is not to say that he wasn't aware of the possibility of war, even eight years ago. He is not feeble-minded, and every man above the intellectual level of a half-wit has been aware of the possibility of war ever since firing ceased in 1918. But the President, like the majority of the American people, rejected war as an instrument of national policy. It was present in his mind, as it was in the minds of us, as a calamity to be avoided as long as possible, not as an opportunity to be carefully studied and considered.

It is doubtless true enough that Hitler never intended to face Roosevelt under the circumstances that now exist. Difficult as it is for us to believe, Hitler evidently thought that he could defeat Britain by psychological weapons and then face Roosevelt, or whoever happened to be President of the United States, with all, or nearly all, the power of Europe solidly organized behind him. For the destruction of free government in this country is a necessary part of any plan of world domination, and Hitler must have envisaged it from the beginning.

Yet in the month of March, 1933, the positions of the two men were strangely similar. Both had risen to power on the crest of a wave of protest set in motion by the same sort of grievances. Both took over countries economically in a state of collapse and visibly disintegrating socially. Both faced the problem of putting millions of idle men back to work immediately, and the even more urgent problem of putting some spirit into an apathetic and despairing people.

There were other similarities. In Germany, as in America, the people were not so much aflame with enthusiasm for the new leader as inflamed with wrath against the old ones. In Germany, as in America, the gravamen of the old leaders' offense was not so much what they had done as what they had failed to do. In Germany, as in America, the indictment of the old leaders included a multitude of counts, but there as here they may all be summed up as failure to obey the injunction of the Constitution of the United States, 'to provide for the general welfare.' Finally, in Germany as in America, the new leader, largely because he was new, was given carte blanche to do what he thought best.

Even if you are one of those who regard the New Deal as Americanism at its worst, it is still Americanism. However distorted you may think its ideas, they are still ideas whose origin is to be found in the Constitution and the *Federalist*, not in Wagnerian opera. Its traditional hero is Mr. Jefferson, not Wotan; and Mr. Jefferson, with all his faults, was recognizably a states- man, and not a baritone singer seven feet high with cowhorns on his hat. We may have come off badly, but at least we came off with something that looks more like a government than like a lunatic stage manager's setting of the Ride of the Valkyries.

The protest that brought both Hitler and Roosevelt to power has been described by Mrs. Anne Morrow Lindbergh as 'the Wave of the Future.' No doubt it is, but it is also the same old wave that has surged up in the past under the same stimulus. Since the beginning of recorded history, the king has never been conceded a right to demand allegiance of his subjects except as he could, and would, protect them from dangers against which they could not protect themselves. In this respect human nature has not changed; what has changed is the enemy. In modern times, and especially since the begin- ning of the Industrial Revolution, the ordinary man has had less reason to fear human robbers with tangible weapons than the impersonal, intangible operations of the economic system. Yet death by starvation is still death by starvation, whether the proximate cause is the irruption of a band of men-at- arms who have ravaged a peasant's farm and taken away all his food or an economic collapse that has deprived a workman of any chance to earn a living. A government not clever enough to prevent starvation through eco- nomic wreckage cannot command the faith and loyalty of its citizens today.

The government owes no man a living, but it does owe every man pro- tection of his life. It incurs this obligation when it exacts of him loyalty and support; and the obligation has never been denied. As far back as human records go it has been acknowledged that, when the ruler can no longer pro- tect the subject, the subject is released from his obligation to support the ruler. In 1933, in Germany and in the United States, millions of men were threatened with death by starvation because the government did not know how, or did not dare, to protect them from the economic forces that were destroying them; so, in both countries, the people revolted against the govern- ment. But this was certainly nothing new, nothing without precedent; on the contrary, it has been the common fate of every government guilty of a similar failure.

But it was none the less a sinister thing. It was the old nightmare that has haunted the dreams of every ruler, and of every ruling class since organ- ized government was established. For time and time again it has been demonstrated horribly that when the *Jacquerie* once gets out of hand there is no limit to its ferocity, nor to its stupidity. It was this that Alexander Hamilton had in mind when he declared, 'Your people, sir, is a great beast!' Leaderless, or led by scoundrels, a people *is* a great beast, capable of rending its friends as readily as its enemies, incapable of distinguishing virtue from vice, patriotism from treason, philanthropy from rapacity. Time and time again it has been demonstrated that a popular movement that starts from the depths cannot be stemmed, cannot be dammed, cannot be arrested. It can be guided, but only by the highest political skill; and rarely, indeed, is it so guided. New? Why, it is the oldest terror that organized government knows.

Perhaps it is the supreme triumph of the American genius for self-government that in this crisis the American people turned to a man of their own blood, steeped in their traditions, and a sincere believer in their way of life. The Germans, on the other hand, turned to a foreigner, little acquainted with the true greatness of Germany, and contemptuous of what he did know. The Germans were perhaps the more logical; since the old system had failed them, why not turn to a man as far removed from it as possible? The old system had failed the Americans, too, but they listened to a man who insisted that the system was basically sound and could be made to work satisfactorily by the use of different methods.

Once in power, though, the two leaders began to diverge at once. Perhaps the essential difference in their philosophies is that Roosevelt believed that the wreckage with which he was surrounded was due, for the most part, to stupidity, whereas Hitler believed that the wreckage of Germany was due to crime. Roosevelt realized that the wealth of America had been dissipated and lost. Hitler believed that the wealth of Germany had been stolen. Roosevelt's aim, therefore, was recovery; Hitler's aim was recapture. One leader said to his ruined countrymen, "Let us make." The other said to his, "Let us take."

They agreed, however, on one point, which was that the sacredness of private property is not absolute but is conditioned on the safety of the nation. Neither hesitated, therefore, to spend enormous sums to establish national safety. By 1939 Roosevelt had spent about 40 billion dollars over and above the ordinary operating expenses of the government, and Hitler had spent a sum which, owing to his incomprehensible methods of accounting, cannot be determined with precision, but which is generally supposed to range between 90 and 100 billions.

But Roosevelt spent the bulk of his money on such matters as roads, bridges, dams, powerhouses, irrigation projects, schoolhouses, land reclamation, and reforestation. Hitler spent the bulk of his on arms. This was the natural result of the difference in the two men's aims. Roosevelt proposed to restore the prosperity of the American people by creating new wealth. Hitler proposed to restore the prosperity of the Germans by taking other people's wealth away from them. In view of Hitler's plans, perhaps Roosevelt would have done better to spend his money on arms, too, but who would have believed it in 1933?

In the end, of course, Hitler forced his scheme on all the world. Under modern conditions no one nation can afford to devote even the major part of its energies to planning for peace while another large nation is furiously preparing for war. People are always referring to this as one of the inherent weaknesses of democracy, but it is hard to see where there is anything in it peculiar to democracy. It is rather the weakness of every nation, democratic or not, that cherishes the concept of the citizen-state as opposed to the concept of the bandit-state. There is no apparent reason why a benevolent and intelligent despot should not regard his domain as a member of a larger community, a citizen of the world-state. Up to 1939 the Russians, for instance, vociferously proclaimed that this was precisely their concept of the position of their totalitarian régime; and until their attacks on Poland and Finland revealed the insincerity of the claim there was so much evidence to support it that many Americans at least half believed it.

There is a school of thought which holds that in this Hitler was the realist, and Roosevelt the idle dreamer, whose drowsy amiability is the real source of his nation's peril. This is the school of the moral defeatists, which has surrendered in advance the principle that is the very cornerstone of American political philosophy. For if men not only lack at present but are incapable of developing the capacity to manage their own destiny intelligently, then the Constitution of the United States is nonsense and the republic itself a futility and a fatuity. Logically, this doctrine is not impossible. Perhaps we are essentially bestial. Perhaps there is in us no capacity for self-government, not even latent. But this is not the doctrine of the republic, hence a man who holds it is not eligible to be President of the republic. A man who holds that office must take it as axiomatic that intelligent self-government is possible, that liberty is an attainable ideal, that a continuing elevation of the cultural level of the masses is practicable, that the people are capable of drawing steadily closer to justice. He must frame his policy on this basis, and not on the basis of barbarism, unless the threat that is offered by barbarism is so close and so plain that none can doubt the necessity of turning to meet it. Roosevelt undoubtedly foresaw the possibility of war in 1933; but he would have been no American had he thrown all the energies of the country into preparations for a war still so far away that few of the people perceived it at all.

In any event, the moment Hitler marched into Poland it made little difference what Roosevelt regarded as the wise course through which to repair the damage of the economic and social collapse. At that moment the threat of barbarism did become plain. From that moment the thought and energy, as well as the money, of the country had to be applied in ever-increasing proportion to the problem of national defense. The New Deal is a peacetime program. The moment the threat of war overshadowed the land it had to be held in abeyance. Mr. Roosevelt tacitly admitted that fact when he appointed to head the War and Navy Departments, and the enormously important Office of Production Management, men who were not New Dealers and not even Democrats.

It is undeniably true, therefore, that of the two great antagonists who came to power in 1933 Hitler was the winner, up to the summer of 1941, not on the field of battle only, but in the field of governmental theory as well. He had forced Roosevelt to abandon his own course and follow that of Hitlerian Germany—that is, the diversion of the national energies from the problems of peace to the single task of creating as rapidly as possible the most formidable military power possible.

There are some Americans pessimistic enough to believe that this represents the loss, not of a battle only, but of a campaign. Strongly anti-New Deal, they hold that the six years and 40 billions devoted to that program represent losses that have weakened us dangerously as we face the menace from abroad. This feeling is natural, doubtless inevitable, in a man who dislikes and distrusts everything Roosevelt has done from the start; yet even in such a man it is hardly justified by the facts.

Grant, for the sake of argument, everything this man asserts. Grant more than has ever been asserted by reasonable anti-New Dealers. Grant that the New Deal was downright criminal, which none except those driven maudlin by hatred of Roosevelt have ever asserted. Nevertheless, the fact remains that 27 million American voters, a clear majority of the whole, more than 55 out of every 100, believe the contrary so strongly that they trampled down the thitherto sacred third-term tradition in order to reëlect the chief New Dealer. If, as few observers doubt, the prejudice against giving any man a third term cost Mr. Roosevelt several million votes, then even the tremendous figure of 27 million does not represent all the American voters who believe that the New Deal was a move in the right direction.

It is important to eliminate Hitler's armed forces as menaces to our peace and safety; it is vastly more important to eliminate Hitler's ideas if we are to enjoy peace for any considerable length of time. But an idea is impervious to bayonets and bullets. It can be killed only by another idea. Now Roosevelt has given a majority of the American people the idea that democracy can be made to work to the satisfaction of the average man, and this idea, whether true or false, is a powerful prophylaxis against infection with the idea that the only hope for common people is embodied in the "leadership principle," the "master race," the "protection of the blood," and all the other fantasies of which Germany has been so fearfully productive in recent years.

The 27 million may be deluded, of course, but the New Deal has given them faith that the American system is, or can be made, the best system of government as yet devised. Being full of faith, they are full of fight. In that sense, the country was being well armed during those six years when more money was going into bridges and schoolhouses than into tanks and battleships. The anti-Roosevelt man, assuming that he is himself profoundly American, can take satisfaction in this. Without those six years, most of the people might not have been so jubilantly confident that theirs is a government worth shedding their blood to preserve. In consideration of this, much can be forgiven by a patriot, even though he is an anti-New Dealer.

As a matter of fact, now that the lines are drawn, not as between Democrat and Republican, but as between American and foreigner, most of us are disposed to welcome those phases of government which we can point out with pride to a foreigner, more than those which we can criticize privately at home. But the years of terrific domestic battling have obscured from its opponents even the incontestable merits of a group whom they oppose. Let it never be forgotten that for eight years it has been politically, and sometimes financially, profitable to paint the New Deal as black as possible; and when blackening is profitable no one need doubt that a good job will be made of it.

Surely it is not mere Democratic propaganda to point out, at this time, those features of the Roosevelt administration which even its opponents admit are not bad, and which shine brilliantly when contrasted with the régime which it now opposes. There have been many things in Washington during the last eight years in which any American can take pride, no matter what ticket he votes, and which he can justifiably emphasize when it is a matter of his country against any other. Certainly now is the time to remember them, without regard to our domestic differences.

The first and greatest of them all is, in fact, to be credited only in part to the New Deal. This is the sharp rise in the level of political debate during the last eight years. The New Deal, simply because it has challenged many long-established concepts, has forced a reconsideration of the fundamentals of our political system, which has been reflected in all public debates but especially in those on the floor of the United States Senate. It is doubtful if the intellectual level of the present Senate is conspicuously higher than that of the Senates of the twenty years prior to the New Deal; but its debates have been markedly above that level. The reason is that a Senator of mediocre intellectual attainments, when he is talking about something important, talks better than a brilliant man who is talking without anything to say. For the last eight years the Senate has had before it a succession of great constitutional questions which could not be discussed at all without some cerebration, and which could not be discussed adequately without long and severe mental effort. As a result, the Senate has talked well.

Perhaps it is not to be listed among the great periods of the Senate. Few would compare it, for sheer brilliance, with the days when 'Old Bullion' Benton stood in the Senate like a bull in the ring, tormented but deadly dangerous, while the incomparable picadors Webster, Clay, and Calhoun circled around and around, prodding him. But it certainly was far above the period when the Republican leader, Senator Smoot, could fill hours of the Senate's time and columns in the newspapers with his horror at discovering a dirty book; and when Heflin, the Democrat, could gain country-wide attention and waste other hours by hurling billingsgate at the Pope. Of late the Senate at least has had too much to do to spend its time considering either *Lady Chatterley's Lover* or the religious prejudices of Alabama. This may be an indication of more distress in the country, but it is certainly an indication of more thought in the Senate.

What is true of the Senate debates is applicable, in a measure, to political debating in general for the period. Neither Mr. Landon nor Mr. Willkie, Mr. Roosevelt's opponents in the Presidential races of 1936 and 1940, is a pettifogging type, but, if either had been, that sort of thing would not have served, for nobody thinks of Mr. Roosevelt as a petty misdemeanant. He may be pulling down the very pillars of the temple, but he certainly is not running away with the altar cloth.

It would be silly to imply that the advent of this President has converted Washington into a serious rival of the Old Academy, but it is sober truth that it has driven Americans to a more careful consideration of the first principles of government than any other administration of recent years has inspired. Among other things, it has had the effect of restoring some validity to party divisions. To be sure, the old party names of Republican and Democrat are still untrustworthy guides to a man's political philosophy, as they have been for thirty years and more; but the terms 'New Dealer' and 'anti-

New Dealer' have meaning. Republicans and Democrats are frequently indistinguishable; but there is a difference between New Dealers and anti-New Dealers.

Another characteristic of the New Deal about which there is no dispute is its notable freedom from the grosser forms of misconduct in office. The spending that has gone on in Washington has been unapproached in time of peace; but the stealing there apparently has been confined to the petty cash and to officials of the rank of clerks and office boys. There have been peculations of considerable size. Several cases have been prosecuted, and it is highly probable that more have been successfully covered; but the stealing was not done in Washington. All the important cases that have come to light were discovered where construction work was going on or funds were being distributed for other reasons out in the country, not under the eye of the administration chiefs.

Nor has the partisanry that unquestionably has stained the record been most blatant and unashamed in Washington. Prodigious efforts were made to connect James A. Farley while he was Postmaster-General—traditionally the Cabinet post of the Politician-in-Chief of the administration—with the improper use of relief and recovery funds for partisan purposes, but none was successful. Of course this did not acquit him. There are people with whom it is an article of faith that Jim Farley bought the election of 1936 with relief funds; and they are quite unshaken in that belief by the complete lack of evidence. If an archangel were Postmaster-General there are people who would believe that he had played dirty politics and was too smart to get caught at it.

It is strange that men are unable to perceive the self-stultification that this belief involves. Anyone who believes that Mr. Farley, or anyone else, could buy the American electorate necessarily believes that the republic is rotten to the core. If the people in the mass are purchasable, then democracy is a fraud on its face, and ought to be abolished forthwith. A man who believes the election was bought has no sound reason for opposing Hitler, or any other conqueror who will reduce a venal nation to the satrapy that is all it deserves to be. A man who believes the election was bought is an apostate American who has repudiated the faith on which the republic was founded. Of course there are men of intelligence and personal integrity who do believe that the republic is thoroughly rotten, and that democracy is a sham and a fraud; but every such man of my acquaintance is also opposed to universal suffrage and to the continuance of the American political system in general. Most of them see no point in opposing Hitler. It is possible to retain respect for such a man, as it is possible to recognize the ability in war and statecraft and the many admirable personal traits of the Emperor Julian, who also was an apostate. But when a man in the same breath proclaims his faith in democracy and his belief that the election was bought, it is impossible to retain respect for his intelligence, whatever one thinks of his sincerity.

The truth is, of course, that Jim Farley all but dislocated his spine leaning backward in his effort to avoid the use of relief funds for party purposes. There is never a doubt that the smaller fry in some of the states were less scrupulous. Some open scandals resulted, and there were evil smells from states where nothing was ever brought to light. But no Cabinet officer was involved.

The noteworthy lack of stenches in the air of Washington ought to be peculiarly gratifying to Americans at this time when they remember the appalling fetors that every breeze from Berlin has brought to their nostrils for eight long years. When the official press was through describing, after the blood purge of 1934, the official and private characters of the men who had stood next to Hitler in the Nazi hierarchy, the average American was pretty well convinced that any plain embezzler or bribe taker would be disgraced by being found in such company. But is there really anything extraordinary in this situation? Is it not, indeed, an old and familiar pattern? When, in all human history, has a revolutionary movement concentrated all power in an individual without being attended by an upheaval in the moral as well as in the political realm? There is a tradition that Vladimir Lenin ruled in an atmosphere of puritanical austerity, and so, apparently, did Oliver Cromwell; but both men are regarded as remarkable on that account. Ordinarily the dictator, for the very reason that he has overthrown the regularly constituted government, is forced to make use of some worse than dubious instruments; and these questionable fellows usually disgrace his régime.

We are not hearing from Washington well-authenticated tales of misappropriation, bribe taking, and embezzlement; of misuse of the sword of justice to gratify private spite; of perjury in the highest places, and cynical betrayal of trust; of great officers of state employing the methods commonly attributed to Al Capone during the prohibition era. Still less are we hearing whispers of disgusting personal habits among the leaders of the government; of strange orgies in official residences; of drug addicts in high office; of men convicted of infamous crimes put in positions of command; of perversion and degeneracy among those who bear the honors of the nation. Mr. Roosevelt himself has been accused of many things, but no one as yet has suggested that there is anything epicene about him, nor has he been seen gnawing the carpet in a fit of hysteria.

It is fatuous to account for this with the smug assertion that such things simply couldn't happen in America. They could happen, and they would happen, fast enough, if there were in Washington a government possessed of supreme power and holding itself accountable to no one. Indeed, they could happen in Washington faster than anywhere else, for the simple but sufficient reason that there is more wealth in Washington than anywhere else; and when the swine are in control their swinishness is in direct proportion to the amount of wealth they find at hand. The relative inoffensiveness of the air in Washington is the most conclusive evidence of all that no dictatorship, but an accountable government, aware that it may be brought to book, holds sway there.

Finally, there is one accomplishment of Mr. Roosevelt which his opponents ordinarily dislike even to consider but in which, at this juncture, they may find a certain comfort. This is his remarkable success in nationalizing our domestic politics.

Franklin D. Roosevelt is the first Democratic President since the Civil War who did not need the support of the Solid South in order to win. He has been supported by the South, to be sure, but that support was not essential. In any, or all, of his three campaigns he might have given his opponent the entire electoral vote of the eleven states that formed the Confederacy, plus the vote of the border states of Maryland, West Virginia, Kentucky and Missouri, and yet have been elected easily. This is a consideration that naturally annoys Republicans under ordinary circumstances, but under the circumstances that exist at present it has a certain nonpartisan value. It proves that our representative in the crisis is a national figure, and not a sectional hero who obtained national office by a political fluke. There is no possibility of a split in our ranks because one section of the country suspects the President of being Jeff Davis in disguise. This gains importance as it applies to a situation in which unity is the first essential.

There is something more than a jest in the apothegm that he who would know the sturdiest manhood in all America should study a Vermont Democrat or a Georgia Republican. The strength of character that can sustain defeat after defeat with no yielding of conviction, that can fight campaign after campaign with no hope of success, and that can bow to the will of the majority without a thought of bowing to its wisdom, is part and parcel of the bedrock on which our political institutions are based. To suggest to a man who has believed all these years that Mr. Roosevelt is wrong that he should now change his opinion, simply because for the third time most of the people have declared that they believe Mr. Roosevelt is right, is more than an insult to the man; it is an insult to the very spirit of Americanism. A man who based his vote for Willkie on conclusions reached after carefully weighing all the facts, and nothing but the facts, would be a poor American if he changed his opinion simply to conform to the election returns.

But Americans, without regard to party, feel an obligation to support the President—any President—whenever the nation is threatened from without. Not all the inhabitants of this country accept that obligation; but not all the inhabitants of this country are Americans. Not even all the natives are American except in a strictly technical sense.

There are some men so blinded by partisan passion that they would rather see the nation remain in peril than see it delivered by a member of the other political party. But they are partisans, not Americans.

There are some so steeped in class and caste prejudice that they would prefer to see Hitler lord of America than see American workmen gain another inch. But they are Tories, not Americans.

There are some so eaten by avarice that they fear a dictator less than they fear the doctrine that property is not as sacred as the duty of the government to see that famine shall not slaughter the poor. But they are not even civilized men, much less Americans.

No one would waste words on these, any more than one would waste words on those who have secretly transferred their allegiance to Hitler, or to Mussolini, or to Stalin. In time of war there is a person officially designated to do all the talking to these people that is necessary; he is the provost-marshal.

To Americans, though, who must support the President, it is not an insult, it is a relief, to consider in as favorable a light as they can the qualifications of the man whom fate has made their leader during the critical years ahead. The fortunate people, of course, are the majority who have believed in Roosevelt from the start. They need no reassurance, for they have no doubts; they can, and do, face the future calmly confident. But in what can a member of the minority find reassurance? Judging the future by the light of the past, what can he reasonably expect of Mr. Roosevelt, not as the leader of the New Deal, but as President of the United States charged with the duty of assuring the safety of the nation against the threat of physical force?

Well, he can expect the first and most essential quality of courage. Whatever else may happen to the man who represents our side in this clash between two worlds, he will not be appalled. Infantile paralysis is a more terrifying devil than Hitler, but Roosevelt faced it. Economic collapse is more terrifying than a bombing raid, but Roosevelt faced it. Whoever may blench, whoever may quail, as we plunge into the fog and smoke, we may rest assured that the man at the top is not afraid, for he has seen worse than this, yet came through all right.

By the same token, we may expect resolution—this not only on the testimony of Mr. Roosevelt's friends, but on the even more enthusiastic testimony of his enemies. They call him the stubbornest man alive. Perhaps this is where his Dutch ancestry counts. At any rate, if he could battle seven long years to reach the point where he can walk limpingly, and could battle seven years more to bring the country to the point where it could get about without crutches, is there any doubt that he will fight quite as stubbornly to prevent the enslavement of the American people? No, another thing that is certain is that the man at the top will not quit.

In addition to courage and resolution, we may expect inflexibility. This will be denied. The idea is firmly imbedded in many minds that Mr. Roosevelt is a master of sinuosity and deviousness, but the idea has been created and propagated by two classes of people—first, those to whose interest it was to make him seem so, including, of course, his political opponents; second, those who have put into Mr. Roosevelt's mouth words he never spoke, and into his mind ideas he never held, and have denounced him for not adhering to these things. An example was furnished by the isolationists, with their denunciations of the President for breaking his promise to keep us out of war. Of course he never made any such promise, any more than he promised to maintain 25.8 grains as the weight of a gold dollar. He said that he hoped to keep us out of war. He said he would do all that lay in his power to keep us out of war. He said he would never send an American soldier to fight in a foreign war. But no man, not an utter fool, would make a flat promise to prevent war, and Mr. Roosevelt is no fool. Neither did he say that he would never send an American soldier to fight on foreign soil. No man not a fool would make that promise either. On the contrary, any man not a fool knows that if we must fight we are lucky indeed if we can fight on foreign soil instead of on our own.

Mr. Roosevelt is a politician, and any politician whose ethics are examined by the standards of a doctor of moral philosophy is pretty sure to show some wavering along the edges. But doctors of moral philosophy do not get elected President of the United States. If it is immoral to accept a man's support simply because he does not, or will not, understand the English language and insists on putting his own false interpretation on plain words, then Mr. Roosevelt is guilty; but so is every man who has held the office of President.

As it happens, the test of this man's straightforwardness is not difficult. Let any fair-minded man take the Commonwealth Club speech, in which he said what he was going to do, and lay it alongside the record of what he actually did—omitting his whirlwind action during the banking crisis, which was not contemplated when he made the speech. The exactness of the parallel between promise and performance will bear comparison with the record of any politician whatsoever, not excluding either Lincoln or Washington.

Mr. Roosevelt has declared that this nation, while he directs its foreign policy, will not submit to domination of the world by Hitlerism. That's that. Whatever else happens, we may rest assured that the man at the top is not going to flatten us with a sudden announcement that he has made a non-aggression pact with Hitler.

All this, of course, still leaves plenty of doubts. Whether or not Mr. Roosevelt will make a good Commander-in-Chief in time of war I don't know. Neither does anyone else. It all depends upon whether he can tell the difference between a general and a stuffed tunic, and that can never be determined with certainty until his selection has been tested in actual battle. They all look alike on the parade ground. Whether Mr. Roosevelt can spur the armament industry to maximum production I don't know; but I do know that he will be accused of fumbling the production program. I also know that if the President were not Roosevelt, but Tubal-cain, father of all workers in metal, he would be accused of fumbling the production program. From now on, denouncing the fumbling at Washington will be one of the easiest ways of impressing the credulous and making oneself seem important. There will be fumbling enough, God knows; but for every fumbler the denouncers will be twice as numerous and ten times as loud. It was so in Wilson's day. It was so in Lincoln's day. Indeed, as far back as 712 B.C. (according to Archbishop Ussher), the Prophet Isaiah was complaining, "Behold, I have created the smith that bloweth the coals in the fire, and that bringeth forth an instrument for his work; and I have created the waster to destroy." Let us bear this in mind.

The editors of the London *Economist* ended their inconclusive attempt to define the New Deal with these words: "Mr. Roosevelt may have given the wrong answers to many of his problems. But he is at least the first President of modern America who has asked the right questions." He is always at his best in a crisis; and in this greatest crisis of all he has certainly asked the right question.

As a nation we are full of imperfections, and it is only too likely that the stresses and strains of the next few years may reveal them horribly. But such as we are we intend to remain, not that we cherish any crazy delusions of being a "master race," and not that we have any God-given mission to regenerate the world, but because we know that the things we value we have created by our own methods and in our own way; and we are certair that if we submit to dictation all that is worth having will slip from our possession, and we shall never again create anything that is excellent or worth the world's attention. We are aware that in determining to live our own national life in our own way we are challenging the aggressors; for even one nation of freemen is a standing reproach and a perpetual menace to all tyrannies. But shall we apologize for living?

Not now. Not while we remain American. Not under the leadership of a man who, whatever his faults, is at least bold, resolute, and inflexible; whose roots are buried deep in American soil; whose blood is American blood, and whose hopes, desires, ideals, and dreams are of and with and for America. Let us stand to arms, then, steadily, knowing that under our latest President, as under our first, we have raised a "standard to which the wise and honest can repair; the rest is in the hands of God."

abridged from AMERICAN HEROES AND HERO-WORSHIP, *1941*

THE CHANGELINGS

M r. Talleyrand, during his exile in Philadelphia, then the national capital, passed by the house of the American Secretary of the Treasury late one night and observed a light burning in the study where the Secretary, having finished his official duties for the day, was slaving over the papers of a private client. Mr. Talleyrand went his way, filled with wonder touched with contempt. "I have seen a man who made the fortune of a nation laboring all night to support his family!" he said later.

It was not a sight of which a thoroughgoing political realist could approve. Alexander Hamilton had handled millions of public funds under an accounting system largely of his own devising; therefore he had no excuse, in Mr. Talleyrand's opinion, for remaining poor.

As a matter of fact, no one in recent years has seriously contended that Hamilton was a realist in the sense that Talleyrand was. All recent studies concede that he believed in the unrealistic concept of honor—indeed, how can any rational man deny it, in view of the fact that he actually went to his death to defend that abstraction? The accepted view of Hamilton seems to be that he was a realist, not in comparison with Talleyrand, but in comparison with his great opponent in this country, Thomas Jefferson. The argument advanced to support this theory is simple but, if true, conclusive. It is that Hamilton's theories worked and Jefferson's didn't—or, more precisely, that the country followed the course of development predicted by Hamilton, rather than that predicted by Jefferson.

Partisan prejudice long ago subsided sufficiently to permit historians of any capacity to perceive that both men were essential. Even writers with a distinct Federalist bias have for many years granted the enormous size of Jefferson's contribution to the making of the nation, and no Jeffersonian who is taken seriously hesitates to admit that without Hamilton the republic probably would have collapsed before its history was well begun. The process of building up one man by attempting to tear down the other was abandoned long ago by sensible students; for the reputation of each is too well supported by incontestable fact to permit any hope for the success of sapping and mining operations.

It must be borne in mind, however, that this truth was never apparent to the men themselves. Hamilton, dying early, while the heat of the contest was still intense, perhaps had no chance to formulate a clear judgment; but it is a sardonic commentary on the value of contemporary estimates that Jefferson, at eighty-one, still lacked any clear comprehension of the significance of Hamilton's contribution. He died believing that the net result of Hamilton's work was to set up a tendency toward disruption and destruction.

Jefferson, however, died in 1826 and there is no lack of reason to assert that in 1826 the pull of the Hamiltonian philosophy was in the direction of disruption and destruction. It was the Hamiltonian philosophy that was drawing the country toward the Tariff of Abominations, which all but precipitated civil war less than ten years after Jefferson's death. Jefferson understood this clearly. He was not deceived by words. He knew that the concentration of legal authority in Washington, under the conditions then prevailing, would end by creating, not a strong government, but a weak one, because the concentration would set up internal stresses that the fabric of the country could not stand. In 1861 he was proved to be right.

Yet this clear-eyed man, after dominating the political thinking of the country for half a century, gradually faded, gradually acquired the reputation of an impractical idealist whose intelligence, although undeniably powerful, did not save him from falling under the spell of dreamy fantasies. For three-quarters of the last century it has been accepted almost as axiomatic that the Virginian was a visionary and the Jamaican a realist—that the hopeful Jefferson was of the poetic temperament as contrasted with the hard-headed, unsentimental Hamilton, who represented the peasant type. Perhaps they were, if you choose, poet and peasant, but one of the ironies of American history is that their roles have been reversed by events and the hard-headed realist is held up as the dreamer, while the poet is reputed to be the materialist.

Men of first-rate ability can never be labeled neatly and thrust into pigeon-holes, for the man of extraordinary talents invariably has a touch of universality, a mentality with many facets. Everyone knows that, but nobody applies it; so it is needful to point out that the suggestion that Jefferson was essentially prosaic and practical is not a denial that he indulged in occasional flights of fancy, nor is the suggestion that Hamilton was romantic a denial that he was capable, when he deemed it necessary, of trudging indefinitely with his feet very flatly on the ground. The emotional natures of the two men do not affect the work they did in the world, nor the influence that each wielded upon the development of the republic; but a misconception of a man's emotional nature blurs and distorts the picture that later generations have of him. It makes it more difficult, if not, indeed, impossible for us to understand him, and so makes the story of his life duller.

But if there is anything in the theory that Alexander Hamilton was the impractical idealist and Thomas Jefferson the clear-eyed realist, there must be some reason for the prevailing opinion that the reverse is the truth. There is an explanation but until it is itself explained it is more confusing than the original assertion. The explanation is that from the standpoint of the last century the popular impression is the true one. The test of an impractical idealist is that his ideas, when applied in practice, do not work out; but Hamilton's did. The realist is the man whose notions stand the test of translation into practice; a good many of Jefferson's have not done so. Where, then, is there an excuse for saying that the man whose advice turned out to be sound was the dreamer, and his opponent the practical man of affairs?

The excuse lies in the fact that these results were brought about by factors that did not exist when the two men died and that could not reasonably have been foreseen by them. The places of Jefferson and Hamilton were switched by two other men who, as far as the material is concerned, were more truly the founders of the existing nation than Washington and his colleagues. These two were not statesmen, and one of them was not even an American, but between them they eliminated the republic of the early days and substituted for it another and quite different country. They were George Stephenson and Samuel Finley Breese Morse, inventors, respectively, of the locomotive and the electric telegraph.

At the time he was writing his *Notes on Virginia* Jefferson assumed that the conquest of the continent would require from four to five hundred years, holding that we should reach the banks of the Mississippi in two centuries. It was a bold assumption, since in the preceding hundred and seventy-five years civilization had marched only about two hundred and fifty miles back from the Atlantic coast. Jefferson's estimate was based on the assumption that the march would be speeded up greatly—in twice the time he expected the conquest to proceed more than ten times as far. This was certainly making a liberal allowance for technological progress. Hamilton probably thought it too liberal; it is unbelievable that any rational man thought it scant. But the thing was done in a single century; and two-thirds of it was done in the half-century following the introduction of the railroad. Any such terrific displacement of the temporal element on which it is based must necessarily have a profound effect upon a political philosophy, probably invalidating it, in large measure.

The Hamiltonian philosophy of a strong central government, supported primarily by "the rich and well-born," necessarily rested upon two bases. One was the permanence of a substantial identity of interest among the rich and well-born; the other was that means of physical control would proceed at least abreast of territorial expansion. If the aristocracy were to be divided, then the chief support of a Hamiltonian government must be split. If means of control were to fall behind territorial expansion, then a strong central government would be a physical impossibility. Without these bases, the theory would have been insane. Hamilton was no madman, hence he must have assumed their solidity.

Jefferson could not assume anything of the kind, hence to him the Hamiltonian scheme seemed fantastic to the verge of madness. To Jefferson it was perfectly apparent that, as the development of the country proceeded, a conflict among the commercial, financial, industrial and agricultural interests was inevitable. The rich and well-born were bound to fight among themselves; therefore, all democratic theory aside, to base support of the government on an identity of interest that was only apparent, and that for no long time, seemed to him hopeless. He was a traveler, too, not only here but in Europe. Abroad he had observed how difficult it was for a central government to maintain control over compact countries with excellent transportation facilities; and he realized how immensely more difficult it would be to maintain it over a continental domain practically without roads. In fact, he believed it to be impossible to exercise anything like intimate control over so vast an area, and he heartily disliked attempts to perform the impossible. So do all intensely practical men. On the basis of the facts before him, Jefferson was entirely right. He was still alive, and Hamilton had been dead less than fifteen years when the country was riven asunder. By 1820 the rich and well-born were fighting furiously among themselves, and the patched-up truce of the Missouri Compromise was a confession of the central government's impotence to impose unity upon so vast and diverse a domain. Hamilton's two basic assumptions had both proved the insubstantial dreams of an impractical idealist, and it is small wonder that to the practical man the news of these events was "like a fire-bell in the night."

But the ironical gods were ready to take a hand. Five years before the Missouri Compromise, the War Department at Washington had so little control over an army at New Orleans, which is to say distant about as far as Warsaw is from Paris, that it could not restrain that army from fighting a battle after peace had been made; forty years after the Compromise it was perfectly feasible for Washington to synchronize the blows of an army operating in the same territory with those of another army operating almost within sight of the Capitol dome. The possibility of effective control which Hamilton had assumed had actually come into existence, so one of his assumptions was established, after all. Again, within that period the industrial interest had advanced so far as to overshadow the agricultural and to contest the supremacy of the commercial, while the agile financial interest was already allied with it, rather than with agriculture. Thus there had been brought about re-establishment of a considerable degree of unity among the rich and well-born. Hamilton's second assumption was also being justified. So was created the appearance that Hamilton had been all along the practical man, and Jefferson the impractical dreamer.

I am not concerned to defend either theory of government; my point is that the misconception of the temperamental endowment of the two men has tended to make American history duller reading than it should be. Idealists, accepting Jefferson as an idealist, have been hard put to it to explain him. Materialists, agreeing that Hamilton was a materialist, have had to spin elaborate and tenuous hypotheses to account for his acts. The result is that the argument, when it is not wholly incomprehensible, can be followed only by devoting to it the closest attention. What men don't understand, they find dull reading; and it is idle to expect men to read dull books unless they are compelled to.

The nation is the poorer for this misconception, especially as it affects Alexander Hamilton. I do not mean to assert that its formal history is poorer. I am not prepared to say that our present conception of events would be radically modified by a modification of our conception of Hamilton. I am inclined to think it would not. There is plenty of diversity of opinion as regards the significance of events, and there is no reason to suppose that that diversity would be eliminated, or very much reduced by the adoption of a different attitude toward the man who started the series of events. What men wish to do, and what they intend to do, frequently has little relation to what they actually accomplish in the world. It is the historian's business to record the event and its significance, if he can determine it. It is the business of the biographer to consider the man's attitude as carefully as his acts. Not the science of history, but the art of biography is the poorer for lack of an adequate interpretation of Hamilton as a poet.

Some attention has been paid to Hamilton's career as the earliest example of the American success story. John Adams' brutal sneer at "the bastard brat of a Scots peddler" made it inevitable that the man's friends should emphasize the wonder of his rise from obscurity to the pinnacle of fame; but there is a subtler and far more moving story in this life than anything ever imagined by Horatio Alger, Jr.

The biographers have paid curiously little attention to the fact that Alexander Hamilton was born and lived to the age of sixteen on an island. His was a narrow world which tends, as every psychologist understands, to produce either men whose eyes are forever on the margin of the land, or men whose eyes are forever on the horizon—insular men, or rovers, the Nine Tailors of Tooley Street, or Raleigh. Hamilton, needless to say, was one of those whose eyes were lifted.

Surely, there is nothing fantastic in the assumption that his fancy ranged, like that of another islander, Corsican Bonaparte, far beyond the line where sky met sea, and painted prodigious visions. Indeed, we have his word for it. The letters of the young Hamilton to his compeers ought not to be taken too seriously; but there is corroborative evidence that he was describing more than the vagrant dream of youth when, at the age of twelve, he wrote his friend, Neddy Stevens, "My ambition is prevalent, so that I contemn the groveling condition of a clerk or the like, to which my fortune condemns me, and would willingly risk my life, though not my character, to exalt my station . . . I mean to prepare the way for futurity."

Thirty-five years later he was still preparing the way for futurity when, on a summer morning, he climbed to a ledge of the cliff at Weehawken and confronted a venomous little man with a pistol. Nothing would have persuaded Hamilton to go through with that grisly farce except the fear that if he failed, he would lose his influence in the future; and the foundation of all his plans was his power to command the respect of men. So he went to his death by way of preparing to live.

From a groveling condition to exalt his station—at twelve Jefferson might have expressed a similar ambition, but not at twice twelve. The Virginian, of course, had the enormous advantages of birth and fortune. His station did not urgently demand exaltation; but John of Austria, Charles XII., of Sweden, and Lucius Domitius Ahenobarbus, known as Nero, are proof that rank and fortune are not enough to extinguish the romantic temperament. It was not his position, but something in the structure of the man himself that rendered Jefferson incapable of being moved by such terms as "groveling condition" and "exalted station." He examined men in the cold, clear light of day, without regard for condition or station; and he saw them as they were, not as they might be.

It is true that Jefferson wrote, "Cultivators of the earth are the most valuable citizens. They are the most vigorous, the most independent, the most virtuous, and they are tied to their country, and wedded to its liberty and interests, by the most lasting bonds . . . I consider the class of artificers as the panders of vice, and the instruments by which the liberties of a country are generally overturned." That seems to be a fairly romantic view of the farmer; but it was written in 1785, which was a long time ago, and it seems probable that at that time there was more evidence to support it than there was to controvert it. The declaration as to artificers, too, at this time seems more like the heartfelt expression of a member of the National Association of Manufacturers regarding the CIO than the considered opinion of a statesman; but factory workers, too, have changed much in a hundred and fifty years. More than that, it is conceivable that a Virginia gentleman of 1940, remembering that the strength of Lenin lay in the cities, and the strength of Mussolini lay in the cities, and the strength of Hitler lay in the cities, would if he told his inmost thoughts, say that "panders of vice and the instruments by which the liberties of a country are generally overturned" is all too mild a characterization of a city proletariat.

The passionate Hamilton, on the contrary, viewed the world with anything but unemotional curiosity. "Your people, sir, is a great beast!" is merely an unusually strong statement of his characteristic attitude. He was committed to the romantic conception that there is an aristocracy of brains and character that is more or less self-perpetuating. His talk of the few and the many nowhere takes into consideration the truth that while there is, in fact, an aristocracy of brains and character in every nation, it is permanent only in the sense that sea-foam is ever-present because, while it is always dissolving, it is always being renewed from below.

The massive proof of Jefferson's impractical idealism is frequently held to be his optimistic belief in the fundamental decency of the average man.

But Hamilton clung persistently to an even more startlingly romantic theory—apparently, in spite of a long career in business, law and politics, he never got rid of the idea that the rich are intelligent. Again and again he urged the policy of making it to the interest of the rich to support the government, thereby apparently believing that their support would be rendered inevitable. He ignored the fact that, to make this come true, the rich must first have the wit to understand their own interest. It is true that this was a century and a half before Thyssen financed Hitler's campaign in Germany and the Dies Committee uncovered the contributions that rich Americans have made to Fascist organizations in this country; but even so Hamilton had plenty of evidence that throughout history the incapacity of the rich to understand where their real interest lies has been their undoing.

It may be argued that this persistent belief in the existence of a superior class was a psychological necessity for a man of Hamilton's obscure origin. The poor and nameless boy had made prodigious efforts, had fought long and bitterly, to batter down the obstacles that stood between him and a place in the favored class; therefore for him to admit that the class itself was a figment of imagination would have been, perhaps, intolerable. It would have left him in the position of the burglars who break into Heaven in Dunsany's play. After long toil they force the lock of the golden gate and swing it open—to discover, on the other side, nothing but stars and the void. It is arguable that Hamilton had to believe in class and caste, on pain of invalidating his own life's effort.

But it is difficult to see how his origin or the circumstances of his early life forced him to preserve to the end his rather adolescent delight in military glory. His wrath against John Adams when that honest but unromantic patriot broke up the war with France in which Hamilton had expected to shine had important political effects; and all his life Hamilton felt a sense of frustration because fate had not permitted him to imitate the exploits of a Marlborough.

Perhaps a partial explanation of this phase of his character is to be found in the fact that he was small and handsome. It is plain to the dullest that a man's inches neither make nor prevent his greatness, but it is by no means so clear that they have no influence upon the quality of his greatness. When one thinks of eminent Americans of unusual stature—the six-footers, Washington, Jefferson, the second Roosevelt; the long fence-rail type, Andrew Jackson, Abraham Lincoln, Woodrow Wilson; and then of the little men, John Adams, Madison, Hamilton, Burr, Stephen A. Douglas, Alexander H. Stephens and so on to Carter Glass and Fiorello LaGuardia—the temptation is strong to declare roundly that there are some moral qualities that seem to be denied to small men. Certainly the small men most prominent in our history have not been distinguished for geniality, patience, or humor.

When a man is not only small, but handsome, as well, his difficulties are increased. He has not only the serious problem of preventing infringement upon his personal dignity, which all small men face, but in addition that of justifying the admiration of the fair. It is hard to escape the conclusion that the quarrel between Hamilton and Burr was inflamed and envenomed by the fact that they were both small and handsome, both favorites of the ladies, both sensitive on the point of physical courage. They would have quarreled in any case. Their political ideas were bound to come into violent collision, and each was under the necessity of attempting to thwart the ambition of the other. But if each had had the seventy-four inches and the powerful frame of George Washington it is rather hard to believe that they would have faced each other with pistols. It is true, of course, that Andrew Jackson was both tall and given to dueling; but Jackson was a frontiersman, who spent most of his life in a country where a man's mere survival frequently depended less upon his intellectual and moral qualities than upon his ability to draw swiftly and shoot straight. Burr and Hamilton lived in a far more orderly environment.

Brooding upon any sort of disqualification, moral or physical, certainly tends to blur somewhat a man's perception of reality. It is a strong stimulant to the development of romantic illusions. When a man wishes fervently that things were different he is disposed to imagine that they are different. Hamilton was one of the finest quill-drivers the country ever produced, and he loathed it; he burned to be the plumed knight. Johnny Inkslinger wanted to be Paul Bunyan, and regarded with contempt the miracles he worked in his own right, and that only he could perform.

One of the kindest things George Washington ever did was finally letting the boy have his way. Right at the end, when the war was practically won anyhow, he permitted Hamilton to have a command and set him to take a redoubt at Yorktown, which he did brilliantly. By comparison with the really great services he rendered, both before and after this incident, the storming of that redoubt was a petty achievement; there were a dozen men on the field who could have done it, and without question one of them would have done it had Hamilton not been there. But there is much evidence that in Hamilton's eyes it was the supreme moment of his whole life. He was prouder of leading that charge than he ever was of being Washington's great adjutant and his still greater Secretary of the Treasury.

The proof of the inextinguishable quality of Hamilton's romanticism lies in the fact that he was at this time already a veteran. Not only had he observed the operations of the army from headquarters in several hard campaigns, but as a captain of artillery he had stood in battle, and after the disasters in New York he had conducted that grimmest and most nerve-racking of military operations, a retreat under pressure of the enemy. Such ample experience is enough to take the romance out of war for all but the incurably romantic; nevertheless, at the end of it, Alexander Hamilton still yearned to charge at the head of troops. He was not merely romantic, he was deeply, basically, incurably romantic.

The argument against any such estimate of the man is, it seems to me, quite irrelevant. It is based on the facts that Hamilton was a shrewd business man, an able lawyer, and an inspired political leader, which are qualities commonly regarded as impossible to the poetic temperament. But Lorenzo de' Medici ran the biggest bank in the world, was undisputed political boss, without holding office, of one of the must turbulent cities in the world, and at the same time was the best poet in Tuscany. William Shakespeare made a comfortable fortune in a business requiring great shrewdness, and retired with it intact. The common belief that it is impossible for a poet to keep books is superstition.

The only verses ever written by Hamilton are some pretty sad productions of his extreme youth, not conspicuously better or worse than those written by most schoolboys and college youths. But surely the world has passed beyond the belief that poet and rhymester are synonymous terms. The vision that can pierce beyond the limitations of space and time, the passionate aspiration for a life larger, more spacious, nobler than the life it is given to mortals to live—these make the poet, and these Alexander Hamilton unquestionably had. He suffered the fate of most true poets in that all his brilliant worldly success was not sufficient to compensate him for the inner frustration which must be endured by any man avid to wring from life more than is in it. Nearly all his biographers have commented on the sense of bafflement and defeat apparent in Hamilton under circumstances in which most men would have been complacent. It is incomprehensible in a thorough materialist; but it is precisely what one would expect in a man whose temperament was fundamentally romantic, although reined in by extraordinarily fine judgment.

It explains, too, why he and Jefferson were bound to misunderstand and, in a very real sense, despise each other. Each respected the other's ability, of course. Either must have been fabulously stupid not to realize that in the other he had encountered a man of superb intellectual capacity. They were not stupid, and each repeatedly acknowledged the power that he felt in the other. But Jefferson had no comprehension of the grandeur of Hamilton's vision of the future republic, and if it had been explained to him in words of one syllable he would simply have said that the man was moonstruck. As it was, seeing that the fellow was far too shrewd to admit of any doubt as to his sanity, Jefferson could make but one inference, to wit, that he was secretly contriving a restoration of the monarchy. Jefferson sincerely believed his great rival to be traitorous, and therefore loathed him. Hamilton, on the other hand, could not understand how any man of Jefferson's incontestably great intellectual powers could fail to perceive the vision that was so plain to him. He could make but one inference, to wit, that it was willful blindness, due to a conscious preference for popularity and present power rather than for a part in the creation of the greatness that was to be. Hamilton sincerely believed his great rival to be a timeserver and a cheat, and therefore loathed him.

Here is a dramatic element in our national history that has been far too much neglected. It was a tragedy in the Greek style, the catastrophe that was no one's fault, but was inherent in the nature of things. Two of the greatest Americans of their time by virtue of the very elements that made them great were doomed to collision, to mutual misunderstanding, and to a contest that, if it had done nothing else, would still have been lamentable because it deprived both of them of the marvelous companionship that each could have given the other.

The friends of Jefferson have frequently pointed out, as evidence of his magnanimity, the fact that he kept a portrait bust of Hamilton in the great hall of Monticello. But it is possible to see it as infinitely sad. It may be read as evidence that, in spite of the dust and fog of party strife, and in spite of the gulf that yawned between their temperaments, the great realist perceived something of his loss, felt vaguely that in failing to draw this man to him he had somehow missed the rarest friend he ever could have known.

The possible effect upon the course of American history of a genuine understanding between Jefferson and Hamilton naturally has fascinated speculative writers throughout the years. The usual assumption is that it would have been not powerful, only, but also beneficent. This does not necessarily follow. It takes no account of the principle of growth through struggle.

Alexander Hamilton was never afflicted with undue modesty. There is good reason to believe that when he entered Washington's Cabinet it was with the secret belief that he was destined to take over the government. It was not that he had the faintest impulse to be disloyal to Washington, but he proposed to give the President what Hamilton considered a higher loyalty than mere subservience—he proposed to give Washington sound advice and discreet guidance, to the end that the fine old country gentleman should stand before the world as a brilliant statesman. The fact that Washington was already a great, if not brilliant, statesman, Hamilton had not grasped, for in some ways he was singularly unperceptive.

This misapprehension of the real situation was a weakness of large significance which, if not corrected, might have worked serious damage to Hamilton's own career, reducing heavily the value of his services to the country. But it was corrected. In the Cabinet the Secretary of the Treasury found, at first with incredulity, and throughout with amazement, that he could not get his hands on national policy, he could not really get at the Chief, because the lanky, awkward figure of the Secretary of State stood in the way. In order to control Washington, it would first be necessary to batter down Jefferson. This task he undertook blithely; but his blithe spirit soon gave way to irritation as the Virginian refused to be swept aside. Then Hamilton bent all his energies to the task, and as Jefferson still stood, immovable, Hamilton worked harder and harder, with a growing exasperation that eventually mounted, as all the world knows, to a baffled fury that made the situation impossible.

The effect of this struggle upon Hamilton himself is, of course, beyond our measurement, but it was probably one of the best things that ever happened to him. Confronted with strong, resourceful and relentless opposition, he was compelled to exercise all his talents, and who can doubt that they were strengthened by exercise?

The effect upon the national history is also a matter of debate, except in one important circumstance. In 1801, owing to the clumsy system of electoral voting, the Federalists, although defeated, found it in their power to choose between Jefferson and Aaron Burr, and it was at the urgent insistence of

Hamilton that they chose Jefferson. The Federalist leader hated both men with equal intensity; but in addition to hatred, he held Burr in contempt and Jefferson in respect. The reason for that was that he had felt the power of Jefferson's opposition in the Cabinet. Had their minds gone along together during that service, he would never have had occasion to appreciate the strength of the great Virginian, in which event it is not beyond belief that he might have been cynical enough to throw the election of 1801 to Aaron Burr. Certainly that seemed to be the preferable move from the partisan standpoint, and any party leader might have been excused for selecting it when there seemed to be no choice otherwise between the candidates presented; but Hamilton was patriot enough not to put partisan advantage ahead of the real interest of the country. If he had to choose between scoundrels, for the country's sake he would at least pick the one with brains. He therefore unhesitatingly stood for Jefferson.

On the other side, there is as much reason to believe that Thomas Jefferson was a bigger man because he had Hamilton as his opponent. Although he came to be one of the greatest of Americans, Jefferson was born with a handicap that might have ruined him, as it has ruined some other men whose intellectual capacity was perhaps as great as his. Jefferson was by nature what a later generation terms scornfully a "Munich-man." He was a natural appeaser. But in the Cabinet no appeasement was possible. Washington did not ask his Secretaries to get together, compromise their differences, and present him with the result. He asked each to present his own policy so that the President might choose no compromise, but the better of the two. Hence there was nothing to do but fight, and fight to the last ditch. Jefferson found, possibly to his own surprise, that, if put to it, he could fight, and fight effectively. For a Munich-man it must have been an immensely valuable experience.

Incidentally, among the innumerable benefits that George Washington conferred upon his country, not the least valuable was the double achievement of taking some of the conceit out of Alexander Hamilton and making Thomas Jefferson fight. Each was a far more valuable man for the experience.

It is strange that this disposition to avoid a pitched battle should have been widely accepted as evidence that Jefferson was an impractical dreamer. It is the dreamers who fight. The genuine swash-buckler is practically always a man whose mental processes are far removed from reality. To call Jefferson's non-combativeness evidence of his impracticality, is much like saying that because in one respect he resembled Neville Chamberlain, therefore he must have been a Cyrano de Bergerac at heart. It is patently absurd.

His non-combativeness is, in fact, the strongest possible proof that there was nothing of the visionary in him. If this obvious truth has been consistently neglected for more than a century, it is because enemies of the Jeffersonian polity, in their anxiety to discredit Jefferson in every phase of his character as well as in every act of his career, have chosen to interpret his lack of belligerence as cowardice. The fact that Jefferson walked serenely in the shadow of the gallows for many years, the fact that again and again he cheerfully undertook commissions that inevitably would have put a noose around his neck had his country's enemies been able to lay hands on him, the fact that none of his contemporaries whose opinion is worth having ever thought of questioning his personal courage, all stand in the way of this charge. But the charge endures because there are so many people who are unable to understand, or at least to admit, that there may be any reason except fear for avoiding a fight.

Fear is a primary emotion, easily understood; Jefferson's disability as a warrior was a much more complex and subtle thing. It was a lack, not of courage, but of comprehension of the war-like impulse. His emotional nature, highly developed in some respects as is evidenced by his devotion to his wife, apparently included not a vestige of the fierce joy of combat. His common sense told him that war is horrible, destructive of all values, material and moral, and rarely productive of any permanent good. He was therefore forever unable to understand why men under some circumstances actually welcome it and regard it as preferable to certain forms of peace.

Yet this mental attitude ought not to be beyond the grasp of Americans, especially of the generation of Americans who are living a century and a quarter after Jefferson's death. It is precisely the attitude of every matter-of-fact realist among us, particularly big business men and research scientists. Business and science, far apart as they are in some respects, agree at least on the rigid exclusion of emotionalism from their intellectual operations. In their calculations they take account of it, of course, as they take account of temperature, velocity, quantity, and other irremovable factors. But they cannot control emotionalism, therefore they dare not employ it as one of their instruments. The axiom, "business is business" has been accepted and adapted by science, and it marks the limitation of both. It is rarely that one finds a big business man or a first-rate scientist who is not genuinely bewildered by the fighting propensities of civilized men.

This is why neither business men nor scientists have been conspicuously successful in American public life. They are too reasonable, too logical, too much afraid to release emotion which they know they cannot control, because they cannot understand it. It is the secret of Jefferson's weakness as President of the United States. As a matter of fact he was, in many respects, a very great President; but in others he was a wretched failure, largely because he saw the situation as it existed and not through a fog of emotionalism as others saw it.

Yet, contrary to the belief of scientists and business men, to see the situation exactly as it exists is not always an advantage. In the first place, the situation may be in process of change. In the second place, the situation may be—indeed, it usually is—affected by what Bismarck called "the imponderables," which elude logic.

Take, for example, the point at which the Jefferson administration has been most consistently, persistently, and successfully attacked—its naval policy. As a matter of fact, it was not a naval policy at all—it was a no-navy policy. Yet Jefferson embedded it so successfully in American political thinking that not until 1890 was it blasted out by Admiral Mahan with his famous book, *The Influence of Sea Power upon History.*

This policy was based upon the much-derided "corn-field gunboats." Jefferson advocated the building of swarms of small craft, each armed with one or two heavy guns. This fleet could not keep the high seas, nor was it intended to do so; indeed, the larger part of it was not even to be kept in commission, which gave the wags their opportunity to assert that Jefferson proposed to keep most of his navy hauled up in corn-fields. It was founded upon the theory that the best defense is simply to repel attacks; and it is a fact that at the outbreak of the war of 1939 the United States navy was maintaining exactly this policy, to a very considerable extent. It was in possession of some 300 destroyers, of which the larger part were laid up in port, out of commission, but ready to be reconditioned and sent to sea in case of a threatened invasion. They were the modern counterpart of the corn-field gunboats.

As a matter of fact, Jefferson saw the situation as it existed in his day and dealt with it adequately. What escaped his observation—and the country's, too, until Mahan's work made them inescapable—were precisely the two factors mentioned above, first, the rate of change of the situation, and, second, an imponderable, to wit, the emotion of fear. The very basis of naval defense was already shifting from securing the coast to the destruction of the enemy's commerce; but it was nearly eighty years later that a naval officer proved it. Furthermore, the only perfect defense is the prevention of war; and one factor in preventing it is the emotion of fear. A nation that is known to have the power to strike heavily a thousand miles, or three thousand miles, from its own coasts, will not have its coasts attacked on any frivolous excuse. But fear is a tricky, unstable, highly dangerous compound; Jefferson was too distrustful of emotionalism, too thoroughly practical, to believe in its employment as a national policy.

But is there anything unfamiliar in this? Have we not heard the same point urged, over and over again, by practical men even after the war of 1939 began? Jefferson could have understood perfectly the reasoning of Charles A. Lindbergh, of Neville Chamberlain and, in part at least, that of Fritz Thyssen, in 1939. These men were all strong believers in facing the facts, in accepting the situation as it existed and working out a reasonable adjustment of conflicting claims. They were all stoutly opposed to what they regarded as romantic nonsense. They were practical men, but their quality as statesmen was worse than dubious.

If Jefferson, in spite of his practicality, made a statesman of the first rank, it is highly probable that one of the main reasons was his collision with a man of romantic temperament who was also a genius of the first order. The impact of Hamilton knocked Jefferson out of his library and compelled him to give some intensive study to mankind in the flesh, and not in the statistical abstract. He was a greater man for it. True, in the Virginian's long career there were other forces driving him in the same direction. The French Revolution exploded right under his nose when he was American minister to France. Before that, he had been a war-time Governor of Virginia, and Tarleton's troopers swarming over the lawns of Monticello could not be regarded exactly in the light either of a sales manager's report, or of a demonstration in differential calculus. On many occasions Jefferson had been handled roughly by an illogical and emotional world; but of all those demonstrations that man is more than either an economic entity or a scientific datum, by far the most impressive was the encounter with Hamilton. All of them together go far to explain why he developed the political astuteness that raised him as a statesman, far above the level of, say, James Madison, who managed to cling to his library.

But what, after all, does it signify? Jefferson has been dead for a century and a quarter, Hamilton for nearly a century and a half. What they did is done. The effects they produced are fixtures in national history and cannot be erased. Suppose Hamilton's mentality was that of the poet and Jefferson's that of the peasant— what of it? Nothing can be done about it now.

That is not so certain. As to the influence upon events of the respective careers of the two men, one's opinion is not likely to be altered by a revision of one's estimates of their respective temperaments; but there may be a very considerable shift in the significance of the two men, not to earlier generations, but to Americans who are alive today.

The ironical fate that has reversed the relative position of Jefferson and Hamilton in the estimation of their successors has little, if any, relation to the qualities of the men themselves. It originated in events that occurred after both were dead, events which they could not have foreseen. The same sort of thing might happen to anybody, may happen to some of the men prominent in public life today. It affects us, not Hamilton and Jefferson; but it may cause us to miss, or to misinterpret, the value of the record.

This view strips Jefferson of some of the "idealism" with which he has been draped; but what he loses is only the cheaper and flimsier sort of idealism. His serene faith in democracy remains and gains weight as one perceives in him the clear-sighted, unimaginative realist. The physical conditions existing in his life-time he expected to change slowly. As a matter of fact, they changed with startling speed. At that, his prevision was justified with startling fidelity before the changes, swift as they were, had their full effect. He saw clearly that, under the physical conditions existing at the time of the Revolution, or under conditions at all resembling them, a strong central government in this country meant, not unity, but disunity. Before he died New England trembled on the brink of secession. Before he died the country actually had been divided along the line of the Missouri Compromise. Less than a generation after his death, the South actually did secede. Lesser men might blind themselves to the inevitable, but not this, the most highly prescient political philosopher America has brought forth.

But it was precisely this man, whose foreknowledge was so precise that nothing less than a revolutionary alteration in the environment in which men lived could invalidate it, who asserted flatly, and never wavered from the faith, that the people, given true information and a fair chance to be heard, are capable of providing for themselves a better government than can be provided for them by any other power.

Institutions are objective, and an alteration in the objective world means an alteration in its institutions; but habits of thought are subjective, and are affected only by subjective changes. As regards American institutions, Jefferson was but an indifferent prophet—only, however, because the conditions on which he based his prophecy were themselves altered after his death. As long as the conditions remained the same, his predictions were astonishingly accurate.

No rational man seriously maintains that the last five generations have witnessed an alteration in the habits of thought of the American people even remotely comparable to the alteration in their living conditions. There is, therefore, no convincing reason to assume that Jefferson's estimate of the capacity of the people for self-government requires any such revision as his estimate of the strength of their institutions. The physical changes, in fact, as far as they impinge upon the people's habits of thought, have been in the direction of making available to more people earlier, more accurate, and more comprehensive information about their government, and should, to that extent, increase, rather than diminish, their capacity to govern themselves. In other words, the clearest, least sentimental, coolest of our political thinkers was the strongest believer in democracy. It is something worth knowing at a moment when repudiation of democracy has gone the lengths it has reached today.

Nor does it necessarily follow that Hamilton is diminished in stature by denial of his capacity to reason strictly on the basis of existing circumstances.

By the insight that is given to true visionaries he sensed the fact that a great destiny lay before this people could they only be united permanently. As against this vision, the palpable fact that, under the circumstances then existing, they could not possibly remain united except in a loosely bound confederation, meant nothing whatever to the visionary. The obstacles in the way of realization of his dream were time and distance, two against which man had been impotent since history began. It is unimaginable that Hamilton foresaw the technical devices by which both were to be brushed aside, but that they would be brushed aside he blithely assumed—insanely, as Jefferson thought, but accurately, as we know now.

So far, this seems to be an argument that, without Stephenson and Morse, Hamilton would indeed have been a madman. But this is not true. Every student of history knows that epoch-making inventions appear when the need of them is sufficiently great. Many men were working on the problem of applying steam to transportation when Stephenson solved it. Many were working on that of the magnetic telegraph when Morse solved it. To an occasional genius is given the power to sense the truth that lies behind logic, to pierce through the deceptive screen of facts to the greater thing that lies behind them. This is poetic imagination, which, over and over again, has proved more accurate than fact-finding, more real than realism. Hamilton had it, and his romantic dream was solider stuff than Jefferson's sober facts.

To the impeccably logical mind, if one exists, this may be distressing. The man who believes that the world actually proceeds in orderly sequence from known cause to predictable effect—if any such incredibly mechanistic individual lives—may find a painful shock in the suggestion that intuitive perception sometimes may overleap scientific method and arrive sooner at the truth; but most of us have seen it happen frequently enough to be sure that there is nothing incredible about it.

More than that, the knowledge is valuable, if only as protective armament against the prophets of doom. When the world is convulsed by war, these prophets multiply exceedingly, and the ordinary man is put to it to withstand them; yet their leadership can direct him nowhere save into the Slough of Despond. America at this moment is full of able, honest, and learned men who, by logical reasoning, based on irreproachable authorities, can show that inevitable ruin lies ahead, and did show it assiduously until military considerations silenced them. From a thousand fora they proclaimed the imminent collapse of the national economy; in a score of learned journals they traced the progress and forecast the continuance of the degeneration of our people, physically, morally, intellectually; in every newspaper they announced daily the cracking of this or that pillar of the state. All this they supported with incontestable facts, with graphs, charts and statistics which a plain man is utterly unable to confute. In this pandemonium it is comforting to reflect—since there is really nothing one can do about it—that perhaps if these people were as clear-sighted as Jefferson, they would be more confident of democracy; and if they were as stout-hearted as Hamilton, the greatness within them might sense and thrill to the greatness of their nation.

The sardonic fates who contrived American history have mocked the prophets ever since it began. Even the mightiest, they have turned somewhat to ridicule. Jefferson, the realist, was right when he trusted the people, and wrong when he distrusted the future; Hamilton, the idealist, was wrong when he distrusted the people, and right when he trusted the future. Therefore, men who distrust both the people and the future, although they may overwhelm us with their learning, do not impress us with their wisdom. For American history is steeped in irony—thank God!

THE AMERICAN SCHOLAR, *Spring 1946*

THE LIBERAL OF 1946

So many of our ideas and attitudes have been vaporized by the atomic bomb that an inventory of what is left has assumed a high priority rating. Not houses and factories only, but concepts and convictions as well, have gone where Hiroshima went; and until an adequate reappraisal is made we shall not know where we stand, politically and psychologically as well as physically.

Consider for example liberalism. Never say that it is unaffected. If liberalism, as liberals like to believe, is simply willingness to adapt one's attitudes to changing realities, it follows that one must know the realities to effect the adaptation. And who is reckless enough to claim that he knows the realities of our present situation?

Behind the atomic bomb looms the shadow of the atomic engine. This is the element of uncertainty that invalidates all our political thinking. The engine will come. It may come soon, or it may be delayed for many years, but come it will and its arrival probably will alter our civilization even more radically than it was altered by the arrival of the steam engine. What was liberalism in an economy based on handicrafts, became rank reaction in the age of steam power. What is liberalism now undoubtedly will be hopelessly inadequate in the age of atomic power.

For the moment the lines of our thinking are hopelessly snarled. Liberals and conservatives are so utterly confused that one finds members of the National Association of Manufacturers advocating radical legislation for the control of atomic power, and members of the Socialist party veering toward the former position of the isolationists. Nobody knows where he stands for the simple reason that nobody knows the realities of the situation. Nobody knows which way is forward and which is backward. We have been spun in the vortex of the atomic bomb until our sense of direction is lost and, to paraphrase Jefferson, we are all liberals, we are all conservatives.

Yet a political philosophy that can be destroyed by any form of high explosive is not, to put it mildly, impressively strong. What has been destroyed is not in fact liberalism, but the program of liberalism. Equality of opportunity remains as desirable in this new year as it ever was; the difficulty is to determine what is equality—indeed, what is opportunity. The prospect of the development of atomic power threatens the validity of all our thinking along this line.

To identify a liberal in 1946, therefore, one must rely less than ever upon his political and economic program and more than ever upon his basic attitude. The touchstone of liberalism today is not advocacy of any specific legislation, or even of any specific idea, but simple equanimity. The genuine, dyed-in-the-wool liberal is interested, but unterrified by recent developments. The atomic bomb to him is simply another weapon, unlikely to affect the central issues of war and peace any more than they were affected by gunpowder. Even the far more terrible spectre of the atomic engine leaves him unshaken. The atomic engine will not destroy Hiroshima, but it might do what conservatives regard as an infinitely worse thing—it might vaporize a large part of Wall Street, which no war hitherto has been able to touch.

Production of nearly unlimited power at nominal cost would make wastepaper of the stocks, bonds and other evidences of indebtedness of every public utility, possibly of every oil company and coal mining company, conceivably of every railroad. A very large proportion of the wealth of the country might be suddenly and violently displaced—not destroyed, but removed from one segment of the population to another, which means, of course, its destruction as far as the losing segment is concerned. The effect upon insurance companies, savings banks and endowed institutions might be catastrophic.

It is not to be expected that the entire possessing class would be displaced, for the blow would fall upon primary power producers. Manufacturers in general would be put to the trouble of making some hasty revisions of their cost-accounting systems, and the whole price structure would be affected, but there is no apparent reason to expect demolition of the entire capitalistic system, even were the atomic engine perfected tomorrow. There would, however, be a terrific upheaval, accompanied by vast transfers of wealth.

It is the nature of conservatives to hold such disturbances in horror, for the conservative always believes the danger of losing what we have is greater than the danger of losing an opportunity to secure something better. To the liberal, however, the disturbance is not of great importance provided it opens the way to an improvement. Atomic fission seems to open the way to such improvement in the conditions of life as the race has never known. It also opens the way to sudden, violent death, but what of that? So did steam; so did electricity. Yet we have made use of them, in spite of their dangers.

Find a man in 1946 who is interested, aware of perils ahead and therefore alert, but who is convinced that the opportunity is greater than the danger, and you will find a liberal. His ideas of what to do next may be all wrong. He may indeed be advocating something that looks like a step backward. Nevertheless, if he inclines to confidence rather than to depression; if, while not ignoring the possibility of the destruction of civilization, he is much more fascinated by the possibility of its reformation—he is essentially a liberal.

That test will be productive of many surprises. Some who went down the line with Franklin D. Roosevelt from '32 to '44, cannot take it; and some who denounced him and everything he stood for may pass serenely. For being a liberal in 1946 calls for resolution in the face of a new danger which the world has not had to consider seriously heretofore. It is the danger of idleness, against which the race has been warned from time immemorial. The conviction that it is good for a man to earn his living by working only a few hours a day is based less on any political philosophy than on a tradition that runs back countless generations; therefore it is exceedingly difficult to uproot.

In fact the evidence against it is as yet far from impressive. Hitherto the people who have lived without labor have done so because others were overworked; and idleness obtained by unfair advantage has not been productive of an admirable type of humanity. To date the man who has had to work least in order to live well has been the American; and our national traits are hardly so conspicuously noble that they furnish incontrovertible evidence of the desirability of leisure.

However, the true liberal is not daunted. Even in America the twelve-hour day existed in the steel industry within the memory of living men, and the forty-hour week is still a bone of contention. We have never tried giving the masses any considerable amount of leisure; our conviction that it would be a bad thing is purely hypothetical. Nevertheless, it is strong; and only the man whose confidence in the possibility of improving humanity is extremely firmly based, can overcome it.

But the possibility of controlling atomic energy brings the question sharply to the foreground of our thinking. It is idle to try to blink it. The possibility exists that our triumph over nature might lead to our moral ruin, for a slave population suddenly released with no preparation for liberty is a fearful thing. The experience of the American southern states right after the Civil War is sufficient evidence. The experience of Russia after 1917 corroborates it. The sudden release of atomic energy, not in explosive, but merely in propulsive force, might make those incidents seem mere child's play by comparison.

This is a possibility that sane liberalism must take into account; yet its effect need not be paralyzing. On the contrary, it should be energizing, for the obvious protective measure against it is one with which liberalism is familiar; it is the goal of all true liberalism throughout history, the far-away but existent goal of the democratization of culture.

The Russian experience furnishes a guide of sorts. The blood-letting in Russia following the Revolution of 1917 was so copious that we find it hard to think of anything but the immensity of the red tide, and we forget the immensity of Russia itself. The most extravagant estimate of the butchery after the fall of czarism runs much below ten percent of the total population. In view of the sudden release of a slave population the wonder is that it did not run to a third or more. It is reasonable to assume that it stopped where it did because of the diversion of energy into a tremendous effort at the democratization of culture. Say what you will of the Communists, they did pour into the darkened minds of the Russian people a flood of light. For one item, they taught something like a hundred millions to read in a space of time so short that, as the history of nations goes, it might almost be called overnight. Mastery of the colossal masses of information suddenly flung at them absorbed energies that might easily have been turned to rioting and bloodshed.

Surely, it is not an extravagant hope to hold that American ingenuity could adapt and improve upon the Russian method, if it set to work in a serious way to do so. To raise the bulk of the American people to an intellectual level still far below that of the membership of Plato's Academy would be a task so gigantic that it might easily absorb all the human energy released by the control of atomic power. If that task were seriously undertaken by our people—as seriously as the Russian masses undertook their task after 1917—the bogy of the evil of idleness would be exorcised in an instant.

But are we preparing our minds to undertake any such task? There is little indication that we are doing so. Our utmost effort at the moment seems to be devoted to preparing some sort of paper defense against misuse of the atomic bomb—Big Three agreements, United Nations Organization trusteeships, even the folly of trying to keep the "secret" which is not and never was a secret except in certain technological details which our own engineers have worked out in at least four different ways and which others will surely work out, possibly in a dozen other ways.

This is a footling and empty task for true liberalism. We know that there are men in the world perfectly fit to be trusted with the secret of atomic power. The United States thus far has exploded three atomic bombs, one as a test and two to force the surrender of the Japanese Empire. The nuclear physicists and the high military command have not wantonly misused the bomb. Nobody believes that it will be misused as long as its control lies in their hands exclusively. The danger will come when atomic power has to be entrusted to large numbers of people. Obviously, the way to avert that danger is to bend every effort to preparing large numbers of people—the ideal would be a majority of the voting population—to handle it as prudently as this group of the élite has handled it.

That means a gigantic effort, an incomprehensible effort if you please, but in the eyes of true liberals not an impossible effort. It means simply an intensification of the effort they have been making all along, for liberalism has ever been based on belief in the possibility of raising the general level of civilization of the masses. It is not belief in the perfectibility of human nature, but it is belief in the possibility of its improvement.

The pseudo-liberal accepts this in theory, but in practice he is more afraid of life than he is of death. His ingrained asceticism makes him regard the sudden release of the slave as almost certain ruin; and the realization that that release may come at any minute, and almost certainly must come within relatively few years, panics him. The true liberal is willing to accept the chance—a bit nervously, perhaps, if he is a man of sense, but not with any deep perturbation. At bottom his equanimity is not disturbed. The prospect of having to work fast, faster than he ever worked before, is troubling; but even if he can't work fast enough, which is highly probable, he does not believe that all is lost. Even if our present world goes into a tail-spin, it will eventually pull out; for no increase in man's control over his environment has ever proved permanently disastrous. Nor will this one.

Never mind the projects and programs, then. Find a man unterrified, and you have found the liberal of 1946.

THE AMERICAN SCHOLAR, *Autumn 1947*

THE DEVIL IS DEAD, AND WHAT A LOSS!

Optimists among us have cherished the delusion, in recent years, that the United States has attained a level of intellectual maturity at which public opinion will no longer tolerate attempts by magistrates to set themselves up as censors of morals, as far as literature and the arts are concerned. But their optimism has been rudely jarred since the day of Japan's collapse; for the last two years have seen a veritable epidemic of attacks on books, plays and other forms of expression—even a statue was removed from one show in New York, although that was done by private, not public, censors. The number and violence of the assaults almost equal those that followed the collapse of the Kaiser in 1918.

Plainly, a recrudescence of Puritanism—meaning, of course, not the theology and ethics of Cromwell and Cotton Mather, but the tyrannical Bluenose—has developed in the United States, and some examination of its nature and origin is essential to an understanding of the prevailing mental climate of the country. There are indications that it differs in important respects from the old Puritanism with which we are familiar; for one thing there is no evidence that it is based upon a revival of belief in theocracy, for there has been none. If you question its strength, though, you should consult one of the publishers who has fought his way through the courts, or a radio commentator suddenly cut off the air, or any script writer in Hollywood. They all know that not in many years has free expression of opinion in America been so dangerous.

In the absence of religious fanaticism, the only explanation of tolerated censorship is fear. Superficially, it would seem to be preposterous to suggest that the United States is terror-stricken. Never before in its history has it possessed military strength so prodigious, absolutely or relatively. Our Navy is by long odds the mightiest afloat. Our Army has recently proved that its high mechanization, rather than the number of its soldiers, has made it capable of shattering simultaneously two of the most powerful armies that the world has ever seen. A hideous war lasting six years has broken down and destroyed the efficiency of every other military power in the world except one, and that one is a land power far removed from contact with our borders except at a single remote point, the extreme tip of Alaska.

Strategically, therefore, the United States would seem to be safer than it has been at any time since 1776.

Economically, the wealth of the United States, as measured in money, is greater than at any previous time, and this in spite of frightful expenditures during the war. The national debt of 260 billions is almost all held by our own people. Paying it will be simply a matter of transferring money from one pocket to another. If every dollar were paid off tomorrow, practically no money would leave the country. Our industrial equipment is enormously greater and more efficient than ever before. Our labor force is larger and better trained than ever before. The productivity of our soil per acre has been increasing, not decreasing, especially since the Soil Conservation Program began to work in a big way. Our forests and mineral resources have been depleted by the war, but intelligent effort can easily restore the forests within one generation. Only in minerals have we suffered anything that can properly be called a permanent economic loss.

Economically, the country is in a far sounder position than it was in, say, 1933.

Politically, the divisions among our people have been eroded and erased to the point at which since 1946 we have had virtually one-party government. The really sharp differences now are not between the parties, but between factions within the parties—between Northern Democrats and "Rankin Republicans" from the South, and between Old Guard Republicans and Sons of the Wild Jackass. Emphatically, there is no danger that the parties will resort to violence to settle their differences, as there was in 1876, when the Hayes-Tilden dispute threatened civil war.

Politically, there is less danger of a *coup d'état* today than at almost any other period in our national history.

Strategically, economically, politically, the United States enjoys in 1947 a security the like of which it has never attained before. Yet terror is the order of the day. Vice societies prosecute authors, even poets, as they have rarely prosecuted them before. Business interests purge the radio. Congress offers to make membership in the Communist party a crime. If this were done, there are grounds for fear that membership in the Socialist party would soon be condemned, and then suspicion of adherence to the New Deal would be enough for an indictment. The President of the United States demands an appropriation of $25,000,000 to delouse the government service of traitors, who must have been put there by his own party, since it has been in power for fourteen years.

Since neither military power, money power nor partisan rancor offers any threat to our safety, it is evident that the threat must be of an intangible kind. Indeed, this is evident from the form our precautions take. Censoring books, gagging radio comedians, purging the civil service, are not defenses against armed enemies, nor against business competitors, nor even against politicians run mad and turned Populist. Such a progam, if it is effective against anything, can be effective only against what the Japanese police called "dangerous thoughts." What we fear desperately is not the Russians, or the cartels, or the Republicans. The real fear is that the American people are about to get out of hand.

This is something contrary to the old tradition. Time was when it was the fashion to rejoice that no one could control the American people—in their morals, in their speech, or in their political ideas.

A proposal to censor books could once draw from Jimmy Walker the scornful comment, "I wish the honorable gentleman would cite one instance of a woman's being seduced by a book."

A proposal to purge the list of government employees could once draw from Thomas Jefferson the remark, "If there be any among us who would wish to dissolve this Union or to change its republican form, let them stand undisturbed as monuments of the safety with which error of opinion may be tolerated where reason is left free to combat it."

A proposal to "knock Mr. Bryan into a cocked hat" once drew Woodrow Wilson's approval, but only on condition that the means to that end should be both "effective and dignified." Failing that, he was against the project.

From Jefferson to Jimmy, in short, it was assumed as a matter of course that the people were never in hand and never would be. Now it is assumed that unless we get them and keep them in hand, ruin is just around the corner. So Edmund Wilson and the concocter of *Forever Amber,* whose name I forget, are haled into court charged with using naughty words. So Fred Allen is cut off the air for making unseemly jests about his sponsor. So we are to spend $25,000,000 purging the public payrolls. The nephews of Uncle Sam are to think none but decorous and immaculate thoughts. They are not to have a mind to sport with Amaryllis in the shade. They are not to giggle in the Cathedral of the Holy Dividends. They are not to suspect that there can be other political parties than the existing Janus-faced organization, Democan on one side, Republicrat on the other.

What in the name of all that is preposterous is the basis of this frowsy idiocy?

I suppose there is no short and simple answer. National hysteria rarely results from a single cause, and usually from a complex of many factors. In the instant case, a number come to mind at once—nervous exhaustion following the emotional orgy of a great war, apprehension at finding ourselves suddenly thrust into the leading role among the nations, mass miseducation conducted by able propagandists, the latent but ever-present fear of freedom in the human heart, resentment at having to solve problems set by others, and the reaction following a moment of intense fright.

There is one element, however, to which analysts of public affairs rarely pay much attention, but which may be more important than they suppose. This is sheer boredom following the death of the Devil.

For the spirit of Puritanism has never been wholly eradicated from the American mind, and it is characteristic of Puritanism that while it may get along comfortably enough without God—witness the host of Puritanical agnostics, from Bob Ingersoll to Clarence Darrow—it has always found the Devil indispensable. He is Protean in his manifestations, of course, but he must exist in some shape if the Puritan is to live comfortably.

Beginning in 1933, we had a highly efficacious Devil in the person of Adolf Hitler, whom we hated with a satisfaction that rose in a steep crescendo into frenetic exultation at the end of a dozen years. But then the inconsiderate Russians shot down his capital about his ears and buried him in its flaming ruins. By the rules of the game we had to thank them, of course, and we did; but it really left a great vacuum in our lives. The Mikado served briefly as a substitute, but he soon bowed himself out of the role, and there we were left, all wound up to hate furiously, and with nobody to hate.

It has taken us nearly two years to perceive the obvious and elect Stalin to the vacancy. In fact, we have not been able to make it unanimous even yet, for Henry Wallace is still howling a contrary vote up and down the land, and until we corral him and his following in concentration camps there will always be doubts that Stalin is the real thing. But time passes. We have no really effective Devil, and the high-pressure hatred generated within our bosoms must have an outlet or we shall choke.

In the circumstances, it was perhaps inevitable that the blushful books, the impudent jokesmiths and the always vulnerable bureaucrats should come in for a vigorous fustigation. It may be, indeed, that it is fortunate that these became the victims, for otherwise we might have vented our uneasiness on negroes and Jews, with results infinitely more damaging socially. After all, jailing a few authors and turning a few radio comedians and jobholders out to starve is not nearly as bad as murdering an indefinite number of persons belonging to racial and religious minorities.

For it is characteristic of the Puritan that he cannot live at ease with his own conscience unless he is persecuting somebody. He has never really accepted the Pauline doctrine of the Vicarious Atonement; in theory he adheres to it, of course, but in actual fact his philosophy parallels the Hindu doctrine of Karma—that is to say, the theory that he must atone for his own sins. He diverges from Hinduism in holding that this is not to be accomplished through reincarnation, but by the neater and simpler process described by Samuel Butler—

Compound for sins they are inclined to,
By damning those they have no mind to.

Censorship of books, for example, is an advantageous katharsis for the semi-literate. Discreetly administered, it may compound for a vast deal of lechery actively practiced. Similarly, cropping the ears of comedians undoubtedly affords relief to the humorless who are troubled by knowledge of their own tendency to extortion and excess. As for applying the bastinado to jobholders, that has been regarded as a manifestation of civic virtue from time immemorial, and none is more vociferously in favor of it than the man who never takes the trouble to vote.

It is rather hard on the novelists, the clowns and the clerks, but if their pains and penalties serve to divert the Puritan rage into channels less murderous than those it would otherwise follow, perhaps they suffer in a good cause. In any event, there is reason to believe that their present disability will not be of long duration.

They are, in fact, rather poor substitutes for a real Devil. They matter so little. If literature and dramaturgy were completely abolished, the lives of huge masses of the citizenry would be affected not at all. As for jobholders, nobody has ever proposed to abolish them; the sport is merely to throw the present ones out and put others in their places. It is for the entertainment of seeing them jump that we propose to spend $25,000,000—not for the abolition of the species.

Once we have a Mephistopheles of real stature, thoroughly established as the orthodox object of hatred for all well-conducted persons, nobody will waste much time and energy pursuing mere scriveners and mimes. Present indications are that this consummation is about to be effected. Stalin is obviously to be the archfiend, whose damnation will compound for all our agreeable sins. Presumably it will not be the authentic, but a synthetic Stalin, one of our own design, a creation much better adapted to the purpose than the somewhat prosaic, matter-of-fact individual who inhabits the Kremlin. His construction is in progress now, and apparently nothing will be taken from the biological Stalin and incorporated in the psychological Stalin except the fact that he represents communism.

As for communism itself, it has long since undergone a metamorphosis that would bewilder Karl Marx. Communism, American style, seems to be the theory that whenever the consumer is robbed, the wage earner should have a large cut of the swag. Old-fashioned Americanism, on the contrary, holds that it should be split between management and the stockholders in the proportion of 60-40 (or, as the progressives insist, 80-20) in favor of management. To the suppression of the current form of communism, all right-thinking men are now being summoned as to a Holy War. And it seems likely that they will soon be so violently engaged in it that books, plays and statues, if not jobholders, may hope to escape in the confusion.

This is not, it must be admitted, quite the ideal solution. In the first place, there is a group of eccentrics who hold that the consumer should not be robbed at all. But these are, at best, only a splinter faction—in numbers and influence comparable to the Dukhobors in the religious world. They are not practical men, and most of them are under suspicion of adherence to the memory of F. D. (Antichrist) Roosevelt, so they may be disregarded.

A more serious objection is the fact that the biological Stalin may get the idea that the epithets we apply to the psychological Stalin are intended to apply to him and so grow peevish. This is serious, for he can hit hard. It is authoritatively stated that he already has at least one atomic fission pile now in operation—which means that he has the material of the atomic bomb. All he needs now is to learn how to detonate it, and he will be in position to come over the Arctic and knock Chicago into the middle of Lake Michigan.

The flat truth seems to be that it is by no means certain that the election of Stalin as Devil-in-chief will be an improvement, even though it may mean a better chance for American novelists to wear their stripes vertically, instead of horizontally. As long as soulful descriptions of fornication and funny business men remain, in American opinion, the most flagitious of all crimes, the pursuit of artists, literary and other, might engage the Puritan almost to the exclusion of the pursuit of Russians; and censorship at its bitterest cannot have repercussions that would vaporize Chicago.

But it cannot be. The artist is, at best, but a bush-league Devil—an Azazel, perhaps, or a Mammon, but certainly not a Beelzebub, still less a Lucifer. The proud Puritan spirit is not satisfied to contend with such; our sins cannot be compounded by belaboring anything less than an out-sized, jet-propelled, supersonic Satan, and Stalin seems to be the only candidate in sight who meets the specifications. There is little hazard in the flat prophecy that he is It.

There are, indeed, now as always, certain antinomians who scoff at the necessity of erecting any Devil at all. Having got rid of Hitler, they are content to do without. Puritanism, they point out, is a religion that prevents nobody from sinning, but does prevent anybody from enjoying it. Since America is obviously bent upon sinning in flagrant and scarlet fashion anyhow, they would have us relax and enjoy it. But this is as impractical as the gift of milk which Mr. Wallace did not recommend for the Hottentots. Puritan we are, and Puritan we shall doubtless remain indefinitely. If that involves us in any unnecessary war, the fact is to be regretted. But to suggest that at this late date we should bend our energies to the elimination of Puritanism from our mental make-up is certainly un-American and perhaps unconstitutional. The Devil is dead, and we must speed the search for another.

For until one is found we cannot hope to return to our normal state of terror and misery. At best, we can only be afraid of a moral collapse, which is not much of a terror, and lament the deterioration of manners and taste, which is no real misery. The Devil that censorship belabors is only *papier-mâché*. We need one that can be worked on by the F.B.I., the Ku Klux Klan, the American Legion, and the heroic taxi-drivers of Greenville, South Carolina. Until we find him our lives will be somewhat empty, somehow lacking in savor.

VOGUE, *October 1, 1950*

NOT TO BE TAKEN FOR GRANTED

Take-it-for-granted cuts the tendons and breaks the wrists of warriors who, uninjured, would face and beat Apollyon himself. If the Koreans have awakened us to an understanding of the extent to which old Take-it-for-granted has permeated American life, it may be that they have unintentionally done us a favor. There is no doubt that they have achieved that effect in part. On New Year's Day, 1950, most of us took it for granted that no tenth-rate power would have the colossal cheek to fire on the flag of the United States; or, if one were so insane, we took it for granted that it would be blasted as by Jove's thunderbolt. But by the Fourth of July, less than ten days after Korea exploded, we were not taking that for granted any longer. In military affairs we take nothing for granted now, and that means that the nation's chances of survival are better than they were at the beginning of the year.

The Korean lesson, however, was strictly military and the attitude of Take-it-for-granted extends into many other fields than the military, but some of them not less important. We could take a pretty heavy licking on the battlefield and still remain America. On the other hand, we might conceivably win all our battles and yet, by taking too much for granted, lose the essence of our nationality. For America, the real America, is not a continent, nor a hundred and fifty million people, nor a collection of things. It is a social pattern, created slowly, laboriously, dangerously, through all the four hundred and fifty years since Columbus landed; and the moment you take a social pattern too much for granted, it begins to fade.

We are aware, of course, that the dominant feature of our American pattern is the dignity of the individual; but we tend to forget how that has worked out in the details of our public services—for instance, public schools, public roads, public health, public safety. Other countries—imperial Germany for a conspicuous example—have been concerned with schools, roads, health and safety, but as the enlightened policy of rulers intent upon creating a strong state; that is to say, as a state policy that incidentally worked for the good of the public, not as a public policy that incidentally added to the strength of the state. If you perceive no difference, or no important difference here, you are already taking the American pattern too much for granted.

For this is of its very essence, this is what makes it American. The ideas themselves are very old—education, communication, sanitation and protection came down to us from the childhood of the race. What is new, and what many men once considered poisonous, is the transformation of these ideas into public property.

Schools are as old as history, but the idea of making them public is relatively modern. Caesar built magnificent roads, but primarily for the use of the legions, not that of the public. Ponce de León sought the Fountain of Youth, but for his own benefit; the science of public health in this country is generally regarded as the creation of William H. Welch, who died in 1934. Prehistoric man sought safety when he fled to caves, but the "Health and Morals of Apprentices Act" passed by the English Parliament in 1802 was the first law dealing with what we now regard as public safety.

Each of these in its time was bitterly opposed and not exclusively by avaricious and cruel men. The formidable opposition came from men who were animated by much more respectable motives. More than that, some motives that to modern eyes are extremely questionable were highly respectable when they drove honest men into opposition.

The first institution worthy of the name of a public school in which our language was taught was set up at Sevenoaks, England, in 1432. At that, it was not supported by taxation; it was endowed by a rich grocer and was public in the sense that anyone was admitted and tuition was free.

If you wonder why public schools started so late, go back another forty years and you will find the basis of opposition clearly, if quaintly, expressed in a bit of popular literature, *Peres the Ploughman's Crede,* supposed to have been written about 1394. Here is the way they looked at it then:

> "*Now may every cobbler set his son to school, and every beggar's brat learn from the book, and become either a writer and dwell with a lord, or a false friar to serve the Devil. So that the beggar's brat becomes a bishop, to sit esteemed among the peers of the land, and lords' sons bow down to the good-for-nothings, knights bend to them and crouch full low, and this bishop's father a shoemaker, soiled with grease and his teeth as tattered as a saw with champing leather.*"

A modern American, reading this, may ask himself, but why did the writer hate the cobblers' children so? There is no proof that he did. What animated him was probably not hatred of the lowly, but dread of what he regarded as subversion of the social order. More than that, he was quite right.

Public school did subvert the social order of the fifteenth century. Where he went wrong was in assuming that the change would necessarily be a bad thing.

Today nobody opposes the principle of public schools because they may enable some shoemaker's son to become a bishop. On the contrary, that is precisely their chief merit—they assist men of brains and character to rise to the top regardless of their origin. Yet Horace Greeley, in the middle of the nineteenth century, questioned the justice of taxing the rich to educate the children of the poor, and at the beginning of the twentieth century William Graham Sumner was flatly asserting that the policy not only robbed the rich, but weakened the moral fiber of the poor. These ideas are now outmoded, but there are plenty of people today who still oppose change and still for the same reason—they are convinced that any change must be for the worse. They have a talking point, too, in the fact that any sudden, violent change nearly always is a change for the worse—witness the rise of Communism. What these opponents of change lack is neither honesty nor patriotism, but that combination of imagination, courage, and energy that enables great men to effect changes for the better.

The miracle of America is that for more than three hundred years the views of men with imagination and courage have prevailed oftener than those of the opponents of change. That is why they have attached the adjective "public" to such things as education, transportation, health, and safety. But it is not a thing to be taken for granted; it is a thing to arouse wonder and pride, and when it ceases to arouse them, then the light of the American spirit will begin to flicker and burn low.

It all goes back, of course, to the extraordinary group who, in 1776, attached the word "public" to national affairs. Up to that time the soldier, the statesman, the judge, even the post-rider, went about "the king's business." In England they claim to be doing so to this day, although every rational man knows that the phrase has lost its meaning; it was here that "the king's business" was first frankly converted into "public affairs." Governments, said our formal Declaration, are instituted among men "to effect their safety and happiness" and when any becomes destructive of these ends "it is the right of the people to alter or abolish it."

That's flat. That is an unequivocal assertion that nothing has a right to survive unless it contributes to the safety and happiness of the people. Change, therefore, is not in itself either good or bad; all depends upon the effect of the change on the safety and happiness of the people. But if that is the very mudsill of our government, how can we take anything for granted? Obviously, we can not; and if, nevertheless, we do, by that very act we are altering or abolishing the American system at its foundation. Of all aliens, therefore, the man who complacently takes America for granted is the most un-American. His ancestors may have come with Captain John Smith, or on the *Mayflower,* and the family may have resided continuously in this country ever since; but notwithstanding that he is as un-American as the loudest howler in the Kremlin.

Indeed, he is more so, if there is truth in the Christian doctrine that those who sin against the light are worse than those who sin in darkness.

The Muscovite knows the prodigious success of the American system only by hearsay, which is a kind of evidence too unreliable to be accepted in a court of law; but the American is an eye-witness.

Hearsay evidence, indeed, is never less reliable than when it purports to convey the secret of the United States. For the real success of America is not to be measured by statistics, or caught on photographic film, or even portrayed, except fragmentarily, by the painter's brush or the sculptor's chisel. The event we see is but a reflection of the vastly more important invisible event that produced the visible success. The factories of Detroit, the banks of New York, the stupendous granary of the Mississippi Valley, the limitless food and fabrics that come from the South, the fleets that cover the seas and the flights that darken the skies, the steel-tipped battalions, are all effects, not causes. Made of steel and concrete they may be, adorned with solid marble, with genuine silver and gold, but they are none the less mere shadows caused by the light that glows within the hearts of men and that is the only reality in American success.

That light is the determination to effect the safety and happiness of the people.

True, it is not yet fully realized. Even after these many years it remains smoky and dim by comparison with what it might be. But it is a light and never since the flame first sprang up has it been utterly extinguished. Far as we still remain from paradise, by comparison with other nations we have contrived to effect a considerable degree of safety and an impressive total of happiness. We have talked too much of our high standard of living as the foundation of our safety and happiness, but we have not talked enough about it as the result. No safe and happy people ever failed to raise its standard of living, but it isn't the standard of living that makes a people safe and happy. Nothing does that but courage, imagination, and devotion.

But name, if you please, the calculus by which the statistician can measure creative imagination. Describe the camera so sensitive that it can photograph the high heart. Identify the artist who has portrayed with scientific precision the devotion, not of Washington and Lee, but of the Unknown Soldier, whose name is Legion, and who did nothing noteworthy but die that America—not you and I, but America—might live. Then, but not until then, you will have a documentary report that you might take to the Kremlin to strike the Muscovite dumb.

Until you understand that success yourself, however, you can not hope to transmit it to another; and you will not understand it as long as you take it for granted as something that came about by the mere operation of the laws of nature, as tides ebb and flow regularly, and weeds cover untended soil. You will not understand it until you have some conception of how much "blood, toil, sweat and tears" not merely hundreds of great men but also millions of little men put into the achievement.

More than that, the very basis of understanding is the realization that our forefathers did not do it all. They merely began a process that is for us to continue, and for our children, and grandchildren, and great-grandchildren to carry on through many generations. For, remarkable as has been our success, a government that will provide adequately for the safety and happiness of all the people is far, very far, in the future. Yet that is a minor matter. The point is that we are nearer to it than we were when the country began— if but a handbreadth nearer, yet nearer. The prime necessity is to keep moving—if at a snail's pace, yet moving; and that requires taking nothing for granted.

We have successfully translated the king's business into public affairs. We are in process of translating the good of the realm into public welfare. Incidentally to those processes, but to the admiration of the world, we have attached "public" to such once aristocratic privileges as education, communication, sanitation and individual security. If we have developed none of them perfectly, we have made a beginning with all.

Nevertheless, there lies ahead a task vastly greater than all this, a task on which, after a hundred and seventy-four years of national existence, we have not made a beginning and have not even learned how to make a beginning. It is the task of attaching the adjective "public" to yet another noun, one so vague that it defies exact definition, yet carries enormous significance. That noun is "culture." The Greeks would have said without hesitation— indeed they did say in different words—that "public culture" is a contradiction in terms, because culture is by definition the possession of the elite.

As far as experience goes, the Greeks were right. A civilization in which huge masses of people, a majority of all the people, are capable of understanding and enjoying the highest achievements of the mind and spirit has never been created. But the men who founded this republic specialized in doing what had never been done and therefore was regarded as impossible; and the men who built on that foundation have not yet admitted that the fact that a thing has never been done is a sufficient excuse for an American not to try it.

No vast economy dependent almost entirely on land carriage had ever been created until the American railroad system was built. There is one instance in which we did the impossible in the material world. No collection of thirty million immigrants drawn from every nation under heaven and adhering to every creed on earth had ever been hammered into a solid, orderly, one-language state until this country did it. That is an instance in which we did the impossible in the non-material world.

If there has never been a public culture—a "democratization of culture" if you prefer long words—so far, that has nothing to do with the case. If the thing is desirable for the safety and happiness of the people, our forefathers have left us under an obligation to try it. Without doubt, the old boys have laid out a long, hard, and exacting job for us, but they were hard men—harder than the oak, the hickory, the ironwood of the forests that fell before them, harder than the rocks of the mountains that they split to carry their highways through, harder than the steel they bent and twisted into whatever shape would suit their need, harder than the savage continent that they subdued. It is idle to expect such men to lay out soft tasks for flabby sons. Such men do not think they can have flabby sons.

To build a country in which the humblest citizen may be perfectly safe and happy would be, unquestionably, to build the New Jerusalem. So what? You and I will never live to see it, but what has that to do with it?

Jefferson didn't live to see San Francisco built on the edge of the Pacific, but he started us on our way, and it is up to us, the living, to keep going. We may be well assured that we shall fall by the road, short of the goal, but to fall nearer, if only by inches, than the last man fell, is to share in the success of America.

It is my belief that one of the best Americans ever heard of never saw this country until he was sixty years old. I refer to Pierre Samuel Du Pont de Nemours, born in 1739 and a new arrival here in 1799. I call him a top-flight American, not because he survived and not because he founded a family that even today is not what you would call unknown, but for a remark in a letter he wrote in 1816 to his friend Thomas Jefferson.

In it Du Pont talked of the stupendous amount of work that must be done before the wilderness could be converted into the sort of country that he and Jefferson desired it to be and believed it would be. Nor was the old Physiocrat thinking in terms of powder factories, and paint factories, and plastic factories to be built, and of billions of dollars to be accumulated. He was thinking, rather, of the vastly greater labor involved in cultivating, not the land, but the minds and spirits of men. He was realistic enough to perceive that the magnitude of the task approached infinity; but he was American enough not to let that stop him.

Mon ami, he wrote in a passage striking then and even more striking a hundred and thirty-four years later, *nous sommes des Limaçons et nous avons à monter sur les Cordillières,* "we are snails and we have to climb the Andes" —a pretty shrewd estimate of the job that lies before Americans now if they are to make good the promise of the Declaration. But it was his comment that raised old Pierre Samuel into the ranks of real Americans and gave him his great share in the true success of America. He might reasonably have written, it is hopeless, it is impossible, it is folly to try. But he didn't; instead, he wrote, *Par dieu, il y faut monter,* "By God, we must climb!"

That was not reasonable. It was utterly unreasonable, but it was the kind of unreason that has made and will keep America great.

THE VILLAINS

Every candid mind must admit that the villains of a nation are as certainly a part of the true picture of it as are its heroes. Cato without Nero is not an accurate representation of Rome; Fouché was as much a Frenchman as Bayard; and if Alfred the Great was an English king, so also was John. Even in our own early history we recognize the existence of the deplorable, if only to point up the virtues of the worshipful. Sir William Berkeley who, according to Charles II, "killed more people in that naked country [Virginia] than I did for the murder of my father"; Judge Samuel Sewall, who hanged nineteen Salem witches; and Benedict Arnold are all authentic figures in the pageant of American history and were they omitted the story would be falsified.

It follows that a survey of the record beginning with the year that saw the foundation of *Harper's Magazine* and coming down to the present would be incomplete without some reference to the incidence of scoundrels in that period. Naturally, an account brief enough to be encompassed in a single issue of the magazine cannot waste attention upon scurvy knaves such as can be dealt with adequately by the uniformed police; but on the other hand it cannot ignore villains in the grand manner, malefactors who operated potently and with an air, for these really affected the course of events as ordinary thieves, swindlers, and fanciers of homicide never did.

Such figures must be very conspicuous indeed, and it would seem that pointing them out should be the simplest of tasks; but an element enters that complicates the apparent simplicity of the operation. It is the influence of geography. The period under consideration begins in 1850, and by 1850 the United States was a continental domain. Texas, California, and Oregon had all been acquired and the writ of the Supreme Court ran from the Lake of the Woods southeastward to Key West and southwestward to San Diego, that is to say, from the sub-arctic to the sub-tropic in mundane geography, and in the spiritual realm from Calvinism to the Spanish Inquisition.

Now it is a matter of common knowledge that villainy, like oranges and barley, is greatly affected by climatic conditions, and if the area under consideration is one with a wide climatic range, it is difficult to find a villain who is equally villainous in all parts of that area. Which of the great rogues of European history appeared equally scoundrelly in every corner of Europe? Madrid's loathsome pirate, Drake, was Sir Francis, the ornament of Elizabeth's court, in London. Peter of Russia, indistinguishable from Shaitan in Constantinople, was an interesting and industrious ship carpenter in Holland. In England prior to 1815 Napoleon was a villain, net, but only there; everywhere else he oscillated with bewildering speed between ogre and hero.

Since 1850 the United States in both geography and demography has resembled Europe more closely than it has resembled any single European country; hence our estimation of villains is European, rather than English, or French, or German, which is another way of saying that it is somewhat wavering and uncertain.

This was brought home to me forcibly some years ago when I, born and bred in North Carolina, compared notes in Baltimore with another newspaper scrivener born and bred in Chicago. He remarked that when he first crossed Mount Vernon Place, the *Siegesallee* of the Maryland city, and on the pedestal of a statue there read the name, "Roger B. Taney," he all but fainted. He would as soon have expected to see a statue of Benedict Arnold. I had just returned from my first visit to Boston, and I understood his emotion; for on Boston Common I had seen a bronze figure representing Charles Sumner, and in a respectable city I should as soon have expected to find a statue of Beelzebub.

It is evident, then, that even as the barley which flourishes in the country around Chicago and much farther north is hardly worth cultivating in the heat of Alabama, so the villainy of the Chief Justice who delivered the Dred Scott decision, strong in Illinois, droops and fails below the Mason and Dixon Line; while the villainy of Charles Sumner can be cultivated in Massachusetts only under artificial conditions, as the oranges that thrive prodigiously in Florida can be grown only under glass in Boston.

Time is another variable that complicates the calculus of villainy in a specimen of any real size. Within my own lifetime, for example, I have seen Woodrow Wilson transmogrified from a demigod into a demon and back into a demigod again, and that within the two decades between 1920 and 1940. In fact, I have seen faster metamorphoses on a smaller scale; it was in 1920 that H. L. Mencken published the second volume of his *Prejudices,* containing the blistering essay, "The Sahara of the Bozart," that made him everywhere below the thirty-seventh parallel the damnedest villain since William Tecumseh Sherman. But that essay heralded, if it did not touch off, a tremendous burst of intellectual production in Dixie which did the region a lot of good; so when Mencken ventured into the South only about six years later his journey became a sort of Roman triumph, beginning with the enthusiasm in Richmond and at the University of North Carolina, and rising to a thunderous climax at New Orleans, where they made him an honorary fire chief and photographed him wearing a large, white fireman's hat. Mencken is the only literary figure of the past century who has collected denunciations that fill an entire volume; so if he rates no higher than a part-time, temporary villain, it is plainly futile to search further among men of letters.

But not even Mencken changed character as rapidly as the one other type whose lightning-like descent to Avernus is remembered by men still in their thirties. In times past the word "banker" before a man's name was not a mere designation; it was an honorific, easily ranking with the French *"de"* or the German *"von"* and approaching in grandeur the English *"sir."* But in the month of October, "the lonesome October" 1929, a "most immemorial year," the word "banker" became practically overnight an epithet so opprobrious that calling a Frenchman a species of camel or a German a pig-dog was hardly worse than hurling "banker" at an American. Even today, twenty years later, although the word has lost its opprobrium, it is still no more than a common noun, denuded of all reverential associations—a classical demonstration of the thinness of the line that separates sanctity from villainy.

Triangulation of an American villain of impressive size is thus an intricate and perplexing operation. It requires a base line not only of known altitude, but also of known latitude and known date. It is quite impossible to measure Thaddeus Stevens, for example, unless it is known whether you are viewing him from the angle of 1869 or that of 1949. The Warren G. Harding of 1921 is obviously not in the same category as the Harding of 1925.

It follows that, disregarding certain persons of murderous and larcenous proclivities from Jesse James to Al Capone, it is difficult to find conspicuous American figures of whom one can say flatly, as Dr. Sidney Painter says in his recently-published life of King John, "he was definitely a bad man." Between 1850 and 1950 the two worst Presidents undoubtedly were Grant and Harding. One is safe in saying that they were bad Presidents; but to say that they were bad men is not merely questionable, it is nonsensical. No doubt Grant had a weakness for bottles and Harding for belles, but villainy, like ambition, "should be made of sterner stuff." When lame Talleyrand brought Fouché into the audience chamber to be presented to the Bourbon king, Chateaubriand, noting how the Prince leaned heavily on the policeman's arm, could remark, "I seemed to see Vice advancing, supported by Crime." No scene in American history since 1850 comes as close to justifying such a remark by an intelligent man, not even when Albert B. Fall went nosing into Woodrow Wilson's sick-room.

Yet, subject to the caveat that American villains are not equally villainous when viewed from different angles, it is possible to arrange the deplorables of the past century in interesting classifications, based first on their intrinsic nature and second on their puissance, as measured by the damage they did to the country.

In considering their generic qualities one admission may as well be stated at once. We have never yet produced a scoundrel who made a real contribution to the refinement of vice, as the Roman emperor Caligula is supposed to have been an ingenious contriver of new perversions, or as the Borgias are said to have developed the art of poisoning, or as Adolf Hitler contrived the new crime of genocide. There is extant a writing attributed to Benjamin Franklin which the prudish have construed as a defense of gerontophilia, but it is in fact no more than a discourse on social manners and customs with some observations on expedience in conforming to them. The American villain is, in comparison with classical and even modern European and Asiatic models, somewhat pallid. Lust plays a relatively unimportant part in his make-up, and sloth hardly any. Pride is usually confined to the narrow limits of personal vanity and gluttony is negligible. Of the seven deadly sins covetousness, anger, and envy are his specialties, if covetousness be understood to cover ambition, and anger, vindictiveness.

  Harper's Magazine was barely two years old before three who may be called the last of the truly statuesque American historical figures died. These were John C. Calhoun, Daniel Webster, and Henry Clay. We have had greater men since, but even Abraham Lincoln was not as monumental during his lifetime as these were, and as John Adams and the Virginia Dynasty were before them. It follows that whatever they did was colossal and, if bad, was worse than anything that latter-day statesmen could perpetrate. For instance, Webster's Seventh of March speech was regarded in New England as a betrayal of such proportions that Whittier spoke of

> _A bright soul driven_
> _Fiend-goaded, down the endless dark,_
> _From hope and heaven!_

an anguished shriek that could hardly be extorted from a New England poet today were the Honorable Harry S. Truman caught down on his knees shooting craps with Joseph Stalin.

  Clay's deal with John Quincy Adams to keep Andrew Jackson out of the Presidency and Calhoun's nullification project were comparable in magnitude. As viewed from the appropriate angle, these were villainies in the grand manner. True, below the Potomac the Seventh of March speech made Webster a hero of tremendous dimensions; and in the perspective of a hundred years it is apparent that its support of the Compromise of 1850 postponed the Civil War and perhaps thereby saved the Union, since time was working against the South. Clay's deal made him a hero in New England and gave the country a nearly-great President in the younger Adams. Nullification made Calhoun immortal in the South and, curiously, has made him something of a national hero since 1932 among those intellectuals who are desperate for effective arguments against the welfare state.

  The Civil War that burst when _Harper's Magazine_ was ten years old stands out in history as the greatest of our national tragedies, and the violent demagogues on both sides who helped precipitate it were highly undesirable citizens, but they were, as a rule, so small that it is difficult for the historian to descry them without a magnifying glass. John Brown, indeed, managed to achieve lasting fame in the same way that Horst Wessel did, to wit, by getting himself hanged for good and sufficient reasons; but Robert Barnwell Rhett, just as vicious if less energetic, on the other side, is known only to historians and other students of political microbiology.

  The men who actually fought the war were long ago acquitted of anything worse than using bad logic in deciding a problem involving divided loyalties. Indeed, the losing side, which normally furnishes the villains in any great revolt, has given us our nearest approximation to Arthur, the Blameless King, in Robert E. Lee; and the brilliance of his military record is a source of American pride although the proud American may be from Minnesota instead of Georgia. Even the momentary victims of war-born fury are now recognized as victims; fair-minded Northerners are ashamed that leg-irons were fastened upon Jefferson Davis, as fair-minded Southerners are ashamed of what their sharp-tongued grandmothers said about Sherman.

The quarter-century following the Civil War is generally accounted bad, so bad that Claude G. Bowers gave his book about it the title, *The Tragic Era.* It was during this period that we elected Grant to the Presidency and almost elected James G. Blaine. It was the time of the Credit Mobilier and the railroad buccaneers, the incubation period of the great trusts. It was the time when the natural resources of the country were expropriated with an effrontery unequaled before or since. It was the time when the corruption of the cities of the Eastern seaboard reached its nadir, and when the legitimate aspirations of the working classes were crushed with a brutal ferocity unparalleled in our history. It would seem logical, therefore, to look to this period for examples of towering villainy, if they are to be found at all.

Villains there were, in plenty, and if theft be accounted the acme of villainy some of them were towering. The cities, the states, and the nation were robbed with brazen recklessness; small business men were stripped of all they had and tossed into the almshouse, and the robbers called it the operation of a sound economy. Labor was robbed of its elementary rights and the robbers had the ineffable gall to name the robbing Christian piety, as when Rockefeller said God gave him the money he extracted from his competitors. Some of them bought judges and prosecuting attorneys. Some of them bought Congressmen on the hoof, as the pork-packers bought swine in Chicago, checking them not by name but by the number purchased.

In the cities, bosses like Tweed, of New York, regimented the ignorant and the poor, and by means of their votes put into municipal offices creatures who looted the public treasury of multiplied millions. At the same time they revived the ancient evil of the sale of indulgences, but this time on the mundane level; they sold immunity from prosecution to gamblers, prostitutes, dive-keepers, and gangsters, and also to "respectable" business men who wished to evade the law for profit.

In the single department of thievery this was truly prodigious, but as a part of the wide realm of sin it may be called rather narrow specialization. Even as a financial operation it is puny by comparison with the Praetorian Guards' putting the whole Roman Empire up at auction, or the course of Warwick in delivering all England to one side or the other as suited his personal advantage. The mightiest of the "malefactors of great wealth" in the Tragic Era could not sell the United States bodily.

Nor could they, as the event proved, do it irreparable damage. This is not to be written down to their credit, for they did their worst. But while the outcome of their operations does not affect their moral quality, it does have a very definitive effect on their stature as villains. The man who steals milk bottles may be as wicked as the man who steals a bank, but he is not as important. Oakes Ames, for example, may have stolen $20,000,000 in the Credit Mobilier scheme between 1867 and 1872; in the abstract this looks enormous, but in the concrete situation it shrinks in importance, because his scheme did get the Union Pacific Railroad built, and the existence of a transcontinental line was so vastly important that the loss of $20,000,000 in its construction counts hardly more than the pilfering of milk bottles counts in the dairy business. Hence, even if all that is said against him is true, Ames is an object of contempt, rather than of terror, not to be compared, for instance, to John Law, whose Mississippi Bubble all but wrecked France in the eighteenth century, or even to Serge Alexandre Stavisky, whose pawnshop swindle almost wrecked it again in the twentieth.

This curious immunity to the attacks of thieves is strikingly exemplified in the history of the cities for the past century. There is hardly one that has not been pillaged by crooked politicians at some time since 1850; and there is hardly one in which the work of the pillagers has not turned out to be in some way profitable to the town. For blatant and shameless criminality it is hard to beat the record of the Tweed ring in New York between 1850 and 1875. Their effect on public morals was utterly destructive, but their effect on public finance was not. Tweed got a $40,000 bribe in stock of the corporation for getting the Brooklyn Bridge project approved, and a very much larger rake-off in connection with the purchase of the real estate that now comprises Central Park. In twenty-five years the Tweed ring certainly stole $30,000,000 and some observers have estimated the loot at seven times that much; but today the value of the park property alone is more than all the gang stole, to say nothing of the bridge and a dozen other public improvements that the Tweed ring put through. For emphasis let it be repeated— this is no credit to Tweed; but it does have the effect of reducing him from the status of a disaster to the status of a petty annoyance to the city of New York.

It is possible to argue with some plausibility that such characters as Oakes Ames, Tweed, and the industrial and financial buccaneers were necessary to the country and worth more than they cost—more, at least, than their cost in money. In the matter of the transcontinental railroads, for example, it is fairly evident that the gentry who were anxious to line their own pockets speeded up completion of the roads anywhere from ten to twenty years. Theoretically, the roads might have been built by honest men; but practically the honest men who originated the enterprises failed to carry them through. Crooks who saw the possibility of vast profits for themselves supplied the driving energy requisite for the last great effort.

Similarly, in the cities the large public improvements should have been made by honest men; but the history of such improvements shows that honest men almost invariably opposed their making. Our social consciousness was not sufficiently developed for us to realize the civic necessity of parks, playgrounds, boulevards, or even, in many places, adequate water supply and sanitary systems. The crooks did not appreciate that necessity any more than the honest men, but they did see in large public works opportunity for large graft, so they heartily favored the improvement of cities and thereby contributed, however unwittingly, to the health, safety, and convenience of all the people. But when a man's work proves, on the whole, beneficial to the public, there is a certain incongruity in describing him as a villain in the grand manner.

Whether one considers the building of the railroads, of the industrial system, or of the cities, it is doubtful that the land pirates were, on balance, an affliction. The real affliction was the inertia, due to lack of imagination, of the honest majority. Had we been socially alert, there would have been no need of crooks; but we were lethargic, almost comatose. Like strychnine in certain cardiac conditions, the poison that the robber barons injected served as a stimulant whose toxic effects were inconsiderable by comparison with the value of the reaction it produced.

It is not to be denied that the United States has suffered lasting hurts in the years since 1850; but the injuries that are felt for generations after their infliction are not financial. They are injuries to the mind and the spirit, not to the pocketbook. It was not the loss of a certain amount of oil that comprised the damage that Albert B. Fall inflicted upon the country; it would have been better to lose ten times as much oil than to lose our former confidence that the President's Cabinet, while it may sometimes be incompetent, or even silly, is never crooked. Huey Long was perhaps the most dangerous demagogue that the country has produced; but he was dangerous not because his gang stole so much in Louisiana, but because he stimulated the latent appetite for fascism in all parts of the country. As an individual, Fall never commanded an impressive following; at most he was but a bush-league rascal; but Long came close to being a villain in the grand manner, one comparable to Bloody Mary with a potential capacity to swell to something like the size of Hitler. Where the pint-size rogues stole money, he had the ability to steal reason and judgment from the minds of men, leaving them furnished with nothing but prejudice and emotion, mostly hate.

That sort of theft is, in fact, the only kind that has had any lasting influence upon the course of American history; so the men who have perpetrated it would seem to be the only kind of villains worthy of serious notice by history. But as one surveys the years since 1850 an anomaly becomes apparent. The men who have embezzled our good sense and substituted for it hatred, suspicion, distrust, and cynicism have only in rare instances been villains by any dictionary definition of the word. Far more frequently they have been holy men, and some of them are enshrined near the top of the secular hagiology.

Consider, for example, the evils that still survive as legacies of the Civil War. The slaughter and destruction perpetrated by Grant and Lee were repaired and forgotten, long ago. The never-dying evils were the hatreds and prejudices that attended the conflict and these were only to a small extent the work of the soldiers. The men in uniform had little to do with establishing the conviction, on one side, that the institution of slavery was the deliberate choice of wicked men, and, on the other, that the tariff was not an economic policy, but one step in an infamous project to obliterate the South as Hitler hoped to obliterate Poland. Yet these convictions were the bases of a cold war that lasted for many years and that has not been entirely eliminated to this day, as witness the frequent recourse to filibustering by the Southern bloc in the United States Senate.

Incidentally, it is worthy of passing notice that the commercial and industrial pirates of the Tragic Era after the Civil War did more lasting damage by debauching politics than by looting the public till. Their wholesale purchase of official and legislative cattle reduced the standard of public service for many years and set up in the minds of the voters a pernicious tolerance of official misconduct of which we can still find lingering traces. Yet it was precisely this, the most anti-social act of which they were guilty, that they could most easily justify in their own minds. They bought judges, legislators, and Congressmen lavishly, yes; but only, as they thought, to prevent their being bought by some villain of a deeper dye. Hence they could quite consistently regard their purchases as measures of public safety.

Among calamities below the level of high tragedy one of the most unfortunate which the nation suffered between 1850 and 1950 was the fourteen years' orgy of criminality inaugurated by adoption of the prohibition amendment. Yet the prohibition movement was semi-religious from the start. After it gained some headway it attracted numbers of spectacular hypocrites, as any movement that is plainly succeeding is bound to do; but in general the prohibitionists were pious, sincere, and rigidly moral. Their aim, like that of the abolitionists, was to do good.

The next great tragedy after the Civil War was the collapse of the moral hegemony this nation attained in 1918. The emasculation and eventual destruction of the League of Nations was but one incident in the larger tragedy of the defeat of the world's hope that in democracy it had discovered a method of government really capable of effecting the safety and happiness of the people. Who was responsible is still a matter of dispute, but the thing happened, and once it had happened the one possible avenue of escape from the second world war was definitely closed.

This country was not solely responsible for the disaster, but it bears a large share of the responsibility, and as far as our part is concerned there are but two possible explanations. One is that the disaster was attributable to the intransigence of Woodrow Wilson; the other is that it flowered from the conspiracy of Theodore Roosevelt and Henry Cabot Lodge, Sr., who planned, before Wilson had reached Paris, to defeat any treaty that he might bring back.

Take your choice; but no matter which alternative you prefer, or even if you embrace both, you are confronted by the fact that the second most dreadful blow the country suffered in the century just past was struck, not by any villain, but by gentlemen of the highest character, whose purpose was to do good.

This leaves the arrant rogues looking somewhat ineffective, which calls for explanation. The most plausible theory is based on the assumption that scoundrelism is a product of social decomposition, as methane is of physical rot. To produce marsh gas naturally in any considerable quantity you must have a cesspool of large dimensions; similarly, to produce a really gigantic villain you need a moral cesspool of formidable extent, and we have had none. Our stink-holes have all been relatively small.

Tweed, for example, was the product of frightful social and economic conditions among the poor of New York City—conditions repeated on a smaller scale in smaller cities and productive of smaller Tweeds. But the slums at that time were urban and the country was predominantly rural, so not even Tweed became a national menace. We have not yet had nation-wide conditions bad enough to produce a Robespierre, a Hitler, or a Mussolini. Huey Long, our nearest approach to the type, came from a state admittedly among the most backward in the Union as far as social services to the people are concerned; and he flourished at a time when the whole country was suffering under an economic collapse that bore hardest upon the poor. But we managed to pull out of the Depression before he, or any of his type, could become highly dangerous. So far, we have always managed to clean up the rotten spots before they had poisoned the whole body politic sufficiently to produce a rogue who would stand among the giants of his breed.

Villainy, however, is determined largely by whether you are on the sending or receiving end. What does me serious and lasting injury I cannot regard as just and right, irrespective of motives. If our worst national disasters are attributable to the pious and respectable—not a uniquely American experience, for Robespierre was justly called "The Incorruptible"—it is plainly relevant to the discussion to examine the calamitous sanctified, to search among secessionists, abolitionists, prohibitionists, and isolationists for some common factor other than the pure desire to do good. There must be some one element present in characters apparently as completely diverse as Calhoun, Sumner, Garrison, Bryan, and Borah.

One comes to mind immediately—they all distrusted the processes of democracy. This charge brought against Bryan, of all people, will evoke indignant and astonished denials, but the charge stands. The Commoner did, indeed, trust the people in all matters strictly political, but he had no faith whatever in their capacity in the moral realm. There he believed in the doctrine of the Elect to whom the truth was delivered and whose duty it is to make it prevail, regardless of the opinions of the unregenerate. Darwinians and wine-bibbers he regarded not as merely mistaken, but as a stiff-necked and forward generation, to be corrected by the rod.

So it was with the others. Each was so certain of the righteousness of his own judgment that he attributed moral turpitude to any contrary judgment. However much he might profess humility, he held himself or, if not himself at least his sect, his faction, his cause as the sole repository of truth. He had never heeded the advice of Cromwell to the Scotch Presbyterians: "I beseech you, brethren, that you pray God to show you that it is possible for you to be mistaken."

It is as certain as anything can be that the man of fixed moral principles is the very bedrock on which civilization rests. But there is a difference, sometimes hard to see yet immensely important, between believing that one's own principles are right and drawing the inference that the principles of all others are wrong and should be extirpated. It is precisely this difference that furnishes the moral basis for majority rule; the genuine democrat concedes not only that the other fellow has a right to his opinion, but that he actually does right in maintaining that opinion by every argument that he can bring to its support. To put down opinion by employing terror, whether it be fear of the hangman or fear of hell, is to repudiate the democratic process, to draw aside from true Americanism and to adhere in some measure to some form of the heresy of the *Herrenvolk*.

Twenty centuries ago Marcus Aurelius was very emphatic on this point. "He is an abscess on the universe," said the imperial philosopher, "who withdraws and separates himself from the reason of our common nature through being displeased with the things which happen; . . . he is a piece rent asunder from the state who tears his own soul from that of reasonable animals."

Marcus Aurelius, however, was an emperor. He made the law, and what he said went. Smaller men must be more prudent. Certainly an abscess on the universe is a villainous thing, but an assertion that to be false to the inner spirit of democracy is, in a leader, the greatest villainy that can be perpetrated on his people, is a stiffer commination than it is becoming for us to utter. It drags one into metaphysical speculations regarding motives and guilt or innocence before God.

So let no inferences be drawn. Let nothing more go on the record than the obvious truth that the lesson of the century since 1850 is something of a paradox; for it plainly implies that within the period the damned rascals have done us little harm, but the holy terrors have very nearly been our ruin.

abridged from INCREDIBLE TALE: THE ODYSSEY OF THE AVERAGE AMERICAN
IN THE LAST HALF-CENTURY, *1950*

ONE ABIDES

He Has Lived

W hat, then, is the American, this new man?" asked French Crèvecoeur in 1782, and wrote a whole volume without framing any very definite answer. In Crèvecoeur's time this new man was, in fact, faith, as Saint Paul described it: "the substance of things hoped for, the evidence of things not seen." A hundred and sixty-eight years later there is not much more to be said. The American is certainly not yet what every liberal believes he may be, and hopes he will be. All hands agree that he is the evidence of things not seen; but what sort of things is the subject of endless debate.

Yet Crèvecoeur really answered his question in asking it. If the American is a new man, it necessarily follows that he cannot fit into any frame of old ideas. If he could, he would be new only in the sense that the last Ford off the assembly line is newer than the one just ahead of it. When Crèvecoeur said "new" he meant "different"; and whatever is different is pretty sure to puzzle many minds and to disappoint some.

Perhaps the genuine liberal has more cause to be apprehensive than anyone else, for he envisages not only the damage that may be incurred but the opportunity that may be missed if the average American proves incapable of coping with the situation in which he finds himself as the century enters its second half.

Consider, then, the case of a man born in 1920. He has known no other century but this. He has known no other international situation than war, hot or cold, or at best an armed truce. His generation is now entering the thirties; it is beginning to be effective in public affairs, but the chief burden of responsibility will not fall upon it for some years. Yet the time is close; another decade, and these will be the men who run the United States. Have their immediate predecessors anything significant to say to them, either of warning or of encouragement? Does the incredible tale of the past half-century really mean anything, or is it "a tale told by an idiot, full of sound and fury, signifying nothing"?

Surely, there is one profoundly significant remark that the ordinary American of fifty can make to the ordinary American of thirty; it is the remark of the Abbé Sieyès: "I survived."

Sieyès was in Paris during the Reign of Terror; and that gives to his laconic statement immense significance. The ordinary American is here—still relatively free, still the final authority in public affairs, still better fed, better clothed, and better housed than the common man in any other country. If he has been here since 1900, the mere fact that he has survived means a great deal; for twice within that period a coalition of empires has risen against him to beat his political system down, once his economic system crashed about his ears, practically every year some part of his social system has had to be remodeled and rebuilt, and for the past five years his form of government, his economy, and his faith have been sternly and relentlessly challenged by the most redoubtable foreign power in existence. Yet he survives.

No great hero is this average American who is now about to turn over his authority and his responsibility to younger men, but no one can question his power of endurance. He has not proved himself master of time and circumstance. He has not proved himself master of his own folly and weakness, but has lost much blood and treasure through both. He has not discovered the answer to any of the governmental problems that worried Solon and have continued to worry rulers ever since. He has found no direct avenue to the good life, but has blundered into countless blind alleys.

Nevertheless, he has attained a certain distinction, if only the second-rate kind that has preserved Sieyès' fame. He has taken the most terrific battering, and by long odds, to which the nation was ever subjected, and he has survived. His life has been attacked by armed enemies, his living has been attacked by impersonal economic forces, his moral certainties have been wrecked by science, art, philosophy and, above all, by time and change, yet he has survived—scarred, charred, maimed, perhaps, but recognizably the same.

If the rising generation is made of material as durable—mentally, morally and physically—there is little justification for the prophecies of doom which have been so frequent recently.

But two items of the hard-won wisdom of the first half of the century the new generation must preserve if an easier time is to bear fruit in greater accomplishments. One is the fact that the efforts of great heroes to save, and of great villains to destroy, the American people are both ineffectual. The passing generation has seen four of the greatest, Wilson, Lenin, Roosevelt, Stalin, and three of the most menacing, Hitler, Mussolini, Tojo, but so much of American civilization as has been salvaged has been saved by the American people; and so much as has been lost, has been lost, for the most part, by their folly.

For they alone endure. Wilson could lead us to a high peak of rational, mature thinking about the art of government, but he died, and we swiftly descended into the Slough of Despond. Roosevelt could lead us to another; but he died, too, and if we do not descend again, it will be because the common people learned something from the first experience.

The second item of wisdom wrung from the past fifty years is that the way out of trouble is to wade straight through, not to try to turn back. We tried turning back after 1918, and again after 1929, and the result both times was confusion worse confounded. In 1945 we could not turn back because Stalin stood in the way; and by 1950 we were no worse off than we were in 1945, and in some ways better off. In Mommsen's phrase, "courage to grasp the hand which beckons to them out of the darkness of the future, and to follow it they know not whither," seems to have paid off, at least reasonably well.

This new man, then, this American, may not be remarkable at all for his beauty, or his wisdom, or his puissance; but he is unquestionably remarkable for his durability. He is a standing encouragement to believe that the worst has already happened, yet here we are; and in the next half-century, that can certainly not be fiercer, and may be far milder, it is impossible to fix a limit on what we may become. So when the next great man appears, he may outstrip all his predecessors, having better followers at his back.

But that is speculation. What is indisputable fact is that the ordinary American who is now fifty or more has been somewhere and seen something. He has escaped the most deplorable of all fates—to be born, to subsist for many years, and then to die without ever having really lived.

ROMANCE AND MR. BABBITT

It is blood-curdling even to imagine the rage of Sinclair Lewis if anyone had intimated to him that his basic philosophy was drawn from *A Child's Garden of Verses*. Yet in the opening chapter of *Babbitt*, describing early morning in Zenith when Mr. Babbitt rose, showered, shaved, dressed, breakfasted and drove to his office, taking a childish and innocent pride in the deftness with which he parked his Buick in a narrow space, there is a passage describing what else had happened in Zenith during the night just past—birth, death, triumph, calamity, high tragedy, and crashing melodrama when a drab, full of cocaine, drew a pistol from her handbag and casually shot her lover across the table. All this was unknown to Mr. Babbitt and would not have interested him much if it had been known. What interested him was the skill with which he parked his car.

Mr. Babbitt was, on the whole, an unhappy man and the insertion of this passage is an intimation of why he was unhappy. He was bored, and he was bored because he didn't know what was going on right under his nose. Without benefit of rhyme, Lewis was reasserting:

The world is so full of a number of things,
I'm sure we should all be as happy as kings.

Probably he would never have said "happy," but he would have said "interested," which is as close an approach to happiness as a realist is likely to make. Lewis was a crusader against dullness and an assault upon dullness is the significance of Stevenson's couplet.

Lewis turned out 21 books—sufficient evidence that he wrote a lot of bilge. A man who wrote 21 masterpieces would be four or five ahead of William Shakespeare. But *Main Street, Babbitt, Arrowsmith, Elmer Gantry* and *Dodsworth* were social documents with a definite effect upon public opinion at the time; and they are likely to remain a permanent part of the social history of the United States. A man who has produced five novels that really meant something to his own generation is an extraordinary man indeed, one sure to be remembered for a long time.

The craftsmanship of these books is a matter of interest mainly to professors of English literature and to aspiring novelists. Lewis observed exactly, reported accurately, and checked, rechecked, compared and verified with the diligence of the dreariest German pedant who ever pursued a subjunctive through nine centuries and 900 volumes. But this was part of the mechanics of his trade. He worked hard. He worked harder than most of us can even conceive of working. But it wasn't industry that won him the Nobel prize. It wasn't industry that made him master of the American imagination for a decade or so.

The magic was an eloquence that arose from a source deeper than syntax and the rules of prosody. Because everyone recognized his own thoughts and his own words in the pages of Sinclair Lewis he was dubbed a realist, and some quirk of the literary mind holds that to be the antithesis of romanticist. But the terms are not exclusive. *Tom Sawyer* was realism. *David Harum* was realism. *Main Street* reported the idiosyncracies of Gopher Prairie no more faithfully than those two books recorded the quirks and oddities of Missouri and upstate New York. But because they are placid and good-humored we list them in a different category.

Lewis was unhappy, and was indignant because he was unhappy. His indignation betrays his essential romanticism. If he had been a realist of the stripe of, say, Montaigne, he might have been just as unhappy, but he would not have been indignant about it, because he would have realized that happiness is impossible anyhow. But this admission is a psychological impossibility to a 100-percent American like Lewis. In the oldest state document issued by us as a nation we committed ourselves to "the pursuit of happiness," and pursue it we must.

Lewis proclaimed—and piled up mountains of evidence to prove—that Americans are unhappy largely by their own fault. Their stupidity renders them incapable of seeing in which direction true happiness lies. Their cowardice renders them incapable of grasping happiness when it is within their reach. Their blind greed sends them chasing after some will-o'-the-wisp that leads them into the mire. All this the average American must admit is very true. There was nothing in the assertion that came into collision with his most profound conviction, so he accepted Lewis as a prophet—of the order of Jeremiah, no doubt, but a prophet.

For he never fell into the heresy of denying that happiness exists *in posse*. On the contrary, in *Arrowsmith* he portrayed its attainment. Young Dr. Arrowsmith went after it the hard way, to be sure, and the happiness of dis- covering what makes a man's liver do what it does is a stern, austere form of happiness that does not appeal to many of us. Nevertheless, it is con- ceivable; and even a Babbitt will readily grant that the happiness of a scientific mind is not necessarily that of a realtor. The point is that by the exercise of indomitable will power Arrowsmith pursued happiness and eventually over- took it. In the assumption that this is possible the book is American to the core.

This was the essence of the literary revolt of the twenties, of which Sinclair Lewis was one of the great chiefs. The whole crew denounced Ameri- cans furiously, and the public loved it, to the amazement of those who over- looked the fact that Americans were being denounced, but not the American ideal. We were, in fact, unhappy, and to be told that it was our own fault was quite bearable; what would have been unbearable was to be told that there is no happiness, and that pursuit of it is utterly vain. If we are unhappy because we are stupid and blind, then to develop intelligence and vision is a way out—difficult, indeed, and a faint hope, but nevertheless possible and a hope.

In that they did not proclaim the impossibility and deny the hope the writers of the twenties remained well within the line of American literary tradition. Their thunderous assaults upon the frauds and imbecilities, the hypocrisies and quackeries of their time were reformist, not revolutionary; and the mood of America has been reformist most of the time since its beginning.

Where Sinclair Lewis will eventually stand in the hierarchy of American letters is not for this generation to decide, but there is no doubt that *Main Street, Babbitt,* and, I think, *Arrowsmith* will survive, if only as *genre* pictures. It is my own belief that future generations will find in them a good deal more, but that may be a prejudiced view because I believe that the American philosophy of life is going to have a long run. We are not ready for quietism. We still believe that when something is wrong, something can be done about it; and a raucous voice bawling out the wrong is not yet to us mere sound and fury, but a trumpet blast summoning the mighty men of valor to stand to their arms.

THE NEW REPUBLIC, "The Superficial Aspect" column, *March 15, 1954*

MUDSLINGING AS A FINE ART

A friend, agitated by the extravagancies he has been reading in the public prints, asks if we have really sunk to a new low in political debate, or if it only seems so because we have forgotten the quality of the mud slung in earlier days. My first impulse was to say No, because I had just been reading Nathan Schachner's book on the Founding Fathers, which brought to mind such characters as Bache, Fenno, Freneau and Dwight—not Timothy, president of Yale, but Theodore, his brother—all of whom had a mastery of billingsgate hardly approached by moderns.

These accused George Washington of plotting the subversion of the republic, Alexander Hamilton of embezzling public funds, and Thomas Jefferson of inaugurating the nationalization of women, which is pretty copious mud-slinging. But they were not Cabinet members, Governors or members of Congress. They were merely newspaper editors, so it is questionable that their mouthings should be compared with the utterances of public officials.

The acme of bitterness in official circles came somewhat later. The two greatest masters of vituperation in American political history were John Randolph of Roanoke and Charles Sumner; but both were something more than poisonous—both were learned and witty. Sumner's characterization of dwarfish Stephen A. Douglas as "a noisome, squat, and nameless animal" had some traces of imagination; and his comparison of Sen. A. P. Butler's defense of slavery to intimacy with a repulsive "harlot, chaste in his sight," while certainly low, was meant to be strictly metaphorical.

The supreme example of that sort of thing is, of course, what John Randolph laid on Edward Livingston: "He is a man of splendid abilities, but utterly corrupt. Like rotten mackerel by moonlight, he shines and stinks." But it took a wit to make that comparison. Even better was his comment when Richard Rush was made Secretary of the Treasury: "Never were abilities so much below mediocrity so well rewarded; no, not when Caligula's horse was made consul." That, though, was perhaps borrowed. Randolph was strictly on his own when he made the attack that provoked the duel—his description of the tie between John Quincy Adams and Henry Clay as "the coalition of Blifil and Black George—the combination, unheard of till then, of the puritan with the blackleg." This was tantamount to an assertion that Clay cheated at cards, which was infamous—but brilliantly put.

There is no suggestion of wit, however, in Senator Jenner's description of General George C. Marshall as "an eager front man for traitors," and "a living lie." There is no wit in Senator McCarthy's description of five Democratic Administrations as "20 years of treason." There is no wit in the slanderous charges brought against Dean Acheson. They are as dull as they are venomous, perpetrated by men who could never come within miles of Randolph's description of two members of Congress as "a Wright always wrong and a Rea without light."

It is regrettable, but true that this world will forgive a great deal to a man who amuses it. Our indignation at an outrageous utterance is always somewhat blunted if the thing is smart; who, for instance, would pursue with righteous wrath the man who said that Adlai Stevenson's motto is, "I'd rather be bright than President?"

So while it is true that American political debate wallowed in the gutter a hundred and fifty years ago, it is also true that the worst of the guttersnipes were private individuals, not representative of any constituency. And while it is true that debate a hundred years ago was fully as venomous as it is today, it is also true that the most venomous of the debaters sparkled, and sparkling slander is less offensive than stupid slander, even when it is uttered by a man in an official position.

Thus it would seem that the modern tone of speakers in public office, being merely ruffianly without wit, is a notch lower than anything that has preceded it. Randolph once excused a descent into sheer ranting by a theatrical simile: "There must be something for the shilling gallery as well as the pit." The inferiority of his modern successors is that they have everything for the shilling gallery and nothing for the pit.

It is to be feared that my friend's agitation is justified. We really have hit a new low when the orations discharged in the halls of Congress make the late Huey Long seem, by comparison, a very Aristides.

THE NEW REPUBLIC, "The Superficial Aspect," *April 12, 1954*

THE STEVENSON BLADE

U ntil recently there has seemed to be little point in taking sides in the debate over whether Adlai Stevenson is or isn't running for President; but when he issued the manifesto, "Eggheads of the world unite; you have nothing to lose but your yolks," the time came to stand up and be counted. If the man isn't running he ought to be.

Whether or not he can beat Dwight D. Eisenhower in 1956 I don't know, but that is irrelevant anyhow. The immediately important thing is not to have him elected, but to have him running; for whether or not he can beat Eisenhower, there is no manner of doubt that he can beat all sorts of preposterous notions that at present pass current for ideas, and a man who can clean out even a few of the idiocies now infesting American politics is a man so valuable that his worth is beyond rubies.

Stevenson is obviously not the right kind of candidate for tranquil times. When all is serene the ideal candidate for President is a solemn ass—a William Henry Harrison, a James A. Garfield, a William McKinley, a Calvin Coolidge. But in stormy weather "motley's the only wear" as we discovered in 1861, in 1913 and in 1933. The second date may give some people pause. Lincoln was a wit, as we all know, and Roosevelt we remember as a gay and jocund fellow; but Woodrow Wilson looked so much like the perfect undertaker that we tend to forget how, when reporters brought him bad news from the convention and clamored for a statement he gave them: "You may say that the candidate received the news with a riot of silence," and how at some whistle-stop he mounted a manure-spreader as the only available rostrum, but apologized for standing on a Republican platform, and how he went into the Presidency proclaiming,

For beauty I am not a star,
There are others more handsome by far,

But my face, I don't mind it,
For I am behind it—
It's the folks out in front that I jar.

The point is that when all is going well a President may only strut and
gurgle generalities and still get by; but when the situation is appalling he
must face reality. Of all people the jester is quickest to see the thing as it
really is. That is why he laughs, if only because he fears, like Figaro, being
obliged to weep. For any man who sees the world clearly must either laugh or
weep; it is the purblind who grunt complacently.

How it will be in 1956 I cannot predict, but as of 1954 the weather is
certainly stormy and it will not be calmed by the incantations of warlocks in-
toning that what is good for General Motors is necessarily good for the
country and that threats of "massive retaliation" will deter an ingenious and
resolute enemy. Such turgid pomposities need puncturing and nothing does it
as effectively as a needle-pointed phrase.

Stevenson is adept at producing such phrases, but if he were retired to
private life he might not find it worth the trouble. So to keep him in the ring
demolishing the sawdust-stuffed guards produced to reassure, and the paste-
board dragons to terrify us, is a highly desirable public service.

Humorless souls may regard this with horror as an incitement to attacks
on everything. The humorless are incapable of understanding that satire never
permanently damaged anything that is solid. It is blunted by coats of mail and
is effective only against stuffed shirts; but the execution it does upon them is
very great. Hit a stuffed shirt with a bludgeon and the club may bounce, leaving the shirt undamaged; but a rapier goes through and lets the wind out with
startling speed.

If "egghead," for example, had been a genuine epithet with substance,
Stevenson's riposte would have fallen flat. But everyone knows that what Senator Fulbright calls "the swinish cult of anti-intellectualism" has been trying to
fit yokes to the necks of intellectuals, and that McCarthyism is far more a war
upon liberalism than upon Communism. So Stevenson's brilliant pun, plus his
sardonic echo of the language of the *Communist Manifesto* was devastating.

While he remains a candidate the campaign will be worth the attention
of the intelligent; for among the stuffed clubs and slap-sticks will be at least
one Toledo blade, and whenever it flashes sawdust and wind will be spilled
like blood upon the field of Gettysburg. In short, while he is a candidate, it
will be a real fight; so let him run forever!

THE NEW REPUBLIC, "The Superficial Aspect," *April 26, 1954*

OPPENHEIMER: THE RIGHT TO BE WRONG

Oppenheimer made a bomb and it went off exactly as it was intended to do.

That much we know for a fact—even we outsiders who are not permitted to know anything important about the new weapons know that much. Oppenheimer's work was good; nobody denies it.

Nevertheless Oppenheimer's reputation has been blasted. He has been denied access to any new information, which of course eliminates him from the front rank of nuclear physicists; and he is being subjected to an investigation by a special commission as if he were suspected of being another Benedict Arnold. He is not accused of crime. Nobody says he has done any spying, but the intimation is that he might spy if he were afforded the opportunity.

On the face of it then, the situation is this: Oppenheimer's work was good, but his thoughts were evil.

Obviously, this doesn't apply to all his thoughts. On most subjects Oppenheimer seems to think like everybody else, and we are not yet ready to make the bald assertion that everybody is a scoundrel. Oppenheimer's evil thoughts must be those that are different from the thoughts of the people who have humiliated him. The one subject on which his thoughts differ from those of the powers that be is that of butchering Communists. Oppenheimer is against it. He holds that Communists are people, and that it is better to try to get along with them than to spend all our effort in preparations to massacre them. This is the head and front of his offending.

An observer of the superficial aspect of things is tempted to say that this is an unheard-of attitude for Americans to take, but that is not true. At least once before the policy of forcible suppression of evil thoughts was urged upon the country, with memorable results. It was a hundred years ago and the great advocate of suppression was not McCarthy, but John C. Calhoun.

Almost as many efforts were made to appease Calhoun as have been made to appease McCarthy, but with no more success. Fugitive slave laws were passed and were given more teeth than an army of crocodiles. Missouri was admitted as a slave state. Abolitionist literature was barred from the mails. Every imaginable guarantee against interference with slavery in the South was offered.

But it was not enough. Not content with security against the overt act, Calhoun demanded that agitation of the question be suppressed—that is, that we punish men for evil thoughts.

It is not pleasant to trace the parallel further, for what Calhoun got was the bloodiest war, in proportion to the numbers engaged, of modern times, a war that effected the ruin of his own country. The demand that men be punished, not for their conduct but for their opinions, made further conciliation impossible and precipitated catastrophe.

It is logically conceivable, of course, that Oppenheimer is wrong and that Communists are so far from being human that the slightest contact with them attaints and works corruption of the blood. But time was when an American was guaranteed the right to be wrong in his concepts as long as he did nothing to force those concepts on others. As long as his conduct was impeccable, his government had no legal right to molest him, or to subject him to scorn and contumely.

Time was, also, when a man who had served the republic well was regarded as due special consideration from the republic; but today special consideration seems to be reserved to those who amuse the public. Lucille Ball is forgiven for harboring evil, if any, thoughts years ago. But she makes people laugh; Oppenheimer only made the atomic bomb, and what is a great scientist that he should claim to be treated with as much consideration as a comedienne?

So "the swinish cult of anti-intellectualism" goes yak-yaking down the road to a culmination as yet unknown and about which nervous persons prefer not to guess. Their small but multitudinous hooves trample into the dirt men who have performed the most distinguished public services if those men lash them across the snout with contumacious words; and if Thomas Jefferson observes from Olympus he must be quoting his own grim comment: "I tremble for my country when I reflect that God is just."

THE NEW REPUBLIC, "The Superficial Aspect," *August 16, 1954*

BEYOND INDO-CHINA

Perhaps there are under the surface deep mysteries that explain the pained bewilderment of our public comment on the affair of Indo-China, but superficially it seems as easy to understand why France left Indo-China as why Friar John quit the monastery. There were seven reasons, he explained, the first being that he was thrown out. Nobody listened to the others.

We, on the other hand, prefer listening to all the others while shutting our ears to the first. Some of our pundits have elaborated a theory that Geneva was another Munich with Mendès-France playing the role of Neville Chamberlain. The fact that Munich was at one end of a war and Geneva at the other is ignored, as is the fact that Czechoslovakia was willing to fight and Indo-China is not, unless, indeed, it fights for the invader.

Without doubt, one reason for the desperate efforts to find some way of accounting for the situation other than an admission that the French were licked is that the admission entails a sharp reduction in our estimate of our own moral superiority. We had announced loudly that the Communists must be stopped at "the bottle-neck" and that we were going to help stop them, and the announcement made not the slightest impression upon the Communists. They assumed that our words were a mouthful of wind and proceeded as if we had never spoken; and events justified them.

This could not have happened to a nation whose moral superiority is recognized by all the world, but it is bound to happen to any nation that is once caught betting on a pair of treys. If the new Administration had told the French in unmistakable terms back in January, 1953, that it was going to risk no more Koreas, we might not have saved the French, but we would have saved face and when the end came we might have been able to exert some sort of influence upon the course of events.

Mr. Dulles did not "lose" Indo-China any more than Mr. Acheson "lost" China; but Mr. Dulles was not one whit better than Mr. Acheson at preventing the disaster. This is a fact that we are extremely reluctant to face, but it will not go away because we shut our eyes to it.

There is no evidence that Russia ever gave the Chinese Communists anything like as much aid as we gave Chiang Kai-shek, and no evidence that the Chinese gave Viet-Minh as much aid as we gave France. Yet in both cases our side lost in spite of its material superiority.

As a mere outside observer, utterly ignorant of high politics, this writer clings stubbornly to the conviction that we do, in fact, have a very decided moral superiority over Communist ideology; but that belief makes inevitable the inference that we have not brought it to bear since we lost in two fields in which we had material superiority to begin with.

Yet the slightest inquiry into why we have failed to employ our best weapon in this struggle leads to embarrassment. The reason is definitely internal politics. But that leads to the question, can a nation that blinds itself to world realities in the squabble over who shall hold office lay claim to any moral superiority at all?

Not a single Russian infantryman has been killed, unless by accident, in the wars that have extended Communist influence in Asia: Communism has advanced by offering the semblance of economic as well as political freedom to oppressed people. The obvious way to stop it was to offer the reality of freedom to the same people; but to do that would have interfered with countless diplomatic and business arrangements throughout the world. More, and from the standpoint of reactionary Americans, worse, it would have afforded aid and comfort to battlers for social justice at home.

So we have laid aside the weapon of moral suasion and have relied on nuclear fission instead. So China has gone, Indo-China is going, and India stands perplexed. The Hindu is not impressed by the moral superiority either of the hydrogen bomb or of a tariff to protect the makers of timing devices for the bomb. He may be impressed by the moral superiority of a system that can win wars because alien people are willing to fight for it.

If India goes, the rest of Asia is pretty sure to go with it; and if Asia goes the bomb may, indeed, become our last hope and a slim one, because Russia has it, too. Too much faith in military and too little in moral force may end by costing us a dozen of our biggest cities, to say nothing of our lives, our fortunes and our sacred honor.

THE NEW REPUBLIC, "The Superficial Aspect," *December 6, 1954*

L'IL ABNER NIXON

L'il Abner Nixon, that Red-Blooded American Boy, achieved one effect in the late campaign that the pious must approve. He drove even the ungodly to prayer. I estimate that not less than 67 percent was added both to the frequency and to the fervor of their petitions for the continued good health of the President of the United States.

But here is a prediction that soon it will appear that he achieved another effect—he used himself up. By 1956, far from standing as the Heir Apparent, he will no longer figure prominently in the Privy Council, and will probably go the way of Henry Wallace in the Democratic convention of 1944.

This is admittedly a risky guess, in flat contradiction of the view of many political observers, some very shrewd, but it is based on observation, not on intuition. As a political operations officer Nixon was guilty of two capital errors: in the first place, his strategy failed; and in the second place it has embarrassed and will continue to embarrass his commander.

It was against his original judgment that Eisenhower was persuaded to engage in bitter partisanship in this mid-term campaign. He knew that he was not elected as a partisan and at the start thought he should and said he would stand as President of all the people. Nixon was one of those who persuaded him to abandon that attitude and throw his great personal influence into the fight to save Congress for the Republican Party.

If the effort had succeeded, success might have justified it; but it only checked without stopping the Democratic landslide. So Ike finds himself in the position of a commander who has been deluded into committing his reserves without achieving victory in an action that is only preliminary to the main engagement. He cannot be enthusiastic about those who urged this error upon him.

More than that, his excursion into partisanship has already inflicted on him the humiliation of having to eat his own words. That unhappy prediction of a "cold war" between White House and Capitol has been publicly swallowed. Eisenhower did it promptly and with good grace; but it could not have been pleasant to tell a roomful of reporters that he had been indulging in the kind of bunk that every soap-box bawler throws around.

Worst of all he knows now, or he will very soon know, that there remains a large and noisy flock of chickens still to come home to roost. When he laid the whip upon Democratic backs he converted what might have been a "loyal opposition" into a vengeful opposition, under no obligation to regard him as above the battle; and the public, having noted his course in the campaign, will hold the Democrats justified up to a point.

In short, by following the course urged upon him by the group, including Nixon, he gained nothing and lost the advantageous position of a man above party. Eisenhower is too wise and too magnanimous to make any public display of irritation with his subordinates, for, after all, it was his own error; but it is beyond all reason to expect him to hold in grateful affection subordinates who gave him what proved to be almost fabulously bad advice.

Even yet it is not entirely clear how bad that advice was, but it will swiftly become clear once a Democratic Congress is installed. Under the best conditions the President would have had great difficulty in retrieving the errors of the past two years, but his difficulties will be multiplied when he has to deal with a Congress justly resentful not only of the President's own talk of "creeping socialism" but also, and more so, of the Vice President's reckless attempts to attaint the Democratic Party of treason, attempts which the President gave his official blessing four days before the election.

So with passing time making it clearer every day that the advice of the Red-Blooded American Boy led not only to defeat, but to a serious loss of advantage in the main battle of 1956, the standing of Nixon in the hierarchy is bound to deteriorate. Such is the position as of the moment, and there may be added the moral certainty that Nixon will continue to add to the embarrassments of the Administration. For pulling the Eisenhower Administration out of the hole is an enterprise demanding skill, tact and discretion, all on a high level; and if the Vice President is conspicuous for any of these virtues the public has not discovered it.

It is true that Mr. Nixon is adept at wriggling out of jams, but this is not an ordinary jam—it is a matter of appeasing a leader whom he has just about wrecked, and I doubt that it can be done.

THE NEW REPUBLIC, "The Superficial Aspect," *December 20, 1954*

IF IT ISN'T JOE

McCarthy's assault on Eisenhower presumably marks the beginning of the last act of this particular burlesque of statecraft. It is typical of such shows. The fatality attending the career of an American demagogue is the necessity of being continuously entertaining, which involves going into wilder and wilder extravagances, attacking shinier and shinier targets. The shiniest of all targets is the President of the United States, and when the demagogue has attacked the President he is usually through.

But when a politician is a true demagogue, that is, one who has nothing to offer except demagoguery, the time comes when he must attack the President or allow the dramatic tension of his performance to slacken and so lose the center of the stage. Thus Huey Long had to attack Roosevelt, thus J. Thomas Heflin had to attack Wilson, and by the same token McCarthy had to attack Eisenhower. Failure to do so would have been followed by boos from the gallery or the silence of a deserted house.

The sorry aspect of it—from the demagogue's standpoint—is that when the attack has been made, the boos and the ensuing silence follow anyhow. For the attack never succeeds. Andrew Johnson was the only President ruined by demagogic assault, but Thad Stevens was a far stronger man than McCarthy, while Johnson was actually a Democrat elected on the Republican ticket. Conditions are far different now. After last month's election every rational politician must realize that Eisenhower is by long odds the greatest, if not the only asset the Republican Party has left. It would be suicide for the party to allow him to be sacrificed to sate the vengeance of one discredited Senator.

It is characteristic of the demagogue facing the awful truth that Nemesis is upon him to develop a Samson complex and decide to pull down the temple to make a defiant and spectacular finish. If McCarthy could, in fact, wreck Eisenhower he would rival his Biblical prototype—he would slaughter more Republicans by his political death than he had slain in all his political life. But it is a safe bet that the average Republican politician is not of a mind to be squashed under the ruins in order to make a fine funeral for McCarthy.

In all probability McCarthy's future is foreshadowed by the last year or two in the Senate of J. Thomas Heflin. The man is so completely forgotten now that the handier reference books do not mention his name, but time was when he was regarded as a Menace with a capital M. He was a Senator from Alabama who gained, and richly earned, the cognomen of Tom-Tom in recognition of his loud and empty clanging. Tom-Tom was opposed to practically everything, but his three pet aversions were the Pope, the negro and his party leader, who was Woodrow Wilson. He assailed them as violently as Mc-Carthy assailed Communists, intellectuals and his party leader.

But Tom-Tom eventually exhausted his entertainment value, and for his last year or two his sole function was to provide frequently an informal recess for the rest of the Senate. Whenever he took the floor, any honorable member desiring the solace of a cigar ambled out into the cloakroom and every correspondent with a yen for a few hands of stud poker quit the press gallery. It was safe to do so, for everybody knew that Tom-Tom would give vent to nothing except vituperation of the Papacy, the Presbyterian and the Brother in Black, as he had 30 times before.

After January McCarthy, deprived of a committee chairmanship, will continue to sit in the Senate and no doubt will continue to bellow; but it is highly probable that ere "Spring comes back with rustling shade and apple blossoms fill the air" he will be bellowing to empty seats and a vacant press gallery. For the vote of censure was well received by press and public, which is a sure indication that the people are getting tired of McCarthy; and no Senator stands in awe of a man who bores the public.

Yet the intelligent should not allow this pleasing prospect to beguile them into being at ease in Zion. McCarthy may be on his way out, but the McCarthyites remain. Jim Farley's secret check of Huey Long's strength in 1936 suggested that the predestined victims of demagoguery constitute perhaps three percent of the population, which would make them five million strong at present. By the time McCarthy is plainly through we may rely on it that some other tin-plate Paladin will be thumping his tub and collecting the plaudits and the cash contributions of the vacant-skulled.

If it isn't Tom-Tom it is Huey, and if it isn't Huey it is Joe, and if it isn't Joe it will be the same old wizard, changed in name but not in nature.

THE NEW REPUBLIC, "The Superficial Aspect," *February 14, 1955*

ATHENS AND SPARTA AND RED CHINA

There are times when a superficial knowledge of history is unpleasant. For instance, when Senator Knowland and some military men call for action to eliminate the menace of Red China the student who has read Grote shudders. They sound too much like Alcibiades urging the Athenians to undertake the expedition against Syracuse.

To assuage this qualm it is useless to cite the maxim, "History never repeats," for if you do some mocking devil will instantly cite the maxim, "Like causes produce like effects." The causes of Senator Knowland's and Alcibiades' perturbation are strikingly similar, and the immediate, first effects are somewhat similar; whether the later effects will bear any resemblance to each other remains to be seen.

In 416 B.C. Athens had Sparta pretty nearly where the United States has Germany in 1955 A.D. and the Dwight Eisenhower of the time, a General Nicias, said, "Hold it!" His idea was that Athens' great need was rest and recuperation after 15 years of war. But while Sparta was down, Syracuse, like Red China today, remained undefeated. Syracuse was on the perimeter of the Athenian sphere of influence, as China is on the perimeter of ours; but Alcibiades was as certain that the task remained unfinished while the Syracusan power remained unbroken as Senator Knowland is that we cannot rest as long as Red China stands.

The agitation of Alcibiades and his friends was so effective that in the end it drove even Nicias if not into approval, at least into a reluctant consent. That carries the modern parallel a little beyond the current date, for as these lines are written the modern Nicias has not given even a reluctant assent; but Eisenhower has advised Congress to make a menacing gesture in the direction of Red China. Two explanations of this course are possible. One, accepted by Congress, is that the gesture was necessary to ward off an impending attack; the other, admitted, of course, by nobody, is that Nicias under pressure of the agitation is beginning to take action against his better judgment.

It is the end of the ancient story that makes the student shiver. Athens learned the hard way that military power is effective in inverse ratio to the distance at which it is applied. What was overwhelming in Greece proved inadequate at the other end of a long sea-lane. The Athenian armies landed in Sicily, bogged down and were frittered away; the Athenian fleet, partly by shipwreck and partly by enemy action, was destroyed; so when a revived Sparta rose again Athens had neither land nor seapower and was crushed.

And all the while Macedon, like Soviet Russia, was looming upon the horizon, to march in when the Greek states had exhausted themselves.

The modern parallel, extrapolated, is even more sinister than the ancient, for Macedon after all was Hellenistic and her conquest of Greece did not involve a social, but only a political revolution. Alexander the Great was a pupil of Aristotle, but if Malenkov ever studied under Arnold J. Toynbee nobody has heard of it. If American armies are swallowed up in the bottomless morass of mainland China, and American fleets and the American economy are exhausted in maintaining the enormously long lines of communication, the conqueror who marches in will impose upon the Western world not merely a new form of political control, but a different and, as most of us believe, a much inferior civilization.

One hopes, of course, that the common sense of the American people will revolt before the process has been carried too far, but it must be admitted that the Athenians were one of the most intelligent populations that ever lived, yet their intelligence did not save them. They were intelligent enough to recognize and to name the threat that hung over them—they called it *hubris,* that pride of power that ruins men and nations by undermining their judgment in moments of triumph.

Not long ago D. W. Brogan, a shrewd Scottish observer, published an essay on the Illusion of American Omnipotence, which was a flat assertion that *hubris* is infecting this nation to an alarming extent. Brogan can be wrong, but he is nobody's fool, and he didn't bring that charge without evidence to back it. Most Americans are still sane enough not to advocate imposing our rule upon the world by the power of the sword, but Senator Knowland does not hesitate to talk of using economic power for that purpose; and pride of power is still *hubris,* even when it is based on the power of the dollar.

THE NEW REPUBLIC, "The Superficial Aspect," *March 28, 1955*

NIXON'S INDISPENSABLE MAN

T he President telegraphed to the chairman of a meeting at which the Vice President was to speak, "I am happy to call Dick Nixon my friend." This certainly warranted assumption by the audience that what Dick Nixon said would be in accord with the President's wishes, since no true friend of a President will make political speeches distasteful to the man in the White House.

What Nixon said was, "The Republican Party is not strong enough today to elect a President. We have to have a man who is strong enough to elect the party."

If this is not Eisenhower's attitude, then Nixon has dropped the watermelon again. If it is his attitude, then what is the meaning of his brusque suppression of any White House correspondent who ventures to mention the Indispensable Man? Over and over, Eisenhower has insisted that there is no Indispensable Man; now Dick, whom he is happy to call his friend, flatly contradicts him and says not only that there is an Indispensable Man, but that Eisenhower is it.

As far as factual accuracy is concerned, a superficial observer is bound to line up with Nixon. In 1952, the voters enthusiastically accepted the candidate, but almost rejected the party; in 1954 they did reject it and turned Congress over to the Democrats. The inescapable inference is that Eisenhower is all the Republicans have, and if he should be lost or damaged they would be sunk.

The interesting thing, though, is not the accuracy of the Vice President's estimate, but the circumstances under which it was promulgated. They can be interpreted in either of two ways. They may indicate that Eisenhower has learned no politics at all in the past two years; or they may indicate that he has learned very rapidly indeed.

If he has learned nothing, he may still believe that he can go on calling people his very dear friends without being saddled with any responsibility for what those people say. If he has learned a great deal, he may have mastered the technique of hypocrisy which dictates that the candidate should shrink in maidenly modesty while his dear friends wallop the gong.

The question is, will either explanation sustain the personal prestige through which he was swept into the Presidency of a country that definitely did not want his party? It is doubtful, to put it mildly. The voters of 1952, knowing that Ike was no professional politician, yet hoped that his mind was supple and realistic enough to learn how to cope with the professionals; but if he has learned nothing, that hope is disappointed.

On the other hand, if he has learned enough to insist coyly on his expendability in public while privately encouraging his friends to shell the woods for delegates, then he has become a politician and is no longer the Eisenhower of 1952. The shoddy tricks of the ordinary vote-grabber do not sit well on the image of Eisenhower in the people's mind. If he is in fact adopting them, that would be a greater disappointment.

Nixon's suggestion that Ike should be the Trojan horse through whose instrumentality a party that the people do not want may be introduced into the citadel is highly practical politics, but it is also monumental trickery; and for Eisenhower to lend himself to trickery on that scale would be a repudiation of his whole character as the public has envisaged it.

The hopeful, accordingly, will prefer the other theory—that the fabulously clumsy Nixon once again has contrived to present the President in a completely false light, by attributing to him a deviousness foreign to his make-up. But how long can that sort of thing continue without disaster, certainly to Eisenhower and perhaps to the country?

A Shogunate is not a practicable form of government for this country at this time. Japan had to abandon it as long ago as 1868 and make the titular head of the state the actual ruler. This country cannot revive the system of keeping the emperor shut off by the Palace Guard from all contact with political reality while persons to whom the nation owes no loyalty conduct public affairs in his name.

So the theory of naïveté is really no more reassuring than the theory of cynical sophistication. Either entails trouble in a big way. Perhaps by exposing the facts nakedly and glaringly Mr. Nixon's ineptitude may for once have served the country well; for the country cannot safely continue to vote for an image that does not correspond to the man.

HENRY L. MENCKEN 1880-1956

H. L. Mencken's *Prejudices,* especially the first three volumes, his *American Mercury* 1924-1934, his *American Language* with its supplements, and his "Days," in form an autobiography but in fact a social history of extraordinary color and texture, constitute a body of work commanding the respectful attention of the literary world. As critic, as editor, as philologist, and as historian the man made original and arresting contributions to the national letters; and a writer who has scored in four separate fields is sufficiently unusual to deserve careful scrutiny and analysis. His passing may be relied on to draw all pundits to their typewriters or dictaphones.

But there was also a character known as Henry Mencken to a relatively small circle in Baltimore and to an even smaller group outside the city; and he was, at least in the opinion of this writer, more remarkable than the H. L. Mencken known to everybody. His passing on January 29 also deserves notice, not in the style of literary analysis, but in the plain speech of the unschooled, in which he was as expert as he was in the language of the Academy.

This man was conspicuously kindly and polite. The information may come as a stunning surprise to those who are familiar only with the roaring invective of which H. L. Mencken was master and the acid wit in which he barbecued heroes and demigods of all sects and fashions; but I refer, not to H. L. Mencken, the public figure, but to Henry Mencken, citizen of Baltimore. He was fully aware of this distinction and drew it sharply himself; as far as he could, he screened Henry Mencken from the observation of press and public, while thrusting H. L. Mencken to the fore.

He once told a friend that when he went into the Stork Club in New York and the diners stared and then turned to whisper to each other, he thought it was swell; but when the same thing happened in Miller's Baltimore restaurant he found himself perspiring and acutely uncomfortable. For that reason he commonly avoided the big places, especially when dining alone. What café society calls "a celebrity" appeared to his realistic eye merely as a curiosity, and he hated the idea of being a curiosity in his home town.

But he was, of course. No such vivid personality could live anywhere without being something of a curiosity, no matter how sedulously he might avoid outward eccentricity. Mencken avoided it. He was of medium height, five feet eight or nine, but stocky enough to look shorter. Clean-shaven and conservatively dressed, with no oddities of posture or gait, he should have merged imperceptibly into a street crowd. But he didn't. He stuck out, for reasons almost impossible to capture and fix in words. The best one can say is that he stood and walked and talked like other men, only more so. He was conspicuously normal.

Into that medium-sized body was packed the vitality of twenty ordinary men. He was surcharged, and the fact was evident in whatever he did, even in the way he put his foot down in walking, or the flip of a hand when he returned a greeting. It was revealed in an immense capacity for work, and in a correspondingly immense capacity for enjoyment. This enraged ascetics, of course, and they called him a sensualist which, in the way they meant it, was nonsense.

But in another way, a quite extraordinary way, perhaps the charge had something in it. Henry Mencken's perceptions were keen, as are those of any man who is intensely alive; to observers it seemed that he could extract more, and more profound, pleasure out of one seidel of beer than most men could from a gallon; certainly he could extract energy and encouragement from apparent defeat; and certainly he could detect and savor lusty humors in situations which to most men meant only tragedy and despair. In seventy-five years he not only outlived the rest of us, he lived far longer; one is tempted to assert that he lived like Noah and Seth and Enoch, those Old Testament ancients.

This gave him a towering advantage over the majority of those with whom he came in contact, and as a rule the man who enjoys a towering advantage is a hateful fellow. The marvel of Henry Mencken is that he was nothing of the sort. H. L. Mencken was hated. Every opprobrious term in the vocabulary of billingsgate was hurled at him, and even honorable terms were applied to him with the force of epithets; he was called a Jew, a Catholic, and a Communist, but never by a Jew, a Catholic, or a Communist, always by their enemies. It would be difficult, indeed, to identify a man who didn't hate H. L. Mencken at one time or another and for one reason or another.

But I have yet to encounter man, woman, child, or beast of burden who knew Henry Mencken and hated him. He was too expansive, too free of envy, too obviously void of any disposition to grasp at personal advantage. Even those most captious of critics, writers who knew that he could out-write them, once they came within the magnetic field of his personality lost the capacity to hate. They could be exasperated by him, they could denounce him with fire and fury; but they had trouble doing it with a straight face.

The explanation is that Henry Mencken was an intellectual philanthropist. Occasionally he would follow some deliverance with the warning, "Now don't you write that. I mean to use it myself"; but as a rule he scattered ideas with the grand abandon, so astonishing to Darwin, of the fir tree in scattering pollen.

Incidentally, the writers who knew Henry Mencken were few. Every semi-literate scribbler in the country knew H. L. Mencken, of course, and those who had met him in the flesh must have numbered thousands; but in Baltimore his intimates, outside the group closely associated with him on the Baltimore *Sun,* included relatively few writers. True, he married the novelist, Sara Haardt, but there was a touch of the Pygmalion complex in that. Mencken had done a great deal toward pruning and strengthening her literary style when she was an aspiring youngster and he was probably a bit in love with his own creation. But this factor was only a touch; the charming lady from Alabama had plenty to account for the romance without seeking explanations in the subconscious. One of her charms was her extraordinary wisdom in being not merely tolerant but gracious to any odd fish that Henry chose to bring to the house.

And odd they certainly were! All the human flotsam and jetsam of the seven seas of literature eventually washed up on the big brownstone steps of the Cathedral Street house—this was during Mencken's married life, tragically brief, as Sara died within a few years—and it included, as H.L.M. once said of the lady drys, "some specimens so dreadful that one wonders how a self-respecting God could have made them." But these were at most friends of H. L. Mencken, more often mere acquaintances, and all too often complete strangers brazen enough to walk in uninvited.

The friends of Henry Mencken were odd, but in a different sense—odd in that they didn't match, could not be listed in any one category. Status of any sort, social, economic, intellectual, or other was irrelevant. They were so different that one can think of but a single characteristic that they possessed in common—they were all vibrantly alive. Whether it was Max Broedel, the anatomical artist, who rarely had a cent, or Harry C. Black, principal owner of the *Sun,* who had dollars and some millions of them; whether it was Raymond Pearl, the biologist and one of the great brains of Johns Hopkins, or William Woollcott, the mucilage manufacturer, who loudly proclaimed that he had no brain at all (although he was a finer wit than his famous brother, Alexander); whether it was a barber or a governor, any man to whom Henry Mencken took a liking was one who savored life, sometimes with a wry face, but definitely.

In the office of the *Sun* H. L. Mencken could work with anybody, although there were some who tried him to the limit. But Henry Mencken's close associates again were various: Paul Patterson, the publisher, diplomatic but as refractory as basalt; Henry Hyde, veteran star reporter, as stately as Mencken was ebullient; the two Eds, Murphy, managing editor, and Duffy, cartoonist, explosive Irishmen; and the Owens pair, John and Hamilton, chief editors, distant cousins and distantly Welshmen. They were all experts, but there were other experts around the place who maintained polite relations with H. L. Mencken, yet never caught a glimpse of Henry. Those who did had something more than *expertise;* they had zest and a fine appreciation of the flavor of life even when—perhaps especially when—it displeased them.

To us smaller fry in the organization he was consistently genial and consistently helpful, although he could be sardonic. To me one day he observed, blandly, "He is a great cartoonist, but in politics, of course, Duffy is an idiot." Since Duffy's politics and mine were identical I got it, all right.

The newspaper man, however, was not Baltimore's Henry Mencken. That character was never to be found in public places, but only in private houses, or semi-private apartments such as the upper room over Schellhäse's restaurant, where he led the Saturday Night Club in wild forays in the realm of music, sometimes murderous enterprises such as playing the nine symphonies of Beethoven in succession—they finished at dawn—sometimes elaborate buffooneries such as orchestrating for ninety instruments Willie Woollcott's ribald ditty about the 100 per cent American; or alone at home devising preposterous communications and mementos. I had on my desk for years a three-pound chunk of rock sent through the mails at terrific expense with a preternaturally solemn document certifying it as an authentic madstone.

But the unforgetttable Henry Mencken, the man who really altered the lives of the relatively few who knew him, was Mencken sitting at ease after the day's work was over, with a cigar in his mouth, a seidel in his hand, and around him a small group who were equal to the rapier-play of his wit— Woollcott, Pearl, Gilbert Chinard, a very few others. In such surroundings Henry Mencken talked better than H. L. Mencken ever wrote—lightly, ironically, extravagantly, but with a flashing perception that illuminated whatever it touched, and it touched everything. A display of intellectual pyrotechnics it was, certainly, but like any fine fireworks display it created in an ordinary place on an ordinary night a glittering illusion; momentarily, at least, life sparkled and blazed, and the knowledge that it can ever sparkle and blaze is worth having. In fact, it is one of the best things a man can have.

It was not optimism. Henry Mencken, like H. L. Mencken, was a pessimist; but his pessimism was more invigorating than the gurgling of any male Pollyanna. "The trouble about fighting for human freedom," he remarked once, "is that you have to spend much of your life defending sons-of-bitches; for oppressive laws are always aimed at them originally, and oppression must be stopped in the beginning if it is to be stopped at all." It is hard to imagine anything more dismal, but I do not believe it will sap the courage of any fighting character.

Mencken would have disliked being compared to pietistic Samuel Johnson, but he played a very similar role in his own city. The difference was that Johnson always and Mencken never took himself too seriously; nevertheless, each was not only witty, "but the cause that wit is in other men." Nor did it stop with wit. They caused a zest for life to be renewed in other men, they touched the dull fabric of our days and gave it a silken sheen. Boswell, greatest of biographers, recognized but never could translate into words the quality that made contact with his hero a milestone in every man's life; and if Boswell could not do it for Johnson, what hope is there that any lesser person can do it for Mencken? One may only record the fact and pass on.

Nevertheless, it is true that when Mencken died there were those in Baltimore who were not much interested in what the world had lost—the incomparable reporter, the critic, the philologist, the social historian, H. L. Mencken. They were too much occupied in lamenting their own loss—Henry Mencken, the unique, who, deriding them exalted them, in threatening them encouraged them, in prophesying death and doom gave them a new, strong grip on life. The man who really knew him will do far more living in the same number of days than he would have done without that contact. If there is a finer gift that a man can bestow upon his friends, I cannot name it. They mourn with cause.

THE NEXT CHAPTER

The race for the Vice Presidential nomination, in which Old Reliable nosed out Young Hopeful in a photo-finish, was the most spectacular event of the Democratic convention, but it rates no higher than third in significance.

The victory of Kefauver makes the ticket a strong one, but it would have been pretty strong with Kennedy in the rumble seat. Much more significant than Kefauver's win was Throttlebottom's defeat, which occurred the day before, when Stevenson threw the race open. What licked Throttlebottom was the issue of the President's health; if Ike were robust, nobody would have been thinking much about Nixon; but with everybody thinking about Nixon, the Democrats simply could not afford to nominate another such. So Throttlebottom was out, and the convention picked the runner-up in the big race.

There is no denying that it is an oddly assorted pair. It is known that Mr. Stevenson is not unsympathetic with the troubles of the Southerners. It is known that Mr. Kefauver is very sympathetic with the troubles of Harlem and the Corn Belt. So no more than the customary campaign exaggeration can make of it the curious combination of an Unreconstructed Rebel from Chicago and a Damyankee from Tennessee. Oh, well—at least it proves that the Civil War is over.

The week's event of first significance, though, was not this, but the exit of Harry Truman skating on his ear. The Republicans naturally are in high glee over this, but their joy is probably ill-founded. Every career must have an end, and how else would anyone expect Battling Harry to go out? Theodore Roosevelt and Grover Cleveland ended the same way, but history attaches more dignity to them than to Rutherford B. Hayes and Benjamin Harrison, who subsided quietly. Weak characters may go out on their own feet, but for a fighter who never quits being thrown out is the only fitting and proper end. Harry propelled through the front door is not the tragic figure that Harry sneaking meekly down the back stairs would have been.

The significance of the incident, however, is not what happened to Truman, but the conclusive proof it offers that one more chapter in the history of liberalism is closed. The Rooseveltian chapter was long and brilliant, exceeded, perhaps, only by the Jeffersonian chapter, but its last page has been turned.

Every such event has its touches of tragedy for there are always some, most of them among the elders, who are persuaded not that a chapter is ended, but that the tale is told. Mr. Truman was one of them in that moment when he denounced Stevenson, but the odds are that he will bounce back and recover his aplomb. Some, less fortunate temperamentally, probably never will be able to realize that while the narrative style has changed the story is continued.

The task of liberalism is, as Woodrow Wilson put it, to "release the generous energies of our people." To accomplish that, liberalism must attack whatever is binding the generous and releasing the ungenerous energies of Americans. In 1932 the chief constrictive influence was an archaic economic organization that had throttled itself and reduced production to a trickle.

In a roaring battle that lasted for 20 years, that specific evil was pretty well remedied. The basic economic doctrine of the New Deal, namely, that the general welfare is paramount to any private interest, is now so firmly established that continuing to fight for it is like adopting the policy of Sandy Mush Precinct of Buncombe County, North Carolina, which, they say, although I think they lie—is still voting for Andrew Jackson.

Yet although Rooseveltian liberalism won its fight, the people are still far from free. The production of material goods has indeed been released, and that is one generous energy that has accomplished wonders that astonish the world. But at the very moment when this was being done other coils were tightening around us; even as the production of goods was increasing wondrously, the production of ideas was being steadily choked off.

The next chapter in the history of liberalism will not be a repetition of Roosevelt's fight in behalf of the ill-fed, ill-clothed and ill-housed, but some other leader's fight—we have hopes that it may be Stevenson's—in behalf of the ill-informed, the ill-taught and the ill-advised. An absolutely necessary condition of freedom is that the free man shall know the truth. Man shall not live by bread alone, and still less shall he live by every word that proceedeth out of the mouth of Madison Avenue copywriters.

This is a subtler menace than the threat of bodily starvation, so the fight against it will be harder and perhaps longer. But it is a fight that must be won unless the Statue of Liberty is to become, as the sardonic Frenchman put it, a monument to the illustrious dead.

from THE LUNATIC FRINGE, *1957*

INDORSING A PHILOSOPHER, A POPE AND A POET

At the beginning of the winter of 1956-57 the business of commenting on the state of the nation became an extra-hazardous occupation. Events were moving at such a tremendous pace that before comment could be transferred from the typewriter to the printed page it was easily possible that it might be invalidated and turned to derision by some totally unexpected upheaval, perhaps in a far corner of the world.

Between the writing and the publication of a book some months must elapse. As 1956 drew to a close, thunder on the left was rising from a mutter to a rumble, and the trembling augurs dared not predict that it would subside instead of mounting into a roar that would encompass the world.

The thunder was the hammering of the guns in Algeria, in Hungary, around the Suez Canal. They were far away, but their menace could not be ignored, for they were a threat to everything American down to and including a book of this kind, able to affect strongly its meaning and its purpose.

For if this book were to appear while the citizens of this republic were engaged in a red-hot, shooting war one of its principal theses would be rendered irrelevant, making the work in part aimless. This is the thesis that Americans in times of relative peace need, or certainly can use handily, some reassurance as to the future of the republic. As late as midsummer, 1956, this was incontestably true, for the air was filled with lamentations and dire predictions. Some of them undoubtedly were fraudulent, for a Presidential campaign was raging and during such occurrences the manufacture of hobgoblins always becomes a leading industry; but many of them were real in the sense that Jeremiahs actually believed their own bunk. The book was planned and produced on the assumption that this atmosphere will still prevail on its publication date.

But if war breaks out it will be a different kind of country, unless all the records of the past are misleading. If war breaks out, the remainder of this chapter will have little more application to the United States of America than to the Tadzhik Soviet Socialist Republic in the fastnesses of Central Asia. For it is characteristic of the American that once he is confronted by a bad man with a gun, by an enemy that he can see and identify, the American becomes grimly confident and briskly efficient. In such circumstances he needs no reassurance and the labor of these pages is in vain. When the American knows that he runs some risk of getting his head knocked off by a cannon-ball he is imperturbable; it is when he fears that he may have his head turned by the siren songs of characters that he classifies vaguely as "subversives" that he falls into blind panic, stampedes, and tramples underfoot the guarantees of his own liberty and even of his physical safety.

But to withhold this comment until there is a reasonable certainty that it will still be apposite six months, or three months after it is written is impractical, for there has not been a day in seventeen years when there was a reasonable assurance that the United States would be even technically at peace six months later. The utmost that a contemporary writer can do is accompany his suggestions with an acknowledgment that events may render them quite useless over night. Hence these lines.

There is a chance, however, that the Day of Armageddon may be post-poned yet a little while, and there is a moral certainty that the Day will pass. For peace is inevitable. That is guaranteed by the fact that the strength of men is not inexhaustible; perhaps it is as true of modern men as of those whom Calgacus denounced that "to plunder, to slaughter, to steal, these things they misname empire; and where they make a desert, they call it peace." Nevertheless peace always returns; and it will return to this earth, even if it finds the terrestrial globe only a cosmic cinder simmering with radioactivity.

So "in time of war prepare for peace" would seem to be an apothegm as sound as its converse, yet it has rarely been seriously applied by the Ameri-can people. Warning after warning we have blithely disregarded. Salem, in 1692, should have been a sufficient warning against all witch-hunts; since it was not, the Reconstruction orgy after the Civil War should have been a warning that witch-hunts may be political as well as religious; since it was not, the Mitchell Palmer delusion in 1920 served notice that they may be ideological, as well as political; but all of them did not prepare us, in the middle of the twentieth century, to realize that patriotism may degenerate into horrible fanaticism as readily as Calvinism did more than three hundred years ago.

Preparing for peace involves, first, accepting emotionally as well as rationally—in bone and blood as well as in mind—the fundamental truth that peace is not static; and, second, cultivating sedulously the ability to contemplate the necessity of taking the next step, not with terror, but with the cool calculation of an engineer figuring the size of the girders that his bridge will require.

There is no impressive evidence—at least none visible to the naked eye—that Americans of this generation are making any effective effort to establish preparation for peace as part of the educational system. The per-ceptible effort is all the other way. The very first principle of any rational approach to the subject, the realization that peace is not static, seems to be intolerable to most of the self-appointed regulators of our schools; they regard any suggestion of change, in economics, in politics, or in social attitudes as a disturbance of the peace, not as part of its normal processes. Hence the present rejection and the occasional persecution of the proponent of any new idea; hence the past inclusion in the Lunatic Fringe of men and women who were proposing what a later generation sees as the most obviously necessary change.

There is, of course, nothing specifically American in this. It is a human failing. It was shared by the Dicastery at Athens that judged Socrates and the Sanhedrin at Jerusalem that judged Christ; it was, in fact, even more conspicuous in them than it was in those Americans who adjudged Robert Oppenheimer unworthy of trust because he hesitated to advocate scientific experimentation that, as we know now, tends to poison the air that all living creatures breathe.

But *tu quoque* is not a logical argument, it is a fallacy, so listed by every elementary textbook. The impulse to murder is likewise common to all mankind, but that is no excuse for a civilized man to give way to it, much less to cultivate it; and the higher his standing on the scale of civilization, the more heinous his offense if he commits murder. The legal penalty is the same for all, but most men would regard a homicidal bishop with deeper horror than they felt for any of Al Capone's gunsels.

It happens that the American republic at this moment in history stands on a very high level of civilization. We may be worthy of it, or we may not; that is immaterial to the argument. Not of our choice, and less by our own efforts than by the inexorable march of events, we have been thrust into the leadership of the free nations. If, as we have proclaimed, free men are peaceable men, it follows that this nation ought to be conspicuously well prepared for carrying on peace—better prepared for that than for carrying on war.

It is hard to understand how any candid man can seriously maintain that we have measured up to our responsibility in that respect. Certainly we talk about peace, world without end. It is doubtful that history ever saw another nation so completely infested with peace societies, foundations for peace, papers and magazines for peace, lecturers for peace, actors, singers, dancers and, I dare say, prize fighters and bar-room bouncers, organized for peace and all giving tongue in such a way as to make Bugle Ann seem a mere stuttering amateur. Unfortunately, while a saving remnant of this motley array may speak with the voice of philosophy, by far the larger part of the noise resembles rather the voice of *Alouatta ursina,* the howling monkey.

But there is a wide gap between talking about peace and preparing for it. Preparing for peace means cultivating a public opinion that will support the government in a program of action befitting the nation that holds leadership of the peace-loving peoples of the world. Effort in this field is certainly not conspicuous. One wing of the peace-mongers, in so far as it contemplates action at all, advocates throwing down our arms in the presence of heavily armed antagonists, which is surrender, not struggle; and others apparently put more trust in compacts among governments than in creation of an electorate adequately informed of the conditions necessary to the maintenance of peace.

One of these conditions is certainly a reasonable hospitality to ideas. There is no lack of historical examples of the folly of the opposite course. Toynbee offers twenty-one, and before more than a handful of Americans had ever heard of Toynbee one example had passed into popular speech in this country. The verb "to chinafy" was used by Theodore Roosevelt; it meant to adhere to a policy of intellectual, moral and spiritual, as well as political isolation, as imperial China did for centuries, with results that horrified Americans.

But while we accept the progression of human thought in theory, we are slow to apply the theory in practice. A fair statement of our actual position was made by a high government official, Secretary of the Air Force Quarles, speaking to a group of educators late in 1956. He said, "When we consider the great potential danger which our country faces and, as far as we can see, must continue to face, I think we are justified in placing something like war-time emphasis on our technological, as distinguished from our cultural needs."

There is every reason to believe that Secretary Quarles voiced the domi-nant sentiment of the country. Probably he spoke for the majority. Certainly he spoke for a large and very influential minority, a group so strong that it has controlled high policy since the end of the Korean war.

For that reason the statement deserves more careful analysis than the unshared opinion of any one man can command. If it is a fact that the country favors, not merely now but for the predictable future, allowing potential—not clear and present, but potential—dangers to thrust technology ahead of culture as the chief concern of education, it can hardly be argued that we are preparing for peace, since the inclination of peace is not toward avoiding potential dangers, but toward improving potential opportunities.

It is also questionable that technology is the best defense against poten-tial dangers. Against clear and present dangers, sharply defined and un-mistakable, yes, technology must be our main reliance; but against potential dangers, not yet clearly defined but merely taking shape—that is, against the thing that may happen, not the one that must happen—the usefulness of technology is limited.

For the highest of all high explosives is not the hydrogen bomb, it is the human mind, as Russia discovered in Hungary in the autumn of 1956. To remove the detonator from this explosive, technology is a clumsy instrument; for this purpose what the bomb-squad needs is not physics, but psychology, not knowledge of the structure of the atom, but profound knowledge of the nature of man.

Hence the first preoccupation of the leader of the forces of peace must be to keep not bombs, but people from exploding; and the most efficient means of attaining that end is to imbue them with hope of better things to come. A man reasonably sure that tomorrow will bring an improvement is not likely to resort to violence today. He has too much to lose. It is when, in the words of the Communist Manifesto, you have nothing to lose but your chains, that you resort to the barricades and attempt to fight tanks by hurling paving-stones.

But the flame of hope is kept burning by one means only, namely, by feeding the flame with a constant flow of new ideas. It flickers and soon expires when the only fuel supplied it is sodden old straw.

Obviously, then, the way for any nation to prepare for peace is to con-vince the world, and first of all its own people, that it is receptive to the point of view of those who are dissatisfied with existing conditions and who can envisage an order of things that comes closer to the heart's desire. The fact that most of them are sure to be wrong, and that a certain proportion are likely to be downright insane, is irrelevant; the important point is that some of them are sure to be right and the maintenance of peace depends upon seizing and applying those ideas that are right even though they run contrary to prevailing opinion.

The point of view represented by Secretary Quarles is in line with this as far as the physical world is concerned. No group of men has been more hospitable to new ideas in their own line than American technologists; the proof is the prodigious technical achievement of the American economy; our productive capacity is the marvel of the modern world and the model even for our bitterest antagonists, who copy our methods and admit it, in fact, boast of it.

But the leadership we are called on to exercise in the immediate future and probably through the remainder of this century is not technical, it is political. To put it mildly, it seems less than wise, then, to devote our energies with wartime concentration to strengthening our technical position, which is already strong, to the neglect of our political position, which is precarious in the extreme. The weak point is the one to reinforce, if our whole position is to be made secure.

A leader who doesn't lead cannot retain his position. But political, like any other leadership, is dependent upon alertness, resourcefulness and ingenuity, that is, upon the constant generation of new ideas in the specific field. Hostility to new ideas presages the decay of leadership. In recent years there has been much talk of the "flight from intelligence" in this country, but it is an abuse of the term. It is in reality a flight from novelty, which is consistent with a high level of intellectuality. John Adams, John C. Calhoun and William H. Taft were intelligent men, among the most intelligent this country ever produced; but their inability to adjust to new political ideas made their political leadership disastrous.

None of them, however, did much damage except to his own party and, in lesser degree, to his own country. None of them was in position to do more. But a mistake by an American political leader today will react not on the United States alone, but on every nation in the world. That is the penalty of leadership. Furthermore, since the selection of American leaders rests with the people, a public opinion hostile to every novel suggestion will inevitably result in the selection of leaders prone to political error.

There is no escaping the truth that when fear of taking the next step is rife among the people, the nation will hang back, even under the most competent leadership; and it is unlikely to have competent leadership for long. The problem is not that of choosing the right President; it is that of creating the right climate of opinion, which involves millions of voters.

"I have but one lamp by which my feet are guided and that is the lamp of experience," said Patrick Henry. "I know of no way of judging the future but by the past."

He spoke the words as a warning, but sometimes there is comfort in them. They should be taken to heart by any American whose courage begins to fail as he contemplates the confusion of fads and fancies, of isms and ologies that in the consulship of Plancus were unknown. Whether *consule Planco* to you means the days of Woodrow Wilson, or those of F. D. R., the principle is the same. We are beyond the point at which the wisdom of those men will suffice.

The temptation is to say, "Oh, no doubt they had their perplexities, but no earlier generation has had to contend with such lunatics as *our* lunatics." But if we say so, we flatter ourselves; they all looked just as bad as the worst before our eyes. Yet the baker's dozen that we have examined had all some intimation of the shape of things to come, some suggestion to offer which, if it had been adopted and adapted by more practical minds, might have delivered us from many of the tribulations through which we have come. If they did no more they at least defied and somewhat weakened the "tyranny of opinion" that John Stuart Mill hated and feared; and in that they are a lamp to our feet and a light to our path.

For the tyranny of opinion can be endured by a free nation no more than the tyranny of George III, and the first step toward throwing it off is to follow the advice of sardonic Pope Julius: "Learn, my son, with what little wisdom the world is governed."

If this process happens to be highly entertaining, surely that is no objection. Rather, it is a merit when the current tyranny of opinion is the tyranny of fear. The colossal grotesquerie, the majestic buffoonery that punctuates American history may be an offense to the prim, but to the ribald it is a constant delight that makes their lives more worth living. So they cherish not only the modicum of wisdom that the Lunatic Fringe presented but also its indubitable lunacies. At least they startle us out of lethargy, they make us more vibrantly alive.

The Stentor of the Illinois prairies phrased it well. Vachel Lindsay may not be the best of American poets, but he has a strong claim to be considered the loudest; and he is a handy bard to have around when the singer's voice must contend against the artillery that is yelling across the sea. Hear him:

> *There are plenty of sweeping, swinging, stinging, gorgeous things to*
> *   shout about,*
> *And knock your old blue devils out.*

Among the "sweeping, swinging, stinging, gorgeous things," the Lunatic Fringe of the past is certainly to be counted: and if of the past, why not of the present? To shout is pleasanter than to shiver; and to shout rather than to shiver at the appearance of a novel idea has the additional advantage that it cannot be a complete mistake. Even if the idea is a bad one, the shout is still partially justified, for the evidence that someone still thinks, and still says what he thinks regardless of prevailing opinion, is ample excuse for jubilation.

THE NEW REPUBLIC, "The Superficial Aspect," *March 18, 1957*

A MEASURE OF DOUBT

Well, Israel has been battered to her knees. She has surrendered her natural defenses and hereafter will exist at the pleasure of the United Nations and specifically that of the United States. She has been compelled to subscribe to the theory that the United Nations will defend her in the future, although it has not defended her in the past; and she had as an excuse for accepting this theory only the word of Mr. Eisenhower and Mr. Dulles. Even that is qualified. They do not say that they will defend Israel, only that they will consider her case.

To a superficial observer this appears to be a bit rough on Israel but no doubt there are underlying motives imperceptible on the surface. As to these, one can only guess, but presumably one is the necessity of maintaining respect among foreigners for the high moral tone of Washington. Nations less elevated morally must not be allowed to get the impression that the United States will ever condone sin, except when the sinner, like Russia, is too strong to be chastised; or, like Egypt, is too tough; or, like India, is sinning only against infidels who do not believe even in the Old Testament, to say nothing of the New.

Israel comes under none of these exceptions. Israel is weak. Israel has always been polite to this country. Israel prays to the same God who receives the devotions of Mr. John Foster Dulles. Therefore Israel, like Britain and France, must be dealt with sternly, lest she begin to get ideas. After all, it is not easy in this sinful world to maintain respect for a high moral tone. The Pure in Heart are always being misrepresented by the Morally Stunted, and steps must be taken to counteract the effect.

For instance, there was the matter of the lavish hospitality we extended to the eminent slave-owner from Saudi Arabia. Some have seen in that a sign of approbation, if not of slave-owning, at least of the general attitude of the Arabians toward this country, which has been, and is, one of studied insolence. It goes without saying that a government taking pride in its elevated moral tone cannot approve of either slavery or insolence. The Arabian was annointed with goose grease for no such reason, but strictly as a matter of business. He is in position, if he were offended, to make trouble for the oil industry which considers itself entitled to the tender care, not only of Vice President Nixon since the days when he was a Senator, but also of the Texas-dominated opposition.

What the Morally Stunted seem incapable of understanding is the fine distinction that the Administration draws between a business deal and a moral attitude. No important industry was threatened by the squashing of Israel, so the Administration in that case was free to take the highest moral tone and happily availed itself of the opportunity. As touching Egypt, India and Russia circumstances are entirely different. Taking a high moral tone with them would upset any number of applecarts, which is not to be thought of.

There is, of course, the danger that Israel itself contains a considerable number of the Morally Stunted, who make take the view that they might as well be hanged for the old sheep as for the lamb, and who therefore may desert morality for business. If they are destined to be squashed in any event they may decide that they would stand a better chance under the Russians than under the Arabs, and so throw out Ben-Gurion and his pro-Western government.

Recent events strongly indicate that if we, or anybody else, should supply the Israeli with, say, $100 million worth of the harrows of hell, there would shortly be no Arabian problem in the Middle East because there would be no Arabs. It has undoubtedly occurred to the Kremlin that this is a possible business deal, but the Kremlin needs cash which the Israeli do not have. Yet the record of Israel is strengthening the belief that if anyone would accept, say, 30-year, 3 percent bonds, the interest would be paid and the bonds retired when due, which would be a good investment, as international deals go. If Ben-Gurion should be thrown out, the Kremlin might stretch a point.

This creates a measure of doubt that the Administration has clearly perceived the truth in this situation. Perhaps this, too, instead of being entirely a moral issue, is affected with a business interest and should be approached with the same moral elasticity we have displayed in dealing with Egypt and India, to say nothing of Russia. It would be a neat irony of history if the event should prove that an Administration priding itself on the equal devotion it has exhibited to the two principles of moral elevation and Business is Business, had confused the two at last and applied moral principle to a business deal. The effect would be terrific; but it would not be the first time that some such irony has crept in—as for example, at Munich in 1938—to reduce the Pure in Heart to confusion and chagrin.

THE HANGMAN COMETH

Last month there was a young biochemist in California who thought he was on to something important. He had discovered what appeared to be a physical link between cancer, certain forms of heart disease, and schizophrenia —three of the worst among the horrors that afflict the human race. The young man may have been a nut; as a layman I have no opinion on that point; but his project looked good enough to induce the American Cancer Society to put up $4,800 a year to keep him working at it. The American Cancer Society figures that even a faint hope of getting at the cause of that affliction is worth a lot of money.

But this month the young man is working no longer. He will never work again. He is dead and the hope that he represented is extinguished. He seems to have died by his own hand because his great ambition had been destroyed and without it life was no longer worth living. It was his aspiration to become a great research scientist, which meant being employed by some research institution, presumably a university. That aspiration had been wiped out by a summons to appear for questioning by the House Un-American Activities Committee.

All over the country Holy Willies will instantly begin to whine that the fellow was all wrong, that no man is really hurt by such a summons. They lie. Perhaps some of the snivelling hypocrites don't know that they are lying, but they could know it, and decent people do.

To become a really great research scientist is appallingly difficult under the most favorable conditions. Thousands aspire to it, but those who make it in any generation you can number on your fingers and toes. In biochemistry, for instance, you must spend many years working with enormously expensive laboratory equipment, which means that you must be employed by a university.

But if this young man had lived, whenever he applied for employment by a university, some fathead on the board of trustees would say, "Wasn't this fellow questioned by the Un-American Activities Committee? I think we'd better hire somebody else." It would not make the slightest difference why he was questioned; the fathead would not go beyond the simple fact. A career in research science, difficult at best, would be impossible under such a handicap. An older man already famous for his brilliant achievements, an Edward U. Condon, a J. Robert Oppenheimer, may survive although he is crippled by such an incident; but a youngster just starting his career is professionally dead the moment he is subpoenaed.

Yet, this imperfect world being what it is, the hangman must earn his fee and Congress must investigate. We cannot well do away with either; but we realized long ago that Jack Ketch has a villainous job, however necessary, and we have gone to great pains to minimize it. We no longer hand a man over to Jack for "imagining the king's death." If imagining that shooting the President would be a good idea were a capital crime, how many members of the American Bankers' Association would have survived the Roosevelt Administration? We didn't execute Zangara even for actually trying it, but because in the effort he did kill the Mayor of Chicago.

A young squirt in college who at 19 years of age imagined that Communism is a better system than democracy is infinitely less criminal than a business man who, at 50, ordered champagne when the death of Roosevelt was announced. Yet the Un-American Activities Committee is steadily sentencing men to professional death, which sometimes brings on physical death, for just that offense.

If we are determined to continue this form of execution we ought, as a civilized people, to surround it with the forms of decency that we use in executions by the rope. I do not go so far as to suggest that members of the committee, when they question a man about his opinions, should adopt Jack Ketch's custom of covering his face with a black mask, although that might not be a bad idea; but I do suggest that the committee should not be applauded for killing a career that ought to be preserved as a matter of national defense.

I am sure that if I had cancer, and if I believed that a Communist doctor could cure it, I should be violently opposed to hanging that doctor, or driving him out of practice. I should oppose it, even if it were proved that the doctor had no more respect for a Congressman than for a cockroach. The young Californian couldn't cure cancer, but he did seem to be on the way to learning something about it that hadn't been known before, and the more we learn about it the better our chances of discovering a cure. To that extent his destruction should be regretted and resented by every victim of the disease; and they should visit that resentment on the politicians who are recklessly destroying professional careers.

THE EARS OF MIDAS

The Triumph of the Egghead is so complete, so shattering, so devastating that it seems rather unsporting to rub it in. Since Sputnik appeared in the heavens the scramble to cram higher mathematics into the head of every sophomore has become a stampede; and at least one genius has come up with a scheme to carry the calculus down as far as the eighth grade. But yesterday it was an Article of Faith that the only brains worthy of respect are such as it takes to meet a payroll; today it is horrifyingly clear that we needed J. Robert Oppenheimer a great deal more than we needed Joe McCarthy, and that would still be true were the scientist surrounded by a whole harem of Communist concubines and the Senator by a whole platoon of Cohns and Schines.

This sudden reversal of the flight from intelligence is not attributable to anything the eggheads have said or done. It is the gift of the Great Bear, but it is not less valuable on account of its source. Indeed it is more valuable, for it cannot possibly be dismissed as an effect of the sophistry of Adlai Stevenson, or the superciliousness of Dean Acheson, or even as a vestigial remainder of the treason to his class of That Man. It is just a fact.

The effect of the injection of brutal fact into the dream-world of the present Administration has been strongly reminiscent of the sudden appearance of a skunk in a hen-house. The fluttering and squawking have beggared description. The President's effort to reduce the clamor to some sort of coherent utterance was far from successful; it was, rather, a betrayal of the fact that Mr. Eisenhower is no less confused than his underlings.

There was a moment when the President, introducing the name of the learned Dr. Killian, seemed about to say something, but analysis of the full text of the speech dissipates the impression. What Dr. Killian is to do, what he controls, the area in which he is to operate—none of this is clear. It is not certain that he is in actual contact with anything on earth. One is driven to suspect that the President was making propaganda after the Russian fashion, only more so; where they used a dog, he has taken a professor and shot him into outer space. But it doubtful that the effect will be as great.

As for the smaller fry, they are so completely unstrung that only one has presented, thus far, anything that hangs together at all. That one is Dr. Von Braun, the German V-2 designer the Army has been using lately, and even his explanation is somewhat shopworn. Dr. Von Braun asserts that it is all Truman's fault for wasting time on the hydrogen bomb when he might have been working on guided missiles. Dr. Von Braun plainly has his uses; so far he seems unable to build a guided missile, but give him credit for building an alibi, and right now an alibi is what the Administration needs.

The one-party press is doing what it can, but even its ingenuity is unequal to the task of covering up the fact that the failure was a failure to use in the most efficient way the brains that were available. The cult of the Balanced Budget was no substitute for the egghead; it has not balanced the budget and it has produced an embarrassing exposure of our lack of respect for non-financial thinking.

Well, the eggheads have been contending for five and a half years that turning the Cabinet into a millionaires' club was not a good idea because the golden touch is not all the equipment necessary for running a nation. Twice the country has voted that the eggheads were addled, but the Great Bear voted the other way, and when the new moon rose upon a startled world it was his, not ours. To recover the prestige lost at that moment will probably cost a great deal more than the men of the golden touch have saved.

The message of the satellite, the radio experts say, was simply "beep-beep," which everyone translates according to his own fancy, from the optimists who hear in it only the Chorus of the Frogs, to the pessimists who translate it as *"mene, mene, tekel upharsin,"* the inscription on Belshazzar's wall.

For my part, I find it somewhat like the sound of the reeds shaken by the wind, according to the tale told by Ovid. Sputnik is unquestionably a revelation of how a nation may fall behind when it casts out the eggheads and intrusts its destiny to men of the golden touch. One such in ancient times, says Ovid, was served by a barber whose professional service revealed to him a secret so dreadful that he dared not breathe it to any human being, yet so sensational that if he kept it to himself he felt that he would burst. So he dug a hole in the ground and whispered it into the earth; but reeds sprang up at the place, and when they were moved by the wind broadcast the secret to the world.

Is there not a parable for us in this? Sputnik has sprung higher than any reed, to be sure, but what it writes across the sky may be translated by the very same words: "Midas has asses' ears."

NEWSPAPER GUILD-SCHOOL OF JOURNALISM MEMORIAL LECTURE,
University of Minnesota, *October 30, 1958*

PERSONALITY IN JOURNALISM

When he was called upon to pay fitting tribute to his fellow-countrymen who in time of war had died in line of duty, Pericles, that master orator, was embarrassed and thought the thing could be done better in deeds than in words. Accordingly he spent most of his time discussing not the men but the cause for which they gave their lives, and in so doing gave the world the perfect model of a eulogy that prudent speakers have been content to follow ever since.

Bon, Cragg, McKoy, the men in whose honor this audience has assembled, need no praise from you and me. Their fame is beyond our power either to add or to detract. The most we can do is to recognize it and that, I think, cannot be done better than by applying to them the words that Pericles spoke of the Athenian dead: "On the field of battle their feet stood fast, and in an instant, at the height of their fortune, they passed away from the scene, not of their fear, but of their glory."

What remains is, in the words of another great orator, for us the living to resolve "that from these honored dead we take increased devotion to that cause for which they gave the last full measure of devotion." That cause, I beg leave to remind you, was and is something more than patriotism; that cause was and is to make men know the truth that the truth may make them free.

This is, however, a statement of the ideal and it is usually the case that the ideal, to be of practical utility, must be restated in terms of our everyday life. My present effort in that direction is confined to one small segment of the whole subject and it is of necessity no more than the reflection of one man's experience and observation in relation to that segment. A man is a fool if he approaches a subject of this size posing as Sir Oracle whose dicta take rank as universal law. The best I can offer is a guess—an informed guess, I hope, but still a guess, to be accepted or rejected in the light of the hearer's own experience. To emphasize that, I have chosen a subject that itself will raise a question, not to say a protest in the mind of every newspaper man. That subject is "Personality in Journalism," chosen at a time when it is generally agreed that the day of what we have known as personal journalism is long past.

I hope, though, that you will bear with me while I define my terms. I submit that the occupation of collecting and disseminating news, like all Gaul, is divided into three parts; these three I denominate as, first and lowest, job-holding, second, newspaper work, and, third, journalism. These three activities are carried by three classes of animate objects, to wit, first, trained seals, second, reporters and, third, stars.

The difficulty with this classification is that it is extremely fluid. A reporter may flash into stardom on one big story and subside again the next day. I have known more than one star who under the erosion of time and circumstance eventually degenerated into a trained seal. Of course, every trained seal poses as a journalist, and with such success among the ill-informed that they have rendered the term "journalist" almost an epithet within the craft. Nevertheless the distinctions, while highly variable, do exist and represent the more or less permanent status of most persons engaged in handling the news.

My concern on this occasion is with one of the two classes that merge into each other rather vaguely. There is no sharp line of distinction between a reporter and a star, but between either and the mere job-holder, the trained seal, the line is very clear. Find a man who says of his connection with any of the media of publicity, "It's a living," and you have a mere job-holder; but find one who says, "It's life," and you certainly have a reporter, perhaps a star.

Naturally, this must not be taken too literally. Catch a very good reporter just after his pet story has been murdered by the copy-desk; or catch even a great star who has spent a week covering a national political convention and is suffering the great-grandfather of all hangovers, and you have a man who takes a dim view of newspaper work or any other phase of human activity. A man is not himself at such times and his comment then should be off the record.

Most of the men who regard the craft of handling news as merely a living need not give us much concern, for they are transients. They soon pass on to some type of work to which they are better fitted. But a few are highly success-ful and they become the real trained seals, performing not for the joy of crafts-manship, but solely in the hope that somebody will toss them a fish. Some of them write brilliantly, but not for the purpose of conveying information, only in the hope of pleasing the front office, or for some even more disreputable reason. Some become nationally notorious, and think they are nationally fa-mous; but none is really part of the craft except in the sense that an infection is part of the victim; and all have the capacity to give honest newspaper men bad moments when they regret that they did not in youth take up plumbing or bricklaying in a serious way.

Let that be enough for mere job-holding. I now invite your attention to the very elusive activity that I have named journalism, but which I cannot de-fine in terms that satisfy me, to say nothing of Noah Webster. It is a sort of emanation from reporting but it is not reporting, for it conforms to no style-book. It is literature, but a very special form of literature, one that baffles the most astute professors of English. And it is an activity so intensely personal that I set above it in that respect only Solomon's great mystery of life, the way of a man with a maid.

The classical model of this form, in so far as it has a model, is Julius Caesar's *Commentaries* on his conquest of Gaul. A modern example of a very high order of excellence is John Hersey's *Hiroshima*. But the oddest with which I am acquainted dates from 1822 and is a report of a prize-fight written by William Hazlitt. I choose it to illustrate my point because this story, viewed strictly as reporting, is almost fabulously bad. Hazlitt violates every rule known to a self-respecting copy-desk. He has no lead. He ambles. He dashes off after every fugitive idea that crosses his path, now to this side, now to that. He is sublimely indifferent to personal names, place names and dates. He actually lost count of the number of rounds, and it is from other sources that we learn that the bout went seventeen. I cannot recall a piece of writing that, judged by the accepted standards of news reporting, would better justify firing the cub reporter who turned it in.

Yet after a hundred and thirty-six years people still read it with delight and many account it the greatest description of a prize-fight that exists in the English language. For when you have read it you know what happened, how it happened and, to a very large extent, why it happened. Hazlitt spotted the blow that really beat Hickman in the third round, and thereafter the reader is in no doubt that it is merely a matter of how much longer he can stand up. But the story does more than that. It presents the event as a whole—the fighters, the crowd, the tension, even the weather. All those extraneous circumstances that at first seemed inexcusable padding contribute to the total effect, and not one could be omitted without some loss.

But if you ask me how he did it, the only answer I can make is, "He did it because he was Hazlitt." Which carries us no further toward an explanation.

Is that, however, a valid objection? For my part, I am inclined to regard as a weakness of the modern world our reluctance to recognize anything that we cannot explain. I am aware that the Great Man theory of history has been largely discredited for good reasons; but I doubt that those reasons do much toward solving the problem of personality.

Sometimes I am inclined to think that they were wiser in the days of the medieval guilds, whose members had a stock phrase to describe their peculiar body of knowledge. They referred to "the art and mystery" of carpentry, or weaving, or brewing, or brick-laying. The phrase was forgotten until H. L. Mencken dredged it up to use in a satirical sense with reference to things about which there is neither art nor mystery.

Nevertheless the words are not meaningless. Every trade, craft, art, and profession has certain techniques that must be mastered before the theorist can practice. These may be taught, and a student of even mediocre intelligence can attain some degree of proficiency in their use. These may be described as the art appertaining to the occupation. But certain students exhibit an aptitude somehow to learn what has not been taught. Let us go back a hundred years and consider two boys, both handy with tools, both interested in wood-working, both serving a long apprenticeship under a master craftsman. When their term is over we have two cabinet-makers. That is the art of the trade. But one of the two is Duncan Phyfe and the other isn't; and that is its mystery.

It is of this mystery that I propose to speak, not to teach it, for John Dewey, Mark Hopkins and Socrates rolled into one could not teach it, but to describe it and to urge recognition, not merely of its existence but also of its high value to the craft of the news handlers and to the craftsmen themselves. Not every man is given the ability to penetrate the mystery of his own craft;

but every man who knows that it exists may cherish the hope of penetrating it, and this hope marks the difference between those who make a living by their labor and those who live by it.

Mencken once made a remark to me that I heard rather carelessly, but remembered; and as I thought it over, its implications became darker and darker until today I consider it a bit of pessimism that is enough to make Schopenhauer look like a humorist. He said, "Johnson, you and I are very fortunate people in that we can make a living by doing what we would do anyhow; not many can say that."

It is true as far as I am concerned, and I fear it is true as regards most men. If I had millions I know that I would still be fevered by desire to write the perfect news story. I know well enough that I shall never do it, nor even come within many miles of it, not if I outlived Methuselah; but I am addicted to the hopeless effort as firmly as a drunkard to his bottle, and through that addiction I have gained the means of sustaining life. How many men, given a fortune today, would return tomorrow to the treadmill on which they had spent their most productive years? A considerable number, certainly—probably all scholars, artists and scientists, and positively all born newspaper men, but a majority of workers? That I cannot believe, and the fact gives a dreary plausibility to Thoreau's remark that most men live lives of quiet desperation.

I do not claim that this signifies any particular merit in either the craft or the craftsmen. Sometimes, indeed, I am inclined to think there may be a touch of the puerile about the whole business and that the greatest of journalists is essentially childish. For the perfect news story would be simply one that transfers from the reporter's mind to another mind an experience, exact to a hairsbreadth, complete in its inclusion of every significant factor, emotional or intellectual, and rigid in its exclusion of everything insignificant or irrelevant. It is an ideal, of course, a feat far beyond human accomplishment, but that is not the point. What is the basis of every journalist's intense desire to accomplish it? Perhaps it is nothing more than the emotion of the excited kid who bursts into the house exclaiming, "I know something that you don't know!" and who is impossible to deter from telling his story instantly. Be that as it may, the emotion is certainly one form of rapture.

Furthermore, I submit that there is nothing more intensely personal in the whole realm of human experience. Then to talk of the elimination of personal journalism is to talk arrant nonsense. We do it because we fall into semantic error. What we mean by "personal journalism" never was journalism at all but propaganda in the sense in which Rome uses the word in the title of the Congregation *de propaganda fide,* that is, propagation of the faith." Henry Watterson, for example, usually accounted the last of the great personal journalists, devoted much of his effort, not to the communication of truth, but to imposing the opinions of Watterson upon his readers—not necessarily an ignoble effort, but not journalism.

To the extent that the opinions of Watterson—or of Greeley, Dana, Bennett, Bowles and the other giants of old—coincided with truth, they were not merely important, they were more important than the most scrupulously accurate narration of events unaccompanied by any explanation of the relation of the events in question to conditions resulting from past events. It is possible, indeed it is common for a man to be in possession of the facts without having an inkling of the truth; and the function of journalism is to communicate the truth. The messenger who brought King Louis XVI word of the fall of the Bastille was a reporter up to the moment when the King exclaimed, "But this is a revolt!" and the man replied, "No, Sire, it is a revolution." With that, he became a journalist.

Every news editor knows this and acknowledges it by his assiduity in seeking to supply "background material" for his current news stories, but we are perversely reluctant to admit it in our discussions of the theory of the business. The trouble is that we have here a factor not amenable to analysis and control, which comes into collision with the necessity for order and discipline in the management of any enterprise as large as even a small-city newspaper. We have accordingly adopted the staff system at the policy-making level, especially on the editorial page. In view of the great and increasing complexity of the operation this is doubtless the only practical expedient available to the modern newspaper; but it ignores the disconcerting lesson of experience, that when it comes to getting at and dragging out the truth behind the facts, one head is sometimes better than two, and usually better than half a dozen.

This is contrary to accepted professional doctrine and I have nothing to offer in its support except the observed fact that influence upon public opinion seems to have shifted from the anonymous editorial to the signed column or, in the case of radio and television, to the identified commentator. This I believe to be the measure of the impact of personality. I cannot accept the explanation that the signed column is powerful because it is syndicated to an enormous clientele. It was years after I had joined the Baltimore *Sun* that Frank Kent and H. L. Mencken first began to appear in any other newspaper; but either of them could shake Baltimore more profoundly than the heaviest thunder of the editorial page.

Superficially, this would seem to indicate that the public reposes more confidence in the columnist than in the newspaper but that, I think, is an oversimplification. It is nearer the truth to say that most of us have more confidence in our own judgment of a man than in our judgment of an organization. There are columnists—some of them widely syndicated—in whose integrity or intelligence I have no confidence whatever, but that they influence my opinions is undeniable. When such a writer adopts an attitude toward a subject to which I have paid no attention I am immediately more than half-persuaded that the opposite attitude is the right one. Since on those subjects with which I am familiar the fellow has been wrong three-fourths of the time, I judge that it is three to one that he is wrong this time. But I have found the composite opinion reflected by the editorial page neither as consistently right as a good columnist, nor as consistently wrong as a bad one; so it is a less reliable guide than either.

I feel that I can understand a man, especially if I know his past record, because he is constituted pretty much as I am; but an institution is different and I am suspicious of my own ability to judge it correctly.

But there is another consideration. I think that most of us feel that the highest social value attainable by an institution is intelligence; the higher value, wisdom, is attainable only by a person. This is because intelligent conduct is the result of following well-known rules, but how a man arrives at wisdom nobody knows, and that applies to the wise man himself. Wisdom implies knowledge, of course, but its essence is the form of a man's response to his learning, and that is a mystery of personality. But while its nature eludes us, we know that it is invariably associated with three other personal qualities, to wit, experience, diligence and integrity. I have never yet seen a really wise man who was not intellectually and emotionally mature, a hard worker, and rigidly honest; he may or may not be brilliant, versatile, witty and so on, but he must be seasoned, industrious and upright.

My conclusion then is that personality in journalism, far from being an inadmissible intrusion, is essential to the highest excellence. But please note well that I have carefully distinguished between journalism and routine reporting. The injection of personality in writing a weather forecast would be a monstrosity; and the bulk of a reporter's daily labor, however much it may differ in form, is basically as purely routine as the weather report.

The fact that all this argument leads up to is that the great journalist is an individualist, but establishing the fact is a waste of effort since nobody denies it. However, there is a truth behind the fact that seems to be unknown to newspaper management in some cases, and in many more cases is consistently ignored. This is the truth that the journalist is one of the few individualists remaining in a world that has less and less room for anybody but the organization man.

In a world driven to more and more minute specialization, I can cite only three classes of men who are in the nature of things generalists, as opposed to specialists. They are the judge, the clergyman and the journalist. As regards these three, everybody's business is legitimately their business. In these days lawyers customarily specialize, but the man on the bench may not. I suppose professors of theology may specialize, but the pastor of a flock may not. Even newspapers employ financial writers and sports writers and dramatic, music, literary and art critics, some of whom have gathered well-earned fame; but for all that they are side-shows. Under the big top are the intellectual acrobats who can land on their feet no matter where they are dropped; and the business of communication is dependent upon them to an extent not approached by any other widespread human activity, the church alone excepted.

And it is not only the press that urgently needs this highly personal trait, this ability to uncover the truth behind the facts. The world at large needs it more urgently than the press. In the current *Harper's Magazine* is an article by one of the most eminent and I may add one of the most highly specialized specialists of our time, Dr. Robert Oppenheimer, the physicist who directed the construction of the first atomic bomb. Oppenheimer notes with alarm the great and rapidly widening gap between scientific knowledge and the experience of the average layman. He makes the startling assertion that

> *nearly everything that is now known was not in any book when most of us went to school; we cannot know it unless we have picked it up*

since. This in itself presents a problem of communication that is nightmarishly formidable.

Who is to solve this problem? Not the specialists, for Oppenheimer points out that they have great difficulty in communicating with each other. They cannot do so at all except by resorting to the common language of mathematical symbols, as medieval scholars resorted to Latin. But the typical American understands mathematical symbolism no better than he understands Latin or Greek; a translation is imperatively required.

Nor can a successful translation be expected of a mere reporter, no matter how highly trained he may be in the matter of factual accuracy. He may get the facts straight enough; but he will not communicate the truth behind the facts unless to the skill he has acquired by training he adds wisdom acquired God knows how, but certainly not by following the rules in any style-book.

Oppenheimer spoke conservatively when he described as "nightmarish" the responsibility that rests upon newspaper men and other servants of the media of communication at this juncture in the world's history. It is all of that; but that isn't the aspect of it that a first-rate man considers most intently. If the job is nightmarish, on the other hand the reward for its successful accomplishment will be fabulous. When I say "reward" I do not have in mind money or fame; I mean the consciousness of having done something in the world, realization that one has exercised power, the assurance that because one has lived and labored the world is not, and never will be again, exactly what it was before.

This is the reward that every giant figure in history has sought, but that very few have attained. It is all very well to assert that great men do not make but are made by history, yet few of us can persuade ourselves that the world would have been exactly the same had Alexander, or Caesar, or Napoleon never lived. Perhaps if they had not existed the work would have been done by someone else; but that is like saying that *Hamlet* was not written by William Shakespeare, but by another man of the same name. The work was done, and whoever did it stamped his image and superscription on the face of the world, which is the greatest accomplishment within the reach of man.

As Oppenheimer points out, a vast new body of hitherto unknown truth has been discovered in recent years, the greater part of which is completely outside the experience, therefore beyond the comprehension of the majority of Americans. This is a situation that cannot be allowed to continue for it is knowledge of the truth that makes men free and without it civilization will not only cease to advance, but will drift back in the direction of barbarism and slavery.

Much of the labor of making this truth available must fall upon the press. But it is not hack-work. None of it is within the capacity of the trained seals, and not much of it can be done by reporters, even good ones. For it is not mere reporting. It calls for a very accurate weighing of the significance of the facts, on the one hand, and on the other, a rare understanding of the average layman's habits of thought.

That kind of knowledge you don't get out of books. It is an element of personality. But the man who has it, and who applies it diligently, exactly, and honestly during the next ten years will hold a plastic world in his hands and will shape and mould it to an extent never approached by any of the tin-pot emperors and strutting dictators who have occupied so much of the front page in recent years. The reward of the great journalist will be to stamp his image and superscription upon the future.

If that is a bit too dramatic for your taste, let us tone it down a bit by substituting a metaphor from the war in which the men whose memories we are here to honor gave their lives. Let us say, rather, that the first-rate journalist, the journalist with personality as well as technical skill, the journalist whose knowledge is transmuted into wisdom, will make his mark as did that shadowy figure known, but never seen, by our armies in Europe. So when the triumphant battalions of liberty sweep forward, driving ignorance and superstition before them, however fast they advance they will always find before them the cryptic inscription, "Kilroy was here."

THE NEW REPUBLIC, "The Superficial Aspect," *May 25, 1959*

JOHN FOSTER DULLES

Cynics may be slow to believe it, but American politics does have its rules of decency, one of which was vividly stated by Old Bullion Benton in explaining why he had instantly ceased his attacks on his enemy, W. H. Crawford, after Crawford suffered a paralytic stroke: "When God Almighty lays His hand on a man, sir, Benton takes his off, sir."

The rule requires that in this space, where the policies and personality of John Foster Dulles have been sharply and frequently criticized, mention should now be made of his conspicuous virtues. His patriotism was flawless. His resolution was granitic. His courage was steely. In an era when a limber mediocrity seems to be the ideal of half the men in public life, these characteristics made Dulles something of a marvel.

It is regrettable that it should be worth mentioning, but Dulles had another quality that made him notable in the Washington of his time. Nobody, not even his sharpest critics, questioned his personal integrity. None dared insinuate that he was a kept man of the oil interests, the real-estate interests or any other interests. There were no vicuna coats, oriental rugs, or receipted hotel bills that he had to explain. No one has produced letters that he wrote on State Department stationery urging favorable treatment for corporations in which he had an interest. He did not include in the circle of his intimate friends persons in whom the FBI and other police authorities took a strong, if unflattering, interest. Like Hughes and Hoover, who sat in the Harding Cabinet, Dulles emerged from a questionable environment without a stain.

All this is attested, not by sycophants and flatterers but by witnesses who are hostile in the sense that they do not agree with the man's official policies, but who are not so obsessed by personal spite as to deny an opponent the credit that is his just due. The danger is that Dulles' real and substantial value may be covered up and lost by an ill-advised effort to pass off upon the country a false image by claiming for the man accomplishments that he did not achieve.

The fact is that in its foreign relations the position of the United States has steadily deteriorated since 1953. It is certainly true that this was by no means the fault of John Foster Dulles alone. There were a great many other contributing factors. But he did not stem the ebb tide. It was not for lack of effort. On the contrary, there is only too much reason to believe that he short-ened his own life by trying to do more than his physical frame could stand. Nor was it due to any moral deviousness or failure in courage.

It was due rather to the lack of imagination that has characterized the Eisenhower Administration from the start, and that has made it the most unrealistic since that of Calvin Coolidge, whose loss of touch with reality led us into the panic of 1929. Such fantasies as the theory that Chiang Kai-shek is China, that Syngman Rhee is a protagonist of liberty, that we are gaining prestige in the Near East, and that Charles de Gaulle is a Great Power, were not evolved but inherited by Dulles. That is an irrelevance. Regardless of their origin, these mythical entities have been accepted by an Administration lack-ing the intellectual agility to discriminate between principle and policy.

The truth that the identical principle may be supported at different times by diametrically opposite policies is one that John Foster Dulles never grasped, and it was his misfortune to serve under a chief hampered by the same dis-ability. They were betrayed by the shifting, twisting course of events to such an extent that their rigid consistency sometimes became inconsistent, and their principles seemed occasionally to come under Cornford's bitter defini-tion: "A principle is a rule of inaction, giving valid general reasons for not doing, in a specific instance, what to unprincipled instinct would seem to be right."

So any attempt to erect this figure into a great Secretary of State is likely to be not merely futile but damaging in that it obscures the admirable qual-ities that he did possess. He was not a great Secretary of State, but he was a man fortunately circumstanced by birth who refused to rely on his good for-tune. He could have lived without labor, but he chose to work hard. He could have worked for himself, but he chose to work for his country.

He could have acquired high esteem and obsequious consideration in his profession without incurring the frustration, injustices and stinging criticism inseparable from public life; but he chose to incur them if thereby he could perform public service. This made him an American whose example any idealist may happily commend to the rising generation. It is enough; and his wiser friends will not risk obscuring it by claiming more.

TIME TO GET UP

It was a sad day for the nation, in the opinion of President Eisenhower, when he had to invoke the sanctions of the Taft-Hartley Act to halt the steel strike.

He can say that again. Indeed, it was the 93rd sad day for everybody in the nation except, perhaps, the steel companies, who could use a summer stoppage of production to reduce their inventories of high-priced steel. But the first 90 days had pretty well done that, so it was beginning to be a sad day for the steel companies, too, which made it unanimous.

Apparently the President was not nearly so much impressed by the sadness of the day when he promptly invoked the law against longshoremen, who struck companies that didn't want a strike. Yet that was a sad day, too, not because the President had to act, but because he had to use a meat-axe to perform a delicate operation. The Taft-Hartley Act is a clumsy implement with which to repair lesions in the economic system, but it is the only one available, and even the Supreme Court can't change that.

This is not only sad, it is also bad. It is a reflection upon American leadership, political and economic, another aspect of the intellectual sterility that has had our foreign relations hung on dead center for the past seven years, unable to contrive any means of buttressing our position in the world except the dubious expedient of terrorizing our potential enemies by the threat of our nuclear arms.

It is both idle and unfair to lay all the blame at the door of the politicians. Political leadership is no more bankrupt than economic. In the steel industry, for instance, when management and labor can devise no other means of settling disputes than a resort to cold war, it ill becomes them to criticize Eisenhower for resorting to the same ineffective and expensive means in the international field.

Labor's charge that management is trying to snatch away advantages gained in a contract 15 years old may be well founded, but it is specious logic, anyhow. In modern industry any contract 15 years old is open to suspicion. However equitable it may have been when it was signed, there is a strong presumption that it is now outmoded. Certainly other features of industrial operation, up-to-date in 1944, are antiquated in 1959, so the burden of proof is upon those who favor retention of the practices of a decade and a half ago. But on the other hand the public's suspicion that the steel companies welcomed this strike as a means of reducing inventories without reducing prices is the suspicion that they are indulging in thinking as archaic as Secretary Dulles' "massive retaliation." To precipitate a strike for any such purpose is as stupidly extravagant as it would be to use an atomic bomb to demolish a termite-eaten flophouse. The late gyrations of the stock market are evidence enough that the steel strike has shaken the whole economic structure, and the fall-out in the shape of collateral unemployment may be costlier than granting all the workers' demands would have been.

Perhaps the flight from intelligence that has impressed and depressed thoughtful observers for nearly 10 years is attributable to fatigue. It is true that the New Deal-Fair Deal era did keep our brains under considerable pressure for 20 years, and perhaps we simply couldn't take it any longer. It may be plausibly argued that only a mentally exhausted country would have taken seriously the kind of campaigning that Nixon did against Helen Gahagan Douglas, and that Joseph McCarthy did against every exponent of common or uncommon sense.

But how long, for Heaven's sake, will it take us to rest up? For seven years we have relaxed under the influence of that cosmic tranquillizer, Eisenhower, a blanket so wet that he could make a dull show out of the capture of John Brown performed by the original cast. Surely, we should by now be showing some signs of recuperation, even from the furious driving of such Jehus as Roosevelt and Truman. But the signs are woefully few and far between; and a counter-indication is the mental and moral inertia that let the steel strike go for 93 days without discovery of a single new approach to industrial peace.

Meanwhile the rising cost of living pinches harder and harder and the presence of 12.5 million "investors" in the stock market sets such analysts as Sylvia Porter to making chilling comparisons with 1928. Yes, it is a sad day for the country, but not because Eisenhower at long last took action. It is sad because of the widespread repetition, in Washington and elsewhere, of that ancient chant of the Sluggard: "Yet a little sleep, a little slumber, a little folding of the hands to sleep."

THE NEW REPUBLIC, "The Superficial Aspect," *April 4, 1960*

COME FORTH, DICKENS!

J. B. Priestley, the English scrivener, may be a shrewd and penetrating critic, or he may be a garrulous old fool, or he may be both, but he comes up now and then with an off-beat idea that gives wings to speculation.

Consider, for example, his recent analysis of Hemingway as an author who developed a style exactly fitting his war experience and has ever since been looking around for experience to fit the style. Not finding it at home, he has had to wander to Spain, to Italy, to Havana, and all over the lot, meanwhile letting the pageant of America pass unnoticed.

The criticism is acute, but its justice hangs upon the assumption that there is a pageant, and that it is susceptible of treatment in the fictional form. The stipulation is not as inane as it may sound. Hemingway is certainly not the only American who seems committed to the theory that his philosophic and spiritual experience for the past few years could be covered as succinctly as Mark Twain did his in the diary he started as a schoolboy. The entries for the first seven days, said Mark, were identical; they all read, "Got up. Washed. Went to bed." After that, he gave up the idea of becoming a modern Pepys.

Like everyone else whose name appears in print regularly, I receive comments from Americans, some friends, many complete strangers, on a great variety of subjects viewed from many different angles. Recently, however, I noticed what seems to be an increasing trend among the majority; it is a tendency to pose like William Morris as "the idle singer of an empty day."

Such communications are hard to answer. Indeed, if a writer is sensitive enough to be galled by the vapidity of the times, shall his complaint be answered with a tut-tut? Should it not rather be approved and fomented? Certainly it is far more admirable than smug complacence, aimless and bootless though it may be.

It is precisely here that the Priestley comment becomes something more than a crack at an eminent literary person. Perhaps it is a comment not on Hemingway alone, but on the American intellectual, whether novelist, historian, philosopher, editor or politician. Perhaps what ails most of us is a vague and fruitless effort to find in the United States of 1960 experience adapted to a previously-developed style. Naturally, such an effort is bound to interfere with, if not to inhibit entirely, any effort to develop a style adapted to our special American experience.

This is not offered as an assertion of fact, or even as a persuasive theory, but purely as a speculation. For my part, I confess that I am at a loss to apply it. To what imaginable human experience, for example, is the Eisenhower style adapted? That it is adapted is obvious from more than the election returns. It affords to millions a satisfaction that neither Pater, nor Proust, nor Faulkner, nor even Mortimer Adler can supply; but the nature of that satisfaction is beyond my grasp; which is certainly a partial explanation of why I shall never be accounted an eminent literary person.

Mr. Priestley argues that a novelist of the caliber of Charles Dickens would know the answer and by supplying it would enchant the *illuminati* and the Philistines alike. No doubt he is right, but why confine it to novelists? A politician throwing an equivalent weight of metal would be equally effective.

For one thing, he would be able to restate liberalism in terms comprehensible to the generation born during the depression, which is more than can be done by one whose style was formed under Woodrow Wilson, or modeled thereon. The mudsill of political liberalism is in the phrase, "The right is more precious than peace," a Wilsonian assertion; but it is my considered belief that the line might be written in Hittite for all the significance it communicates to the present generation.

Why? It may be a matter of style. It must be something of the kind, for the alternative, that there has been some biological mutation of the species in the past thirty years, is nonsense. But if the modification that interrupts communication is psychological, then the onus of understanding it rests upon liberal leadership.

Is it conceivable that instead of diligently laboring to master the new style we have been wandering to Spain and Italy and Havana seeking experience adapted to our old style? It is a disconcerting idea, but it cannot be shrugged off. It explains too much.

Incidentally, it throws us back toward the Great Man theory of history; for if a man endowed with a political or philosophical genius comparable to the literary genius of Charles Dickens is the liberals' one hope of being renaturalized in modern America, then all most of us can do is stand by and pray.

THE ATLANTIC, *July 1960*

TO LIVE AND DIE IN DIXIE

As the twentieth century swung toward its three-quarter post, the American who felt left furthest behind was probably the citizen of the late Confederacy who was unfortunate enough to be able not only to read the newspapers but to understand something of what was in them.

The ability is not universal, not even, as our semanticist would say, "coterminous" with literacy. All America, but the South especially, seems to be afflicted with great numbers of citizens who apparently do their reading through spectacles equipped with lenses having a special property of fluorescence that enables the reader to detect infrared and ultraviolet where nothing appears to the naked eye except prosaic black and white.

These persons are happily free of any feeling of retardation. On the contrary, they are convinced that they move in the van of civilization and are irate when their certainty is questioned. To me they appear to be insane, but they are not unhappy, and who knows? they may be the only sane people in a mad world. There is profound philosophical penetration in the sweet singer's immortal lines:

> *See the happy moron;*
>   *He doesn't give a damn.*
> *I wish I were a moron—*
>   *My God, perhaps I am!*

Nevertheless, irrevocably committed to the illusion that I am sane, I see in the antics of the region of my birth in recent years evidence of a cultural lag appreciably greater than that of the rest of the nation, and to say so is to accuse the South of being far behind indeed. When Eisenhower dispatched federal troops to occupy the city of Little Rock, Arkansas, he retreated behind the year 1877, when President Hayes withdrew the last of the army of occupation; but Eisenhower did so because the state of Arkansas had retreated behind the year 1833, when President Jackson embalmed, cremated, and buried the doctrine of nullification.

The genesis of this lag is easily detected. In 1868, the year of its ratification, the Fourteenth Amendment bore no more relation to the facts of human experience than the axioms of non-Euclidean geometries bear to them. The South, living of necessity in a factual world and under compulsion to adjust to nonfactual law, resorted to subterfuge as the only way out of the impasse, and the rest of the country, unable to devise any workable alternative, tolerated the subterfuge for many years.

But the departure from candor bore the fruit that it always bears. In the course of time, the South came to believe its own bunk. The grandfather clause was written into the constitutions of various Southern states by men who were perfectly aware of its disingenuousness. It provided that the literacy test might be ignored if the applicant for registration as a voter was a descendant of a citizen qualified to vote before 1867, and its purpose was to disqualify illiterate negroes—at that time, the great bulk of the negro population—while admitting illiterate whites to the suffrage.

It was frankly a device for defeating the purpose of the Fourteenth Amendment while apparently complying with the letter of the law. In some cases the quality of this device was kept in mind, and when white illiteracy had been sharply reduced, as in North Carolina in 1908, the grandfather clause, having served its purpose, was abrogated. But in other states it remained until it was struck down by the Supreme Court of the United States. By that time, its essential fraudulence had been forgotten and it was regarded by many not as a doubtful expedient to gain time until the negro could be prepared for full citizenship but as the embodiment of a sacred principle; to wit, the principle that the negro should not ever be admitted to full citizenship.

Acceptance of a fraud inevitably involves some deterioration of character. In that sentence is compressed the political history of the South since Reconstruction. Its exegesis is the whole corpus of William Faulkner's work, admittedly the greatest artistic achievement of the South in this century. The tale that Faulkner tells in many volumes is that the very section in which once the concept of honor was so highly esteemed that for even a fantastic idea of honor men did not hesitate to sacrifice life itself has now accepted fraud for three generations and has become, as one critic put it, "tricky and mean." It is a tragedy worthy of the novelist's genius, tragedy on a more than epic scale.

Yet I have never encountered a white Southerner without pride in his heritage. Some no doubt exist, but they are invisible, presumably because they conceal their Southern nativity. For the rest, the danger in which they stand is not that of losing their pride of birth but that of permitting it to swell into a foolish and offensive arrogance. Men whom ambition or economic or professional necessity drove out of the South decades ago still tend to proclaim, rather than to conceal, their origin. Even those who fled from the intellectual sterility of their early environment realize that its emotional wealth is prodigious; they may be able to think better almost anywhere else, but nowhere else can they feel as intensely, so they are aware that their voluntary exile is not all gain.

On the face of it this is a paradox, and to resolve it should be interesting and possibly instructive. That it can be done completely is incredible, but even a partial resolution may contribute somewhat to a clearer understanding of the continental confusion that is the United States of America today.

The greatest enemy of the late Confederacy was certainly not Ulysses S. Grant, or even William T. Sherman. They were, in fact, its political and economic liberators—a trifle rough in their methods, careless of life in Grant's case and of fire in Sherman's, but in the end highly effective. They had a job to do, and they did it; the modern South has no just cause to regard either with anything but a somewhat grim yet very real respect.

Far more lasting damage was done it by men whom the South adores: at the head of the list, Stephen Collins Foster, the Pennsylvania magician who betrayed the South into hugging the delusion that melody is all in all, in complete disregard of the tonic value—nay, the harsh necessity—of counterpoint. Deceivers of the same kind were orators of Henry Grady's school and a long procession of literary gents, beginning with John Pendleton Kennedy and culminating in Thomas Nelson Page.

They meant no harm, and, to do them justice, they told no lies. But a lie does not have to be told; by what they did not tell, these fictioneers propagated the titanic lie that Keats has preserved in the amber of great poetry:

Beauty is truth, truth beauty, — that is all
Ye know on earth, and all ye need to know.

The South believed it, and since the South is beautiful, it developed a complacency that has wreaked more permanent devastation upon it than Sherman perpetrated all the way from Atlanta to Savannah and thence up to Durham Station, where Johnston surrendered. Atlanta was soon rebuilt on a greater and finer scale, and before they died, such great ladies as my old friend Mrs. MacMaster, of Columbia, had acquired other spoons. That damage was temporary. But to this day there remain far too many otherwise intelligent Southerners with an implicit faith that the beauty of the South compensates for all else that it lacks.

Precisionists will promptly argue that when these Southerners say "beautiful," what they mean is "pretty." There is some force in the objection, but not much. Even the geographical South defeats it; to call pretty the Valley of Virginia, or the view from Mitchell, highest peak east of the Mississippi, or old Charleston, or the enclosed gardens of New Orleans would be to perpetrate a semantic crime. The magnificence of Daytona Beach, the sullen menace of Hatteras, the Potomac before Mount Vernon, and Old Man River himself command reverence, not delight. Even the magnolia, which cynics have made almost a term of disdain, is superb—somewhat spectral, perhaps, but far beyond mere prettiness.

It is beauty of a different type, however, that worked the ensorcelling of the modern South and, like Vivian's spell upon Merlin, put its strong magic to sleep. It is the beauty of the legend, informing and irradiating the landscape but distorting the vision and paralyzing the will. It is the fashion of the moment to denigrate that beauty, calling it sickly sentimentalism; but beauty it was, and is, and ever will be—Circean, indeed, but real.

From Kennedy's *Swallow Barn* to Mitchell's *Gone with the Wind,* just a hundred years apart, it has enchanted men of every section and undoubtedly will continue to enchant them as long as the telling of tales delights the human heart. It is, in fact, a recrudescence of the Arthurian legend, of loyalty, love, and derring-do all compact—in short, romance. Tara and Red Rock were never built of brick and stone but of the same dream stuff that composed the walls and towers of Camelot; yet when all is said and done, it is the only building material that is utterly indestructible.

A man from Iowa or Maine can read this legendry with no sense of personal involvement, therefore with no more damage than he sustains from reading the exploits of the Round Table. Who in his right mind would seriously claim blood kinship with Gareth or Pelleas? But in the South, all this is told as of grandfather's day; it is close, it is intimate: hence, the Southerner is moved by a dangerously strong impulse to maintain the legend, and "that way madness lies."

Nevertheless, the beauty is there, it is real, and it is imbued with potent sorcery. It involves the three great verities, poverty and love and war, whose acquaintance every man must make if he is to be completely educated; and no amount of abuse by the mawkish and the maudlin can destroy it. The calamity of the modern Southerner is that of Don Quixote—his wits were already lost before the curate arrived to sort out the meretricious from the sound.

But the South is in fact beautiful, whether you construe the South as meaning the land or the legend, and the memory of its beauty grips the emotions of its sons, no matter how long they may have been away. The misfortune is that all too many Southerners believe Keats not only when he says truthfully "that is all ye know," but also when he lies by adding "and all ye need to know."

However, nothing absolute can be said of forty million people, not even that they all exist; for within the time that it takes to make the statement some will die and others will be born. Not all Southerners have succumbed to Vivian's spell, and relatively few have succumbed entirely. O. Henry's former Confederate colonel turned editor of *The Rose of Dixie* is a recognizable type that survives to this day, but even fifty years ago his obsession with the legendary South was recognized as an oddity which was not to be taken seriously.

As recently as the spring of 1960, the British critic D. W. Brogan considered it worthy of note that, although when he began reading American history as a boy in Scotland he sided with the South, after he became a mature man he realized that "the right side won" the Civil War. As I am some years older than Mr. Brogan, it may interest him to learn that, as a boy in North Carolina, I heard and heeded an uncle who had served the Confederacy faithfully and well but who told me, "Yes, they had more men, and more artillery, and more rations, and more everything else, but, boy, don't you ever believe that was what whipped us. We lost that war because God Almighty had decreed that slavery had to go."

Mr. Brogan is quite right in noting that, although the legalists, citing Abraham Lincoln as their chief witness, have proved conclusively that slavery was not the issue, the fact remains that the war was about slavery because the legal issue, secession, arose out of slavery. But Mr. Brogan is quite wrong in assuming that the South had not realized that as early as fifty years ago. It was known in North Carolina that the right side won, even when boys in Scotland were still siding with the South.

The argument against the South that would be conclusive, if it were sustained by fact, is that having appealed to the arbitrament of the sword, the South refused to abide by the judgment it had invited, and so was forsworn. But the argument is only doubtfully sustained by the fact. The undisputed fact is that the judgment was that slavery had to go, and it went. Even the furiously reviled Black Codes of Mississippi and Louisiana did not attempt to re-establish legal slavery and were less rigorous than the apartheid legislation of South Africa ninety years later. If the North, victorious but stung by grievous wounds, imposed, after hostilities had ceased, new conditions not nominated in the bond, who was then forsworn? It is a pretty question, one that has given Southern casuists their opportunity.

After so many years, however, even to admit the argument to debate is casuistry in the pejorative sense. Attempts at the attribution of blame hinder, do not help, the search for a solution of current problems, most of them arising from the refusal of the South to grant the negro all the rights and privileges appertaining to the status of first-class citizenship.

Note well the phraseology: "to grant him the rights"—not "to recognize his status"; for the latter is a refusal based on the simple and solid fact that, taken in the mass, the negro is not a first-class citizen. There is no convincing evidence that he is biologically inferior, but even Gunnar Myrdal admits that there is every evidence that he is culturally inferior. Two hundred and fifty years of bondage have left their mark, which ninety-five years of freedom have not erased.

The casuists of the South contend that this is in itself evidence of the negro's irremovable inferiority. Those of the North contend as fiercely that it is evidence only of the irremediable wickedness of the white South. Both contentions are empty gabble, innocent of logical consistency or historical perspective. Logically, the existence of this republic can be justified only on the assumption that the status of a freeman is favorable to the development of political competence; were it not so, we should have done better to adhere to some other system. Historically, Runnymede, starting point of the English-speaking peoples' struggle for political liberty, is nearly seven hundred and fifty years in the past; yet he who thinks that we have perfected our competence is an optimist indeed. Shall we then brand the negro as inferior because he has not accomplished in ninety-five years what the white man has not completed in more than seven centuries? Or shall we brand the white South as wicked because it has not performed the miracle of endowing another race with qualities it is still struggling to develop in its own character?

Citing individual exceptions is no rebuttal. Certainly to call Ralph Bunche a second-class citizen would be as preposterous as to call King Arthur a second-class Briton. Thurgood Marshall is a first-rate lawyer, Marian Anderson a first-rate artist, and so it goes down a long and scintillant roster. But these are examples of what the negro is capable of becoming, not of what he presently is; and what he presently is determines his influence upon the situation existing here and now.

The difficulty of the South is that, although it sees clearly enough what is directly before it, its distant vision is blurred. It is weak in applying the logic of its own experience to test the hypothesis now presented. It is beyond belief that many Southerners will concede that their political history since 1776 has been so complete a failure that they have made no advance in the art of self-government. It may be admitted that they have produced no masters of the theory of government superior to Jefferson, Madison, Marshall, Clay, and Calhoun, but the masses certainly know more about the management of public affairs than their great-great-grandfathers knew, and the development of their skill they owe to long practice under political freedom.

The hypothesis now presented is that the same conditions will produce in negroes the same effect. The method of testing it is, of course, to proceed as if it were true. The objection to applying that method is the necessity of risking the whole social structure upon the outcome. For this a courage is requisite that to many Southerners seems temerity, not to say foolhardiness. Their opinion is perfectly honest and could be correct. The sole answer to their objection is Danton's advice to the Convention, that audacity is the only way out.

Above and beyond all this, there is a psychological, or perhaps a biological, block, ignored by the thoughtless, but formidable nevertheless. It is the primeval impulse, not monopolized by man but shared by bird and beast and creeping thing, to equate "alien" and "enemy." Jeremiah, who antedates the Confederacy by a very considerable time, took note of the speckled bird that "the birds round about are against her." Whatever is not of our kind is *ipso facto* objectionable, and a definite exercise of the intelligence is required to neutralize the repugnance. The negro merely by his coloration is, of all other races, the one most completely alien to the white man, hence the one surest to arouse—and to reciprocate—this ancient hostility. The primitive, or in ordinary parlance, the natural relation of black and white is one of dislike.

This is no defense, but it is a partial explanation of such policies as segregation. Morality may be defined as the conscious suppression of destructive biological urges, and the advance of civilization is measured by the success of that suppression, so the appearance of any instinctive reaction is a slip backward toward Neanderthal man. But that such reactions do appear constantly is attested by trials everywhere and every day for homicide, theft, rape, and abduction. It will be a very long time before they are eliminated. Race prejudice will not be eliminated soon; the hope is not to eliminate it but to prevent its expression in race injustice, at least as far as the forms of law are concerned.

The theory cherished by idealists that race prejudice is exclusively the product of miseducation and bad environment is only about 90 per cent true. There is a residue that can be traced back certainly into prehistory, and the attitude of the animals toward a variant strongly suggests that it can be traced back into prehumanity. However well suppressed, the thing exists, in Detroit as certainly as in New Orleans, in Massachusetts as in South Carolina. Latent everywhere, it needs only a certain combination of evil chances to become manifest. And its existence is one more complication added to the other troubles of the South.

This adds up to a dismal sum. The odds are plainly against the South, and if the region survives as more than a mere Boeotia, as an effective participant in American civilization, it will be only by dint of bitter travail, for it contends against itself as well as against adverse outward circumstance. The passions and frailties common to all humanity are doubly dangerous to the South, made so by the peculiar course of its history; while it must also contend with all the dangers and difficulties that bring woe to other regions, because they are inherent in the democratic process.

What, then, is the reason, if there is a rational reason, for a Southerner's pride in his birthplace? Why, its difficulties, of course.

"I," said Saint Paul when they taunted him with being a nobody from nowhere, "am a citizen of no mean city." Every Southerner knows how he felt. We are the sons of a land that has paid its way. For a century, in fact, it has been paying not only its own debt but that of the whole nation, first incurred in 1619 when that Dutch ship of evil omen cast anchor off Jamestown and, among other items, sold the Virginia colonists "twenty negurs"; and that was augmented for the next hundred years by the middle passage of New England shipmasters, running rum to Africa, bringing slaves to Southern ports, and thence carrying molasses to Medford to make more rum.

For their part in that crime the North and the West were let off at the price of four years of blood and agony a century ago. But the South paid that price, and in addition to it, ten years of military occupation, thirty years of poverty and grinding toil, ninety years of harassment, anxiety, frustration, and moral deterioration. The South has been granted no favors. The South has paid in full.

Every historian is aware that, up to about the year 1900, it labored in economic thralldom under a fiscal system that exploited it ruthlessly for the profit of the industrialized sections, but that loss was merely monetary. Far more galling to intelligent Southerners has been the inevitable result of the acceptance of fraud as a legitimate device in politics. Heaven knows, fraud is no stranger to the politics of any part of the country, but elsewhere it enters furtively and is killed by exposure. It is a vice that pays to virtue the tribute of hypocrisy. But in the South the grandfather clause and, later, innumerable tricky registration laws were adopted for the open and avowed purpose of doing indirectly what the Constitution forbade being done directly. Political leaders otherwise of good repute publicly justified this course, and in order to sustain it did not hesitate to appeal to every villainous prejudice and passion in the lowest elements of society.

The inevitable result was the reduction of the political process to a level so ruffianly that it became a national scandal, and this in the very region that in the early days had produced more brilliant thinkers on the art of government than came from any other part of the country. The South that had once graced the halls of Congress with Pinckneys, Randolphs, Clays, and

Calhouns now sent Heflins, Bleases, Bilbos, and Eastlands. The South that had given to the presidency the Virginia dynasty—Washington, Jefferson, Madison, and Monroe—could furnish only one President in ninety-five years, and that one by first having him processed by twenty years' residence in New Jersey.

The South has paid in money. It has paid in toil and trouble and anxiety and humiliation. But it has paid in full, and it still survives. More than that, even as it staggered under its backbreaking load, it has accomplished a feat unparalleled in the history of the white race. In less than a century, it has brought a formerly illiterate and servile population numbering many millions from tutelage to a point so close to the van of civilization that they are now ready to assume the most difficult citizenship in the world, that of responsible members of a self-governing nation that is also a great power.

In this, the white South did indeed have assistance, but not from the victors of the Civil War. It was the assistance of the Southern negro himself, who wrought the major part of his own transformation and therefore is entitled to the major part of the credit. But not to all. The ignorance, prejudice, and stupidity that would have blocked the negro's advance have always been combated valiantly and not without success by Southern whites.

The very Alabama that produced Tom-Tom Heflin also produced, and in the same generation, Edgar Gardner Murphy. The same Georgia that is in socage to the Talmadges also tolerates Ralph McGill. "Our Bob" Reynolds flourished in North Carolina, but so did Howard W. Odum, and so do Frank P. Graham and Jonathan Daniels. If it can ever pay off its debt to the past, the South still has the germ plasm to produce great men, and they will be tempered and toughened by the tribulation through which they have come.

With the eyes of a child I once saw the process at work, although it was many years before I understood what I had seen. At the age of perhaps ten, I was one midsummer noon at the house of a kinsman when he came in to dinner from the cornfield where he had been stripping fodder, one of the nastiest jobs attached to farming in those days. This man had taken his degree at the University of North Carolina just in time to spend the ensuing four years as a trooper in Wheeler's Cavalry, C.S.A. But as he stepped up on the back porch that day there was nothing about him suggestive of either the scholar or the soldier. The oven heat of the cornfield had had sweat rolling off him all morning, and the black soil's powdery dust had settled and caked until he was inky except for his teeth and the whites of his eyes. On the shady porch I pumped, and he held his head and then his arms under the spout for a long time before it became evident that he was actually a white man.

But his comment on his own state has rung in my ears ever since. When he had mopped his face and was toweling his hands and arms, he looked at me with a sardonic grin and broke into the thundering strophes of one of the *Georgics* of Virgil: *O fortunatos nimium, sua si bona norint, agricolas*— O most happy farmers, if only they knew their good fortune!

The small boy was merely startled by the rolling Latin measures, but an aging man knows now that he had there before his eyes the South triumphant. The soldier had returned from the war ruined, like everybody else. Like everybody else, he had moiled through thirty years of a depression that made the episode in Hoover's time a trifle by comparison. Not for his own fault, but by the ruin of his country, he had been sentenced to hard labor for the term of his natural life, with small hope of ever achieving ease, none of achieving luxury. Yet in the stifling heat of the cornfield, in a land of poverty and defeat, so far was he from broken that the ear of his mind could hear a great poet singing and his stout heart could laugh at the absurdity of human fate.

The small boy gaped, but the aging man remembers how Desdemona found " 'twas strange . . . 'twas pitiful, 'twas wondrous pitiful. She wish'd she had not heard it . . . yet she wish'd that heaven had made her such a man." I, too, Desdemona, would to God I were such a man!

But he was my kinsman. However far I may fall short of his strength, we are of the same blood, of the same origin, we are of the South. Therefore, I would be ashamed to fall into despair because the rising generation in our land is hard put to it to cope with the same problem, unchanged except in the degree of its urgency. Time is running out, and the South must not only lift itself by its own bootstraps, but lift suddenly. The problem is what it has always been—to raise 30 per cent of the population, now handicapped, to the level of the rest, politically, economically, and culturally; the change is that it must be done more quickly than most of us had believed was imperatively necessary.

But to accomplish the feat, the white South must first lift itself to a moral and intellectual level higher than it has ever attained, or than has been attained by any dominant race anywhere in the world. It is a formidable task. It is so formidable that the Southern lower classes—lower, even though some have millions and pedigrees of enormous length—have shrunk back and re-nounced it. But the lower classes have always failed in every great emergency, so Faubus and Eastland and Talmadge are not of any great significance. The men who will count are the saving minority, unbroken and unbreakable, men who can respond to a challenge after the fashion of sturdy old Pierre-Samuel, the original Du Pont de Nemours. In 1816, when a swarm of troubles seemed about to overwhelm the new republic, he wrote to his old friend Jefferson: "We are but snails, and we have to climb the Andes. By God, we must climb!"

The South will climb. A romantic illusion? Possibly, but a living faith at this moment, nevertheless, and one not destroyed by reports from Little Rock, or even Poplarville, not shaken when presumably sane men talk of interposition, of concurrent majorities, of the compact theory of the Consti-tution. For it is precisely by wrestling and overthrowing the giants of mad-ness and despair that the thews and sinews of the South will regain their old-time power, endowing it with the moral and intellectual vigor to become again the great instructor in political philosophy that it was when our history as a nation began.

I am a Southerner, and I wish the fact to be known; for the land of my birth is right now enduring the discipline that makes a nation great. So, in the midst of its current tribulation, I can think of it as my toilworn kinsman did, and can echo his chant: *O fortunatos nimium,* O most happy, land!

I'M FOR ADLAI STEVENSON

The *New Republic's* invitation to switch to Kennedy is doubtless all right for those who are liberals first and eggheads afterward, but some people are so peculiarly constituted that they are the other way around. For one, I believe that for the past seven years the country has suffered less from lack of liberalism than from lack of realism—if, indeed, there is a difference. I am accordingly persuaded that our most urgent need is a leader who not only knows what is going on in the world, but has a pretty shrewd idea of what it means.

Without prejudice to Senator Kennedy, I believe that Adlai Stevenson's grasp of the essentials of our present situation, at home and abroad, is firmer than that of any other man in public life in either party. And I believe, considering what we have been through recently, that this qualification is more important than any other that a candidate might possess in 1960.

The Republican Party, thanks to superior organization and more money, has frequently won with a second-rater or worse; but the Democratic Party has never achieved a signal success except when it puts up its very best man. Truman? He was not only the best, he was the only man who could have beaten Dewey in 1948. Truman was no egghead, but at that he had more brain-power than a majority of his critics and—which is the supremely important thing—what he had he used.

At this moment it is worth remembering that every really damaging criticism aimed at Truman was based on his judgment not of measures, but of men. When great issues were presented he was right with astonishing consistency; but some of his appointees let him down lamentably. I think he is wrong again in his judgment of the man Stevenson. Truman calls him indecisive; but four years ago Stevenson decided not to make any effort to obtain the nomination in 1960, and he has been adamant on that point despite more pressure than has been brought upon any potential candidate since Teddy Roosevelt in 1912. Having made up his mind, he has been harder to shake than Woodrow Wilson.

But all that he has ever said is that he will not seek the nomination, not that he would not accept it with pleasure if it were offered. That is to say, he has not attempted to use his position as titular leader of the party to throw obstacles in the way of any other candidate. They have had a fair field to show what they can do. If Kennedy runs away with the nomination on the first ballot Stevenson can and will support him heartily; but he has not sunk the knife into either Johnson or Symington. Therefore, if Kennedy can't make it, Stevenson would be the logical compromise because nobody has cause to feel aggrieved by him.

So much for his position. That of the Stevenson men, however, is a little different. Some, no doubt, are more afraid of a reactionary Democrat than they are of Nixon and in view of the odds against Stevenson's nomination they may be justified in switching. But there are some who feel that Stevenson's two campaigns, although he lost, did far more to introduce common sense into national politics than the winner did. Hence they can contemplate a third experience of the kind with tranquility; Stevenson might lose, but the country would gain.

This is a bit ruthless as regards the candidate. It is, in fact, using him as a whipping-boy. But it is emphatically not to his discredit. On the contrary, it is the last full measure of confidence, implying that to lose with Stevenson is a more valuable public service than to win with a lesser man. In any event, Jim Doyle is not the only man who feels that way, not by many thousands. It may be bad politics, but it is the way the genuine eggheads are made. When they descry in the offing a man who was built by nature to cope with just such a situation as now exists, they are for him and they will remain for him whether he can be nominated or not.

The Battle Hymn of the boys of North Carolina includes the defiant pronunciamento:

I'm Tarheel born, and I'm Tarheel bred,
And when I die, I'll be Tarheel dead.

A similar spirit informs the embattled eggheads. I was a Stevenson man in 1952. I was a Stevenson man in 1956. I am a Stevenson man in 1960. And I suspect than when what Dr. Samuel Johnson called "lapidary inscriptions" are in order an appropriate epitaph on my tombstone would be, "He voted for Stevenson till the cows came home."

No, I don't know that he can be nominated. No, I don't know that if nominated he can be elected. But I do know that he would make a good President, and I am immovably persuaded that he would make a great one. Therefore I am for him, forward, backward, and starting in the middle and going both ways at once. And with that my duty is done.

IF HE SCRAPES OFF THE BARNACLES

In New York campaign lapel buttons reading, "Neither." In Califorina windshield stickers reading, "For President—Vote No." Two weeks before the election Dr. Gallup concedes defeat.

These are political phenomena unprecedented within the memory of this writer, which goes back a long way. Perhaps they are trivialities without significance; but perhaps they are more significant than anything given out by the candidates or their press agents.

In the year 1900 William J. Bryan, who had been terrific, but had used up all his ammunition, ran against William McKinley, who looked like six Presidents but was not even one—an exploded firecracker against a punctured windbag. Near the end of the campaign Mr. Martin Dooley, the philosopher of Chicago's Ar-r-rchey Road, was quoted by Dunne, his creator, as remarking to Hennessy, "Did ye iver notice how much th' candydates looks alike, an' how much both of thim looks like Lydia Pinkham?" Lydia's bland countenance was used to advertise a patent medicine warranted, according to the ribald ditty, to cure "all female weakness and the pimples on your face."

To the present situation, this is the closest parallel that can be recalled. Mr. Nixon clearly recognizes the desperate pass to which things have come. Through a female intermediary he has gone so far as to exhume the mouldering carcass of McCarthyism, accusing his opponent of being "soft on Communism." Now there is something—a Catholic in good standing accused of being friendly to Communism! Tell it not in St. Patrick's Cathedral, publish it not in the streets of Vatican City, lest the daughters of the Philistines rejoice and the uncircumcised triumph!

Dr. Gallup throws up his hands and announces that the winner in this contest is utterly unpredictable. Maybe so, but it is easy to spot the loser. The loser this year will be the two-party system. Last summer intelligent Republicans wanted Rockefeller and intelligent Democrats wanted Stevenson. They got neither, and it is their firm conviction that both conventions were rigged to deprive the people of any chance to vote for a man they really like. The professional politicians have us neatly bound, gagged and delivered. Who can respect a system that leads to such results?

But wailing and breast-beating do no good, and not to vote at all would be to abdicate the sovereignty that is a free man's most precious political heritage. The practical means of ending the sorry farce is to elect Kennedy precisely because his election will split the Democratic Party completely.

Nixon, with a Democratic Senate certainly, and probably a Democratic Congress, would mean four years more of Ike-ism, that is, of inertia, while the future slips beyond our grasp into that of Communism.

The Democrats, given full power, would be saddled with full responsibility. They could not, as Alibi Ike could, blame every failure on Congress. Then when Kennedy tries to meet his responsibility, he will find the barnacle-encrusted Democratic Party responding so sluggishly that it will certainly move to disaster four years hence. His sole chance of survival will rest upon scraping off the barnacles—the partisans of John C. Calhoun and Stephen A. Douglas—and putting the conduct of public business in the hands of men who live in the 20th Century.

If that means lumping in South Carolina and Mississippi with Maine and Vermont, so be it. That is where they should be, for the political philosophy of all four states is an anachronism not consonant with survival in the modern world. A truncated Democratic Party that has an idea and a purpose would certainly be more useful to the country, and probably more successful at the polls than the existing contraption, held together with the Scotch tape and bailing wire of professional politics, contemptuous of everything save the loaves and fishes of public office.

Besides, there is the possibility that Kennedy, like Coolidge and the singed cat, is better than he looks. There is no possibility of that in Nixon's case. He has been tried in high office and has been found wanting—without an idea, without a purpose, without a philosophy other than the philosophy of office-holding, without any of the qualifications required by a man who is to lead this country successfully through the next four years. If Kennedy has not shown much, remember that his first necessity is to get elected. Remember, too, that FDR didn't show much in the campaign of 1932. Not until he assumed office did the country realize that it had a leader, and not merely a nice, amiable fellow with the gift of gab—very much as John F. Kennedy looks today. Better take a chance on an unknown than accept a demonstrated dud.

THE NEW REPUBLIC, "The Superficial Aspect," *November 21, 1960*

HE WILL BE GREAT

The constant reader, if any, has not hitherto found in this space a single confident assertion that John Fitzgerald Kennedy is a great man, nor is it asserted here today.

But he will be.

Rabbits, complained the Little Boy when told of the narrow escape from Br'er Fox, can't climb trees. "Honey," Uncle Remus answered, "Br'er Rabbit he 'bleeged to climb." Kennedy is in a similar strait. To survive at all, he 'bleeged to be great, and here is a flat prediction that he will survive.

It is not a reckless guess. It is based on evidence that if not conclusive is certainly persuasive. Kennedy has courage. He has honor. He has intelligence. And he has the Presidency. It is enough. If a man starts with courage, honor and intelligence, the stresses and strains of the Presidency will make him equal to the task; and if the task is unusually great, the office will make him a great man.

There is certainly no lack of evidence that Kennedy's task is formidable. The economic boom is plainly sputtering out. Communism has crossed the Atlantic and now squats 90 miles off-shore. Our position in the United Nations is precarious and deteriorating. Worst of all, vast numbers of our own people, including many who voted for Kennedy, have no more idea of what is the real situation than Don Quixote had when he tilted against the wind-mills.

All these things spell trouble for the next President and the man who leads the country safely through the labyrinth cannot be less than a great man.

In his favor are two circumstances, one general, the other affecting Kennedy alone. The former is the fact that the American people are slowly recovering from their pipe-dream of invincibility and invulnerability. This year not even Ike, the master tranquilizer, could get them hopped up on that kind of political goof-ball. Therefore, when President Kennedy tells them the truth they will perhaps believe it, as they would not believe it coming from Stevenson in 1956, and at that time probably would not have believed though one had risen from the dead to tell them.

Historically, when Americans have once realized exactly what's what, they have been willing to take action, and on most occasions it has been pretty sensible action. Mr. Kennedy will have a better chance of getting a reasonable program through Congress than has been offered since Eisenhower's first year.

President-elect Kennedy was probably helped more than he was hurt by the attacks of the genuine bigots. Nevertheless, he started with a serious handicap in the fact that many intelligent and relatively unprejudiced Americans were disturbed, not by Kennedy's religion, but by the strictly political claims asserted by the Roman Curia. It is really amazing that he did not fall, like the Philistines, slain by the jawbones of two asses in Puerto Rico.

But he survived even that calamity, and he did so because a great many of his fellow-citizens stifled their doubts and voted for him on his personal assurance that those doubts do not apply to him. It was a compliment so high that its equal is rarely, if ever, to be found in our political history. The man who received it must be inspired and invigorated by it; after such a brilliant assurance that the American people believe his word is good, Kennedy will redouble his efforts to make it good, as who wouldn't?

So the position of the incoming President is far indeed from being altogether bad. There was very little difference between the popular vote he received and that received by Mr. Nixon. But there is all the difference in the world between having won and having lost. Kennedy's foes are strong and ferocious, but his weapons are excellent. The trust of the people is the best blade that comes to the hand of any President, and when its metal has been tempered in the heats and pressures of religious strife, it is a very Excalibur.

It will not be asserted here that Mr. Kennedy today is perceptibly a bigger man than he was on the seventh of November; but he is entering the lists where in times past men have been made great "not without dust and heat." The real measure of Kennedy will be his stature two years hence. He may not stand at all on that day, for the fight is going to be tremendous; but if he stands, the ground will be littered with dead dragons and this country will be on the march again, under a leader again, and again happy in its resolution to achieve, not merely survive.

THE NEW REPUBLIC, "The Superficial Aspect," *June 14, 1961*

WHAT EVERY MAN KNOWS

Do you suppose she really can make it? The question refers to Mrs. John F. Kennedy and the growing suspicion that she may take us back to the days of Dolley Madison when charm was part of the atmosphere of the White House. The reports in the Parisian and Viennese newspapers leave no doubt that Mrs. Kennedy was a hit, not merely with the street crowds, but with de Gaulle and Khrushchev, with President Schaerf and with the curators of museums and proprietors of restaurants she visited.

This, of course, has nothing to do with the progress of affairs of state, but that is precisely its value. As long as no one suspected Mrs. Kennedy of intruding, all could enjoy her presence and conversation without reservation; and a friendly atmosphere is certainly no handicap to successful diplomacy.

That is what Dolley contrived to supply for 16 years—for she acted as hostess for the widowered Jefferson as well as for her husband—and the memory of it has survived for a century and a half. Nothing so memorable is unimportant, and if Jacqueline Kennedy can reproduce it she will add her name to the very short list of President's wives who have made an impact on American history on their own account.

That list at present is composed of three names, Dolley Madison, Mary Todd Lincoln and Eleanor Roosevelt, for "the fierce white light that beats upon a throne" has the effect of bleaching out all but the most vivid personalities among the women who stand close to it. But a vivid personality can be an asset to the President—or the reverse. Mrs. Lincoln's activities were often unfortunate and embarrassing, but Mrs. Roosevelt's independent status as a great humanitarian unquestionably helped FDR in many a close corner; and Mrs. Madison served well not only her "withr'd little apple-John," but the great Jefferson and the party down to the time of Andrew Jackson. No President's wife since has shared her peculiar talent of charming all sorts and conditions of men and women.

Yet if one judged by outward show, the last person one would pick as the logical successor to Dolley would be Jacqueline Kennedy. One was majestic, the other svelte; one was blandly ignorant—Dolley insisted on a superfluous "e" in her own name—the other as blandly, and highly, educated; one was born in genteel poverty and endured it all her days; the other has always been accustomed to great wealth; one's taste in personal adornment was nothing short of calamitous, the other is the pride and joy of the fashion kings.

Perhaps there is in fact no real similarity and Mrs. Kennedy's gratifying success in Europe was due to a fortuitous combination of circumstances not likely to be repeated. That remains to be seen. But one is permitted to hope that the modern First Lady shares the quality that made her predecessor unforgettable. That quality was genuineness.

There was nothing phony about Dolley Madison. Even in the highly artificial atmosphere of official Washington, where it is as rare for a woman to remain herself as it is for a man to remain what he was down in Guilford County, North Carolina, where Dolly Payne was born, she remained just that —Dolley Payne to the end; and Mr. Madison, Mr. Washington, Mr. Jefferson, and Mr. Jackson, the Marquis de Lafayette and M. de Talleyrand were merely half a dozen men and like all men entitled to amiable, good-natured sympathy as long as they did not behave outrageously. Dolley honestly liked people and wanted everybody around her to have a good time. But because there was nothing very much that she wanted from anybody, there was no occasion, or she could see none, for her to be especially nice to one because he was powerful and to another because he was rich. She was nice to everybody and everybody adored her.

Dolley was naïve, but what has that to do with it? There is no known reason why a sophisticated, rich, educated woman should not have the same authenticity. Jacqueline Kennedy has that quality or she hasn't, and in neither case can anything be done about it. But her first European tour more than hints that she may have it; and in that case not only is her husband as lucky as James Madison, but the country has reason to rejoice. For another really inspired hostess in the White House, merely by attending to her job and rigidly avoiding the role of Aspasia, could work wonders. She could soothe the savage Senator, smooth the ruffled ambassador, reinflate the deflated candidate, and make the governmental machinery run more smoothly in a thousand ways.

Incidentally, she might have a wholesome effect on our taste in art; although even she can hardly make Americans appreciate the humor in Manet's "Olympe."

THE NEW REPUBLIC, "The Superficial Aspect," *July 24, 1961*

WHAT IS KENNEDY?

The Kennedy Administration is now six months old—one-eighth over— and the most striking thing about it is the fact that its essential character is not yet clearly apparent unless, perhaps, to observers far more penetrant than this one.

There are two explanations of this, equally plausible, but leading to diametrically opposite estimates of the value of the régime. One is that Mr. Kennedy is an exceptionally wise leader; the other is that he is shrewd, but essentially hollow. In either case it was to be expected that after his first six months his superficial aspect would still be puzzling observers with no inside information and not gifted with second sight.

One thing is certain: his election propelled him into a situation as nasty as any new President has faced, certainly since Roosevelt II, and perhaps since Lincoln. In such circumstances a wise man seizes any stopgap available at the moment, but develops his long-range plans slowly and without premature publicity. A shrewd man also resorts to stopgaps, but if he is merely shrewd and nothing more, he is incapable of developing long-range plans. Either would act precisely as Kennedy has acted.

Kennedy is a first-rate politician, therefore he is bound to be a shrewd fellow; but so is every really effective statesman. When it came to playing smart politics, Lincoln could run rings around Douglas, Seward, Chase and other presumed masters of the art; so the fact that Kennedy put the skids under Truman, Stevenson, Symington and Lyndon Johnson, to say nothing of the Honorable Richard Nixon, is no proof that he hasn't the making of a great statesman. But neither is it proof that he has.

The Cuban fiasco was bad. It would be fatuous to deny it, but the fact that it was so very bad argues against the theory that the President is a smart political operator and nothing more. Animal cunning might have kept him out of that trap, and after he had fallen into it a weasel-minded man would have used every device to dump the whole thing into Eisenhower's lap. Instead, Kennedy grimly assumed full responsibility. Whatever else that may have been, it wasn't slick politics; and it may have been his way of notifying the country that he has put back on the President's desk the sign that Truman had on it: "The buck stops here."

As much may be said of the allegation that he wasted his time in Europe because he got nowhere with Khrushchev. That may be, probably is, significant. But it is at least equally significant that in Europe he pleased everybody except Khrushchev, and he went there fully resolved to please everybody except Khrushchev. He seems to have accomplished what he set out to do.

After the interview Khrushchev decided to devote to additional armament money that everybody knows he desperately needs for other purposes. That may, or may not, presage an attack; but it certainly means that Khrushchev has decided that he can't scare this fellow with mere words and therefore he must be ready with cannon, the last argument of kings. If cannon also fail, Khrushchev may fight, but it is at least conceivable that he may abandon terror as an instrument of national policy and fall back on some form of compromise.

If the event proves that Kennedy has provoked a war, then he is a flatter failure than John Foster Dulles, and the United States is guilty of having sent a boy to do a man's job. But if he has brought the Russians to the point at which they will eventually see reason, he is not only assured of a place in history, but assured of a high one. At present, the argument in favor of one point of view is about as strong as the argument in favor of the other. We simply don't know.

As usual, there are many thousands who are quite certain that they do know—Mr. Nixon, for a conspicuous example—and they constitute a threat to the country rivaling that of the Red Army. The besetting sin of democracies has always been their tendency to make up their minds on insufficient evidence, as in 1812, when we fought England on the certainty that she would never revoke her Orders in Council, whereas she had already revoked them. But the shooting had started before we heard the news.

Liberals and conservatives alike are in danger of making a comparable error with regard to Kennedy—and they may make it either way, by attribu-

ting to him either virtue or villainy in excess of reality. We don't know, and
to what Walter Lippmann once called "the omnicompetent citizen"—not
without irony, of course—that is an unendurable state of mind. Suspension of
judgment is torture. Rather than suffer it we risk calling Washington a tyrant,
Lincoln a baboon, Roosevelt a traitor, and Kennedy—well, you name it, and
somebody will immediately call him something worse.

THE NEW REPUBLIC, "The Superficial Aspect," *September 11, 1961*

GOD WAS BORED

A friend, not critical, merely curious, writes that he has seen in this place
recently more than one reference to Thucydides. Then in a commencement
speech that Adlai Stevenson wrote for Amherst—he never delivered it because
he was suddenly dispatched to South America, but it was printed—he found a
pair of quotations from Thucydides; and he wonders why people have this old
Greek writer on the brain these days.

What Mr. Stevenson may have had in mind is unknown to this observer
of the superficial aspect of things; but if Thucydides has slipped into this page
from time to time it is because his book applies to our present situation to an
extent that raises the hair on the back of a thoughtful American's neck.

It is apt even in being incomplete. We do not learn from Thucydides
how it all came out; for that, we must turn to Grote, or some other historian
of ancient Greece. We do not know how our own very similar situation is
going to turn out, and there is no Grote to inform us. If we undertake to guess
on the basis of the facts in hand we find no comfort in the process.

Thucydides' theme is the Peloponnesian War in the first phase of which
Athens was as triumphant as the United States was in 1945. Sparta was prostrate, but the inspired leader of Athenians, Pericles, was dead and to replace
him the democracy turned to a general who by genius or luck had made a
good record in the war, and was universally regarded as an honest man.

This was bumbling Nicias, who saw what ought to be done, but never
had quite enough vigor and resolution to do it. Incapable of coping with
Cleon, he allowed that demagogue to undermine the morale of Athens even
more than McCarthy did that of America. The so-called Peace of Nicias was
actually a Cold War, which drifted inevitably into a hot one because nobody
knew how to organize a genuine peace.

When the hot war was launched with the Syracusan expedition, worse
bungled than the anti-Castro raid on Cuba, Athens, although powerfully

armed, was psychologically incapable of waging successful war. At a critical moment the one general of some real capacity, Alcibiades, was yanked out of the theater of war by the Un-Athenian Activities Committee. Since it was known of all men that anyone summoned by that outfit was already as good as hanged, Alcibiades defected to the enemy. And so it went. Nicias contrived to lose both the fleet and the army in an operation as insane as would be an American invasion of Laos.

It is about there that Thucydides quits, but Grote continues the dismal story. By frantic efforts Athens managed to raise a new army and build a new fleet, dragging out the war for years. She even recalled Alcibiades, who did brilliant work for awhile. But it was all to no avail. Cleon had done his work too well and the city was morally disarmed. There was no such thing as confidence and trust in Athens. Everybody was suspected as a traitor, and if a man had lived an honorable and useful life for many years, that only showed what a shrewd deceiver he was. Athens' state of mind was that of the John Birch Society, and ruin was the inevitable result.

True, her conquerors profited little. Sparta was so weakened by the 27 years' struggle that she was easily smashed by Thebes; and presently both were overwhelmed by Macedon—all the while lurking in the background, the Red China of the ancient world.

Is it necessary to draw a diagram to show why Thucydides is horrifying reading for a modern American? Athens, the one great democracy of the ancient world, was a suicide, driven to self-destruction by fear. Yet she had faced and beaten the overwhelming power of Persia. She had defeated Sparta. She had won more small wars than the United States won against the Indians. She had been unchallenged mistress of the sea, her land forces were formidable.

But she died of fear—not of fear of the Persian, or of the Spartan, or of any barbarian. It was fear of the Athenian. Even as the John Birchites, taking their cue from McCarthy, howl that the real enemy is the enemy within, so Cleon howled against any man of real ability in Athens until it came to pass that the only reward for conspicuous public service was to be regarded as a subversive character. Only the stupid were beyond suspicion, only the dull could be entrusted with command.

Naturally the story chills any American who lived through the McCarthy affliction and who had hoped that McCarthyism died with its originator, but who now finds it revived in a more pestilential form under the name of a brainless character who got himself shot for no purpose at all. Napoleon collapsed, said Victor Hugo, because "God was bored by him." But a nation afraid of itself is a greater bore even than Napoleon.

THE NEW REPUBLIC, "The Superficial Aspect," *November 6, 1961*

THE CULT OF THE MOTOR CAR

All false gods resemble Moloch, at least in the early phases of their careers, so it would be unreasonable to expect any form of idol-worship to become widespread without the accompaniment of human sacrifice. But there is reason in all things, and in this country the heathenish cult of the motor-car is exceeding all bounds in its demands. The annual butchery of 40,000 American men, women and children to satiate its blood-lust is excessive; a quota of 25,000 a year would be more than sufficient.

No other popular idol is accorded even that much grace. If the railroads, for example, regularly slaughtered 25,000 passengers each year, the high priests of the cult would have cause to tremble for their personal safety, for such a holocaust would excite demands for the hanging of every railroad president in the United States. But by comparison with the railroad, the motor car is a relatively new object of popular worship, so it is too much to hope that it may be brought within the bounds of civilized usage quickly and easily.

Yet it is plainly time to make a start, and to be effective the first move should be highly dramatic, without being fanatical. Here, then, is what Swift would have called a modest proposal by way of a beginning. From next New Year's Day let us keep careful account of each successive fatality on the highways, publicizing it on all media of communication. To avoid suspicion of bigotry, let the hand of vengeance be stayed until the meat-wagon has picked up the twenty-five thousandth corpse; but let the twenty-five thousand and first butchery be the signal for the arrest of the 50 state highway commissioners.

Then let the whole lot be hanged in a public mass execution on July 4, 1963. The scene, of course, should be nine miles northwest of Centralia, Illinois, the geographical center of population according to the census. A special grandstand, protected by awnings from the midsummer sun of Illinois, should be erected for occupancy by honored guests, who should include the ambassadors of all those new African nations as yet not quite convinced that the United States is thoroughly civilized. The band should play the Rogues' March as a processional, switching to "Hail Columbia, Happy Land!" as the trap is sprung.

Independence Day is the appropriate date as a symbolic reminder of the American article of faith that governments are instituted among men to secure to them certain inalienable rights, the first of which is life, and when any government becomes subversive of that end, it is the right of the people to alter or abolish it. The highway system is an agency of government, and when it grinds up 40,000 Americans every year the government is destroying its own taxpayers, which is obviously a silly thing for any government to do.

Hanging the responsible officials would not abolish the government, but would emphasize its accountability for the lives of its individual citizens, which would certainly alter it, and definitely for the better. Moreover, the salubrious effects would not be exclusively political, but at least partially, and perhaps primarily social. It would challenge sharply not the cult of the motor car itself but some of its ancillary beliefs and practices—for instance, the doctrine that the fulfillment of life consists in proceeding from hither to yon, not for any advantage to be gained by arrival but merely to avoid the cardinal sin of stasis, or, as it is generally termed, staying put.

True, the adherents of staying put are now reduced to a minor, even a miniscule sect, and their credo, "Home-keeping hearts are happiest," is as disreputable as Socinianism. Nonetheless, although few in number they are a stubborn crew, as tenacious of life as the Hardshell Baptists, which suggests that there is some kind of vital principle embodied in their faith. Perhaps there is more truth than we are wont to admit in the conviction of that ornament of Tarheelia, Robert Ruark's grandfather, who was persuaded that the great curse of the modern world is "all this gallivantin'."

In any event, the yearly sacrifice of 40,000 victims is a hecatomb too large to be justified by the most ardent faith. Somehow our contemporary Moloch must be induced to see reason. Since appeals to morality, to humanity, and to sanity have had such small effect, perhaps our last recourse is the deterrent example. If we make it established custom that whenever butchery on the highways grows excessive, say beyond 25,000 *per annum,* then *somebody* is going to hang, it follows that the more eminent the victim, the more impressive the lesson. To hang 50 Governors might be preferable except that they are not directly related to the highways; so, all things considered, the highway commissioners would seem to be elected.

THE NEW REPUBLIC, "The Superficial Aspect," *March 5, 1962*

OUR NEED TO KNOW

Hell-gate is ajar in Vietnam and is plainly swinging open. All the skill in dialectic of the President cannot alter the fact that large numbers of Americans are daily coming under gunfire in those steaming jungles, and the number is being increased. A soldier shot to death is dead, whether on Omaha Beach, or on Heartbreak Ridge, or in Vietnam. To the man who stops a bullet, this affair in Vietnam is just as big as the Battle of the Bulge; and to his family and friends the pain is as keen, the desolation as complete.

To this outside observer it seems that the President tends to ignore this aspect of the situation. It is no cause for wonder if, busy with the conflagation in front, he tends to ignore the possibility that the woods may take fire behind him. Yet he has a striking example, for it happened to Truman. There is no doubt that the Korean affair was one of the chief factors contributing to the Republican victory in 1952.

Consider, then, that the reasons for the "police action" in Korea were much easier for the average American to understand than are the reasons for our present activity in Vietnam, and it begins to appear that President Kennedy is taking more of a risk than President Truman took. It may be that he is entirely right, but the risk is there. Truman was right, but that did not save him. The trouble was that the operation was little understood by the American people.

There is small reason to believe that they are better able to understand such complicated relations today. For eight years the Eisenhower Administration made no effort to inform them. Its policy was to feed them soothing-syrup, not the iron-and-quinine tonic that they needed. So Kennedy has inherited a constituency whose grasp of our real situation is, if anything, less adequate than it was when the trouble started in Korea.

The American people's loyalty to the flag is not in question. It is a matter of their loyalty to Kennedy and the Democratic Party, which is altogether different. If we must pour thousands of men and billions of dollars into Vietnam, we will do so; but that will not prevent us from highly resolving to take an axe to the party that seems to have dragged us into the mess, and that at the earliest opportunity. Unjust? Certainly; but it's politics.

Kennedy's rather snappish response to the reporters who were trying to get an approximate idea of what this adventure is costing in men and money hints at some lack of realism in his own thinking. He said that he had already told them all that it is safe to tell and they ought to be satisfied with that. But why should they? For eight long years it was the consistent policy of the Eisenhower Administration to tell just as little as possible, and on occasion, as in the U-2 incident, to tell what was not true. This has accustomed the reporters to expect attempts to hoodwink them and even to lie to them. Thus getting at the truth has come to be a game of matching wits. Whether at the White House, the State Department or the Department of Defense, the official spokesman is assumed by the reporters to be a liar and the truth not in him. If they have unfairly carried that attitude over into the Kennedy Administration, the fact may be deplorable, but it is not astonishing.

Among Mr. Kennedy's burdens, in fact, is that of reestablishing confidence in the Presidency. He has to prove, first, that he is acquainted with the true facts, for his predecessor often was not, and, second, that he will speak candidly of what he does know, which his predecessor often did not. It is irritating, no doubt, but it is inescapable, for failure to do it will result in souring public opinion on our whole foreign policy.

How much does the typical American really understand about Vietnam's importance? Not too much, Mr. Kennedy may be assured. He may have read reams of explanation, but none of it was authoritative. He has had no such blazing illumination as he got in that early Fireside Chat when Roosevelt explained the banking and currency situation. That, too, was an obscure subject to the typical American; but in 30 minutes it was lighted up to such a degree that most of us were satisfied that what was being done made sense, and that was all that we wanted to know.

It is all we want to know about Southeast Asia. Whatever is really necessary to do, we will do, and with a right good will even though the cost runs high in both blood and money. But we do want to know that it is necessary, and why, and we will not take the word of any press secretary, or even of any Cabinet secretary. We want to hear from The Man himself because our first need is to know that he knows.

THE NEW REPUBLIC, "The Superficial Aspect," *April 16, 1962*

BY HOOK OR CROOK

The Hon. Richard M. Nixon seems to be one of those unfortunates whose doom it is always to be ill-served by their friends. Those well-wishers who put up the slush fund while he was in the Senate came within an ace of ending his political career in 1952; those Washington advisers, presumably friendly, who urged him into that South American adventure against the advice of the men on the ground did worse—they almost got him lynched; Allen Dulles, who is not known to have been unfriendly, unwittingly did him an ill turn when he failed to explain to Nixon that Kennedy was not informed of the Cuban invasion preparations, leading Nixon to make a serious mistake in his book; and now it appears that even his research assistant let him down by permitting Nixon to insert in the same book a passage making it apparent that Alger Hiss could have been framed.

Since Hiss has been shouting for years that he was, in fact, framed, this was much worse than merely a typographical error, since it adds another wisp of smoke to the murkiness that already clouds that incident; and the wisp is not cleared away by the chief researcher's assertion that the passage was inserted through error by one of his subordinates. What else could the man say? It's a poor hireling who will not take the rap for his employer in such a case.

It is pretty generally agreed that it was the typewriter that sunk Hiss, and it sunk him because the jury believed—and Hiss's own counsel at the time believed—that it was authentic because there was no possible way in which the prosecution could have planted a fake. Now Nixon's own book reveals that there was a way; and while the assertion that it was all a mistake by a subordinate may be perfectly true, it is the kind of truth that has too much the look of a lame excuse.

If the Hiss Case had been otherwise clear of suspicion this episode would have been shrugged off by fairminded men. But it is not clear. On the contrary, throughout it has been clouded by the way in which it was conducted. There are many who, without any idea whether Hiss was guilty or innocent, look with strong distaste on the methods by which the man was prosecuted by Nixon, among others. By such methods, they believe, you could convict anybody of anything—you could convict George Washington of having shot Abraham Lincoln. The use of such methods, in this view, inflicted more permanent damage on the United States than what Hiss was alleged to have done.

The basic error of the men who handled this case for the government is one into which police and prosecuting attorneys are all too likely to fall—the error of believing that there can be no greater evil than that a criminal should escape paying the penalty for his crime. But there is a greater evil and a very great American man of the law pointed it out more than 40 years ago. "I think it a less evil," said Holmes, "that some criminals should escape than that the government should play an ignoble part."

The statute of limitations was embodied in the law because it is a matter of common knowledge that it is difficult, sometimes impossible, for an innocent man to defend himself against charges based on something that happened 10 years ago. By using technicalities, the government evaded that statute in Hiss's case; and there is no doubt of what Holmes would have thought of governmental evasion of its own laws even to prevent the escape of a criminal. But since Mr. Nixon is not another Holmes, perhaps it is less than fair to hold him to the rigorous standard that the old judge set.

But it was Richard Nixon who, albeit inadvertently, brought the Hiss case back into the news. Accordingly he has only himself to blame if his conduct in that case comes again under public scrutiny and arouses again the distaste that some have always felt. To say that the blame is not his, but lies upon his misguided friends—well, if not friends, certainly associates—is to beg the question. A man always chooses his friends and usually his associates; so if they are characteristically misguided, it is a reasonable inference that the man's own judgment is none too sound.

Partly (and many people think largely) at Nixon's instigation, the government played a controversial part in the Hiss case. Hiss himself is now out of it; guilty or not, he has paid the penalty and his account is squared. But if in the process the government played an ignoble part, then in Holmes' opinion—and Holmes was a wise man—a greater evil has been inflicted upon the country by those who managed the case for the government, of whom Mr. Nixon was one of the most active, than could possibly have been inflicted on us by Hiss's escape. This is the issue revived by Nixon's book, and it is not one he can easily dodge.

THE VIRGINIA QUARTERLY REVIEW, *Spring 1963*

MEDITATION ON 1963

*To encourage all valorous hearts, and to show them honorable examples,
I, John Froissart, will begin to relate the actions of the noble King Edward of
England, who so potently reigned, and who was engaged in so many battles
and perilous adventures, from the year of grace 1326, when he was crowned
king.*   —Opening lines of Froissart's "Chronicles"

> *The Knight's bones are dust,*
> *And his good sword rust;—*
> *His soul is with the saints, I trust.*
>
> —S. T. Coleridge, "The Knight's Tomb"

Baltimore, January 1, 1963

Brilliant and bitter, the New Year, the one hundred and first since Lincoln freed the slaves, opened with a cloudless sky overhead, hard-packed snow furnishing a treacherous surface underfoot, and a saw-toothed wind cutting between. One hundred years since Lincoln freed the slaves—not in fact, but in tradition, which is much more solid and enduring than fact. Even more than most first days of January it would seem, therefore, an appropriate occasion on which to write with the aspiration of old Sir John: "to encourage all valorous hearts, and to show them honorable examples."

Since it is a national holiday there is no mail delivery, but the public journal shows up as usual—that institution known to all faithful Baltimoreans not as a newspaper but as "the Sunpaper," and so described by the sign on its building. The front page announces that the United Nations will hold what it has gained in Katanga. What that may be, I do not know. Senator Dodd, of Connecticut, says it is a reputation for imperialistic aggression, and Senator Goldwater, of Arizona, intimates that it is the brand of Cain. One hopes, naturally, that the United Nations, like King Edward, has "potently reigned," but at this writing one simply does not know. The story, therefore, is but indifferent encouragement to all valorous hearts. Like the day, the operation seems to have been brilliant and bitter; but it was certainly bitter.

On January 1, 1863, the Emancipation Proclamation went into effect. It declared that all slaves not within the jurisdiction of the United States should be considered free. It is still in effect. For instance, all slaves in Katanga are considered free. Two years later the Thirteenth Amendment decreed that slavery should not exist even within the jurisdiction of the United States, but whether that has ever gone into effect was still a matter of dispute on January 1, 1963. A few weeks earlier James Baldwin, a negro, writing brilliantly and bitterly in the *New Yorker,* had confessed to hearing, in the back of his mind, echoes of the strident assertions of the so-called Black Muslims that the white man is a devil, incapable of wishing to release any thrall once held to service, and incapable of doing so, even if he wished it.

As to what are the rights of the matter I do not know. All I am quite sure of is that Lincoln is dead "and his good sword rust." The Emancipation Proclamation was a brilliant coup; of that there is no doubt, since all historians agree that it put new heart into the North, through which defeatism had been creeping. Six months later the tide turned at Gettysburg; but in the intervening six months, without some such stimulus as the Proclamation gave it, the North might have decided to quit. Thus as to the brilliance of the stroke there can be no doubt; but decision as to whether it was as bitter as it was brilliant must depend upon one's estimate of subsequent events. If the object of the Emancipation Proclamation was to constitute every man in the territory then in arms against the United States a free citizen, whether of this republic or some other, the thing was obviously a failure. Baldwin is but one of a cloud of witnesses testifying that to this day no man whose skin is black has become a full and free citizen; which is justification for viewing the event of January 1, 1863, with a certain amount of bitterness.

A week after the centennial anniversary one James Meredith, known as a student at the University of Mississippi and a negro, announced that he will not continue there because his situation "is not conducive to learning." Whether membership in the University of Mississippi ever was conducive to learning is debatable, but not a point at issue. Meredith was protected at the university by three hundred United States marshals and, whatever the general atmosphere may be, living under such conditions is obviously not conducive to learning.

Meredith's purpose, in fact, was not acquisition of knowledge. It was to prove that a negro citizen of Mississippi has a legal right to become a student at the state university. He has made his point. He has at the same time made another, to wit, that a negro who chooses to exercise his legal right to enter the University of Mississippi is not seriously in pursuit of education, since he will not get it there. He seeks martyrdom, not instruction, and such characters, sometimes brilliant, are always bitter.

There is no omelet without broken eggs, no new freedom without some martyrs. What Lincoln gave the negroes was emancipation, not freedom. All that any emancipator can do is strike off the bondman's chains. He then becomes a freedman by grace of another; but to become a freeman he must move under his own power. A college man protected by United States marshals is not automotive. He is not a student, except in name. He is a demonstration, a symbol, a token, what you will, but not a student because his situation is not conducive to learning.

He may indeed receive encouragement from others, but not by way of armed men. At Wake Forest, a college in North Carolina privately endowed and therefore not subject to the Supreme Court ruling of 1954, on petition of the student body the trustees ordered the admission of any student who can meet the entrance requirements, regardless of race. Not many negroes could, for the requirements are pretty stiff, but two or three made it and were duly admitted with not a single United States marshal on the premises. Doubtless they, too, are to an important extent symbols, tokens; but they are also students. Perhaps their situation is not altogether conducive to learning, but at least it is not prohibitive. They are in transition from freedmen to freemen, but while the path was cleared for them by others, they move under their own power. It is the only approach to real freedom.

The bitterness in this contrast is that the Wake Forest story was not newsworthy to the extent that the Mississippi story was. The experts of the press figured the ratio as of the order of one inch to one column, and competent journalists don't make mistakes in that kind of calculation. The idea that people will read whatever appears in the newspapers is merely the sales-talk of advertising solicitors. It is not a fact. The newsworthy is what people will read, and what they will read is what stirs their emotions. A stockbroker doesn't read the financial page, he studies it. A politician studies the editorial page and the political commentators. Some women study the society page. But what everybody reads is what stirs their emotions—astonishment, pride, fear, hatred, and love, roughly in that order. The big news story is the astonishing story, and the biggest of all is one that touches all five emotions perhaps with some stirring of cupidity and lechery as well.

Many good people can't get it through their heads that newspapers don't make the news. The special skill of the journalist is that of knowing what people will read, not that of deciding what they shall read. Occasionally, by brilliant writing and clever display, he can induce them to read what ordinarily they would skip over; but it is possible only occasionally. The news makes the newspapers, and the news is what people will read, which is not necessarily what is important.

A negro quietly attending classes at Wake Forest is many times more important to the destiny of this country than one guarded by United States marshals at the University of Mississippi, but he is merely important. He is not news. Bitter? No doubt, but true.

The sage whose advice was never to read a new book without immediately reading an old one might, I believe, have extended his dictum profitably by suggesting that one should never read the day's newspaper without reading a book that is not merely old, but very old.

There is, for example, Sir John Froissart. If you wish to understand what is news, read Froissart. What is news he understood so well that men still read him although the events he chronicled are six hundred years out of date. He gives two lines to the death of Richard of Bordeaux, although he had previously devoted many pages to him and his doings; justifiably from the news standpoint, for this Richard of Bordeaux had been, but was no longer, Richard II, King of England. With a sword at his throat he had surrendered the crown; so much for him. Thereafter he rated about as much news space as that fellow who ran against Kennedy does now; the fact that he was once headline material means nothing.

In the case of Richard, Froissart's estimate of his news value fairly parallels his historical value; Sir John furnishes a better commentary on this morning's paper by his early insistence on the enormous importance of the Duke of Ireland, accompanied by only slight and passing references to one whom he regarded as a minor functionary, a certain Sir Michael de la Pole.

Small acquaintance with English history is enough to acquaint the student with the fact that de la Pole was one of the great masters of intrigue of the fourteenth century; but one must have specialized a bit to be able to identify Ireland as Robert de Vere, a character as inept, politically, as a man who bet on Dewey in 1948. Ireland, indeed, may rate as the prize chump of the era. Starting by allowing his suspicious intimacy with the young Richard to get the King in bad, he ended by tangling with Gloucester, a fighter more vicious than a dozen Trumans. With that, even Froissart saw the basic insignificance of de Vere and dropped him; he doesn't even bother to kill him off in his exile on the Continent.

Naturally Sir John, intent on the newsworthy, never heard, or doesn't admit having heard, either of a scrivener named Geoffrey Chaucer, or of a pulpit-pounder named John Wycliffe. It is idle speculation, but one does meditate on the possibility that the Sunpaper, printing thousands of words on Nehru and Mao, may have omitted from its columns all mention of some poet or some theologian whose name will thunder six hundred years hence.

Joinville was even older than Froissart by about a century, but as a commentator on current events he, too, is not without merit. In recent years I know I have read some hundreds, and I think some thousands of columns dealing directly or indirectly with the question of civilian defense against nuclear warfare. It appears that if we stay above ground we shall be incinerated, and if we go below ground we shall be suffocated; or if, by great good fortune, you and your wife should avoid being either charred or smothered, yet in merely escaping from the place that was smitten you may receive that which will cause you, for time untold, to generate offspring with three eyes and thirteen fingers. It is a dilemma to which the pundits of the press have addressed themselves with great assiduity.

But I have read in none of their columns, no, not in those of Lippmann himself, anything more to the point than the words of the old Seneschal of Champagne, recalling the days when he sallied out on crusade with Saint Louis. Joinville and another knight, ordered to guard a certain outpost, were attacked by the enemy with Greek fire, the new and dreadful weapon that was the medieval equivalent of the atomic bomb. Says Joinville:

> *The fashion of the Greek fire was such that it came frontwise as large as a barrel of verjuice, and the tail of fire that issued from it was as large as a large lance. The noise it made in coming was like heaven's thunder. It had the seeming of a dragon flying through the air.*
>
> *When my Lord Walter of Ecurey, the good knight who was with me, saw it, he spoke thus: "Lords, we are in the greatest peril that we have ever been in, for if they set fire to our towers and we remain here we are but lost and burnt up; while if we leave these defences which we have been set to guard, we are dishonored. So my advice and counsel is, that every time they hurl the fire at us, we throw ourselves on our elbows and knees, and pray to our Saviour to keep us in this peril."*

Translated into our modern tongue: when the Intercontinental Ballistic Missile comes over, down on your all-fours and pray! In all the columns of print I have read, I have thus far seen no advice that is better, or more practical. Thus far we have come and no further since Louis IX warred against the Saracens, more than seventy-five years before Edward "so potently reigned" in England. Walter of Ecurey is only a name in Joinville's book;

> *The Knight's bones are dust,*
> *And his good sword rust;—*

but his pious admonition rings down the ages to a generation that has vastly increased the potency of Greek fire, but that has found no better way of dealing with the infidel than to cut him down.

"Lords, we are in the greatest peril that we have ever been in." The words are different, but such is the message conveyed by the headlines whenever we open a newspaper in 1963. As the year began Castro, the Cuban, although under rigorous pressure he had removed the more obvious menaces, was suspected of having hidden in his mountain caves God knows what evil things that might fall upon us at any moment. Khrushchev, the Russian, was boasting that, lost in the vast reaches of his land, were engines of destruction capable of burying us all. Mao, in Peking, was threatening to set the whole Orient ablaze to no apparent purpose; but, as every American knows, "the heathen Chinese is peculiar," so we hardly doubted that he might do it.

In far-scattered places—the mountains of Montana, for one—we ourselves had poised in secret dens more than a hundred, soon to be two hundred, sleek messengers of death, each carrying a charge, not of Joinville's Greek fire, but of Greek fire raised to the nth power of destruction. With scientific precision each was aimed at a different target half-way across the world; each was poised, ready to go at a touch, with "the seeming of a dragon flying through the air." How many similar monsters are poised, aimed at our own cities, we can only guess—and fear. Unless those persons in authority to whom we have committed our destinies are lying unanimously—which is incredible —we are indeed in the greatest peril that we have ever been in.

We have taken the temperature of Venus, and observed the other side of the moon, and bounced electronic waves off Mercury. Our heroes have ridden the thunderbolt at twenty-four times the apparent speed of Apollo's chariot, circling the terrestrial globe in the space of an hour. We have measured the incomprehensibly large, and in the other direction ingenious extensions of our fingers have taken the atom apart, revealing in its supposed indivisibility at least thirty-seven constituent parts. Yet the most powerful of our necromancers, put to the question, is compelled to make the age-old admission:

> *I cannot ease the burden of your fears,*
> *Or make quick-coming death a little thing,*
> *Or bring again the pleasure of past years,*
> *Nor for my words shall ye forget your tears,*
> *Or hope again for aught that I can say.*

Froissart we can easily tag as "the idle singer of an empty day," but what about the brilliant and bitter voices of our own time?

Moreover, while Sir John, the reporter, may have been no better than the modern Mr. Gigadibs, he was no worse. He did not miss the significant every time. True, he wrote pages about Robert de Vere and ignored Chaucer, but he also wrote a great deal about old Lancaster, constantly frustrated, often defeated, but always faithful and always brave. For which he lingers in memory. De Vere is dead and gone, Richard of Bordeaux was buried privately with only four knights in attendance, and who can remember which of the eight Edwards it was that "reigned so potently?" But even in our own time, after six hundred years, a rhymer in search of an allusion that glitters, a name that will put a spark in his lines, succeeds when he writes,

> *"Proud pump, avaunt!" quoth John of Gaunt,*
> *"I will dine at the Mermaid Inn."*

John of Gaunt, archetype of the futilitarian, who wore out his life in a bootless effort to prop up a king who was hopelessly non-royal, John of Gaunt, who lived and died a vassal, yet became ancestor of all of European royalty that survived into the Victorian Age when royalty shone brightest—this John was not overlooked by Froissart who, for all his basal frivolity, did believe that loyalty and valor are important. So, perhaps, his successor, Mr. Gigadibs, in the endless columns he turns out about Miss America, the Ten Best-Dressed Women, and tin-pot dictators, may be, unknown to him and to us, including an occasional paragraph about the doings of some contemporary Lancaster whose faith and courage, however lightly esteemed, even now are generating a royal line destined to be the glory of centuries to come.

The fantasy is not entirely without support. For instance, the brilliance of the administration's Cuban coup is self-evident, but there was within it an element that may continue to shine long after applause of our diplomacy has died away. That element was patience under severe provocation. Showered with insults and objurgations by a pygmy, we disdained to strike. In time to come this may be remembered as a more notable feat than photographing the back of the moon, for it was evidence of a political maturity that pessimists have regarded as further from us than Uranus.

After many centuries men remember how the wrath of soldierly Abishai was quelled when across the gully Shimei kept pace, cursing and casting stones. "Why," asked Abishai, blowing his top, "should this dead dog curse my lord the king? Let me go over, I pray thee, and take off his head." But David the King knew that Shimei had supported Saul in the late campaign, and a life-long Republican cannot be accounted a traitor to the administration, even though he throws dirt and maledictions. "Let him alone," said David the King. "It may be that the Lord will requite me good for his cursing this day."

On New Year's Day the Cuban, Castro, stood untouched even though there were forty generals in the Pentagon, any one of whom would have been pleased to go over and take off his head. It could be that his immunity will be recalled as something notable when the technological, scientific, military, and economic triumphs of 1962 will be mentioned only in reference books. Why not? The restraint of the King, and the fidelity of John of Gaunt

are remembered now that most of their battles and sieges and feats of arms
have faded into oblivion. They persist as wingéd names, potent to lift a
modern singer's verses off the ground, able to achieve John Froissart's purpose
"to encourage all valorous hearts."

Froissart is dead. His kings and knights are dead and their feats of
derring-do are to us tedious repetition signifying nothing. Turning over his
pages on the first day of a year promising to be as brilliant and bitter as the
weather and the year just past, we are conscious of one incessant refrain: "All
our yesterdays have lighted fools the way to dusty death." Then we turn over
the pages of the Sunpaper, so fresh from the press that the ink smudges the
fingers. Twenty new long-range missiles have been emplaced in the Montana
mountains, each aimed at a different target. The sword of Damocles. Then in
the Ural mountains and in the mountains of Kamchatka, how many are poised
and waiting aimed at my city, and at yours, ready at the touch of one reckless
hand to hurl obliteration upon us? We do not know how many, but we
know there are some, and one is enough to establish the threat. We have
come far since Edward was crowned king in the year of grace 1326. Far?
Just far enough to bring us into the greatest peril that we have ever been
in. The journey of six centuries has brought us under the sword suspended
by a hair. So say the pages of the Sunpaper, repeating in 1963 the refrain
about fools and dusty death.

The lady whose colors were borne by the winning knight was the Miss
America of her day. She is dead. Her knight is dead. How curiously, how
terribly alike are Froissart and the Sunpaper! Yet there was John of Gaunt.
Yet there was that good knight, Sir Walter of Ecurey. Only a taper, each, in
a great darkness; but "how far that little candle throws his beams!"

THE NEW REPUBLIC, *December 7, 1963*

"ONCE TOUCHED BY ROMANCE"

As an exercise in futility nothing exceeds trying to recall today what one
thought of John Fitzgerald Kennedy last month or last year; for what anyone
thought of him pales into insignificance by comparison with what the nation
feels about him now and will continue to feel through the predictable future.
Logical analysis will certainly be applied to Kennedy's career, and will have

about as much effect on his position in history as Mrs. Partington's mop had upon the Atlantic tide.

For Kennedy has been touched by romance, a magic stronger than Prospero's; so

Nothing of him that doth fade
But doth suffer a sea-change
Into something rich and strange.

Historians may protest, logicians may rave, but they cannot alter the fact that any kind of man, once touched by romance, is removed from all categories and is comparable only with the legendary.

We are told that at a Mass celebrated by Cardinal Spellman before members of the American hierarchy in Santa Susanna's Church in Rome the afternoon after the President's death, the Cardinal called John Kennedy "the martyr of this century." Yet he had flown West with no more exalted purpose than to meet his opposition, patiently explain his case and win the people of Texas to his side.

Already it has happened to two of the 35 men who have held the Presidency, rendering them incapable of analysis by the instruments of scholarship; and now Washington, the god-like, and Lincoln, the saintly, have been joined by Kennedy, the Young Chevalier. No matter that Washington had no faintest aspiration to be Olympian, Lincoln for beatification, or Kennedy for idealization—regardless of their own inclinations, reverence will attend the first, adoration the second, and heart's-delight the third for many a year to come.

It is inevitable, for the dry, factual record is the very stuff of song and story. The Paladin who overcame the manfullest who met him openly, but at the height of his fame fell to a skulker who struck from behind, has always been legendary. Achilles, Agamemnon, Caesar, Roland, William the Silent, Lincoln simply are not measurable by the standards applicable to ordinary historical characters. They are epic, and when Plato threw the poets out of his Republic he acknowledged that the epic defeats philosophy.

Then endow the hero with courage, strength, youth, beauty, gaiety, and consider realistically the chance of aligning him with ordinary mortals. Zachary Taylor, Franklin Pierce and Benjamin Harrison also were elected Presidents; but what ridiculous pedantry would hang the picture of the Young Chevalier in that gallery?

Perhaps Dr. Dryasdust may rail at the emotionalism that in a dramatic moment blots out the record of a man's factual achievements and over-writes the page with poetry; but he will rail in vain. Wiser men than Dryasdust will not rail. Instead they will weigh the wisdom of him who, if he were allowed to write the songs of a nation, cared not who wrote its laws. There are times in the history of a nation when a symbol is worth more than a sage; and there is much reason to believe that Americans are living through such a moment. We have acquired wealth and power beyond the dreams of the men who founded the nation; but that we still possess the high hearts of the group that met in Philadelphia long ago is, to put it mildly, open to question.

If the tragedy of the President stings us into a new awareness of the value of that possession, it cannot be said that he died in vain. The ancient Greek held that pity and terror and awe, the components of high tragedy, produce a katharsis of the emotions, expelling the baser and lifting men above themselves, at least for the moment. During the days of mourning, man after man who knew him personally commented on Kennedy's ability, whether as President, or before that as party leader, and in the early days as naval officer under fire, to spur the men he led to efforts of which they did not deem themselves capable. If his death has lifted a nation above itself, even for a moment, then his last moment will have marked his supreme achievement.

That remains to be seen. What is already evident is that the national pantheon has a new figure and a shining one. It is, above all, the ideal of youth; which is to say, it will continue an inspiration to the rising generation for longer than we can see; and when a nation has gained a symbol that can release the generous impulses of its young men and women it is fortunate beyond computation.

That alone is value enough. Why try to carry the calculation further?

THE NEW REPUBLIC, *December 26, 1964*

JUDGMENT IN MISSISSIPPI

But *somebody* killed them," said a despairing woman of Philadelphia, that sardonically misnamed town in Mississippi. She referred to the three young idealists—Michael Schwerner, Andrew Goodman and James E. Chaney —murdered and buried in a mud bank. She was presumably unaware of the mangled pride, honor, truth and gallantry whose butchery was the gravamen of the offense. Twenty-one were arrested by the FBI in connection with this murder, and then released, but that is legalism; the terrific significance of the act is that it was not merely homicide, but homicide tainted with genocide. Homicide is an assault upon the law, but genocide is an assault upon civilization, specifically upon the American theorem that all men are created equal and endowed with inalienable rights. In the persons of three obscure individuals, somebody has murdered Lincoln, and Jefferson and George Washington; and that blood will not cry out from the ground to no purpose.

For the moment, the Twenty-one are free with no charges pending against them. A grand jury willing, however, they or others may someday be charged and be summoned to appear before competent authority. By law, that competent authority is a Mississippi jury, but it is not so in fact. The Mississippi case will be heard, is being heard, by an unseen, nameless jury, scattered over thousands of miles. It is as dreadful a jury as the one empaneled to hear the case of Daniel Webster against the Devil. If that larger jury is not convinced that justice has been done, it will hand down its own verdict, in the form of a shot from the dark through a lighted window, a stick of dynamite wired to the ignition system of an automobile, an ambush similar to the one laid for the three idealists ... anything that the ingenuity of terrorism can invent.

Anyone who questions the likelihood of this development must have paid little attention to the public deliverances of the extremist minority in the negro revolt. Is it imaginable that they have had no effect on potential John Browns among their followers?

As it always is, retributive terrorism would be senseless and useless. Consider against whom it would be directed. These Twenty-one, for example? —a couple of peddlers, self-designated "salesmen," three filling-station greasemonkeys, two delivery truck drivers, an ex-Marine heaved out of the Corps with a yellow ticket, a trailer-park manager, a sawmill hand doubling as a hell-roaring religious exhorter, a sheriff, a deputy, and a cop ...?

What force could conceivably propel any man into commission of a crime more hideous than plain murder? The answer is not far to seek. It is the policy, pursued for generations by the proper gentlemen of Mississippi, of controlling and manipulating the wool-hat boys, the rednecks, the lintheads, by stuffing them with lies that blind their eyes to the real world. The policy of white supremacy could be justified, of course, only on the theory of white superiority. In the realm of physical force white superiority did and does exist; the lie was in extending this superiority into the realm of moral and intellectual force, and attributing it to a biological factor, which is to say, the propagation of racism.

Without doubt the proper gentlemen of Mississippi to a large extent were self-deluded. They gulped the nonsense of de Gobineau and Houston Chamberlain and despised such correctives as their native Edgar Gardner Murphy and Howard Odum. Thus infected with the perennial heresy of the *Herrenvolk,* they regarded as legitimate any measures necessary to hold the inferior masses in order. The shock of the Populist revolt at the end of the 19th century steeled their determination to maintain control at any cost. The negroes they could handle with shotguns, but the far more savage poor whites had to be cajoled, even if it meant using such instruments as Bilbo, Blease, Heflin.

The smoothest and most effective method, however, was not political ruffianism, but prostitution of the legend of the Old South. It is so bedraggled and degraded now that the contemporary generation finds it hard to believe that it was once touched with the romantic glamor that induces in men a wish to believe so ardent that they do believe.

In the hands of statesmen of the first order of greatness this might have been a powerful engine of statecraft. It is the tragedy of the South that in the hands of second-raters it remained powerful, but as an engine of petty politics. It was potent to transform the yahoo, in his own eyes, into a *preux chevalier* inhabiting a realm of moonlight and magnolias instead of the moonshine and skunk cabbage of his actual ecology.

Of course, the fantasy was not universally accepted. The stronger intellects in the South perceived the sham and reacted characteristically— Erskine Caldwell, Lillian Smith, Tennessee Williams. The greatest, Faulkner, brooding, became the country's most perfect anatomist of moral and intellectual deterioration. But in general the fantasy prevailed except in the upper South, where the spell was partially shaken off after the First World War. Florida, flooded with alien sun-worshippers, also escaped. But the strip on the Gulf Coast, including Mississippi, remained enthralled. So now we have Philadelphia and Twenty-one men walking at large, but not in the familiar ways of men, walking still in the shadow of death, possibly at the hands of the law, but probably under the claws of the fiend that has been conjured up, the terrorism from which America has been almost free for many years. This monster, once released, never stops with the execution even of the roughest justice; always it brings destruction to the innocent and inoffensive. That is why the mere passing-by of the Grinning Twenty-one chills the blood of bystanders.

THE VIRGINIA QUARTERLY REVIEW, *Spring 1965*

AFTER FORTY YEARS—DIXI

In brief, if he is not to become a barbarian the Southerner must become something not readily distinguishable from the saints in glory."

That dictum appeared under my by-line in the *Virginia Quarterly Review* for July, 1925. It was the conclusion of my first contribution to the *Review*, a consideration of the state of civilization at that time in the region below the Potomac. When I was informed that the fortieth anniversary number was in preparation I dug that article out of the files and reread it, with the intention of offering to the editors such corrections and emendations as might seem appropriate after the lapse of forty years.

I have none to offer.

There are, to be sure, some passing references to then current events that time has rendered obsolete. For instance, there was a remark that abandonment of the policy of separation of the races was unthinkable. It is thinkable now and it is immaterial that the abandonment was involuntary on the part of the white South.

The article was colored, also, by the disastrous political campaign of the preceding year. In 1924 Alfred E. Smith and William G. McAdoo, calamitously abetted by Father Duffy and William J. Bryan, had wrecked the Democratic party over an issue that had no legitimate place in American politics, the quarrel of the Ku Klux and the Catholics; the result being that the colorless nominee, Davis, lost everything but the then still Solid South. This inspired the observation that the late Confederacy had performed one final service for the Democracy—"she furnished the organization's burial party and accomplished the last sad rites over its mangled remains." It was premature, but at the time no other soothsayer foresaw the coming, eight years later, of Roosevelt, the fabulous Resurrection Man, under whose incantations the party, like John Barleycorn, "Got up again, And sore surprised them all."

Today, it seems more likely that the party will bear the South to its last resting place, rather than the other way about.

The substance of the article, however, and the conclusion I believe still sound forty years after its writing. I am aware that this position will be challenged by observers who can cite impressive evidence that the moment of decision has gone by and that the Southerner, or at least the white Southerner, has become a barbarian. Disregarding a multitude of minor incidents, they may be expected to mention these undeniable facts, all dated within the past year and a half:

Item: In the South a President of the United States has been assassinated by a Southerner.

Item: Even before the assassination the United States Ambassador to the United Nations was assaulted and spat upon, an incident less heinous but more vulgar than murder.

Item: In the South four little girls were blasted to death in a Sunday-school room, undoubtedly by white Southerners.

Item: A reserve officer of the United States Army, who had gone to the South in obedience to military orders, was murdered for no known reason except that he was a negro.

Item: Three young idealists, exercising their legal right of American citizens to travel, were murdered in the South and not even allowed civilized burial, but concealed in a pile of clay.

Item: An agent of the National Association for the Advancement of Colored People, going about his lawful occasions, was murdered from ambush.

Disregard an uncounted number of beatings, jailings, maimings, and tortures, most of them without even a pale shadow of legality, and consider these six items alone. They constitute a fearful indictment. Standing alone they are enough to persuade a fair-minded observer that the society in which such things are tolerated more closely resembles that of the headhunters of Borneo than that of the heavenly host; but they do not stand alone. They are merely the most spectacular incidents in a reign of terror that has flailed the South ever since the Southern negro began to make a serious claim to the rights guaranteed him by the Constitution of the United States.

In the circumstances the burden of proof rests upon one who asserts, or implies, that freedom of choice rests with the Southerner; for not cynics only but all superficial observers are persuaded that he has definitely, if not irrevocably, chosen barbarism. They may be right, but the case is not closed. There is a formidable mass of evidence on the other side. Hitherto it has been obscured by the dust and smoke of controversy, but it is there, and it must be weighed before a just judgment can be reached.

To begin with, nearly one-third of all Southerners are black. This immediately acquits a large Southern minority of the charge of regression; for the Southern negro has given, especially in the years 1963 and 1964, a demonstration of political maturity that is among the most impressive in all history. Having decided upon a policy of non-violent protest he has adhered to that policy through years of intense provocation, resorting to violent retaliation only in sporadic and isolated instances.

That record is written. Such is the speed of the historical process today that before these lines come under the reader's eye the record may have been blotted by black men whose nerves could no longer stand the strain, but it cannot be blotted out. Two years of steadfast adherence to a considered policy of quietism cannot be ignored by any honest historian. Adherence under fearful pressure to any kind of policy is a notable achievement for a democracy; and when the policy is one of non-violent protest, it is an amazing achievement, indicative of a degree of political maturity that Periclean Athens never reached.

Furthermore, the feat was accomplished by the Southern negro under Southern leadership. Of course he was stimulated, encouraged, and assisted by Northerners, white and black; but when he rose en masse it was at the call of his own kind. It has always been so. The Northerners, Frederick Douglass and W. E. B. Du Bois, are negro heroes and deservedly so; but the men who really shook the race in the South were Booker T. Washington and Martin Luther King, both from Alabama. It is the fashion now to look scornfully on Booker Washington, and it is becoming fashionable to sneer at King, because both were to some extent quietists. But Gandhi also was despised and at last was murdered by a Hindu. Nevertheless, it was his policy that succeeded.

In addition to that, these people led off. The so-called "negro revolution" had been in progress for many months before Harlem, Rochester, Jersey City, Chicago, and Chester, Pennsylvania, exploded. It is generally assumed that the Northern negro's educational and economic position is distinctly superior to that of his Southern brother. Nevertheless, it was the Northern negro who was guilty of the folly of aimless and self-defeating violence. The first sit-ins were staged, mostly by college students, in Greensboro, North Carolina. The first streetcar boycott occurred in Montgomery, Alabama. The first economic boycott was organized in Albany, Georgia, by negro citizens of Albany, without even the participation of Martin Luther King until the movement had been under way for a month or two. But the first great riots broke north of the Potomac; and it was the riots that provoked the "white backlash."

On the face of these facts it is evident that nearly one-third of the South, the black third, far from regressing has been rapidly advancing toward a level of civilization rarely attained by any race. If one-third of the remainder, that is, a third of all white Southerners, are as mature politically as the mass of the negroes, we have a numerical majority of the whole population against a reversion to barbarism. Statistical proof is impossible, but there is evidence that more than one-third, indeed, more than one-half and possibly sixty per cent of white Southerners are civilized.

In witness whereof I cite another passage from the essay of 1925. It reads: "to educate the negro, to safeguard his rights in the courts, to encourage his spiritual development is unquestionably to make him more formidable and more resolute." This statement evoked no comment whatever at the time. In the South of forty years ago it was regarded as so trite that nobody thought of questioning it.

There is no manner of doubt that the Southern negro of 1965 is more formidable and more resolute than any of his ancestors were; and most competent observers agree that this is the case because he is in fact a new man— better educated, less intimidated, more spirited by far than was the Southern negro of forty years ago. I have designedly repeated the word "Southern" not only because this development occurred in the South, but because white Southerners in 1925 knew that it was bound to occur unless they took vigorous and effective measures to prevent it. They took no such measures. On the contrary, such measures as they did take were designed to assist, not to retard, the cultural advance of the black South. Nor were these measures as half-hearted as critics of the white South assert; the notorious Tom-Toms, such as Watson and Heflin, were much louder but less effective than such Southern leaders as Edgar Gardner Murphy in the earlier days, and Howard W. Odum in the latter.

The adoption of this policy can have but one explanation. It is that an effective, which is not necessarily a numerical, majority of white Southerners, although they realized that the cultural and economic advance of the black Southerners would make them more formidable and resolute, realized that it would at the same time make them more valuable cultural and economic assets; and they estimated that the increase in value would be greater than the increase in danger.

But this is a highly civilized view. Indeed, it is so highly civilized that it is difficult to maintain consistently. If passion and prejudice have occasionally obscured the white South's vision of its ideal, it is certainly not unique in that respect; and to glimpse the ideal at all is not characteristic of a people sinking into barbarism.

In sum, the theory of reversion is flatly and obviously contradicted as regards the black South and is not sustained by the record as regards the white.

It must be admitted, however, that this estimate imposes upon optimists an embarrassing obligation—that of explaining why an essentially civilized people submit to being misrepresented and traduced by yahoos whose public careers reflect the intelligence of a chimpanzee and the ethics of a gorilla. There, at last, we come upon a failure that no white Southern apologist can evade or avoid; but it is an intellectual, rather than a moral lapse, inability to grasp the implications of an unprecedented situation.

The fact seems to be that the dimensions of the problem that intelligent Southerners of both races face has been but dimly appreciated by themselves and hardly at all by others. The problem, as it is generally conceived, is that of assimilating into a culture derived from western Europe many millions of people drawn originally from the completely alien culture of Africa. But it may be plausibly argued that that problem was solved two hundred years ago. The negro arrived in what is now the United States in 1619, a full year ahead of the Pilgrim Fathers; chronologically, at least, he is as fully American as any descendant of the *Mayflower's* company.

The unsolved problem is not that, but the one posed by the Emancipation Proclamation, just over a hundred years ago. It is the problem of the incorporation of the negro in our political system, and the central difficulty there arises from the fact that the white man himself has never fully mastered the management of that system. The negro, after his long exclusion, has every right to expect from the white man competent instruction in the management of the system, which is to say, in the art of being free. But how shall we teach him what we have not yet learned, except fragmentarily and uncertainly?

Specifically, the Southern white man lies under another inhibition, imposed upon him by two really great Southerners, John C. Calhoun and Roger B. Taney. Both were men with powerful minds; their fault, indeed, was that they were too intelligent. Both fell into the characteristic folly of the intellectual, that of identifying intellectuality with reason, ignoring the fact that reason includes both cogitation and emotion, both thinking and feeling.

Biographers mention, but without stressing the fact, that the young Calhoun indited a poem to his lady-love, each line of which began with the word "whereas." But, surely, it is highly significant. Such a mind would naturally fall into the error of believing that the binding force holding the Union together was the Constitution, not a deep emotional attachment to the ideal of the Founding Fathers.

Taney, in his turn, unquestionably believed that in blasting the Union he was saving it. Like Calhoun, he conceived of law as more powerful than love, and therefore assumed that animosities adjudicated by law were thereby abolished. He persuaded himself that the quarrel between the sections, if brought within the field of law, could be juridically composed; ignoring the fact that logic applied to emotion is equivalent to the very best butter applied to the works of the Mad Hatter's watch.

Calhoun and Taney are long gone, but their misconception still clouds Southern political thinking. The heresy that equates legality with morality is far from being confined to the South, as the rise and fall of prohibition proved; but its evil effects have been conspicuous in the South because it affects the immense social problem of race relations there; and that very fact is illustrative of the immensity of the problem.

The arguments of the more fanatical segregationists may be dismissed; they are not based on thinking, but are simply repetitive of the exploded theories of Calhoun. But some Southerners who are anything but fanatical are hard put to it to distinguish the basic philosophy of *Brown v. Board of Education,* the school integration decision in 1954, and that of *Dred Scott.* They are uneasy lest the Supreme Court should be repeating the error of applying strictly juristic thinking to the solution of strictly political, which is to say, largely emotional, problems.

But if the Supreme Court has, in fact, made that error, it was in *Plessy,* the "separate but equal" decision of 1896. In *Brown* it was trapped. There, after long and sometimes tortuous evasions, it was confronted squarely with the question, "Is or is not the Fourteenth Amendment part of the supreme law of the land?" I do not see how any nine rational men, to say nothing of nine learned Justices, could have given any other answer than, "It is." Yet inescapable though it was, *Brown,* like "the gallant Hood of Texas" in the Confederate infantrymen's doleful lament, "played hell in Tennessee."

The grim fact is that the South is trapped in a worse predicament than that of the Supreme Court. After a hundred years of evasion, avoidance, and intricate sophistry, it has learned that such a course leads only to what James W. Silver euphemistically terms "The Closed Society," although it is actually the anteroom to barbarism. That string has run out. The hideous events in Dallas, in Birmingham, and in the Mississippi hell-hole ironically named Philadelphia prove that the next step is into a state of savagery that the civilized part of the nation, including the civilized South, will have to extirpate, with tanks and machine-guns if necessary. The issue is squarely before us and must be met.

But the South is less fortunate than the Court in that the answer cannot be yes or no. For the question does not involve the Constitution or the statutes. It is not legal; it is political. It is, by what procedure may some ten million members of a formerly dominated race be inducted into full participation in a self-governing society without subjecting the whole social and political fabric to a strain that it cannot withstand?

That is the question, and it has never been answered yet. On rare occasions it has been answered as regards a class, or a caste, and it doesn't even arise as regards a miniscule minority. But when it applies to many millions, sharply distinguished by physical characteristics, that is, to a race, human wisdom has not yet been able to supply even a reasonably adequate answer.

But Southerners, black and white inclusive, must supply an answer because the alternative is to descend below the lowest level of civilization that the United States of America can afford to tolerate. The negro, once a slave, is now a freedman; and the problem is how to convert him into a freeman, with all that the word implies. Scoffers may say that the answer is easy: through the same process by which the white man was made a freeman with all that the word implies. But if the scoffer is asked, "And how was that? And when and where was that?" he has no reply—not if he is an honest man. We won our independence nearly two hundred years ago, and therefore call ourselves freemen. But if the word implies the enjoyment of equal justice under the law, he is an optimist indeed who would claim the status for every American—in grim truth, for any American.

The historical significance of this republic is simply that it affords men an opportunity to learn how to be free, unhampered by the bonds that Church and State have laid upon the generations of the past; but every rational man knows that the heaviest bonds of Church and State were not as weighty as the gyves locked upon our wrists by passion, prejudice, ignorance, and superstition. Then to expect the white South to teach the black, or the black the white, how to strike these off is to expect it to rise to a state of wisdom and grace that only the sanctified have attained, and they but rarely.

The fact that we have not attained it in the past forty years is insignificant; the pertinent question is, have we moved, if only by an inch, in that direction? The conclusive answer is supplied by the "negro revolution" itself. The utterly hopeless do not rebel, but these have rebelled, proof positive that they have seen a gleam of hope not apparent to an earlier generation. They do not yet know how to be free, but they are trying harder to learn than they ever tried before.

There, no doubt, is the answer, so far as there is an answer this side of the New Jerusalem. The endeavor to learn how to be free is an activity not characteristic of a people reverting to barbarism, but of one struggling upward on the scale of civilization; and it is through that struggle that some men have developed such moral and intellectual power that their names are inscribed in the calendar of the saints.

This is why, after forty years, I have nothing to add to, or subtract from what I wrote in 1925. Without complacence, but equally without cynicism and without despair, I repeat: "If he is not to become a barbarian, the Southerner must become something not readily distinguishable from the saints in glory."

ADLAI STEVENSON*

T his must be the context of our thinking—the context of human interdependence in the face of the vast new dimensions of our science and our discovery. Just as Europe could never again be the old closed-in community after the voyages of Columbus, we can never again be a squabbling band of nations before the awful majesty of outer space." That quotation from his speech at Geneva on July 9, the last that he made, may well serve as the obituary of Adlai Ewing Stevenson.

What to most of us appear as mighty confrontations of power, he could see as the "squabbling" of nations "before the awful majesty of outer space." It is a reduction to absurdity of the ideologies, the dogmas, the so-called immortal principles which men use as excuses for cutting one another's throats and ravaging with fire and steel the planet on which all must live. It suggests that the conquest, or even the destruction of the terrestrial globe may be a triviality that the high gods hold in derision.

To attain such a view a man must be either a supreme cynic or imbued with a faith that escapes the comprehension of men of more modest capacity. Cynicism, however, is not impressed by "the vast dimensions of our science and our discovery." This leaves faith as the only explanation of the power of Adlai Stevenson.

This explanation of him is extraordinary, certainly, but not unprecedented in the experience of Americans. On the contrary, every great leader in our history has possessed faith in a principle of moral and intellectual development analogous to the biological process of growth, not as the endowment of an elite, but as a potential of all mankind.

This is not, as the scornful assert, the theory of human perfectibility. It is the theory that human improvement is subject only to the mathematical law of the limited series that may forever approach without ever attaining unity. Without this faith Washington, Jefferson, Lincoln would be inexplicable; with it, the obscure and humble have faced life and death steadily and undismayed.

Adlai E. Stevenson was honorable, wise and witty. Any one of those traits would have made him distinctive. Together, they made him distinguished. He was a political liberal, but his liberalism was not so much a studied philosophy as the resultant of the countervailing forces of his faith in his fellow men, and the sharp perception of reality that we term common sense. This balance is

---

*Written the day of Adlai Stevenson's death.

distasteful to fanatics on both left and right, but it fascinated moderates, who felt that they were understood and appreciated.

Mr. Stevenson qualified under the schoolboy's immortal definition of a friend: He knew all about us, and he liked us anyhow—more, he had faith in us anyhow. Thus he gave us the inestimable gift of faith in ourselves; and for this largesse we mourn him as few Americans have been mourned by this generation.

THE SATURDAY REVIEW, *December 2, 1967*

LAUGH, CASCA, LAUGH!

I durst not laugh, for fear of opening my lips and receiving the bad air." Thus Casca, observing the beginning of the end of the Republic. If Casca had laughed perhaps it would have made no difference, because by that time things had gone too far to be reversed. But, while exercising reasonable prudence as an individual, he was remiss in his duty as a Roman citizen, for without doubt there had been a moment when a mere snicker might have tipped the scales toward the side of sanity. Laughter, says Dr. William Sargant, is the best prophylactic against brainwashing. He should know, for after attending the wreckage of two world wars, the London blitz, and the survivors of the concentration camps, Sargant has had probably as much experience as any psychiatrist in the world with the disintegration of the personality under long-continued, unbearable tension.

Assuming that, in the field of psychology, what is true of a man is also true of a nation is reasoning by analogy—which is always dangerous, but not always wrong. Sargant finds that if at any point in the long and difficult process of brainwashing—in formal terms, "psychological reconditioning"— the subject laughs, the whole process is wrecked and must be begun all over again. This is pretty well proved in regard to men, and there is some historical evidence suggesting that it also applies to nations, or at least to the United States. The most blatant case in point was that of the Eighteenth Amendment. From the start in 1919, Prohibition was opposed by some earnest souls on the ground that sumptuary legislation is morally wrong; yet what killed it was not that, but eventual realization by an effective majority that it was ridiculous.

An older and better example was presented in 1785 when commissioners from the states of Maryland and Virginia, having finished their business at Alexandria, paid a courtesy call on the gentleman farmer at Mount Vernon, no longer a general and not yet a President, but plain Mr. Washington. The commissioners had been called together to settle an interstate quarrel. Virginia held—and still holds—legal title to the capes at the mouth of Chesapeake Bay. Maryland held—and still holds—legal title to the Potomac River, for the interstate boundary is not the center but the right bank of that stream. Virginia undertook to exercise its sovereign right to levy toll on Maryland ships passing between the capes. Maryland undertook to exercise its sovereign right to levy toll on Virginia ships passing up the river to Alexandria. But the robust breed of ship captains paid small attention to anybody's sovereign rights, and "incidents" had been multiplying into a shooting war. The commissioners quickly agreed on the basic point—to wit, that the whole business was idiotic—and each state undertook, in consideration of like forbearance by the other, to stop interference with its neighbor's commerce. So they adjourned to call at Mount Vernon.

The ensuing discussion hinged on the possibility that the many other interstate quarrels might be as absurd and could be as easily composed by the exercise of sanity. This colloquy started the chain of events that culminated, two years later, in the Philadelphia Convention that wrote the Constitution of the United States. The call for the Convention, written by Alexander Hamilton, stated as its purpose, "to render the Constitution of the Federal government adequate to the exigencies of the union." It was an admission that the whole setup was ridiculous and that most of the bawling and bellowing about the sacred rights of sovereign states might have been compared to the braying of jackasses, except that the true jackass, *Equus asinus,* is too intelligent to bray when braying is likely to be suicidal. The country saw the point, laughed, and set up a government that could govern.

Seventy-four years later the mood was reversed. On that occasion nobody laughed, although a government that could not govern was no more absurd than a self-styled democracy that held 4,000,000 human beings as chattels. But in those days we were ruled by Men of Principle, according to Cornford's famous definition: "A principle is a rule of inaction giving valid general reasons for not doing in a specific instance what to unprincipled instinct would seem to be right." The unprincipled instinct of such leaders as Washington and Jefferson told them, even in 1787, that slavery should be eliminated, but the sacred principle of state sovereignty was too strong for them. By 1861 unprincipled instinct had become very nearly a monopoly of Abraham Lincoln, while the rest of the national leadership was divided between Garrison's principle that the Constitution was "a covenant with death and an agreement with hell," and Calhoun's principle that slavery is "a good, a positive good." The outcome was almost the destruction of the republic.

It is, speaking mildly, disconcerting to realize how far we have reverted toward that state of mind in recent years. There is still an objective reality, a man, *Homo sapiens,* inhabiting the White House; but of late the effective

President is less often the man than the image he projects, and the image is not even of the genus *Homo*. It belongs, rather, to the Menckenian classification of *Boobus americanus,* although we label it with the legal appellation of the specimen of *H. sapiens* then resident in Washington. The image is a fraud by definition, but it carries the weight of authority with a population so humorless as to be allergic to reality. The sawdust-stuffed father image that we called Eisenhower, the fake Prince Charming that passed as Kennedy, and the television cowboy furiously applying quirt and spur to his bucking swivelchair we designate as Johnson are our three most recent images. The Bantu, the Hindu, and the Shinto may laugh, but the modern Casca dare not, lest his opponent in the next primary accuse him of un-American activities—the bad air, or the hot air, most certain to stifle a flourishing political career.

A realistic appraisal of the state of the nation viewed *in situ* is, in all conscience, grim enough, but the successive steps by which we reached our present condition were of such a kind that their adequate description might strain the genius of a Voltaire. The current situation is that we are dribbling away a great army and a magnificent air force in a war 9,000 miles from our borders against an enemy less than a third as numerous as our field forces—ill fed, ill clad, and ill armed but, so far, indomitable. As of this writing we have lost 14,000 men killed and several times as many crippled, temporarily or permanently. We have lost at least 700 planes by enemy action and an undisclosed but certainly large number by accident and by wear and tear behind the lines. We are supposed to have had, in the beginning, 20,000 qualified pilots, but of these only some 1,500 had had the long and rigorous training that alone can qualify a man to take a huge bomber off a carrier, accomplish its mission, and bring it back safely. How many of these we have lost is known only to the high command, but certainly we should need every man of the 1,500 in case a really big show started. In money, the war is costing about $2 billion a month.

Even for a nation as large and rich as the United States this is a very considerable effort for which the country can be compensated only if the fruits of victory are lavish. Here the element of comedy begins to intrude. The United States abjures the ordinary fruits of victory. We do not intend to extort money from the Vietnamese, or to seize their territory, or to reduce them to servitude. Our sole objective is to vindicate the honor of the United States. The point of honor that is challenged is an implied commitment by a former Secretary of State never to permit the South Vietnamese to follow the leadership of Ho Chi Minh, a Communist leader of the revolt against the French, who had become President of North Vietnam in 1954. The reason offered for our interdiction of Ho was Mr. Dulles's theory that if South Vietnam were permitted to accept him, all the other nations of Southeast Asia would go Communist, as a row of dominoes falls when the first one is tipped over.

This was a *non sequitur,* as Sukarno discovered to his cost in Indonesia, but we have been trying ever since, at great expense, to establish it as truth. The reasoning seems to be that if we admit that it is untrue, we thereby admit that John Foster Dulles was a fool, and to admit that any Secretary of State can ever be a fool would dishonor the nation. So, to prevent national dishonor, 14,000 men have already died and more are being sacrificed daily. It is hard to recall another instance in which the honor of a nation was believed to hang on a successful demonstration that Simple Simon was in fact Socrates. Perhaps it is worth doing as a matter of principle, but to unprincipled instinct the cost seems excessive.

In the meantime, in the summer of 1967 thirty-odd American cities burst into flames, ignited by the fury of a tenth of the population in revolt against what they choose to consider intolerable tyranny and oppression. Our professed aim in Vietnam is to deliver the South Vietnamese from intolerable tyranny and oppression. For this there is, if not a historical, at least a fictional parallel: It is Dickens's Mrs. Jellyby, whose own children went ragged and neglected because she spent her time making red flannel nightgowns for the infant Hottentots. If the Vietcong seem to have no more use for American-style democracy than the infant Hottentots had for red flannel nightgowns, that only goes to show how backward those peole are.

Yet the cumulative effect of all this doesn't rise quite to the summit of our absurdity. That is touched only by the loudly vocal dissent; for the alternative that the dissenters offer is not a renunciation of folly, but an even stronger adherence to the cult of diabolism, holding that every evil is the work of a personal devil. The dissenters would have us believe that Eisenhower, Kennedy, Johnson, all of them—however hollow yet highly moral gentlemen—were, as Presidents, not quite monsters of iniquity but at least moral imbeciles incapable of discerning good from bad. If there is a greater absurdity than regarding Dulles as a man of wisdom, it must be regarding the three Presidents as deficient in rectitude. It was, indeed, just their excessive anxiety to avoid contamination by the Communist Powers of Darkness that drove us unwittingly into the labyrinth of nonsense in which we have been wandering for the past ten years.

Obviously, we will not emerge until some force compels us to face reality, and it is the plain duty of every citizen to exert that force if he can. Wrath will not accomplish it. If Sargant is right, the best available corrective of tension-produced hallucinations is laughter. It is risky, and, of course, it may be too late. If Casca had laughed, he might have been lynched. But it is just possible that his laughter might have been infectious and that sanity might have been swept back into the Forum on a gale of guffaws.

THE END OF INCREDULITY

Eighteen years ago at the end of the first half of the twentieth century I published a book-length dissertation based on a misconception so fantastic as to make Plato's detailed description of the lost Atlantis as prosaic as an ordinary travel guide. The misconception was that the first fifty years of the century had been so theatrical that Americans might reasonably echo what Aeschines, the Athenian orator, said to his contemporaries: "Our lives have transcended the limits of humanity; we are born to serve as a theme of incredible tales to posterity." In my infatuation I named my sketch of the semicentury "Incredible Tale."

The second half of that century is now one-third gone, and with two-thirds still ahead, the appropriate comment on my exploit is the old yarn of the bar-room braggart who proclaimed that he was a much-traveled man, in fact he had been everywhere and seen everything. A lush, painfully lifting his head from the bar, asked, "Mac, you ever had the d.t.'s? "

"Certainly not! " snapped the braggart.

"Well, Mac, you ain't been nowhere, and you ain't seen nothin'."

Reviewing the years 1900 to 1950, it seems now that, from the American standpoint, nothing really spectacular happened except the murder of Mc-Kinley, a couple of World Wars, and a Depression.

There were, of course, numerous minor episodes touched with a measure of gaudiness. The two Roosevelts, for example, were dramatic, but in conventional ways with no relation at all to the contemporary theater of the absurd. Prohibition may have been a forecast of the modern unfunny comedy, but if so, it was a pale one. Teapot Dome and the jailing of a statesman for malefactions committed while he was a member of the President's Cabinet were a jolt, but not one severe enough to break the Republican Party's grip on power. A rougher one was Truman's campaign of 1948, for it did to the political soothsayers what Darrow did to Bryan at Dayton, Tennessee; that is, stripped them of their hypnotic power.

The World Wars were, indeed, apocalyptic in their size and the physical destruction they wreaked, but there was nothing *outré* about them, nothing that could not be explained by the familiar laws of causation. The crimes and follies of the nations had eventuated in death and devastation—a harsh and alarming sequence, but in no way mysterious, and with the hopeful implication that if in the future crime and folly could be avoided, we might escape death and devastation.

As for the other startling, but lesser, sensations of that period, all, from Prohibition to Truman, are susceptible of explanation by perfectly logical, if sometimes intricate steps from cause to effect. They, as they should have, gave rise to anxiety as to the future of the republic because they revealed in the American spirit deplorable infusions of stupidity and malevolence. But with such things we have always had to deal, and we know by experience that they are, if not eradicable, at least reducible to an infection less than fatal.

Now, with thirty-two years yet to go, the second half of the century has already presented us with six events of tremendous public import, and for none can we find a readily comprehensible cause. To cite the proximate cause is frivolous. Kennedy, King, and Kennedy again were all hit by bullets. That was the proximate cause of their deaths. The Korean war, the Vietnam war, and the developing civil war were caused by the lack of political and diplomatic competence to settle the issues without resorting to war.

The mystery is why the bullets, why the blundering incompetence? Balaam, the bought prophet, is, of course, voluble with explanations. Everything wrong is due to the Communist conspiracy or, if not that, to capitalist aggression. You and I and the next-door neighbor are sinless. All trouble is created by outside agitators misleading dupes. In the spring of 1968 there was a disturbance at a Maryland state college, one formerly 100 per cent and still 90 per cent negro. Students demanded that the Governor visit the college and hear their complaints. When he did not come, some of them marched on the State House at Annapolis and when told that the Governor was not in his office (this was quite true; he was across the street, and stayed there) they sat down to wait for him. After three hours, State police entered and arrested 117 of them. It showed, said the Governor, how unrest is being fomented by outside agitators, perhaps Communist, or Communist-inspired.

The students' bill of complaint asserted that, *item,* they had found roaches in their food, *item,* they had found rats in their dormitories, *item,* they had found defective plumbing in the bathrooms, *item,* they had found plaster falling from classroom ceilings. Why it took outside agitators to persuade them to object to such things the Governor did not explain.

Balaam doesn't go so far as to claim that Martin Luther King, an ordained Christian clergyman, was a member of the Communist party, but does assert that he was a Communist dupe. But King never objected to capitalism; he objected only to the practice of injustice, oppression, and abuse by capitalists, or by any others. Furthermore, he cited chapter and verse. He told when, where, and by whom these practices had been pursued, and the facts were not to be denied. He refused to shut his mouth. He was killed.

This was nothing unprecedented. Tellers of unbearable truth have been done to death many times. Socrates, Jesus of Nazareth, Gandhi come to mind at once. But those three were all destroyed by their own people. Even Garrison, the American, had his narrowest escape from violent death in Boston, not in Richmond. King, on the contrary, fell at the hands, not of his own people, but of the dominant race. This afforded a proximate, but not a final cause for what immediately ensued.

Two days after his murder, as the hands of the clock moved past midnight ushering in Palm Sunday, I stood at a back window of my house and watched Baltimore City burning in seven places. The slight elevation on which the house stands affords me only a narrow view of the city, which explains why I could observe only seven out of many other incidents of the kind. To be exact, within the next four days there were 1,124 fires in Baltimore. By the most generous estimate half of them may have been accidental, which leaves between five and six hundred that were expressive of the blind fury of a people whose most reasonable and clear-sighted leader had been cut down. Cause and effect thus far were clear enough; the actual assassin had not been apprehended, so, failing him, the dead leader's people vented their wrath on a society that they believed approved, if it had not instigated, the crime.

It took 12,000 men, 4,900 of them regular army troops from North Carolina and Georgia (all the regulars in Maryland and Virginia were busy in Washington at the same time), to subdue Baltimore. Seven people died, three in fires, two in accidents, one fire department officer whose heart failed from over-exertion, and one looter shot when he pulled a knife on a city policeman trying to arrest him. Hospitals treated over 700 injured, including 50 policemen and 17 firemen. Property damage was variously estimated at ten to thirteen million dollars. General York, of the regular army, arrested over a thousand looters and about four thousand violators of the curfew, but his men never fired a shot. Even under attack they defended themselves with clubbed rifles, not with bullets. Yet thirty-six hours after his arrival the situation was in hand.

So for a week the Baltimore newspapers were loaded with letters to the editor venomously attacking the General, the Mayor, and the Police Commissioner because only one looter was shot and he not for looting, but for threatening the arresting officer with a deadly weapon. Apparently the writers believe that the authorities should have turned the machine-guns loose and set the gutters of Gay Street awash with blood. Apparently it didn't matter that most of it would have been the blood of teen-agers and of fool women who swarmed into the street during the excitement, very little that of the genuine terrorists. The argument was that more blood might have saved some property, although all experience supports the opposite view. Baltimore howled like a Congo jungle, although a thousand looters were punished for their crimes by the courts.

Not much thought is required to convince one that this is more terrifying than 1,124 fires. The rioting, while senseless, was the effect of a definite, comprehensible cause, but denouncing law-enforcers for acting lawfully is completely irrational. If the black population went crazy without just cause, part of the white population went as crazy without any cause. If madness is prevalent in both races, what is the future of the country? Nothing promising, we may be sure.

Then within the month Robert Kennedy, a Senator of the United States and a candidate for the Presidency, was shot to death, apparently for expressing the opinion that Israel's case is better than that of her enemies.

This, too, was not unprecedented. Merely approaching the Presidency is a risky adventure. Both Roosevelts were murderously attacked under similar conditions, although neither was killed, thanks to the bad marksmanship of the assassins. The reason is not far to seek. Even to be seriously considered for the Presidency a man must demonstrate his possession of some quality that lifts him above the average, and a display of any kind of excellence mortally offends men gnawed by a sense of their own nonentity. The malice of bad losers is hideous, but explicable.

The eerie factor in the Kennedy case is not the crime itself, but its evocation of Greek tragedy in the antique mode, the mode of Aeschylus, not that of Sophocles or Euripides. The latter tragedians dealt with cause and effect, but Aeschylus wrote of effects without cause other than the inscrutable will of the gods who "kill us for their sport."

It is the numerical factor that introduces this ghastly concept into the Kennedy story. Steadily, remorselessly, in strict order of seniority, they have died violently before reaching middle age. What, then, had they done to invoke this pursuit by the Furies? There is no answer, and it is that silence that chills the blood.

Joseph Patrick, father of the family, in the course of his career made business enemies who have accused him, with little convincing evidence, of various financial misdeeds. If bankruptcy had fallen upon him, unctuous moralists no doubt would have asserted that the punishment fitted the crime; but instead, he prospered exceedingly. Joseph Patrick, Jr., on active service in time of war fell in the line of duty, a fate that war inflicts on blameless and blameworthy with complete impartiality. Kathleen, next in order of birth, died in an airplane crash, cause unknown. John Fitzgerald was elevated by the will of the people to the highest office in the land and, far from demeaning it, added to that office grace and dignity, in testimony of which the heads of most of the civilized nations walked in his funeral procession after his murder. Robert Francis, like Caesar, was accused of ambition, but "when that the poor have cried, Caesar hath wept:/Ambition should be made of sterner stuff." All are dead, all by violence, and two by appalling crime.

Aeschylus felt that to add the last grisly touch to his tragedies, he must deal exclusively with the exalted; demi-gods, heroes, kings, and princes are his dramatis personae. Even this is not lacking in the Kennedy saga. Kings and princes are no longer in style, but a hero, a President, an Attorney-General, and an Ambassador will serve, especially when they are touched with the glamor of enormous wealth, and the public adulation heaped upon habitual winners of every kind of contest. All the blazonry was there, masking sorrow, horror, and the grinning skeleton with the scythe.

Reason and religion agree in teaching that it is rank superstition to explain this by positing a cosmic warfare between Ormazd and Ahriman for possession of the world, with the upper hand gained, now by one, now by the other. But reason and religion balk at explaining to us why, when "the sons of God came to present themselves before the Lord . . . Satan came also among them." Our only certainty is the uncertainty of our understanding of the laws of causation. At the same time, complete eradication of the teleological view of our existence seems more than human nature can achieve. We shudder, but not entirely from the shock administered by the dreadful events themselves. A deeper chill strikes into us because of our inability to ascribe to the sequence either a basic cause or an imaginable purpose.

Shuddering, however, is a strictly somatic reaction, the prelude more often to hysteria than to rational thought, and a fit of hysterics is precisely what the nation can least afford at this juncture. For this is the year in which we must make, according to law, choice of the persons to whom the conduct of public affairs will be entrusted for the next four years. It is the moment when it is most important for us to make the closest approach to reality that we can manage; for while the Kennedy tragedy dissipates any assurance that rational conduct will guarantee our safety, the King tragedy demonstrates that irrational conduct will destroy all security.

The King tragedy also had its part in shaking our confidence in the logical sequence of cause and effect. Baltimore was a city in which race relations, up to Palm Sunday, had been conspicuously good. It was the only American city in the million-population class that did not burn in the lurid summer of 1967. It had been, in 1954, the first big city to set about implementing the Supreme Court's school integration decision. It equaled any city, and surpassed most, in the number of its committees, commissions, and other organizations, secular, religious, or political, devoting their energies to eliminating racial friction by promoting equal justice for all. Leaders of both races were in constant and close communication, endeavoring to understand and adjust varying points of view.

Nor had it all gone for nothing. The status of the negro population of Baltimore has improved appreciably since the 1954 decision, whether viewed from the economic, the educational, the cultural, or the political angle. Futhermore, the rise showed no sign of slackening but seemed rather to be accelerating. Every surface indication pointed to a progressive easing of tensions and strengthening of confidence in the stability of the city's political, economic, and cultural institutions.

Whence, then, this harvest of seven dead, seven hundred injured, five thousand arrested, and ten to thirteen million dollars' worth of property destroyed? Clearly, there must have been sub-surface indications, unobserved, but pointing in the opposite direction.

I know that as Palm Sunday dawned many a thoughtful white Baltimorean began to harbor an icy suspicion that all this time we have been working at cross-purposes. I do not know, but I strongly suspect that many thoughtful negroes were in a similar state of mind, for I do not believe that blacks understand any better than whites the profound significance of a collision of ancient, disparate cultures.

Nearly thirty years ago, Gunnar Myrdal startled us—and obtruded his presence into the minds of millions who had never heard of the Swedish sociologist—by asserting that there is no such thing as a negro problem, that the American Dilemma is entirely a white man's problem of making his conduct conform to his conscience. Many of us accepted this as wisdom, whereas it was only proof that Scandinavians also are white. In Baltimore, as elsewhere, fair-minded whites set about the task of making their conduct conform to their consciences, and, especially for the past fifteen years, they have been working at it persistently and vigorously.

But our consciences dictate that right conduct consists in allotting to the negro a fair share of what we should desire were we in his place. To a measurable extent we have done just that and we have evinced a disposition to continue doing it on a more comprehensive scale in the future. The outcome, certainly in Baltimore and apparently everywhere else, has been rioting, conflagrations, bloodshed, and such an eruption of hate as makes Etna's worst a triviality.

Balaam is on hand with an instant explanation, of course. In his mind— if it may be so called—all is explained by the irremediable inferiority of the negro. But in one trait, at least, the negro is obviously not inferior. He has exhibited the courage—desperate certainly, insane perhaps, but superb—of Ajax defying the lightning. There is, however, an alternative explanation, not flattering to white perspicacity, but a possibility demanding consideration. If the negro is not in fact merely a sunburnt white man, then to offer him merely what a sunburnt white man desires might be anything but placatory. It could be and, it would seem, has been the reverse.

Disregarding the considerable infusion of white genes through miscegenation, black Americans are descendants of people who have developed certain cultural patterns far more ancient than those developed in Europe, Judea, and Islam, or the Buddhist and Taoist patterns of Asia. It is a matter of common knowledge that ancient cultural patterns are deep-rooted and not easily eradicated. To assume that their transmission is genetic may be heresy, but to admit that patterns perhaps sixty centuries old cannot be completely extirpated by three and a half centuries of intensive brain-washing is attested by the survival of obeah, or its equivalent, in Georgia as well as in Haiti, and the complaints of contemporary social workers about the practice of polyandry among black Americans on the lowest rung of the economic ladder.

The rigidity of our own cultural pattern compels us to regard these things as perversities. Even if we can bring ourselves to see them as vestigial remainders of once dominant patterns based on polytheism, matriarchy, and tribalism, still they are perversities that must be extirpated, and if persuasion will not do it, then police power must be invoked. To take any other view is to admit the possibility that monotheism, patriarchy, and the familial rather than the tribal unit as the building block of the social structure may not be absolute truths, equally valid for all species of humanity. For American whites to make such an admission probably is, at our present level of cultural development, impossible without psychic disaster.

The white man has been in close contact with ancient and disparate cultures for rather less than two centuries, too short a time for an appreciable change in his cultural level. Yet, while he has made no adjustment on his own part, he has worked out a rule-of-thumb method of dealing with the situation that sufficed as long as his power to enforce it was overwhelming.

It was applied in Asia, Africa, and America, but perhaps most ingeniously and smoothly in the South Atlantic states of this republic. It is notorious that, certainly until quite recently, Southern courts and police treated leniently polygamy and polyandry, devil-worship, and the *lex talionis* practiced among the blacks. The unadmitted but true basis of this procedure was the theory that the black man is a sub-species of the genus *Homo* and could not fairly be held to the degree of social responsibility imposed upon *sapiens,* the dominant species. This bland insult the black man swallowed as long as his strength was insignificant. But as he increased and multiplied and replenished the earth—500 per cent in less than a century, the fact as well as the theory of Black Power emerged and his smothered hatred changed into open defiance. So Baltimore burns and so do a hundred other cities and towns. Until the spring of 1968 a civilized government had managed to handle the turmoil without much bloodshed, but with Washington and Baltimore afire at the same time it had to reach down into North Carolina and Georgia for troops, and by the time these lines come under the reader's eye it may have to be reaching into Vietnam.

This problem is one of many on which the American voter must pass some kind of judgment in November, but it is so far the most dangerous that by comparison the rest are mere petty annoyances. In the spring we were profoundly moved emotionally by having four or five hundred men killed every week in a war that to half the country seems endless and aimless. But a rising of the Jacquerie involving not the few thousands of 1358 but more than twenty millions would blot out in blood the very memory of Vietnam.

Every solution thus far advanced is so obviously defective that it is fair to say that no solution is as yet in sight. Yet failure to find one threatens us with more than a ghastly form of civil war—it threatens a rude awakening from the great dream of 1787, when men dared hope that they were founding a nation in which domestic tranquility would prevail because every inhabitant felt assured of equal justice under law.

But how can we find the answer, when we are still uncertain that we have heard the question? It is evident—we have vociferous black testimony to it—that the negro is not, and has no desire to be, a sunburnt white man. What then is he? Is he a man whose deeply-rooted racial traits fall into a pattern that can be adjusted to fit smoothly into the pattern of the dominant white majority? It is beyond belief that such an adjustment can be made without some alteration of both patterns. Then arises the question, is it psychologically possible for the dominant race to concede anything beyond certain status symbols which, as is already apparent, are not nearly enough? To answer with an unhesitating Yes is to assume that the white American is capable of questioning the universal validity of his theology, his monogamy, and his political philosophy. It is a bold assumption.

Yet unless some adjustment more profound than either black or white America has yet imagined is made in race relations, the prospect for the next ten years is forbidding. Another Jacquerie is improbable—if anything can be called improbable in a year when the unimaginable has become routine. But let us not forget the great cost, in both tangible and intangible values, to the British of dealing with the Irish Republican Army that commanded the secret sympathy. although not the active participation, of three million people, and remember that we have to deal with twenty million. A handful, relatively speaking, of bold and agile negro terrorists whom the rest of black America does not approve but will not betray could make Britain's trouble with the IRA sink into insignificance historically.

This is the problem facing the men, and especially the President, to whom the conduct of public affairs must be entrusted in November. Not one is demonstrably capable of handling it, but some have demonstrated glaring incompetence to deal with it. All, however, must be given credit at least for the virtue of physical courage, for the exercise of leadership in this country has become deadly dangerous. The tragedy of King showed that to speak reasonably is to invite destruction. The tragedy of Kennedy showed that destruction may fall upon a man without discernible cause. The tragedy of Vietnam showed that pious aspirations not guided by realistic intelligence can land us in hellish situations. The voter trudging to the polls in November, then, is fortified by the assurance that if he votes reasonably and intelligently and has luck he may avoid voting for a blatantly incompetent man, although he cannot choose one known to be competent, for none exists.

Incredible? And how! But true.

THE AMERICAN SCHOLAR, *Winter 1969-70*

PROGRAM FOR THE MINI-INTELLECTUAL

When the University of Basel celebrated its five hundredth anniversary in 1960 Karl Jaspers delivered an address containing a passage that is curious, considering the time and place of its enunciation. It reads:

> *Having the will to know is not a harmless business. The consequences of knowledge are not within sight. The beginning of modern science is also the beginning of a calamity. . . . From time to time terror has come over investigators and caused them a tormenting conscience.**

---

*The translation is that of Professor Don Travis, Jr. It appeared in the University of Texas' *Graduate Journal,* Spring issue, 1962, and had limited circulation for in those days the *Journal* was not available by subscription and was distributed only to those persons to whom the editors chose to send it.

At a casual glance Jaspers' words seem to deprecate research, strange doctrine to preach at the semimillennial of an institution of learning as distinguished as the University of Basel. But Jaspers knew his audience. "Whoever has had the experience of knowledge," he said, aware that that included them all, "is acquainted with the appeal of the *sapere aude,* the appeal to the courage not to stop." This resembles an academic version of Hillary's reason for climbing Everest: "because it was there."

But the references to calamity, to terror, and to the "tormenting conscience" are not in that category. They reflect the philosopher's conviction that scientific research today gives far too much of its time and energy to producing ever more efficient instruments of destruction. Evidently, not all research scientists are troubled by a tormenting conscience, or, if they feel it, are not deterred by it. This is partly explained by the fact that when one does revolt, he may expect to be rewarded by being officially branded as untrustworthy, as Oppenheimer was when he balked at helping develop the hydrogen bomb. Honors and decorations are reserved for scientists who feel nothing but pride in the feat of packing the horrors of hell into portable containers that are themselves, like their contents, disposable with great malignancy.

Einstein, Fermi, Szilard, as well as Oppenheimer, and a host of their scientific colleagues only less prestigious have cried out against this practice, but thus far they have cried in vain. Even with the backing of Jaspers and practically every other philosopher of any real eminence, they have been impotent. It is clear that if they are to accomplish much they must have massive reinforcements, and the only available source seems to be the very large body of Americans who are intelligent without being austerely intellectual—people who have brains, but customarily use them for other purposes than the extension of knowledge.

They outnumber manyfold the scientists and philosophers, and their influence on the conduct of public affairs is greater than their numbers, which makes them a potentially effective force. But they are hamstrung by the belief, widespread among them, that they have no armament that would enable them to give any worthwhile support to the Einsteins and the Oppenheimers in intellectual warfare. To engage in battle without a weapon is obviously not intelligent; so this large class of the citizenry tends to stand aside.

They delude themselves. To oppose maleficent science they have already in their hands a deterrent more efficacious than both terror and a tormenting conscience. Its name is disgust. If the procedure described in academic language as the rejection of value judgments, and, in the vulgate, as denial of moral responsibility, were smitten by widespread public disgust, its popularity among scientists and technologists would decline precipitately.

It is not so simple to wield as the broadax, for disgust implies some acceptance of moral responsibility by the disgusted, and the intellectual middle class finds the acceptance as burdensome as do the scientists. But the burden cannot be evaded except by relinquishing any claim to competence in self-government. Science, considered apart from the scientist, is neutral, capable of operating indifferently to better or to worsen the human condition. But the scientist who undertakes to be as neutral as science becomes, not neutral but a neuter, characterless, commanding no consideration favorable or unfavorable, because his quality is not his own but merely a reflection, a sort of mirror image of the purpose that he serves.

Although he has always been with us, only within the past twenty-five years has this neuter figured importantly in the conduct of public affairs in this country. But he is now very important indeed, so his correct placement in the scheme of things becomes urgent, not to Jaspers and his colleagues only, but to the commonalty as well, for by the selection of its heroes the quality of a society is indicated and to no small extent determined. Learn the accepted archetypes of a people and it is easy to deduce its present types. Among us it is considered an accolade to call a physician a modern Galen, or an astronomer a new Galileo. Of course, the prosaic truth is that, enriched by the accumulated knowledge of the centuries, the modern is a far better physician than Galen ever was, and the astronomer than Galileo. Nevertheless, the honorific bestowal of a famous name is assuredly no insult.

Those scientists whose genius is applied to devising instruments useful only to make life shorter and more miserable also have their archetype, although the bestowal of his name falls short of being an accolade. It is Jack Ketch, eponym of hangmen and other professional executioners. But if the fabricator of megaton bombs and superlethal gases is hardly flattered by being dubbed a present-day Jack Ketch, in fairness it must be noted that neither is he thereby condemned to the stake or to the galleys. Jack's operations were perfectly legal. He was merely the agent, not the principal, in his transactions, playing no part in deciding who should die, merely seeing to it that they did die. Yet his occupation exuded an effluvium not grateful to sensitive nostrils. Generations before there was any widespread opposition to capital punishment, only a man of dull sensibility coveted an invitation to dine in the hangman's house.

In a world as ill-managed as ours still is, it may be that Jack's services remain indispensable, but not so his society. The aversion to accepting Jack as a boon companion is now becoming strikingly apparent in American youth. The company that produces napalm has found that of late its recruiting agents are definitely and increasingly unwelcome on many a college campus. It has been reduced to issuing plaintive explanations that it produces dozens of other items of commerce that are harmless and useful. No doubt this is true, but the fact remains that it also produces napalm, a weapon exceptionally dreadful because, for one thing, the death that it inflicts is excruciatingly painful and, for another, its use cannot be restricted to the elimination of combatants, for it as readily roasts alive women, children, and old people incapable of bearing arms. The upperclassman who contracts to participate in that business now finds his classmates regarding him with a fishy eye, and even the prospect that he will be well paid cannot restore any warmth to their sidelong glances. It has always been customary to grant Jack Ketch a handsome fee.

To the brassy this is a triviality to be brushed aside, which, perhaps, is not altogether regrettable. The thoroughly brassy are now, as always, a minority, and in a world insanely turbulent and therefore copiously productive of garbage, there may be need of a small caste of Untouchables to do the kinds of work so dirty that they sicken the more civilized. The drawback is that too complete tolerance of these tends to induce the greater numbers who are not really brassy but only thoughtless to "first endure, then pity, then embrace" the craft of the devisers of ever more scientific death. The thoughtless will refrain, however, if the business carries a touch of odium.

This reaction of youth is one of the few encouraging signs of the times, for the ruling generation, case-hardened by lifelong exposure to war, cannot be expected to take the lead in a profound reconstruction of our thinking. A man of fifty-five has not even a childhood memory of world peace, for war has raged somewhere as long as he has lived. It calls for a profound reconstruction of his thinking to wrench his mind from the dubious theory that war is a necessary condition of survival and concentrate it on the indisputable fact that war is the summation of all evil. Historically, such extensive reconstructions have almost always been initiated by youth, from which it is a reasonable inference that they are a function of youth. Thus an indication that American youth is on the job is emphatically no occasion for discouragement.

The fact remains, however, that the air is burdened with forebodings of revolution voiced by people who consider "revolution" a synonym for ultimate disaster. This adds interest to a comment of Walter Lippmann in an interview occasioned by his eightieth birthday last September. In answer to a question Mr. Lippmann remarked briskly that he does not anticipate the early coming of a revolution, for the simple but sufficient reason that the revolution is already here, although not many recognize it for what it is.

He might have added, using terms to which he was partial in earlier days, that most of us fail to recognize it because of our addiction to thinking in stereotypes. The American stereotype of revolution includes a Robespierre and a Saint-Just followed by a Bonaparte, or a Lenin and a Trotsky followed by a Stalin. Since none of those stigmata have appeared in this country, so the stereotyped argument goes, Lippmann must be wrong, and what we have cannot be a revolution. But revolution, correctly defined, covers any change in manners and customs so profound and far-reaching as to amount to a reorganization of society. It is commonly, but not necessarily, associated with violence and bloodshed. In the Industrial Revolution, for example, disorder was a minor factor, but the changes it induced were of a depth and reach unprecedented in history.

Yet it was in fact a revolution, and its manner of developing highlights another of our stereotypes, and one perhaps even more solidly petrified. It is the delusion that government is primarily, if not exclusively, political. The so-called Industrial Revolution overthrew no political organization, beheaded no king, produced no incident comparable either to the Reign of Terror or to Stalin's purges, hence it was not revolutionary.

The fallacy in that argument is exposed by the common knowledge that he who persuades does rule, legally or extralegally. An example is furnished by this very man, Lippmann. It has become a cliché to remark that in fifty years he persuaded more Americans to change their minds than any President in the same period, the second Roosevelt perhaps excepted. In or out of office, a man who causes his ideas to prevail is a ruler. An influential journalist is one, in effect, if not in law.

It is fashionable to describe Lippmann as the most influential of his time, but that is doubtful. Among the intelligentsia, yes, but it may be that, numerically, Drew Pearson changed more votes than Walter Lippmann ever did. The point, though, is that both were among the *de facto* rulers of the United States, and in a high echelon at that, although neither held elective office.

As much may be said of various other types. For instance, what governor ever had half the power to produce and control action that was exercised for many years by the pedagogue, John Dewey? What official authority on any level changed the face of America as did both the technologist, Thomas A. Edison, and the technician, Henry Ford? Even among professional politicians, whose badge of success is supposed to be a majority vote, one finds not a few of the prime movers who shook up and sometimes eventually overthrew the existing establishment, not in the list of Whitman's "elected persons," but in that of O'Sheel's "who went to battle forth and always fell." Best remembered among them was Henry Clay, but there were also Representative—not President—John Quincy Adams with his constantly rejected petitions, the original La Follette, the eccentric Bryan, and, only yesterday, Adlai E. Stevenson. All were potent, all in their day were among the rulers of the republic.

Yet each of these attained power by a process that was not merely democratic, but quintessentially democratic. No outside pressure compelled any man to read Lippmann if he preferred to read Pearson. Only his own rational processes could drive a man to believe Dewey. One might despise both movies and the Tin Lizzie, but the presence of Edison and Ford was as undeniable as that of Pike's Peak. We are, we say, governed from Washington and from various State Capitols and City Halls, but it is true only within narrow limits. Four fifths of our active lives are directed and controlled, not by any part of officialdom, but by men in whom we, for reasons of our own—or perhaps for prejudices and superstitions of our own—have chosen to repose confidence. This is an admission that we are not a self-governed nation, but there is no such thing as a self-governed nation, because a nation has no self. There is only a self-governed man, and his authority extends only to choosing the ruler whom he will obey. But that choice is real, and it is effective.

Thus by a transition that, I do protest, is natural and easy, we come back to Jaspers and his *sapere aude*. He opened the way himself, when he insisted in this same lecture on the identity of truth.* His demonstration, it must be admitted, has a tendency to coagulate the thought processes of a brain not attuned to the subtleties of existentialism, but the principle that scientific truth and philosophic truth are organs of a symbiont that embraces

---

* "Are there perhaps two kinds of truth unrelated to one another, the truth of science and that of philosophy? Not at all. Rather in all sciences the separation and unification of both are consummated."

all truth admits the hypothesis that even the plain citizen who is neither scientist nor philosopher and not much of an intellectual, may yet apprehend some fragment of the whole.

For instance, "the will to know is not a harmless business" is obviously a qualification. Otherwise it would be senseless, for the will to know has been the matrix of all civilization. The problem, then, is to define the qualification as sharply as possible so as to mark clearly the point at which the harmful element enters, and then to deduce what, if any, obligation lies upon nonscientists and nonphilosophers to erect a roadblock at that point.

I confess to being staggered by the suggestion that any obligation to correct science rests upon me, or upon the millions of Americans who are only slightly more intelligent, but a little thought reveals the dismaying possibility that it does. For what a nuclear physicist tries, or in fact accomplishes, I have not the slightest responsibility, but for my reaction to his purpose and his accomplishment I am responsible.

The difficulty comes in reconciling this responsibility with the salutary prohibition of intrusion by unskilled persons on the field of science—prohibited because it must be pernicious to the extent that it is not ridiculous. But frank disesteem is not intrusion. To learn "what" is the beginning of knowledge and to learn "how" is its continuation. As to the absolute value of both no question arises. But to learn "why" is higher education, in philosophy or in science, and the injunction, "know why" does evoke another question, to wit, "why know?"

If the end in view is the amelioration of the human condition in any respect, it is the plain obligation of us, the unilluminated, to applaud. Even if the effort is abortive, or perhaps harmful, the effort itself merits approval. But if the aim of the project is to devise means of destroying human life faster, more extensively, and with a greater measure of impunity, our equally plain obligation is not to applaud, but to hiss.

To what end? The answer is statistical. The influence upon science of any unschooled individual is too small to be calculated even by the physicist who can easily weigh the electron, but multiplied by a figure approximating two hundred million it becomes perceptible, and if it is possible that the figure may eventually be increased to four billion, the present population of the earth, it may become decisive.

The usual rebuttal is an assertion that the inventors of armament ever more scientific propose, not the destruction of Ah Sin, resident in Peking, or of Ivan Petruski Skavar, resident in Moscow, but the preservation of John Doe, resident in Washington. The rebuttal is vulnerable because it is based on an unproved hypothesis, namely, that the said Doe is endowed with an absolute value so much greater than that of the other two that their destruction to assure his safety is right. That is, of course, merely the ancient superstition of the *Herrenvolk,* the Master Race, a superstition proved iniquitous many times, most recently and most hideously by the Nazi regime in Germany.

Yet it continues to pervade the world, somewhat diluted and disguised under the name of nationalism, a euphemism for patriotism become paranoiac. Nationalism bears much the same relation to true love of country that Tantric

Buddhism does to the doctrine of Gautama, or that the morality of John of Leiden did to that of St. Paul. The United States, unhappily, is as massively infected with this virus as any country in the world, and it will be correspondingly difficult to eradicate. But the task is imperative, for the thing is more virulent than the craziest political ideology dreamed up by lunatic utopians.

So the menace does apply whip and spur to every citizen who can read the newspapers, regardless of how ignorant he may be of nuclear physics and existentialism. To be sure, it is not within his province to judge among scientists which should be exalted and which hanged or jailed, but it is obligatory upon him to consider carefully which he shall applaud, and which regard with dubiety as very questionable associates for politicians in office. With the world in its present state he cannot dismiss the fabricators of napalm and new biochemical weapons as totally worthless. They have a certain value, but it is ambivalent. In one direction it points toward the value of Socrates, and in the other toward the value of a trained monkey, who also is worth money as long as his destructive capacity is kept under strict control.

The duty of the plain citizen, then, resolves into a negative one. He is not required to do anything, but it is incumbent upon him not to regard the intellectual heir of Jack Ketch as the successor to Aristotle, not to mistake a trained monkey for Socrates.

THE NEW REPUBLIC, *February 7, 1970*

PRESIDENTIAL BOWSTRING

The feeble health of liberalism in the United States at present is observed by all observers. The lady languishes. So much is beyond dispute. She keeps her room, she pines, she cannot take the air. Her voice is reduced to a murmur, which allows the trumpeting of the Vice President to dominate the sound waves. Her state is deplorable and her hereditary foes, wringing their hands publicly and rubbing them privately, aver that she has gone into a decline that cannot be arrested because it is due to an irremediable thinness of blood.

It could be. But before the observer buys it, he should explore the alternative theory, that liberalism suffers, not from anemia, but from garroting by the most expert manipulator of the bowstring since the days of Abdul the Bulbul Ameer. The high efficiency of this method of execution lay in the fact that, once the bowstring was properly looped around the throat, the more the victim struggled, the tighter he drew the noose and pious sophisters could write off his end as suicide.

A relatively short memory lends credibility to this explanation by recalling Mr. Nixon's efficiency with the political bowstring, braided of hatred, prejudice, and superstition, in the cases of Jerry Voorhis, Helen Gahagan Douglas, Robert Oppenheimer, and, through alliance with Joseph McCarthy and his wrecking crew, of many others. Once only did it snap in his hands, when he described one of the most brilliant eras in our political history as "twenty years of treason."

It is not surprising, then, that Mr. Nixon has neatly throttled criticism of the Vietnam war by announcing that he intends to get out, and withdrawing rather better than 10 percent of our troops. Can a liberal object to that? He cannot, without creating suspicion that he secretly favors war, pestilence, and famine, all of which we have been inflicting on wretched Vietnamese since July 8, 1959, the date when the first American soldier was killed in combat.

In the old days the expert garroter frequently doubled his bowstring and Mr. Nixon has not failed to follow that practice. In fact, he has cleverly converted one of his most exposed positions into a strong point against criticism. We have at present a huge army in a very perilous position. By a combination of bad civilian diplomacy and worse military strategy we have contrived to land that army, whose fighting quality bears comparison with the best in our history, in such a position that it can achieve nothing worthwhile by moving forward, yet cannot move back without undertaking one of the most difficult operations known to the art of war, a retreat under fire through a hostile country. Xenophon managed it, and thereby became immortal, but it was too much for Napoleon and too much for Hitler. MacArthur, like the British at Dunkirk, was saved by the sailors.

Perhaps General Abrams has the necessary genius. We must hope so, but it is a delicate maneuver in which he will need all the help that intelligent diplomacy can give him. In the circumstances, any deliberate attempt to joggle the President's elbow is thought unthinkable.

At the moment liberalism, half throttled, can only gasp wishes for the President's success in his present policy. But perhaps that is not the whole story, for a sequel is possible. One recalls the commander in Victor Hugo's novel who was proceeding to the Vendee in a warship when, in a gale, one of the huge cannon on the gun-deck slipped its lashing and began plunging about the deck threatening destruction of the ship. But an agile sailor leaped down to the deck, caught up a rope and, after escaping instant death half a dozen times, managed to take a hitch round the piece and secure it. The commander, who had watched the feat, learned that the same man was responsible for the insecure lashing in the first place. So when the sailor was brought before him the commander detached his own highest decoration, the Cross of St. Louis, and pinned it on the sailor's breast for his heroism— and then had him shot for his carelessness.

That, however, is by the way. The immediate problem is how to withdraw from Vietnam without losing most of that magnificent army. If Mr. Nixon solves that problem he should have the highest decoration available—and be defeated for reelection.

THE SUNDAY SUN, *August 2, 1970*

REFLECTIONS AT 80

The occasion of Mr. Walter Lippmann's 81st birthday brought an extraordinary round of tributes to which has now been added one that, if not exactly unique is certainly unusual. The publishing house of Liveright has brought out a volume of his very early writings and James Reston, assuredly no dispenser of critical goose-grease, marvels at the quality of those youthful productions. "It is really ridiculous," says Mr. Reston, "for anybody to be so smart so soon."

With due deference to Mr. Reston, I hazard a different opinion. I doubt that the young Lippmann was particularly smart, in the ordinary sense. What made him conspicuous in his 20s, and a monument in his 80s, was that he was highly educated and at the same time extremely fair—a combination of qualities able to make any man of the Twentieth Century as remarkable as a white blackbird.

Evidence of this quality is furnished by what was intended to be detraction—Charles A. Beard's waspish comment that "Lippmann has been on every side of every question." Of course! His approach to any important issue was to think all around it. I first saw him when I was sent to report a commencement address he made in North Carolina. Later in the course of conversation the subject of H. L. Mencken came up. "I delight in reading him, especially when he writes about politicians," said Mr. Lippmann, "but he is too rough. After all, we have to have them, you know." Years afterward, he wrote the best one-line characterization of H.L.M. that I know: "He denounces life, and makes you want to live."

Furthermore, he lived in a period that made life hard on a man equipped with vast information and an obligation to be fair. He was bound to be constantly disappointed, because every idol has clay feet. I assert this flatly, because I lived through the same period, bating a single year, and it was the century of the iconoclasts. Idols were set up and pulled down with a speed and profusion almost, if not quite, without historical precedent. It is probable, though, that I had a better time than Mr. Lippmann, being untrammeled by his burdens, either learning or a dominant impulse to be fair.

A gaudy period it was! I cast my first vote, and probably Mr. Lippmann cast his, for Woodrow Wilson, but I have always remained proud of it and he hasn't. But if I had a chance I would ask him if before that, he, being 12 in 1901, got the curious shock that I did in realizing that Englishmen would no longer sing, "God Save the Queen"? Of course the "sea-king's daughter, from over the sea, Alexandra," was a queen, but not regnant, and to American small boys the Widow at Windsor was the only Queen that *was* a Queen. And she was gone.

Well, "the wheel is come full circle" and they are singing "God Save the Queen" again, but four—or at least three and a half—kings later, they no longer recite, confidently,

> *For the Kings must come down and the Emperors frown*
> *When the Widow at Windsor says "Stop!"*

which alone would signalize a great change in the world during Mr. Lippmann's lifetime even without reference to Ford, Marconi, the Wright brothers and Robert Oppenheimer. They did, indeed, change the physical aspect of the world beyond the recognition of President Benjamin Harrison, but to rate them among the real earthshakers of the Twentieth Century would be reckless, considering that spectators of that pageant have seen Wilson, Lenin and Gandhi pass by, not to mention the Roosevelts and Churchill, or the grotesques, Hitler, Mussolini and Stalin.

Adlai Stevenson once took me aback by remarking, after an hour's discussion of countless evil portents, "Still, I am glad to have lived at this time." But a little thought revealed what he meant and without doubt Mr. Lippmann would say as much. After all, we have not been bored—dismayed, at times, and at other times infuriated, horrified, exalted or dejected, but never bored. Of the two absolute evils in the world, pain and boredom, Schopenhauer contended that boredom is much the worse, a view supported by many other pundits of types ranging from Freud to Scott Fitzgerald. It is a point on which Mr. Lippmann's generation hardly has a right to an opinion, for we have had little more experience of boredom than a man on the highest roller coaster in the world. The plunge from Wilson to Harding, for example, was breathtaking beyond all precedent and the curves round which we went screeching in the time of the second Roosevelt started perspiration in showers. Of heartstopping fright and apoplectic rage, we can speak with authority, but about tedium we really don't know much.

Is that why an "intruder on posterity," as Franklin called himself at 80, finds it so hard to understand what ails contemporary hippies and dropouts? Incessant repetition does destroy the power of attention and perhaps even battle, murder and sudden death may in time become dull—battle in the streets, murder on the campus, sudden death in an apparently endless and aimless war. Mr. Lippmann has admitted that he doesn't know and most certainly I don't.

The Ten Commandments say that honor to one's parents is the secret of longevity which perhaps ought to settle it, but to me it has always seemed that curiosity is also a strong factor. If a man is firmly convinced that there is something worth seeing around the next corner, he will make it to the corner—on crutches, or in a wheelchair, perhaps, but he will get there. Of course, he is usually disappointed, but there is always another corner ahead and his ignorance of what may be on the other side will not permit him to lie down and die like a well-conducted person. When he does pass out, it will be in the act of heading for the corner.

It is the appropriate end for a newspaperman, as I think Mr. Lippmann would agree. Very Important Persons, with no more questions to ask, may die properly in bed, with a Doctor of Medicine on one side, and a Doctor of Divinity on the other, but the Inquiring Reporter should go with a pencil in one hand and a wad of copy paper in the other.

This occurred to me after an exchange with my sometime colleague and longtime friend James H. Bready a couple of weeks ago, when he wanted to ask me a series of questions on the past 80 years. At first I demurred on the ground that if he wrote anything along that line he would incite some sourpuss to ask the obvious question, "What for is he still hanging around?" and that one, I feared, would stump Oedipus, the great riddle-solver.

But I was wrong. I can't answer for Mr. Lippmann, but for me there is a very powerful incentive to stick around. It is my conviction that within a short time something very important indeed is going to happen to the third republic going by the name of the United States of America. The first was the tentative republic that lasted only 13 years under the Articles of Confederation, the second the national republic operating, except in time of war, under the Constitution, and lasting a century and three-quarters, the third the imperial republic, whose mode of operation is still undetermined, but must be decided very soon. Two courses are open to it. It can steer onto the rocks that have wrecked every empire in the past or it can steer into the fog and bring up God knows where. Since empire was thrust upon it by the Second World War, it has wobbled, with the Marshall Plan heading into the fog, then, with the invasion of Vietnam, heading for the rocks, but shortly it must settle upon one course or the other.

That I should like to see, because it will be a fateful decision and to a newspaperman it is the breath of life to be around when the big story breaks. In 1789 the national republic plunged into the fog and came through very well, but that is no guarantee that the imperial republic will be as lucky. Either course may end in disaster, but if so, it will be a honey, possibly involving the end of civilization, but probably clearing the way for some other nation to take up, where we have left off, the age-old quest for liberty under law.

There is always the possibility, though, that, as the second republic invented a new form of democracy, the third may invent a new form of imperialism and prosper immeasurably for a length of time that we cannot measure.

What is just around the corner for this nation is certainly no triviality. It may very well be hellfire and damnation, but it might be a period of greatness beyond our imagining.

Is it an appropriate season, then, for a man who has made it from
Benjamin Harrison to Richard Nixon, through earthquake and fire and
whirlwind, now to close his eyes and lie down with a lily in his hand?
Bosh!

THE AMERICAN SCHOLAR, *Autumn 1972*

THE TURKEY-GOBBLER STRUT
A Dangerous Political Infection

To play fairly with the reader, a writer who touches any political subject
in a campaign year ought to begin with a frank statement of his own position
to make possible a reasonable discount for bias. Accordingly, I acknowledge
that as a lifelong Democrat I regard the election of Senator George S. Mc-
Govern as rather to be desired. But as merely a democrat, not as an item
in either party's herd of livestock, I do not believe that a McGovern victory
in November is essential to the salvation of the nation. The nation has already been salvaged. McGovern accomplished that in June, when he yanked
his party out of the slave galley of the military-industrial complex and restored it to its rightful status as the party of inveterate opposition to war,
famine, pestilence and Nixon. Reequipped with a real opposition, the two-
party system is restored, and with a real, not a nominal, two-party system
the nation is reasonably safe, no matter what the name of the occupant of the
White House for the next four years.

The point is that an alert, vigorous and intelligent opposition is a president's best immunization against the most insidious of political ailments,
loss of perspective in relation to his own position. Humor, said Hazlitt, is
comparable to the slave who stood behind Caesar in his chariot to remind
him in the midst of his triumph that he was bald. That is probably the best
immunizer of all, but our presidents, Lincoln excepted, have not been notable
for a sense of humor, and a lively opposition is the next best protection
against delusions of grandeur.

The incumbent of the office is a case in point. Every professional observer of American politics has taken note, some with approval, some with
distress, of what they call Mr. Nixon's sharp turn to the left in the past year

and a half. The designation is questionable. A sharply increased concern with problems that sharply concern the people seems rather to be a turn to the facts of life, but let that pass. Ever since his demand that the electorate give him a Republican congress was met with a flat refusal, Mr. Nixon has been struggling with the grievances of the people with marked assiduity, if less marked success.

Unquestionably, he is a chastened man. Therefore the possibility of his reelection may be viewed, if without enthusiasm, yet equally without fear that it would portend the collapse of the republic. More plausible is the theory that he would, like Coolidge and the singed cat, be better than he looks. Thus at the time of writing, in midsummer, a Democrat might expect to vote for McGovern, but with no faint impulse to commit suicide if Nixon wins.

In this comfortable frame of mind one may find it possible to look forward to the campaign with pleasurable, not to say gleeful expectations, for it bids fair to be one of the most entertaining in our political history. For one thing, the incidence of whirling dervishes on both party platforms already surpasses anything known since the first (1896) campaign of William Jennings Bryan, and this without forgetting the Bull Moose eruption of 1912, with its marches to Armageddon to the tune of "Onward, Christian Soldiers," and the prayerful exhortations of George W. Perkins, Morgan partner and both financial backer and spiritual adviser of the movement.

This year, the announced withdrawal from the arena of Mrs. Martha Mitchell is a loss, but it is doubtful that she could have rivaled the entertainment value of Maryellin Lease, of the Bryan days. In any case, Maryellin's advice to the Kansas farmers, "Raise less corn and more hell!" is already being promulgated by voices sufficiently raucous. If, as some predict but others deny, the vice-president goes into action at the height of his form, we shall hardly miss Ignatius Donnelly's long-worded and -winded eloquence, while the McGovern cohorts already include an amply sufficient contingent of Sockless Jerry Simpsons. Imagination balks at attempting to guess what other apparitions may materialize, but it is small risk to prophesy that they will be numerous and incredible.

It is well within the bounds of probability that it will be a hard season on the humorless, but they live a hard life anyhow, mistaking the jarring of every passing oil truck for the first shudders of the crack of doom. Their own temperament dooms these poor wretches to months of intense suffering, and nothing can be done about it. It is immaterial that some of them see McGovern, and others Nixon, as the personification of the Foul Fiend. Their sufferings, like action and reaction, are opposite but equal.

It is possible, however, that as the campaign reaches its highest intensity, even the majority who usually maintain a fairly firm grip on reality may have moments of trepidation when the very earth seems to be giving way under their feet. When the bongo drums are reaching their highest intensity and the spinning witch doctors approach the speed of particles in a cyclotron, even a pretty hardheaded citizen may be swept by the excitement into making a fool of himself. It is very much in order then, indeed, it is elementary prudence, to consider whether there may be any factor in the situation that may act as a febrifuge, reducing the temperature of the body politic below the danger point.

One that comes to mind at once is the lack of novelty in the current manifestation. This holds good, even though it flatly contradicts the out-giving of numerous pundits who aver, "There never was anything like it before!" Bah! Something like it has been happening at intervals ranging from fifteen to thirty-five years since the first presidential election that was really contested, that of 1800. True, the exterior decorations, the trinkets and gewgaws that dazzle our eyes, are always different, but the fundamental cause of the upheaval is always the same. It is a deep and wrathful disgust with the way the country has been ruled in recent years.

How pervasive it is, is a question that will not be answered conclusively until November 7, but the nomination of McGovern, contrary to the predictions of all the experts, is conclusive evidence that it is widespread. If it is strong enough to force his election, then one may say with assurance that we have been through another upheaval similar to those that occurred in 1800, 1828, 1876, 1912 and 1932. The election of 1860 was in a different class, for that one did provoke an effort to disrupt the Union. There is not the slightest evidence that anything of that sort threatens us today, so it is a reasonable assumption that, regardless of the outcome in November, the net result will be pretty much what it was after the other upheavals.

The election of 1876 also was a special case. Few historians today doubt that Samuel J. Tilden won that election. In the popular vote he had a majority of two hundred fifty thousand, but the electoral votes of three states were challenged and the matter was not referred to the House of Representatives, as the Constitution provides, but to an *ad hoc* electoral commission composed of eight Republicans and seven Democrats. Two of the challenges were supported by pretty strong evidence, but all three had to be thrown out to give Hayes an electoral majority of one vote. It was done, regardless of legality, because there was serious danger of a renewal of the Civil War unless the remnants of the Army of Occupation were removed from the South. Hayes was elected and the army was removed. There is no documentary evidence of a deal, but there wouldn't be. No participant in a job like that would leave written evidence.

In each of the other cases, what happened was the ejection of the group in power—in 1800 and 1828 not the party in power, for the parties had not yet crystallized—a group of men who were believed to have arrogated to themselves power that belonged to the electorate, and for several years thereafter there was a marked increase in at least outward deference to the will of the majority.

But after the passage of one to three decades it all had to be done over again, for in the land of political lotus-eaters that is Washington politicians tend to forget their politics and to assume that the power to rule the country is theirs by right, not by delegation. Thus they drift into the crime of *lèse majesté,* not recognized by the penal code, but punishable by political exile. Usually it is unconscious. It creeps upon the victim like an insidious disease, and when he is accused of arrogance he is genuinely astonished—which merely adds to the complainant's sense of outrage.

A peculiarity of the present situation is that the disgruntled cannot ease their surcharged bosoms by voting against the party in power because, since 1968, the feeling has been growing that both parties are about equally guilty of arrogating to themselves power that rightfully belongs to the voters. The sharp rebuke to the leadership of the Democratic party given by the nomination of the rank outsider, McGovern, is proof enough on that side. If Mr. Nixon is re-elected in November it will be because it is not as great, or certainly not as energetic, in his case.

Naturally, this analysis of the situation will be greeted with hoots of derision from professional politicians, Democratic or Republican. In all probability their scorn will be no pretense, but quite sincere, reflecting an actual belief that the suggestion offered here is ridiculous. But it must be taken into account that one reason for their unbelief is the embarrassing implication that they have been mismanaging their own business, just as any merchant who contrives to outrage more than half of his customers is thereby convicted of being a poor businessman.

Things move with such speed these days that by the time these lines come under the reader's eye they may seem as antiquated as a description of the battles between Commodore Vanderbilt and Daniel Drew, but as the time for the Republican convention drew near it was fairly clear that the issues on which the voting was likely to turn would be Vietnam, inflation as reflected in the high cost of living, unemployment, and the disaffection of various minorities, chiefly but not entirely ethnic. The displeasure of the Zionists, for instance, is not ethnic, nor strictly religious, for some Jews who are Zionists in politics are freethinkers in religion, and many who adhere to Judaism in religion are not Zionists in politics. The blacks, by far the largest ethnic minority, up to forty years ago were solidly Republican, so far as they participated in politics at all, and if they swung Democratic in 1932 it was not by reason of their devotion to the gold standard, or the protective tariff, but because Franklin Roosevelt—and especially his wife—showed them the respect that is due to people who are, *de jure* if not *de facto,* fully entitled to the rights of citizens of the first class. That is not a purely ethnic motivation.

Optimistic Republicans were predicting that Vietnam would not be an issue because the president, by some brilliant improvisation, would remove it before the balloting. Less optimistic observers regard that as rather a thin chance, but assume, for the purpose of argument, that he does achieve, not merely a cease-fire, but a negotiated peace, signed, sealed and delivered. Will that remove the issue?

That depends on one's conception of the real issue. It is obvious that the war has grown increasingly hateful to an increasing number of Americans, but do they hate it simply because of its heavy cost in blood, money and time? The history of the country hardly justifies that assumption. This war has outlasted any in our previous experience, but we have spent more blood and more money in other military clashes without producing such an effect. The Civil War was the effect, not the cause, of a deep division in the country, and in the Second World War the resolution of the country hardened, not softened, after each lost battle.

Much more plausible is the theory that the present disaffection is based much less on the fact that we got into a long, frustrating and expensive struggle than on the way we got in. Our original involvement in Vietnam was due to the eccentric diplomacy of John Foster Dulles, and the effects President Kennedy inherited. But he did not inherit a war because President Eisenhower had been too wise to permit Dulles to throw troops into Southeast Asia. Kennedy did that on his own, at first only drill sergeants and commissioned officers as "advisers." There is some evidence that Kennedy grew very uneasy about the whole adventure and was edging toward withdrawal when the assassin's bullet struck. What is not guesswork is that his successor had no such qualms. Johnson increased the commitment and, once elected president in his own right, went at it in a big way.

All this was done by the relatively small group of men who held power in Washington, not all of the same party. Prominent among advocates of strong action was Richard M. Nixon, who had a large following among Republicans. But it was done without any consultation with the electorate, not even with the constitutionally ordered formality of asking for a declaration of war from Congress. The nearest approach was after the Tonkin Gulf incident when, at the request of the president, Senator Fulbright—of all people!—put through a resolution authorizing the president to use all necessary force to repel attacks on our warships. Later Fulbright became convinced that the "incident" on which his resolution was based was of doubtful authenticity, but that is a detail of no great importance as regards the real issue.

The real issue was whether the people's right to rule, which they necessarily delegate to certain agents chosen by ballot, had been arrogated to themselves by those agents. A declaration of war is so momentous a function of government that the Constitution denies it to the executive. He may request the legislature to do it, but it is only a request, never a demand. But President Johnson never requested authorization to make war on North Vietnam and received only the right to repel attacks on our forces.

That issue remains and will remain even if an armistice shall be arranged at once and a formal peace established before Election Day. We cannot erase the past, but we can make a repetition of the mistake less probable by an unmistakable declaration that it was a mistake.

The other issues are less sharply defined, but through all of them this same question is raised. Inflation and unemployment, for instance, raise the question of whether the economy, to the very large extent that the government can affect it, is being managed in the interest of the whole people, or only in that of a favored few. Is race prejudice—a term more exact than that vague and wooly "racism"—being subtly encouraged to undermine the Fourteenth Amendment's decree that no citizen of any state shall be denied the rights and privileges enjoyed by citizens of the United States?

So, also, with the rest. All of them, on analysis, come down to the one question, "Who's running the show, anyhow, and for whose benefit?" Does the final power still rest in the hands of the people, or has it been arrogated to themselves by the people's agents, to be used to the profit of their friends and accomplices?

How seriously this question is being taken by the country as a whole is a question that can be answered with finality only when the ballots are counted in November, but the whole campaign is, and must be, directed by the Republicans to provide an answer favorable to President Nixon, and by the Democrats to provide an answer favorable to Senator McGovern.

Here is a guess, however, that by and large, the answer will be favorable to the people. That guess is not based on the statistical analyses of Dr. Gallup, or any other of the popularly accredited soothsayers, still less on the out-pourings of the tub-thumpers on the hustings. It is based in part on the political history of the republic, and in part on the essential reasonableness of the people's demand.

For what was it that they required in the previous upheavals that were direfully pronounced apocalyptic and turned out to be only mildly reformist, and what do they require today? Only a modicum of politeness in their chosen agents.

Do they repudiate leadership? Far from it. They adore leadership and search for it constantly. Do they loathe dictators? Not a bit of it. By general consent the most dictatorial president in our history was Andrew Jackson, whose popularity steadily mounted until at the end of his eight years he was able to dictate the election of Martin Van Buren as his successor. Does their commitment to democracy, like that of the sansculottes, mask a thirst for the blood of aristocrats? Nonsense! The three American presidents who came nearest to making their lightest word the law of the land, Washington, Jefferson and the second Roosevelt, were all aristocrats, but all approached the people with a punctilio that Chesterfield could not criticize.

The perfect diagnosis of our current malaise is to be found, I believe, not in the record of any exalted figure in history, but in the fall of a far more obscure personality, Roscoe Conkling, a Senator from New York, now forgotten, but in his time regarded as a very Goliath of politics, who spent eighteen years in Washington, four in the House and fourteen in the Senate. In his early days he earned his reputation, for he laid out the opposition in windrows; but by little and little he came to regard power as his, not by delegation, but by divine right, and in the end he was brought down by a gibe. It was when an opponent, with deadly accuracy, objected to "his haughty disdain, his grandiloquent swell, his majestic, supereminent, overpowering turkey-gobbler strut."

Alas, it seems that the Turkey-Gobbler Strut may justly be described as an occupational disease among American politicians, regardless of party, who have lived too long in Washington. It is not always politically fatal, but its mortality rate is high, and it sometimes results in banishment to the quarantine station of a man showing few, if any symptoms of infection, but known to have been in close contact with strutters in the terminal stage. For proof of this, ask Humphrey.

WATERGATE: ONE END, BUT WHICH?

Watergate was, is, and as far as American history is concerned, will remain a terminus of some sort, but whether it is the beginning of the end, or the end of the beginning, will never be known with anything like certitude by the living generation, and only doubtfully by the next. The third will perhaps be able to assess the real significance of the thing with reasonable assurance.

Yet it is the hard fate of Americans now living to have to work in the dark, knowing that what they do will go far toward determining the eventual outcome. It is a particularly ruthless demonstration of Mr. Justice Holmes's observation that every year, if not every day, "we have to wager our salvation on some prophecy based on imperfect knowledge."

The government established by the American Declaration of Independence in 1776, and implemented by the Constitution of the United States in 1789, was precisely such a wager. Our ancestors explicitly admitted that they were staking "our lives, our fortunes, and our sacred honor" on the success of an experiment testing the unproved theory that democracy is a viable form of government. The knowledge then available was worse than imperfect, it was definitely negative. Every previous effort to test the theory had ended in the same way—a reversion to tyranny, rarely blatant, but thinly masked by lip service to the old institutions.

According to John Adams, one-third of the Americans of 1776 did not believe that the experiment had a ghost of a chance. These were the Tories, thousands of whom left the country, while some of the bolder ones actually took up arms in support of the king, being less fearful of the familiar tyranny of the monarchy than they were of the imagined tyranny of the mob that they supposed was implied in the sovereignty of the people.

At first it seemed that they were right, because the hastily erected structure of government in the Articles of Confederation proved hopelessly inadequate, and within eleven years was visibly collapsing. But in 1787 a convention dominated by and substantially composed of the very men who had written the Declaration, produced, in the Constitution, a new structure which proved solid enough to endure, with occasional patching, for nearly two hundred years.*

> *Observers as different as Albert Camus and Sir Denis Brogan*
> *have overlooked this point in refusing to accept the American*
> *experience as a real revolution, in any wise comparable to the Russian*

*and French. But it may as logically be argued that ours is the only
complete revolution because it was finished by the same men who
began it, and therefore followed one idea from beginning to end.*

But circumstances over which we had little or no control very suddenly
altered the world status of the republic in 1945 and subjected our governmental structure to strains that were unprecedented and very severe. Some
warps and cracks were to be expected and did occur, but they were far from
serious enough to justify the spasm of terror that swept the country, producing the witch-hunts that subsided only when the excesses of the egregious
Joseph McCarthy made them ridiculous.

The most blatant abuses of that unhappy era have been abandoned, or
at least abated, but some of the effects of that period still linger, one of the
most pernicious being a resurgence of federalism, not that of John Adams,
but of Timothy Pickering. Adams' federalism assumed the inevitable dominance of superior men, but he, like Jefferson, based superiority on "virtue
and talents." Pickering based it on power, whether acquired by the man's
own efforts, or inherited in the form of property. Inherited status is, of
course, the difference between natural and synthetic aristocracy. On the day
when each was inaugurated president, Jefferson was a richer man than
Adams, so it is preposterous to assume that the affluent Virginian thought it
impossible for a man who was rich, even by inheritance, to be a superior man.

It is the Pickering brand of federalism that inevitably drifts toward
tyranny. Dictatorship is not necessarily identical with tyranny. Cincinnatus
was twice a dictator, but never a tyrant. Al Smith observed long ago that in
time of war "we adjourn the Constitution," but Al had in mind hot war,
shooting war, when concentration of authority is imperative. Furthermore,
Al said "adjourn," not "abolish," implying that on the cessation of hostilities
the Constitution would resume its sway. The sole excuse even for adjourn-
ment is what Justice Holmes called "a clear and present danger," emphatically not a supposed or imagined one.

But it is precisely the alleged danger to national security that has been
advanced as the reason for the steady increase in the power of the executive
for the past dozen years. Yet we have the word of no less an authority than
Henry Kissinger that total national security is impossible in fact, from which
it follows that no threat to it can be clear and present, therefore a valid
excuse for denying or impairing the sovereignty of the people. But sovereignty is definitely and perhaps fatally impaired when the sovereign is
denied access to the whole truth about the state of the realm.

This was the trend of American politics long before the first administration of Richard Nixon. It can be traced at least as far back as the temporary
domination of the political scene by Joseph McCarthy. It became glaringly
apparent at the beginning of Kennedy's tragically short tenure of office,
when the Bay of Pigs folly revealed that our policy was dominated by what
the second Roosevelt had called the only thing we have to fear, the "nameless, unreasoning, unjustified terror which paralyzes needed efforts to convert
retreat into advance." True, Roosevelt was not talking about fear of an invasion by an armed enemy, but he *was* talking about distrust of the com-

petence of the people to cope with the difficulties of statecraft in the modern world.

Lyndon Johnson would have denied violently that the same distrust was what impelled him to use a very dubious incident in the Tonkin Gulf to wangle through Congress a permissive resolution that he used to justify escalation of the Vietnam War—a ruinous policy that was the fountainhead of a flood of woes that now torment us.

Nixon, while he must be acquitted of having inaugurated the trend, consistently approved and encouraged it from the time of his first appearance in politics. If there ever was a "nameless, unreasoning, unjustified terror" it was that of the Californians whom he persuaded to believe that Jerry Voorhis was practically a Communist and that Helen Gahagan Douglas was a "pink lady." He was a member of the administration while the Bay of Pigs fiasco was being organized, and if he knew nothing about it, it must be because he never read the newspapers, for they carried amazingly detailed information about it. Not until it proved so unpopular that it forced Johnson out of the race in 1968, did he, being then a candidate, disavow the Vietnam War and promise to end it, which he did by spreading it into Cambodia and Laos, and when his diplomatic agent, Kissinger, did negotiate a cease-fire agreement, the president—the election being safely past—tore it up and launched the disastrous Christmas bombing of Hanoi, which cost us more than a hundred airmen and $165 million worth of planes—eighteen B-52s at $5 million each and five of those swept-wing calamities at $15 million each, only one of which was shot down by Hanoi, four having simply fallen down without ever reaching the combat zone. Not three months earlier an unidentified Air Force officer had explained to the newspapers that we had not used the B-52s against Hanoi because they were too vulnerable to SAM missiles. Yet it was coolly explained to the public that the bombing had forced Hanoi to accept a much better agreement, although the newspapers were never able to discover wherein it differed materially from the original.

Nevertheless, Nixon was overwhelmingly reelected in November, 1972. The endorsement was the most emphatic since James Monroe was reelected by every electoral vote except one. It has since become apparent that the election was tainted with fraud, but that it was bought is an inference not supported by convincing evidence. The fact that a slush fund of at least $50 million was assembled supports the belief that every vote that could be bought was bought, but it does not prove that the venality of the electorate gave Nixon his victory, and it assuredly did not give him the landslide. Henry Kissinger's misleading announcement, made just before the voting, that "Peace is at hand" gave Nixon ten votes for every one that was purchased.

There is no evidence whatever that Dr. Kissinger knew that his statement was false. On the contrary, there is every reason to believe that he spoke in complete good faith. His instructions had been to arrange for a cease-fire on the best terms possible, and he had done so. His assumption that peace would follow rapidly was unwise, but natural; in fact, it was what everybody else thought, except inveterate skeptics. Not until the election was over did Nixon tear up the arrangement and virtually throw it in his agent's face.

If the learned doctor emerged with his reputation somewhat damaged, it is not because he knowingly lied, but because he did not instantly resign, instead of meekly swallowing the insult.

As it was, he forgathered again with Le Duc Tho, and the pair of them, the cynics aver, shifted a semicolon and dropped a couple of commas, whereupon Nixon, appalled by the wreckage of the Air Force, claimed that it was a new agreement, and signed.

But by that time the election was over and it was still some weeks before the lid really blew off Watergate.

Yet to this writing it is still questionable that anything like a majority of the voters have grasped the real significance of the affair. They are appalled and disgusted, of course, except for a minority of considerable size who believe that it is all a pack of lies invented by a depraved and dissolute press. They are not in the least impressed by the fact that the investigation and subsequent publication cost all the communications media, including radio and especially television, far more than they can hope to recoup, except in the nonnegotiable form of increased prestige for the performance of the public service. But the unconvinced would not change even if Moses and Elijah rose from the dead to testify. Indeed, they can't believe, because to do so would be an admission that they have been played for suckers, and for a certain type of American to admit that he has bought a gold brick is a psychological impossibility.

But even the majority who are not blinded by their own conceit show little indication of having realized that something of this sort is to be expected whenever the people allow their sovereign power to be usurped by a dictator or an oligarchy. It is not always so crass. Indeed, Watergate seems to have come close to setting a record for what Whitman—I believe—termed "the audacity of elected persons." But however suavely it begins, it ends in the brutality of the barracoon, the pen of the slave traders.

It came as a traumatic shock to ordinary Americans to learn that the tenant—the people are the owners—of the White House was capable of associating and staffing the place with men of such character that they would defile the edifice into a thieves' kitchen where malefactors would gather to plot burglary, bribery, perjury, forgery and slanderous defamation of honest men, not primarily to stuff their purses, but to fasten their grip upon power that belongs to the people. Half a century ago Harding had smirched the premises with thieves, mountebanks and at least one man who had been tried for murder, but acquitted for lack of evidence, yet such commonplace rascals seem almost respectable by comparison with men who would forge letters accusing honorable men of addiction to dishonorable sexual practices.

The stench was powerful enough, in all conscience, to distract attention from other aspects of the situation that, while less noisome, are more sinister by far than the degradation of a mere building, for powerful disinfectants, lavishly applied, can make even a lazaretto safe for human occupancy. The realistic American should pinch his nostrils long enough to give consideration to what this implies with respect to the theory that democracy is a viable form of government.

Many of us are committed to the belief that it is more than viable, that it is the best form of government that it has as yet entered into the mind of man to conceive. We assume that Jefferson was neither drunk nor crazy when he asserted that a society of free men, given all the facts necessary to intelligent judgment, can govern themselves better than anyone else can govern them. Of course they cannot act directly, but only through agents of their own choice. They must, however, retain the power to veto any policy that they deem inconsistent with their safety and happiness, for it is the sovereign power, as every absolute ruler has recognized. Ivan the Terrible and Nero ruled through agents. Harun al-Rashid, in all his snooping expeditions, was attended by Giafar, the grand vizier, and Masrour, the sword-bearer, and they, not the caliph personally, attended to the disposition of expendable persons.

But Nixon is the twice-attested choice of a majority of the electorate for president of the United States, and Nixon chose to install a palace guard that has brought disgrace upon the nation. What does that suggest as to the ability of the people to govern themselves better than anyone else can govern them?

The prodigious clamor over whether he was acquainted with all, or any, of the details of his men's rascalities is really beside the point. He chose them, and the rascalities were committed. He, in turn, was unquestionably president by the will of the majority; therefore the final responsibility rests squarely upon the shoulders of the majority.

Of course there are pleas in extenuation. There always are. For four years the people had been consistently kept in ignorance of what was actually going on, and every realist knew it. Why was the war extended into Cambodia? The excuse that it was done to protect our men in Vietnam was serious enough, but only as a revelation of the contempt of the president for the intelligence of the American people. Is it protecting men to order them to attack an additional enemy on unfamiliar and difficult terrain? In any event, an army is supposed to protect, not to be protected by the nation at the expense of another war. Ho had answered that argument long before. Asked by a European war correspondent if he would attack the Americans if they started to withdraw, he replied, logically, "Attack them? I would throw flowers in their path!"

Even when Nixon adopted a policy that was obviously correct, as when he sent Kissinger and then went himself to Peking and Moscow to try to make somewhat more rational our relations with China and Russia, he concealed his intention not only from the American people, but also from our friends abroad, who were disconcerted by the surprise, especially those in Britain and Japan. We have since learned that part of the price for conciliating Russia is the sale of an enormous quantity of wheat just when we are threatened with a shortage. What Kissinger offered China is still unknown. Perhaps it was nothing at all, but it is a credulous American who can believe that, in view of the administration's past record.

Whether or not he ever put it into words, as he is said to have done, his course of action is convincing evidence that Mr. Nixon believes that the masses of Americans are children and must be treated as such.

Nevertheless, the fact remains that he was the people's choice, and that raises a question, not about Mr. Nixon, but about the validity of the experiment we launched in 1776. It was undertaken to test the viability of democracy as a form of government, and, as tried on the national scale, it has been more than moderately successful for nearly two hundred years.

But our past record is no guarantee of the future because the conditions have changed. The New England town meeting was a success, too, when hardly more than a hundred people were involved. But it had to be abandoned long before cities of a hundred thousand and more dotted New England. The republic is fifty times as populous and more than fifty times as rich and powerful as it was in 1776. But in 1945, it emerged, willy-nilly, from national into imperial status, and new conditions imposed new responsibilities upon us, which we were in no wise prepared to meet.

Since then, we have been floundering, and a perplexed and uncertain people are especially vulnerable to the kind of fears that F.D.R. regarded as our only real danger, because they paralyze the will. If we remain much longer in that condition, we may be reasonably sure that our system is not viable in the new circumstances, and the adoption of a new one is imperative. For the experiment has failed, and Watergate was indeed the beginning of the end.

But we don't know. One is tempted to liken the present confusion to Balaam's time, in that any ass may speak, but prophecy is struck dumb. All that is certain is that the average American has suffered a terrific shock and, as regards individuals, when a patient is just beginning to emerge from such a shock, an honest doctor is wary of predicting what the permanent effects, if any, will be. They are unpredictable.

It is by no means unheard-of for the permanent effect to be beneficial, especially if the patient had previously been subjected to a long, exhausting nervous strain. That is undeniably true of twentieth-century Americans. From the First World War through the binge of the twenties, the depression of the thirties, the great wars of the forties, the small wars ever since, with the possibly spectral but constantly present cold war looming over all, the average American has passed successively every known state of mind with one exception—he hasn't been placid for fifty years.

The analogy with a psychiatrist's patient may be unscientific, but it is not irrational, for nations are composed of people, and mass hysteria is a well-recognized phenomenon. To people already under serious nervous strain the shock of Watergate was sudden, violent and brutal. It may also be ruinous. Mention has been made of the segment of the population that is determined to believe that the whole thing is a pack of lies concocted by those notorious Communists, the multimillionaire controllers of the *New York Times,* the *Washington Post* and the television networks. People who so believe have already gone into the screaming meemies, and it is possible that the rest of us may follow ere long.

On the other hand, it is equally possible that the very violence of the jolt may tend to restore our contact with reality, for instance, with a renewed appreciation of the truth in the old adage, "Eternal vigilance is the price of liberty." In that case, Watergate may come to be recognized as only the end of the beginning, the point at which the old experiment entered a new phase, that of adjusting to a new state of affairs at home and abroad.

It is a possibility that may be faced with some satisfaction, but not with unalloyed delight, for the process of readjustment is pretty sure to be long, arduous, dangerous and expensive, with no guarantee of success in the end. That has always been characteristic of serious efforts to renovate long-established social and political institutions, and for that reason, now as ever, the most formidable of all threats is fear itself, for timorous men who undertake such a venture are doomed to failure from the start.

Nevertheless, a certain number and perhaps a sufficient number of Americans will pursue the quest through the years immediately ahead. Not rejecting the phrase that Dr. Milton Eisenhower picked up from the Cubans, "The wine is bitter, but our own," they will counter with the cynics' boardinghouse motto, "Only the brave can stand the fare," and they will proceed with the endeavor to establish Watergate as the end of the beginning and the opening to a possibly stronger and better republic in a possibly better and stronger world.

Win, lose, or draw, their effort will be the most interesting thing in the world in the years immediately ahead. For if they conquer the fear of fear itself, they will lose nothing that cannot be replaced.

THE AMERICAN SCHOLAR, *Spring 1974*

POSITION PAPER FOR THE AMERICAN REALIST, 1974

Define your terms, sir!" If memory serves, it was old McCosh, of Princeton, who used to flatten an argumentative student with that admonition, but, regardless of its source, it is a good one, and so:

Definition: What a position paper is, I am not sure, but after reading scores, I deduce that the term is gobbledygook for a propaganda sheet, and proceed on that assumption.

Definition: A political realist, at least in this country, is a man whose perception of reality is as clear as that of a jackass of average intelligence and often clearer. Indeed, the realist is a jackass from the standpoint of the porcine element on our continent-sized Animal Farm, for he has only a languid interest in getting both forefeet, as well as his snout, into the swill trough. This relative lack of interest is no proof of his moral superiority, but is owing, chiefly, to his observation that an animal as sinewy, swift, and surefooted as the jackass seems to enjoy life more and to live longer than the fattest and greasiest of the swine.

As far as ideology is concerned, the realist may belong to any party, sect, or faction—except the far-out—right or left. He may be a Democrat, a Republican, a conservative, or a liberal, but never a Communist, or a John Bircher, for extremism of any kind is unrealistic.

In the light of these definitions, the position of the American realist in the early fall of 1973 cannot be outlined with two or three swift strokes because in this fateful year all political outlines have become blurred. Everything is fluid, "the center [does] not hold," and he who aspires to stick to the middle of the road has to be more nimble than Jack jumping over the candlestick. Indeed, the very concept of the middle of the road becomes unrealistic when no road leads to anywhere, and any to everywhere.

Under such conditions, to establish a realistic position that has any sort of credibility, perhaps the best approach is by way of negatives. In the first place one must concede that the American realist is as badly jarred as the most fanatical party man, but not by Watergate. Startled a bit he was, not by the operation, but rather by the fabulous clumsiness with which it was carried out. Dirty politics we have had ever since the first secretary of the treasury, Alexander Hamilton, leaked information to the British minister in Washington about the instructions given John Jay on a mission to England. But that operation was done so smoothly that the identity of the leaker remained concealed until some descendant of the diplomat made his ancestor's papers available to historians nearly two hundred years later.

The large significance of Watergate, on the other hand, began to be realized hardly fifteen minutes after the arrival of the seven burglars at the police station. Burglary is commonplace, but why Watergate? The most dim-witted cub reporter knew that no professional would crack that crib in the ordinary course of business, because it was notorious that the Democrats were desperately hard up, so that little money and less portable property easily convertible into cash would be found in their office. As for incriminating papers, what could a burglar do with them? It was as plain as the traditional pikestaff that this was a hired job, and since the cops had nailed no fewer than seven raiders in the room, it meant cash in such impressive wads that only an extremely affluent employer could have put it up. That meant somebody very high up in the Republican campaign, for to the Republican campaign committee, as the president may or may not have remarked, a million or so was no problem.

Nor was it the subsequent revelation of corruption in high places that knocked the realist off his perch. After all, Fall went to jail for taking bribes while a member of the cabinet, and every casual student of American history is sure that at least a dozen others of high standing in various administrations should have gone, but didn't. The cover-up is one of the oldest dirty stories in American politics.

What really griped the realist was the discovery of how far utter contempt for the sovereignty of the people has permeated our political system. Certainly that sovereignty has been evaded and avoided many times. But hitherto, it had always been done with a certain finesse, or a face-saving hypocrisy, if you prefer, that took the arrogance out of it. The second Roosevelt, for instance, was a far more effective dictator than Nixon has ever been, but he was careful to go about it with a fine show of deference to public opinion. The fireside chats, in particular, although they were couched in rhetoric so masterly as to completely conceal the rhetorical, in logic boiled down to apologies. "I hate to do this, but I have to, for these reasons . . . so I am going ahead. But you see how it is." So he got away with it, and was cheered to the echo as he did so.

But this administration, especially as represented by Mr. Nixon's personally elected handymen, has chosen to follow a different line. Oh, they were suave enough in their choice of language, but witness after witness for the defense, especially when testifying before the Senate committee, has said, in effect, "We are running this show. We have told you that we have done nothing illegal. By what right, then, do you have the temerity to question our word? We know what is essential to national security and you don't. So shut up and attend to your own business without interfering with ours."

Well, Louis XIV said, "I am the State," and made it stick throughout his reign and the next. But realists harbor some doubt that Richard Nixon is Louis XIV, and are dead certain that his palace guard is not. Furthermore, what eventually happened to the French monarchy is one of the prime horror stories of modern history. Hence realists are given some queasiness by promulgation of the doctrine that the executive is beyond all questioning, to say nothing of restraint, by the other branches of the government. Theoretically, of course, the legislature, plus the chief justice, has power to behead the executive by impeachment and removal of its chief officers. But to date the administration's reply to that is, "Try it, and see what it gets you!"

If this theory is accepted in common practice, no realist can deny that one of the important structural elements in our governmental fabric has given way. This element is the principle of checks and balances implemented in the Constitution by the separation of powers.

By the dictionary definition, checks and balances are restrictive, not destructive, and this is true of their practical application in the separation of powers. Nobody dreamed of giving any branch of the government the power to destroy any other branch, but only to check one if it showed a disposition to invade the province of either of the others. The power of impeachment and removal is quite another matter. It does empower the Senate to destroy a man's public life without touching his person by making it impossible for him ever again to hold any office of trust or profit under the government of the United States. But this is a desperate measure, to be invoked only against a man found guilty of treason, bribery, or some offense so heinous as clearly to disqualify a man for the office. It is obvious that removal by impeachment is too severe a penalty for a man whose most conspicuous fault is nothing worse than bad judgment.

But as the year wore on, and almost weekly a new scandal erupted while the fumes of its predecessor were still causing honest men to gag, the attitude of realists hardened progressively. Suspicion increased that here was not merely a recurrence of Harding's bad judgment in appointing arrant rogues to positions of trust and honor, but a reflection of the belief of the man at the top that a popular mandate, once issued, is irrevocable, no matter how much it may be abused. This suspicion made a resort to impeachment seem far less drastic than at first it had appeared to be, until at last an extremely reluctant House of Representatives was driven to appoint a committee to determine whether impeachment is necessary or, indeed, possible under the wording of the Constitution.

This has revealed a serious defect in the Constitution not attributable entirely, if at all, to its writers. They knew that some time in the future a man elected to the presidency might turn traitor or accept bribes, so they made either crime ground for removal by impeachment, and they did not doubt that time might reveal offenses equally heinous, so they added "other high crimes and misdemeanors." But the only president hitherto impeached was charged only with invading the powers of Congress, of which he was acquitted, so we have had no occasion for a judicial interpretation of "high crimes and misdemeanors," and it is apparent that we can secure one only by the process of impeachment. The need is to secure an interpretation that will make the remedy effective without subjecting the president to attacks based on nothing more substantial than partisan rancor.

To effect that will obviously require hard work and great skill, which is a sobering thought, but a worse is behind it. If the separation of powers is giving way under modern pressures, what about the other main supports of our governmental edifice? To a man who sees things as they are, and not as they are supposed to be, and as demagogues assure us that they remain, which is to say, a man who has not sunk into romanticism, but is still a realist, it is appallingly plain that some of the other pillars are sagging and cracking.

Equality before the law, for example, is obviously in bad shape. True, it was always more of an ideal than an actuality, but if the rule is established that the president, and not the Supreme Court, may decide when and to what extent he is amenable to the law that applies to all other men, then legal equality is no longer even an ideal. Everyone who is merely rational, not to say realistic, knows that the six aims of government posited in the Preamble to the Constitution are ideals that, like mathematical "limits," may be approached indefinitely, but never attained short of the New Jerusalem. What daunts the realist is the intrusion of new forces that tend to impede even the slow progress we have made in the past.

One, and perhaps the most spectacular, although not necessarily the most dangerous of these, was never even imagined in 1787, and therefore was not taken into account by the framers of the Constitution. It is the weight of international responsibility imposed upon the United States by its relatively sudden emergence in 1945 as potentially the most powerful death-dealer among the nations of the world. That was due at first to our armament, which was for the moment supreme, although it was soon largely neutralized by Russia. A more lasting element of strength was and is our economic power, which was and is capable of exerting terrific, perhaps fatal pressure on any nation against whom it might be brought to bear.

In 1947 we temporarily allayed the general alarm by a masterstroke of statecraft, the Marshall Plan, that reversed the historical role of victors. Instead of grubbing through the wreckage of Europe for what loot might be recovered, we offered $20 billion and actually spent $12 billion helping the stricken continent to its feet. We could afford to do it because, at the time, our political stance was based on confidence, not on fear. Aware that nobody could attack us with the remotest chance of success, we could view the situation as rationally as a businessman, one of whose best customers has suffered a disastrous fire. The businessman, if he is really smart, will help the fellow rebuild, knowing that it will cost him nothing, for what he spends today he will get back next year in the increased business the customer will be able to give him.

The American merit in the Marshall Plan was not our good hearts, but our good sense, and we were able to exercise good sense because we were unafraid. The odds are ten to one that whatever a badly scared man does is not going to be sensible, and the history of the United States since the Russians exploded their first atomic bomb is dismal evidence that this is as true of a nation as of a man.

To the wave of terror that swept this country—wantonly fomented by Joe McCarthy and his cohorts, prominent among whom was Richard M. Nixon—can be traced every one of the more egregious errors in our foreign policy for eighteen years. Dulles's refusal to sign the Geneva agreement on Vietnam was the first, but Nixon's refusal to sign the Kissinger agreement in 1972 was the climactic one. It precipitated the calamitous Christmas raids on Hanoi, which cost us over one hundred airmen and $165 million worth of planes, but did drive us back to the conference table sheepishly to sign, after all, substantially the original agreement.

The miraculous part of this achievement was its successful presentation to the country as a famous victory, "peace with honor," although it did not bring peace, and only a high-powered microscope can discern the honor.

Obviously, the country's most desperate need is eyesight that at a single glance can tell the difference between a hawk and a handsaw—in the specific case, between a glorious victory and the damnedest licking taken by a supposed great power since France crashed in 1940. The proximate cause of this dimness of vision was the politics of fear, assiduously promulgated by some politicians of all parties, but most effectively by the party that happened to be in power.

But in this case, as in most others, the proximate was not the final cause. The Red army is big and tough, and no man in his right mind wants to tangle with it, but in the minds of our lords and masters—the effective, not the nominal ones—Communist military power is only a secondary danger. Their fear of Communism is trivial by comparison with their fear of Americanism—distrust of its power to withstand, not the threats but the blandishments of the Red artists in hokum. That is the really valid explanation of the steady erosion of the Bill of Rights, especially freedom of speech, freedom of the press, and freedom of assembly to petition for the redress of grievances, or in modern vernacular, freedom to demonstrate. "Your people, sir, is a great beast!" said Hamilton, voicing the real, although not the avowed, basis of Federalist political theory. It has been repeated by every spokesman of that party since, although the modern designation is not Federalist, but elitist. It was murmured by Kennedy, spoken aloud by Lyndon Johnson, and bawled by Nixon, but it is essentially the same, except that the moderns strike out "great beast," and substitute Robert Burns' "wee, sleekit, tim'rous, cowerin' beastie." By an opposite approach, certain segments of the supposed liberals have arrived at approximately the same position, but that is another story.

The position of the realist, however, is that this doctrine necessarily repudiates the experience of fifty years, and a realist doesn't believe in defying experience, preferring to be, not ruled, but guided by it.

Since 1917, which is nearly sixty years now, the smartest artists in hokum that the great empire of Russia could produce have been working on the ordinary American with only sporadic repressions, never involving tanks and rarely machine guns, usually nothing more lethal than tear gas, and what have they accomplished? According to J. Edgar Hoover, never one to underestimate the numbers of the wicked, at their top they mustered perhaps as many as fifty thousand card-carrying Communists, but shortly before his death he estimated that they had been reduced to no more than fifteen thousand—statistically negligible in a population of two hundred million.

As an ideology, political freedom has proved invulnerable to either Communism or Fascism. What, then, is the excuse for renouncing it?

Nevertheless, the realist has to admit that the Constitution has been badly battered, not by enemy artillery, but by the pounding of time and events. He perceives that some repair work is imperative to prevent collapse of the whole structure.

All realists therefore dread the next few years, knowing that any extensive renovation of the Constitution will afford cover to pretended repairmen who are really saboteurs intent on removing parts of the structure that are still perfectly sound, notably the Bill of Rights. Hence realists divide into two types. The optimists believe that the job will be done, after a fashion. The pessimists are already exploring the possibility of obtaining Swiss citizenship.

THE NEW REPUBLIC, *June 22, 1974*

ON VOTING DEMOCRATIC
Confession of a Party-Liner

My first vote in a presidential election I cast for Woodrow Wilson, of which I am very proud. Subsequently I have supported every Democratic presidential candidate, of which I am not very proud, as it implies an affiliation, of which I am not proud at all, with an organization that in the past has included, and at present, I doubt not, still includes some of the damnedest rascals unhung. In confession and avoidance, as the lawyers say, I plead that the alternative was adhesion to the Republican party which includes, I believe, even more of the same. Furthermore, in congressional, state and local elections I have occasionally voted Republican, albeit only when the Democratic candidate stank so abominably as to be beyond endurance.

I am, in fact, a man imbued with the black pessimism of Thomas Jefferson. Of course I know that Jefferson is popularly regarded as an optimistic idealist, but that is simply a legend of our American mythology. The man was profoundly realistic, and no realist is unremittingly cheerful. Consider two of his characteristic utterances. One is from his first inaugural, a guarantee that it was carefully considered and exactly phrased. It reads, "Though the will of the majority is in all cases to prevail, that will, to be rightful, must be reasonable." If it is not, it becomes oppression. The other was in a private letter and in such writing Jefferson, like the rest of us, tended to become more vehement but not necessarily less truthful. He said, "Whenever a man has cast a longing eye on offices, a rottenness begins in his conduct."

The first is a plain implication that democracy is capable of abandoning reason, and when it does so, is transmuted into tyranny. The second is an equally plain implication that under any form of government, including the democratic form, there will always be some rotten eggs. Together they amount to corroboration, almost two centuries in advance, of Winston Churchill's judgment that no form of government is good, but that all the others are worse than democracy.

Churchill spoke generally, but I submit that specifically his reasoning applies well enough to the American two-party system. Allowing for temporary deviations from the norm, my reason for fairly consistent adhesion to one of the two major parties is not that the Democratic is a good party, but that the Republican is, as a rule, appreciably worse. "To prove this"—again I quote Jefferson, capital letters and all—"let Facts be submitted to a candid World."

Then—not as conceding a point, but as due courtesy to holders of the adverse opinion—let the first two facts submitted be the incontestable truth that the Republican party did elect Abraham Lincoln and Theodore Roosevelt. Both, to be sure, encountered venomous opposition within their own party, but that is the usual reward for getting something done. Every Democrat, also, who has had a lasting effect on our political history has endured the like.

Delving into ancient history is, however, rather beside the point. Washington, the pre-party President who had both Jefferson and Hamilton in his cabinet and was tough enough to fire both, is beyond debate. But Jefferson, Madison, Jackson and Lincoln were unquestionably shakers and movers, and most scholars agree that the Adams pair, John and John Q., were masters of statecraft, the science of government, and so command respect despite their woeful incompetence in politics, the art of getting elected. Yet the skills that bolstered, though they did not establish the reputations of the first five, and to some extent that of Lincoln, were markedly different from those most useful to 20th-century Presidents. (Note well, if you please, the word "skills"; probity, courage and energy are not skills, they are elements of character.) So the fact that John Quincy Adams was a superb Secretary of State is no proof that he could have handled the kinds of problems with which Kissinger has had to deal. And while the integrity of Washington had an intrinsic value that has never altered, Lincoln was too wise to try to use his iron hand, Theodore Roosevelt fumbled it, and Wilson's attempt to use it, after he was physically disabled, was a disaster.

My steadfast adherence to the Democratic party did not enable me to vote for the Virginia Dynasty, but it has influenced me to vote for two Presidents of the first rank—indeed, to vote for them six times—for another who, in the estimation of historians is not only in the second, but edging close to the top of that rank, and for another whose personal charm exceeded that of any occupant of the White House since Martin van Buren, most graceful of all Presidents. True, it also influenced me to vote for James M. Cox, John W. Davis, Alfred E. Smith and Lyndon B. Johnson, although in the last case the stronger influence was my impression that Johnson's opponent, Mr. Goldwater, was an evocation from the political Stone Age—an impression since shaken but not yet eradicated. I concede that, had I been old enough, partisanship might have betrayed me into voting against Theodore Roosevelt in 1908, but I balance that potential error by pointing out that party loyalty did cause me to vote for Cox against Harding. In 1924 the murderous combat between the Ku Klux and the Knights of Columbus gave the voters in November a choice between a zero and a cipher, so I voted for Davis, and why not? In 1928 I was for Al Smith with real enthusiasm. Not until some years later did I realize that he and Hoover were opposite sides of the same coin, and it a plugged nickel.

In the next seven elections, 1932-1956, I had not the shadow of a doubt that my party alignment was the right one. In five of them the majority of the voters agreed with me, and in the other two the party's error was a tactical one. In the aftermath of a great war, to run the best man you have against a successful general may be honorable conduct, but it is a long way from realistic politics, for in such circumstances the best man who walks in shoe-leather cannot beat five stars.

In fine, for the 16 elections for President in which I have participated, I remember my adherence to the party line with pride in seven cases, the two for Wilson, the four for F. D. Roosevelt and the one for Truman. Two for Adlai Stevenson I regard with personal satisfaction, although they were hopeless. In three, Harding-Cox, Nixon-Humphrey and Nixon-McGovern, sticking to the party saved me from being in the winning majority, which I remember with increasing satisfaction. In one, 1960, party loyalty had nothing to do with it. Kennedy was glamorous, to be sure, but had he been uglier than Caliban, he would have had my vote, for his opponent was Richard M. Nixon. In 16 tries the Democratic party, I believe, has nominated the better candidate 11 times, elected him eight times, and won again with Johnson, although that victory was a donation by the Republicans.

As a gambling system, then, I submit that nine out of a possible 16 wins, plus two that it deserved to win, make party regularity a pretty good bet.

But as a political philosophy I believe that dyed-in-the-wool Democracy rates much better. When the donkey is high he usually takes off in the direction of the New Jerusalem, the elephant, in like condition, toward Nineveh and Tyre. Obviously neither can arrive, because the New Jerusalem never was and the glories of Phoenicia never will be again. The practical problem is to determine which crash landing will afford the better chance of some survivors. There is no definitive answer, but the historical facts are that the donkey's trip ended in Johnson's Great Society and McGovern, the Elephant's in Watergate and Nixon. Which was the more terrific smash only time can tell, but my prediction is that the donkey will recover consciousness somewhat sooner than his rival will. I am well aware that this prediction may be attributable to a shot of wishful thinking, but I maintain that it has a factual basis that many Democrats frequently overlook.

I think that these facts are incontestable: 1) that the fight that historians call "our brush with Spain" demonstrated that the newly rebuilt United States Navy could move fast and shoot straight; 2) that in the days when the Wright Brothers and Marconi were still obscure, any nation with such a navy was either a great power or on the verge of becoming one; and 3) that the emergence of a new great power would compel readjustments of policy by all nations, including the new great power.

Add to these a fact still unsuspected when Wilson was first elected in 1912, but that is frightfully apparent now: that from a world viewpoint the 20th is the most terrible century since the time of the Hundred (really 116) Years' War, beginning in the 14th and running half through the 15th century.

Finally, consider a fact that half the Democrats and three-fourths of the Republicans in the country will deride as pure hallucination: that the three incontestably great leaders of public opinion in this century, Wilson and the two Roosevelts, were only incidentally reformers, being in the main hard-headed realists who not only observed the first three facts but perceived some part of what they implied.

When the first Roosevelt was President the century's nightmares had not begun, but he saw clearly that his first duty as President was to prepare the country for the inevitable change. The first step toward that end was to get rid of innumerable obsolete ideas and practices that would prevent us from profiting by our new opportunities. He went about it with a boldness and energy that continually startled and often scandalized the beholders.

Wilson followed the same line, but with a more realistic perception of the whole situation. He too was intent on preparing the nation for a new role in the world, but the first of the successive hurricanes struck the world as he was halfway through his first term, and thereafter he was preoccupied more by preparing the nation to shoulder its new responsibilities than to profit by its new opportunities.

The second Roosevelt, not in Wilson's class as a political philosopher but greatly his superior as a practical politician, spent his entire first term and part of his second clearing away some of the wreckage that the ineffable Harding, Silent Cal and bewildered Hoover had hardly touched. But the job was less than half done when the first blast of the second hurricane struck, and thereafter his time was all taken up by efforts to persuade the nation to face the storm rather than try to outrun it. He might have failed at that, had it not been for the thoughtfulness of the Japanese in giving us a terrific kick in the rear as we were in the act of cowering before the blast.

Certainly the three leaders all urged upon Congress and the country many and varied reforms, most of them long overdue and some, especially in the case of the second Roosevelt, frankly tentative, but the idea that they were soul-savers is one of the most fantastic of our political myths. It was our hides, not our souls, that they were out to save, and did save but by a frighteningly narrow margin.

Of the three Wilson was by long odds the hardest-headed realist. I make this flat assertion on the basis of an insight into his character that I gained before I ever heard of him, in fact before I was 10 years old. It derived from attendance at Sunday school in two Presbyterian churches whose congregations were almost exclusively Scottish-Americans and rigidly Calvinistic. There I became acquainted with the Session, a committee that was the ruling authority in matters of faith and dogma, and composed of the elders and the minister. In childish eyes these figures were majestic, holy and hateful, all in the superlative degree.

Therefore in later years I received placidly utterances of President Wilson that drove into frenzy friends and neighbors imbued with Arminian, Socinian, Papist or Judaic errors. My own reaction was, well, the man was a Scotch Covenanter, so what else could you expect? Case-hardened he certainly was, ruthless he certainly was, arrogant he frequently was, but a hypocrite he was not. A very cursory examination of his chief propositions will reveal that they were designed to adjust the republic to its new position as a great power so that it might function smoothly and with the greatest attainable measure of security.

When he declared that the highest function of government is "to release the generous energies of our people," he spoke with machine-tooled precision. The ungenerous energies require no release because they rampage throughout the world, as witness the national cemeteries and the national debts.

It is the glory of the second Roosevelt that he understood the core of Wilson's political philosophy and approved it. But he inherited a nation with its economic system in ruins and with the people's confidence in themselves and in their government buried under the ruins. His first task was to dig it out, which he did with a political skill of which Wilson had not an iota. But his administrative ability fell far short of his perception of the truth that you cannot establish respect for law until the law has been made respectable, and he was only halfway through that task when the second hurricane struck him, and eventually killed him, but not until victory was in sight. He died firm in the faith that the only national security is in the people's faith that the nation is worth securing.

But his post-mortem good fortune was to have as his successor Mr. Truman, a man thitherto regarded as rather less considerable than Chester A. Arthur, but who had the courage to erase from the Democratic banner Marcy's swinish slogan, "To the victor belong the spoils" and substitute, "On the victor devolves the duty to give first-aid to the injured," and with that the world prestige of the United States touched the highest pinnacle it has ever reached.

Because I was a party-liner I had voted for him. So, my lords and gentlemen, despite Boss Tweed, the Tonkin Gulf Resolution, local stinkers and all, I remain a Democrat unabashed.

THE NEW REPUBLIC, *September 21, 1974*

THE NOTHING KING

The consensus at which we have lately arrived is not the one of which Lyndon Johnson dreamed, but it is a pretty solid opinion that the chief occupation of the American citizen for some time to come will consist of trying to pick up the pieces of his late government and fit them together before the next hurricane hits.

But before we become absorbed in the salvage operation, it is certainly advisable to give ear to the political arson squad that is trying to tell us that the catastrophe was by no means as simple a thing as some of us find it convenient to believe. Part of it, but only part, is due to the fact that there came three unwise men, curiously antiphonal to "Casper and Melchior and swart Balthasar"—bright John and dulcet Lyndon and oily Richard M.—not from the East, but successively from Massachusetts, Texas and California, all bearing hallucinogenic gifts. The first created the dazzle of gold in his evocation of King Arthur, the second the fragrance of incense in his materialization of Santa Claus, the third offered a revival of Machiavelli as bitter and narcotizing as myrrh.

Each of these contributed somewhat to the misdirection that brought us, unwittingly, very close to deposing the Sovereign Citizen and replacing him with a usurper, the Sovereign President. It was a narrow squeak, how narrow is not yet realized by probably a third of the American people. The deadly factor is that the proposed usurpation was strongly assisted by the Sovereign himself, and unless this is recognized and taken into account by the majority who are capable of thinking, no adequate barriers will be set up against a recurrence of the attempted subversion.

The frightening truth is that within the past 25 years the Sovereign American Citizen has acquired much of the intellectual and moral coloration of the late Merovingian kings of France, the *rois faineants,* "nothing kings," who couldn't be bothered with ruling and were content to let power drift into the hands of the mayor of the palace. The inevitable end was that there came a mayor more vigorous than Nixon and as ruthless. He deposed the king, seized the crown and begot Charlemagne, since when the Merovingians have been as inconsequential as shadows on the wall. And why not? For that matter if the American Sovereign Citizen is too indolent or too stupid to retain final authority in his own hands, it will be better for the world when some new Pepin the Short takes over.

Nixon was not the man for that job, and his unfitness became plain before successful subversion was possible. But if the Sovereign Citizen refuses to drag his rump off the cushioned throne and chase out the fake magi, American democracy, like the Merovingian dynasty, will become "as a tale that is told."

THE NEW REPUBLIC, *May 31, 1975*

TRUMAN NOSTALGIA

Memories of Competence in the White House

Shortly before his death Walter Lippmann was asked by an interviewer to name the last really competent President of the United States and, after a moment's thought, replied "Madison." Mr. Lippmann, being a man of good judgment, was probably speaking sardonically, for if not he was certainly wrong on a least one count. In the list of Presidents, Truman came later than Madison, and was, if anything, more competent.

No man of sense, and emphatically not Mr. Lippmann, ever equated "competent" with "perfect." In business, and there is no reason to doubt in politics also, a competent man is one who is steadily on top of his job, keeps it moving, abstains from graft and nepotism and when he retires leaves the company, or his section of it, in better shape than it was when he took over. Thus a President who has announced in advance and with complete candor what he intended to do if elected, and then proceeded to do it, cannot fairly be called incompetent. If great damage results it goes to prove the incompetence, not of the President but of the electorate that, knowing the man's quality, elected him.

In Truman's case perfervid moralists were joined by the overeducated intellectuals who are committed to the proposition that no man can know anything unless he has learned it by the method of sitting at the feet of Gamaliel, that is, by learning it from certified and authorized pundits, usually in university faculties. By such intellectuals it can never be granted that a farmer, for instance, can learn anything important through being whipped by a combination of poor soil and dry weather in northwestern Missouri, or being whipped again trying to operate a retail merchandising business in a postwar depression, or by fighting, with success, the wolfpacks of crooked contractors and grafting politicians that swarm around every sizable construction job in a county being rapidly urbanized. Most emphatically they do not believe that a man learns anything important by tongue-lashing back to their guns a battery of half-trained artillerymen who had panicked when enemy shells first started bursting around their ears. But the men knew that the captain knew what it is necessary to know in the front line and before the cease-fire came that same battery had fired 10,000 rounds at the enemies of this country.

If the question is raised, what has this to do with the operation of a democratic system of government? the answer is, everything that is essential.

Civilized men of course prefer to see their government conducted with dignity and, as far as may be, with grace. But it must at all cost be conducted with honesty and courage or it will inevitably blow up, as the United States exploded when Watergate exposed the perfidy and mendacity that had been rampant in Washington. Nixon, to be sure, wasn't the only President who was unfit for the office; he was merely the one who went too far and got caught. Nor is it likely that he was the last. Considering the imperfectibility of mankind, it is a safe guess that there will be others in the future. If too many are elected in succession, the republic will not survive but that, *Deo gratias,* will be our grandchildren's problem, not ours.

Harry S. Truman was propelled into the presidency with no training for the ordeal he was destined to endure, which is the greatest blot on the record of Franklin D. Roosevelt. Truman didn't even know that the atomic bomb existed, although it was almost ready for its first test, and he had only the ordinary newspaper reader's knowledge of the intricate military arrangements among the Allies then sweeping down upon Berlin from east and west, to say nothing of their various postwar plans, joint or individual. It is hard to imagine how a man could be more unfairly thrust into a position of immeasurable responsibility. It is no wonder that he said that he felt that the weight of the moon and all the planets had fallen upon him.

But he knew and faced the terrible truth that was being sedulously avoided by every ambitious politician who was nothing more, but which it was the President's duty to face. It was the truth that, with the exception of the United States, 90 percent of the western world was wrecked. The United States, too, was seriously hurt. The republic had spent both blood and money lavishly in Europe, having at the same time to fend off a deadly attack from Japan, but we were still on our feet. Germany was nearly finished. The Japanese navy was virtually wiped out but the home islands were not yet invaded and to judge by the way their army had fought on the islands to the south, the invasion would be very difficult. Truman's ablest military advisers told him that he might expect a million casualties, with Japanese losses two or three times as heavy. The Pentagon figured that three or four million people, counting ours and theirs, would be killed or wounded in an invasion and the land would be completely devastated. The generals wished to avoid that if it could possibly be done, but the militarists still in power in Tokyo were adamant and our people felt that the fanatics' will would not be broken without some terrific shock. So President Truman was informed and he had no just cause to reject the Pentagon's judgment.

It so happened that the necessary shocker was at hand, but the scientists who had fabricated it stood appalled by the effectiveness of their own work. To produce the necessary effect it must be used against a huge industrial complex or a very large military installation, either of which would catch great numbers of civilians and 100,000 casualties might easily result. But an invasion, the experts told the President, would produce three or four million casualties, one-fourth to one-third of them ours.

The President's decision was prompt and realistic. We had two bombs. They were to be dropped on two ports used by the military and naval commands of Japan. Hiroshima was an army port of embarkation as well as a naval station at which two divisions, some 30,000 men, were assembled but had not been shipped out because there was very little chance that they could escape our submarines, surface craft and planes. The other port was Nagasaki, used more for shipments of supplies than for personnel. In obedience to the President's order Hiroshima was hit on August 6, 1945, and Nagasaki on August 9. On August 14, the Japanese government asked for terms. By the most careful estimates available—admittedly none too exact—in the two cities 120,000 people were killed or died of their injuries. For that decision Truman has been denounced as a fiend, regardless of the fact that three or four million, including one million of ours, did *not* die in an invasion of Japan.

There is and has always been as good reason for calling Truman a great humanitarian as a ruthless butcher. He was, of course, neither. He was simply a man who turned a deaf ear to the ballyhoo and acted on such facts as were known to him. He died serenely confident that in a hot spot he had done his plain duty, no more and no less. His decision may or may not have been barbarous, but there is no doubt that results followed fast. And that supports the trend of this argument that Truman was a competent President.

In any event, his case does not rest entirely, or even chiefly, on his handling of the bomb. In addition he had to make four other decisions, each of which has profoundly affected the political history of this country for 25 years, and *every single one of them was right!* They were the Marshall Plan, the North Atlantic Treaty Organization, the Berlin airlift and Korea.

To call the Korean decision right will set some people's teeth on edge—and very honest people, too—but only because they do not understand that I refer to Truman's Korean policy, not to MacArthur's. Truman's error, for which he paid a terrific penalty, was in not adhering to the assertion on the plaque that he kept on his desk in the White House: "The Buck Stops Here." Why he slipped is anybody's guess, but the one offered here is false modesty. The only time he had stood in battle was as a mere captain of artillery, so who was he to dispute with a four-star general on a point of strategy? The correct answer was, he was the commander-in-chief, outranking any number of stars. But he faltered about pulling his rank and permitted the general to proceed on, as the event proved, incorrect intelligence and out-dated maps, straight into a Chinese trap and the worst licking inflicted on an army of the United States since Bull Run. Truman paid the price and not unjustly, for there can be no toleration of faltering in the top command. True, he busted that general and put in one who could, and did, drive the enemy beyond the line to which the United Nations had authorized Truman to advance, and stop there. But it was too late. Truman still bears the blame for a messed-up campaign, and Eisenhower gets the credit for salvaging it. Both judgments are technically correct, but factually completely wrong.

So also with NATO and the airlift—political opposition has found plausible pretexts on which to denigrate both, but the discredit is achieved only by some very tortuous reasoning. On the face of the facts, NATO gave the European democracies a chance to pull themselves together, and the Berlin airlift was a fast and sharp but not excessive reaction to calculated

Russian aggression. Both were indicative of high competence in the White House.

However, all these are relatively small matters as compared to the great feat of the Truman administration, for which, incidentally, he tried to pass the credit in very large measure to his Secretary of State, Gen. George C. Marshall. The general demurred, pointing out that at least half a dozen men, some in, some out of office, played important parts in devising the scheme. But Truman authorized it, and Truman ordered Marshall to proclaim it— thereby getting his name attached to it—in a speech at Harvard. So if Truman must bear the chief blame for Korea, he cannot fairly be denied chief credit for the Marshall Plan.

Of course it was misinterpreted both ways, which proves nothing about the idea itself but is simply another demonstration of mankind's disposition to believe any romantic fairy tale rather than a dull narration of colorless facts. The sweetest of the romantics rhapsodized over the Marshall Plan as the most glorious act of magnanimity in the history of nations, and the sourest of the same breed denounced it as the most vicious demonstration of sentimental imbecility in the history of nations.

Both were off the target by a long sea mile. The Marshall Plan was the act of a man of sense who knew, as everyone capable of knowing anything knew, that the free nations belonging to Western civilization were, with one exception, completely devastated. Getting them into production again would take many years unless they were given an initial push by someone who could. The only nation that could was the United States. These facts were no official secrets.

The one fact that all romantics, sweet or sour, ducked, but that Truman faced was that in the matter of giving help, if the United States could, the United States should. This applied even on the narrow ground of advancing our own interests, for the prostrate nations had been and could again be our best customers.

That, howled all the romantics, is a lie! We should always act, said the sweet ones, "in the name of the Great Jehovah and the Continental Congress," but mainly in the name of the Great Jehovah, for we are the holiest of all tribes of men, and appointed by God to lead those who sit in darkness into the white light of sanctity. The sour also demanded inaction, but on different grounds. They held that Silent Cal, greatest of all political gurus, in two maxims had prescribed our proper course in such cases. One was, "The business of America is business," the other, "They hired the money, didn't they?" But with the advantage of hindsight we know now that Coolidge prosperity led into the crash of 1929 and the Great Depression, while the Marshall Plan led into the biggest and longest boom in our economic history.

The proposal of the Marshall Plan was, in brief, that if the chief financial officers of the war-damaged nations of Europe, including our late enemy, Germany, and our late Communist ally, Russia, would calculate what immediate repairs were required to get the European nations operating again, the United States would take their word for it and foot the bill up to $20 billion. In Russia the offer met with a surly refusal, and even Russia's captive nations, such as Poland and Czechoslovakia, were forbidden to accept. Many Americans forget that the financiers of the other nations calculated that $12 billion would turn the trick, and that was all that we acually put up. But it worked a near miracle of restoration, and it won us a measure of confidence and respect such as we had never enjoyed before. In retrospect we can see that, at the moment, the American republic touched a level of power and prestige above any in its previous history. And it was accomplished without firing or threatening to fire a single shot.

But all that is now history, finished, water over the dam and of contemporary value only as a suggestion of what can be done when we are resolved on action. But the suggestion acquires immense significance when we consider who did it. Literally, the answer is millions of Americans, but what we mean is who gave the word to go and pointed the way. To that, the astonishing answer is, no mental giant, no profound master of statecraft, or philosophy, or science, or art, nobody but Harry S. Truman, so completely the average man that you and I would not fear to match wits with him, although we might back off a bit from a comparison of our honesty and nerve. Croesus couldn't buy nor the devil scare him, but only in those two qualities did he stand head-and-shoulders above the rest of us.

What of it? Why, nothing, if you can see nothing in it. But it is possible that you may see a great light in the story if you are one of those who, knowing how dark is the future and how great the difficulties in our way, have been praying to whatever God you worship that of His grace he send us a Washington, a Jefferson, a Lincoln to lead and deliver us. In the light of this gleam from the past, you may be moved to moderate your demands upon the Lord. We can make do with less. If a beneficent Providence would grant us, say, two-thirds of the clear vision with which Truman saw what he ought to do, and even half of the courage he needed to do it, the republic would be safe. And who knows? Those gifts might be enough to carry us to a summit on which the air perhaps is purer and the light brighter, even than on the level to which that very average man led us in 1947.

THE END OF THE BEGINNING

Bertrand Russell's *Human Society in Ethics and Politics,* published when he was eighty-three, ends with these lines: "Those who are to lead the world out its troubles will need courage, hope, and love. Whether they will prevail, I do not know, but, beyond all reason, I am unconquerably persuaded that they will."

You may dismiss this as the dithering of a sentimental old fool. If you do you will find yourself in the company of a great many Americans, some of them adjudged very shrewd fellows. His Lordship was a man of tremendous intellectual capacity, especially in mathematics, but also in philosophy, which does not rule out the possibility that in other phases of existence he may have spoken on the mental level of a retarded child. The point is arguable but for the purpose of this essay without significance.

What lends this statement vivid interest in this country twenty years later is the fact that an impressive number of Russell's moral judgments that were laughed out of consideration when they were delivered subsequently proved to be based on very solid fact. Some have been absorbed into the corpus of conventional tuition, especially on the upper levels.

The point of interest today, therefore, is not the state of mind of the noble Earl, but whether there is any tenable reason to hope that this is another instance in which he was talking very uncommon sense when he seemed to be dithering. Russell acknowledged that he spoke "beyond all reason" in predicting that the people he described will in time prevail, but he certainly did not speak beyond all emotion, and no rational observer will deny that the emotional drive has frequently produced results, and sometimes desirable results, that cold reason would never have predicted.

However, there is no fruitful dialectic without a definition of terms, in this case courage, hope, and love. Lucifer unquestionably had courage, hope is the sustaining force of the gambler as well as of the saint, and we have the highest authority for it that there are those who "love the darkness rather than the light because their deeds are evil." Russell was not speaking derisively; so I think he would not have objected to having his terms defined as the courage to learn the truth, hope that a better structure of government than any now existing can be designed and constructed by our generation, and love of that ancient ideal of all mankind, freedom from fear.

With its terms so defined his statement becomes obviously true. But the evidence that contemporary Americans possess the qualities so defined is far from conclusive. The records of the police courts and the penal institutions attest that great numbers are devoid of any trace of the three, while some have courage only to inflict injury on others, some have hope that has corroded into gluttony, and some are consumed by a self-love that has become maniacal.

So much is obvious, but so it has always been, and the fact remains that within the span of recorded history human life, for a great many millions, has risen somewhat above the level of the primitive as described by Hobbes: "solitary, poor, nasty, brutish, and short." It is evident, therefore, that for the level of civilization to be raised appreciably it is not necessary that every living man shall be honest, industrious, and just. To establish a tolerable form of government it was not necessary in 1787, and has not become necessary in 1975, for every living American to practice all the virtues of good citizenship. John Adams said that in 1776 not more than a third of the American people favored independence. Another third preferred the familiar tyranny of the King to the unexperienced but fearsomely described "tyranny of the mob" which they were assured was the inevitable end of democracy. The remaining third favored nothing except being on the winning side. But the energy of the positive third was enough to sweep the apathetic along and so to become a majority.

The outlook at the beginning of 1975 is gloomy, and it is not merely silly to deny it, it is very dangerous, for until we face our difficulties realistically we shall do nothing intelligent toward overcoming them. Heilbroner, for instance, is perfectly logical in asserting, on one condition, that the springs shall become silent, the seas polluted, and the atmosphere heated to a degree destructive of all life as we know it. But his one condition is so improbable that it invalidates his prediction. It is that we shall continue our present insensate follies for anywhere from 150 to 300 years.

Every high school mathematician knows that in extrapolation the factor of error increases exponentially with extension. In political affairs extension through three centuries raises the factor of error to, or very near to, 100 per cent—in other words, no prediction is valid at such a distance in time. To do him justice, Heilbroner never presented his statement as oracular, but only as logical, which it certainly is.

But many less cautious savants have conceded to democracy a chance of survival so thin as to be no chance at all in any practical sense. To judge by their public utterances, the opinion of academics runs heavily against the continuance for more than a very short time of the experiment in self-government begun in 1776, and miraculously successful for nearly two hundred years.

Yet while these predictions cannot be dismissed lightly, it is an error to assume that there is nothing whatever to be set against them. In particular, there is one historical fact whose significance cannot be quantified but that certainly exists and that may be highly significant. It is the fact that we have been here before.

That is to say, there is registered in our history and therefore in the consciousness of every schoolboy the fact that once before we faced a similar problem and solved it not, indeed, perfectly but well enough to permit the nation to survive and prosper exceedingly. Consider then the core and center of our present difficulties. It is simply that the pre-existing governmental structure of Western civilization has been demolished and nothing has been erected to take its place. That structure was the Balance of Power fabricated by Castlereagh, Talleyrand, and Metternich in 1815, which crashed in 1918. It was not a good system. It was merely an equipoise of imperialisms, all rapacious and all vulnerable, which even its architects did not expect to last forever. Nevertheless it did, after a fashion, maintain itself for a hundred years before becoming such a threat to the safety of all the world that it had to be demolished, which was accomplished, with our assistance, in 1918. But nothing effective was done to replace it and in 1939 a convulsive effort to revive the menace had to be put down, again with our assistance, but at far greater cost in both blood and money.

Our first experience of the kind involved the overthrow of a governmental structure covering not a whole civilization but that part of North America held by the British King, roughly the area between Maine and Spanish Florida and between the Atlantic ocean and the Mississippi river. It was strictly our idea, and although we had very effective assistance from the French in carrying it out, after the cessation of hostilities they left us to our own devices. What was done toward replacing the demolished political structure was done according to strictly American plans.

In the first instance, we started the war and the French saw fit to join us. In the later instances others started the war and we saw fit to join them. Thus when a new governmental structure to cover a whole civilization was to be designed we were very far from having a free hand. Indeed, in 1919 Wilson did not have even his own country solidly behind him, and although in 1945 Roosevelt had much more solid support at home, he also had a much more difficult task because our late allies were prostrate.

Most literate Americans are aware that in 1776 we asserted the Right of Revolution as defined in the Declaration of Independence, but not all Americans and almost no others understand it in full. Every Fourth of July orator is eloquent on the first half of the Right, but few Americans and almost nobody else have emphasized the fact that it is the second half that gave the American revolution a distinctive character setting it apart from the French and the Russian, the other great upheavals of the last two centuries. The American Revolution alone was finished by the same people who started it.

The French Revolution, started by the Girondins, was snatched from them by the Jacobins, from whom it was snatched by Bonaparte, who converted it into a tyranny. The Russian Revolution was started by the liberal Mensheviks, was snatched from them by the Bolsheviks, and, after Lenin's death, snatched from the Old Bolsheviks by Stalin, who converted it into a tyranny.

But the men who signed the Constitution were in many cases men who had signed the Declaration of Independence, and the others were almost all either junior officers who had served under Washington or civilian officials who had acted under the Continental Congress, that is to say, original revolutionaries.

And why not? The Right of Revolution as defined in the Declaration of Independence consists of two parts. The first reads: "Whenever any Form of Government becomes destructive of these Ends"—i.e. the inalienable rights—"it is the Right of the People to alter or to abolish it." The second part adds without interruption, "and to institute new Government . . . in such Form as to them shall seem most likely to effect their Safety and Happiness." The duty is an inseparable part of the right, neither being valid if separated from the other.

One can read the whole story on the green side of a dollar bill. The reverse upper part of the Great Seal of the United States carries the motto *Annuit Coeptis,* "He hath smiled on our undertaking," the reference in the original being to Jupiter, the god worshiped by Aeneas. The lower part explains the undertaking with the words *Novus Ordo Seclorum,* "A new order of the ages." The old order is ignored as being merely an obstruction removed to give place to the new.

That national experience, drilled into them as schoolboys, accounts for a characteristic of Americans that has puzzled Europeans and exasperated Americans less indoctrinated with the spirit of the Revolutionaries. It is the modern American's "of course" acceptance of Woodrow Wilson's insistence, echoed by Franklin Roosevelt, that winning the war, either that of 1914-18 or that of 1939-45, was not an end in itself, but only a process of clearing the way to the real job, which was the establishment of a *Novus ordo seclorum* not for this country alone, but for the whole Western world.

By the time of the second Roosevelt Europe had been forced by ghastly experience to understand what Wilson had in mind, but for us the ordeal had not been severe enough to eliminate a sweetly stupid romanticism that still permeates the minds of a formidable number of Americans—the notion that the source of our woes is a fabulously clever Devil, not mainly our own stupidity. Stupidity we can overcome, by dint of enormous labor, no doubt, but by labor, not by spells and incantations. But who can contend with the Foul Fiend except a shaman equipped with powerful spells, incantations, charms, and fetishes unknown to the common herd, which the witch-doctor alone can handle without disaster. Yet thanks to the protagonists of fear, the tireless recounters of tales of Raw-Head and Bloody-Bones continue to flourish.

Of course, it may be that this is their time. According to Toynbee the time must come to every civilization when the challenge it meets is more powerful than any response that it can muster, which, historically, has always been the beginning of the end. But while candor compels the admission that this is possible, nothing compels the admission that it is inevitable.

Americans, on the contrary, are under a very strong obligation not to make any such admission until we have exhausted every effort to apply to the new situation what our experience with the old has taught us. The obligation is imposed by the sharply different relation to the other democracies in which we found ourselves in 1945. This relation was not of our choosing; it arose from the fact that at the end of the Second World War with the whole world in chaos, the United States and Russia were the only nations left with strength enough to do anything effective about cleaning up the mess.

Russia, still completely authoritarian despite the switch from Czarist to Communist dictatorship, repudiated any responsibility for areas not occupied or controlled by the Red Army. We drew no such line, but it was quickly drawn for us by Moscow. Such borderlands as Czechoslovakia and Poland were forbidden to accept aid under the Marshall Plan, although it was offered on the same terms given to France and Great Britain. So, also, it was offered to Russia, only to be curtly refused. This naturally swung American opinion sharply to the side of those, including Sir Winston Churchill, who had been urging us to follow Kipling's advice:

> Make ye no truce with Adam-zad—the Bear that
> walks like a Man.

It was certainly a part, possibly the central part, of the beginning of the Cold War.

Theoretically, of course, we should have remembered that up to the time of Peter the Great Russia had been a hermit nation as far as participating in the political development of Europe was concerned and to the time of Alexander I and Napoleon had been very slightly Europeanized. It had not undergone the bruising experience that had taught Western Europe and, through Britain, the budding American republic the lesson that, in an increasingly crowded world, possession of power imposes responsibility for keeping some kind of order so that the mutually profitable exchange of goods and services throughout the world may not be totally inhibited. If we had kept that fact in mind we might have acted more realistically and effectively.

But that is water over the dam. Lost opportunities are gone forever and the only ones open to us—and therefore worth discussing—are those presenting themselves now and hereafter. Furthermore, many of these are not really open because we are entangled in a web of old superstitions and so prevented from grasping them.

This is the reality of our difficulty. Dr. Milton Eisenhower startled Marquis Childs by using, as a chapter heading in his book, *The President Is Calling,* the words: "America has the wisdom and wealth to solve its most pressing problems; it is only sufficient will that is lacking." Mr. Childs undoubtedly would concede that in the items of sufficiency of wealth and insufficiency of will Dr. Eisenhower is right; but can wisdom exist in the absence of wit enough to distinguish reality from fantasy? The history of the United States for the past fifty years gives an answer less than flattering to our national complacency.

The Nixon episode is the most recent and most startling case in point, but that particular danger is probably over except for assorted remnants and reminders with which we shall be dealing indefinitely. Theoretically, it may recur, but not until some aspiring dictator organizes a junta less crassly stupid than Nixon's, which is unlikely for some years.

But the removal of that danger served only to unveil a cluster of problems vastly more complicated than any mere power grab. Some are economic, some juridical, some technological, and all with important political and social implications. The question is, are there credible reasons for believing that the American people have some special qualifications for dealing with these things? If such reasons exist it is important to reveal them now, for possession of any qualifications, or the mere belief that we possess them, would go far toward supplying Dr. Eisenhower's missing factor, the will to grapple with our problems.

I believe that we can credibly claim three. One has been mentioned. It is the fact that we have been here before, in the sense that we have overthrown an existing government and replaced it with a sounder one. This ought to enable us to view with more equanimity than any other modern nation the possibility of having to make some radical political changes. To people convinced that it is blasphemy to lay hands on anything that is old the fact that something new would obviously work better is irrelevant, but it is not so to us, or it has not been so in the past.

A second is the fact that we have had extensive experience in adjusting to a condition that to date has affected the rest of Western civilization but slightly. It is adjustment to the difference made by modern technology in the influence of time and distance on social and political operations. In communication this difference amounts to abolition of time and space, and as regards people, animals, and ponderable objects it has worked an immense reduction in the influence of those barriers. For Mr. Kissinger, London is an overnight journey from Washington, and for an Intercontinental Ballistic Missile, Moscow is twenty minutes from Montana. This has resulted in an intimacy of contact of cultures unprecedented in history.

But more than any other nation the United States has been for two hundred years the locus of a reproduction of this process on the laboratory scale. Nowhere else have so many representatives of every known culture been forced into intimate contact with so many others. One result is that Americans have perforce become very knowledgeable about knocking off knobs and protuberances and smoothing jagged edges in order that heirs of the most widely different civilizations may live together with the minimum of abrasive contacts. This expertise, very considerably developed and refined, one hopes, should be of great value to the civilization of the twenty-first century, since the combination of the population explosion and extreme mobility has subjected the former imperial powers to the melting-pot experience of this country. If our own record of adjusting has not been too encouraging, still it seems to be the best procedure available so far.

Finally, our population includes a certain proportion of men and women, probably not a majority but an impressively large minority, perhaps approximating John Adams' one-third who favored independence in 1776, who are imbued with what can hardly be called anything but a metaphysical faith. It is best expressed by a curious remark of Woodrow Wilson when asked to comment on some badly aimed but nobly motivated outburst of the youth of his time. He called it "the effort of nature to release the generous energies of our people."

The implications of that are staggering. It assumes, first, that there are generous energies in our people; second, that they are capable of being released; and third, that there is a force in nature that operates toward their release. The Covenanter in Wilson of course would have identified this force as God, specifically, the Presbyterian God of the Westminster Catechism, but the modern American in him knew that this identification would be rejected by the non-Presbyterian majority of his fellow-countrymen, so he substituted "nature," a term with no sectarian implications. Yet aside from all theological implications the gist of this utterance is its assumption of the persistence of generous energies in the American people. A good many still accept that persistence as a fact independent of sectarian dogma.

In sum, then, it is historical fact that the American people have had the experience of overthrowing one form of government and erecting a new one to replace it. It is a fact, also, that the new one has worked with spectacular success for nearly two hundred years.

It is probably a fact and it is certainly a tenable theory that Americans may have acquired some skill from their indisputable experience in dealing with the demographic jamming that technology has thrust upon the modern world. Intimate contact of diverse cultures has been part of our experience since that day in 1619 when a Dutch ship, name unknown, landed what John Rolfe described as "20. and odd Negroes" at Jamestown. Thus we should be able to realize better than any other great power how indispensable are countless adjustments to make civilized life possible under that condition.

Finally, there is evidence supporting the hypothesis that a very large number, possibly a third or more, of the American people are convinced that the highest possible achievement of statecraft is to release the generous energies of our people, this based on the faith that those energies, when actually released, are capable of achieving triumphs beyond the wildest dreams of Hammurabi, Lycurgus, Solon, or any other famed lawgiver of fact or fable.

Certainly all these are inference based on evidence that is less than conclusive. It is conceivable that from our experience in statecraft we have learned nothing, that our efforts to adjust to demographic shifts and changes have merely piled up trouble for the future, and that our theory of generous energy in Americans is doubtful, the possibility of its release more doubtful, and the assumption that if released it would do good rather than harm, preposterous.

All these doleful predictions are within the realm of the possible but the only one that reaches the level of high probability is the prediction that we are going to have plenty of trouble for the next four or five and perhaps the next twenty years. But to assume in advance that the trouble will be more than we can handle would be the equivalent of pleading *nolo contendere* before the case comes to trial, which may be the philosophy of Spiro Agnew but not that of Abraham Lincoln.

Fifty-five years ago Mr. Justice Holmes described our position with characteristic precision: "Every year, if not every day, we have to wager our salvation on some prophecy based on imperfect knowledge." That's democracy for you, and if you can't stand it the alternative is to go totalitarian, thereby shifting the necessity of choosing to some overlord. Whether the master you choose is Fascist or Communist, the effect is the same—thereafter you will be relieved of the necessity of choosing among the possible ways of life, and the burden of choosing is intolerable to the slave mentality, for to it any tyranny is preferable to responsibility.

Toynbee—I do not apologize for mentioning him, although I am aware that he has been demolished by some Spaniard, for Herodotus, Thucydides, Gibbon, and Mommsen have all been demolished at least once in every generation since they wrote—Toynbee presents a different hypothesis which, while doubtless flawed, as all hypotheses are at their first presentation, accounts for more of the established facts and therefore commands a livelier interest than any other of recent date. That is his theory, mentioned above, of challenge and response as the pattern of the history of civilizations.

It seems to be applicable to the history of the United States since 1945 on account of the position of leadership into which we have been thrust rather than climbed. The theory is that each nascent civilization meets successive challenges to which it makes responses whose energy exceeds that of the challenges—overcompensates, in the modern term. But eventually comes a challenge that the response cannot quite meet and that is the beginning of the end. The descent to Avernus may be steep and short, or gradual and long, but a descent it is.

The challenge facing us, that of devising a "new order of the ages" not for ourselves alone but for Western civilization, may be more than we can meet. If that is true, we are facing the beginning of the end of the experiment in self-government by free men that we launched in 1776 and that our forebears have continued with startling success for nearly two hundred years.

But consider the other half of Toynbee's scheme. As long as a civilization meets its successive challenges with successive responses each more energetic than the challenge, that civilization proceeds from triumph to triumph along whatever road it has chosen. If, then, we can contribute largely to the erection of a stronger and finer world than the fallen Balance of Power, then this Time of Troubles means only that we have completed our apprenticeship to statecraft and are now prepared to undertake some masterwork greater than anything that we have done hitherto or that we can now imagine.

This is the choice that appeals to the mentality of the freeman. It involves labor and danger, both great, but what of that? Freedom has never been easy or safe, and democracy is the most difficult of all forms of government. But a certain number of Americans are committed to it and they have some of the qualifications necessary to preserve it. The question is, are they numerous enough and skillful enough? And the only answer to that is, God only knows.

BIBLIOGRAPHY

OF LONGER WORKS BY GERALD W. JOHNSON

in Chronological Order

The Story of Man's Work. (with W. R. Hayward). New York: Minton, Balch and Company, 1925.

What Is News? A Tentative Outline. Series: Borzoi Handbooks of Journalism. New York: Alfred A. Knopf, 1926.

The Undefeated. New York: Minton, Balch and Company, 1927.

Andrew Jackson: An Epic in Homespun. New York: Minton, Balch and Company, 1927. Reprint, New York: Bantam Books, 1956.

Randolph of Roanoke: A Political Fantastic. Series: Biographies of Unusual Americans. New York: Minton, Balch and Company, 1929.

By Reason of Strength. New York: Minton, Balch and Company, 1930. British edition, *The Strength of Catharine Campbell.* London: G. P. Putnam's Sons, 1931.

Number Thirty Six. New York: Minton, Balch and Company, 1933.

The Secession of the Southern States. Series: Great Occasions. New York: G. P. Putnam's Sons, 1933.

A Little Night Music: Discoveries in the Exploitation of an Art. New York: Harper and Brothers, Publishers, 1937. Reprint, Westport, Connecticut: Greenwood Press, Publishers, 1970.

The Sunpapers of Baltimore: 1837-1937 (with Frank R. Kent, H. L. Mencken, and Hamilton Owens). New York: Alfred A. Knopf, 1937.

The Wasted Land. Chapel Hill, North Carolina: The University of North Carolina Press, 1937. Reprint, Freeport, New York: Books for Libraries Press, 1970.

America's Silver Age: The Statecraft of Clay-Webster-Calhoun. New York: Harper and Brothers, Publishers, 1939.

Roosevelt: Dictator or Democrat? New York: Harper and Brothers, Publishers, 1941. British edition, *Roosevelt: An American Study,* with introduction and notes by D. W. Brogan. London: H. Hamilton, 1942.

American Heroes and Hero-Worship. New York: Harper and Brothers, Publishers, 1943. Reprint, with introduction by Ralph Adams Brown, Port Washington, New York: Kennikat Press, Inc., 1966.

Woodrow Wilson: The Unforgettable Figure Who Has Returned to Haunt Us (with the collaboration of the editors of *Look* Magazine). Series: *Look* Picture Books. New York: Harper and Brothers, Publishers, 1944.

An Honorable Titan: A Biographical Study of Adolph S. Ochs. New York: Harper and Brothers, Publishers, 1946. Reprint, Westport, Connecticut: Greenwood Press, Publishers, 1970.

The First Captain: The Story of John Paul Jones. New York: Coward-McCann, Inc., 1947.

Look at America: The Central Northeast (in collaboration with the editors of *Look* Magazine). Series: Look at America. Boston: Houghton-Mifflin, 1948.

A Liberal's Progress: Edward A. Filene, Shopkeeper to Social Statesman. New York: Coward-McCann, Inc., 1948.

Our English Heritage. Series: Peoples of America. Philadelphia: J. B. Lippincott Company, 1949. Reprint, Westport, Connecticut: Greenwood Press, Publishers, 1973.

Incredible Tale: The Odyssey of the Average American in the Last Half-Century. New York: Harper and Brothers, Publishers, 1950.

This American People. New York: Harper and Brothers, Publishers, 1951.

Pattern for Liberty: The Story of Old Philadelphia. New York: McGraw-Hill Book Company, 1952.

The Making of a Southern Industrialist: A Biographical Study of Simpson Bobo Tanner. Chapel Hill, North Carolina: The University of North Carolina Press, 1952.

Mount Vernon: The Story of a Shrine. New York: Random House, 1953.

The Lunatic Fringe. Philadelphia: J. B. Lippincott Company, 1957. Reprint, Westport, Connecticut: Greenwood Press, Publishers, 1973.

Peril and Promise: An Inquiry into Freedom of the Press. New York: Harper and Brothers, Publishers, 1958. Reprint, Westport, Connecticut: Greenwood Press, Publishers, 1974.

The Lines Are Drawn: American Life since the First World War as Reflected in the Pulitzer Prize Cartoons. Philadelphia: J. B. Lippincott Company, 1958.

America: A History for Peter. 3 volumes: *America Is Born, America Grows Up, America Moves Forward.* New York: William Morrow and Company, 1959-60.

The Man Who Feels Left Behind. New York: William Morrow and Company, 1961.

The Government. 4 volumes: *The Presidency, The Supreme Court, The Congress, The Cabinet.* New York: William Morrow and Company, 1962-66.

Hod-Carrier: Notes of a Laborer on an Unfinished Cathedral. New York: William Morrow and Company, 1964.

Communism: An American's View. New York: William Morrow and Company, 1964.

Franklin D. Roosevelt: Portrait of a Great Man. New York: William Morrow and Company, 1967.

The British Empire: An American View of its History from 1776 to 1945. New York: William Morrow and Company, 1969.

The Imperial Republic: Speculation on the Future if Any of the Third United States of America. New York: Liveright, 1972.

America-Watching: Perspectives in the Course of an Incredible Century. Owings Mills, Maryland: Stemmer House Publishers, 1976.

334

INDEX

This index may be consulted for full names of persons identified partially in the text.

Abishai, 261
Abolitionists, 189
Abrams, General Creighton, 292
Abrams v. United States, 102
Absolutism, 306
Academic freedom, 96-100
Acheson, Dean, 186, 191, 215
Achilles, 263
Adams, John, 9, 125, 144, 146, 174, 209, 302-303, 315, 326, 330
Adams, John Quincy, 10, 48, 174, 186, 289, 315
Adler, Mortimer, 229
Aeschylus, 281
Africa, colonialism in, 106, 284
Agamemnon, 263
Agnew, Spiro T., 291, 297, 331
Agricultural production, 113, 160
Alabama, 22, 134; civil rights movement in, 268
Albany, Georgia, negro economic boycott in, 269
Alcibiades, 195-196, 249
Aldrich, Nelson W., 47
Alexander I, Tsar, 329
Alexander VI, Pope, 73
Alexander the Great, 196, 223
Alexandria, Virginia, 275
Alfred the Great, King, 171
Allen, Fred, 162
American: definition of an, 180; history, teaching of, 121, 144, 148-155, 210; intellectual, 228-229; leaders, philosophy of, 273; leadership, 226; literary tradition, 185; philosophy, 185; people, characteristics of, 325-332
American Cancer Society, 213
American Dilemma, An (Myrdal), 282
American Language, 199
American Legion, 54, 165
American Mercury, 199
American Revolution, 57, 302-303, 326, 327, 330, 331

Americanization, 64
Ames, Oakes, 175-176
Amherst College, 248
Anarchy, 125-126
Anderson, Marian, 234
Annapolis, Maryland, 78, 79, 279
Antietam, 79
Anti-intellectualism, 190, 206
Antinomianism, 164
Anti-Saloon League, 15
Anti-Semitism. *See* Jews
Apartheid, 234
Appeasement, 150, 152, 191
Arabs, 211-212
Architecture, 98; Baltimore, 17-18, 78
Architecture of the Universe, The (Swann), 98
Aristides, 118, 187
Aristocracy, early American Republic seen as, 9-10, 11, 12
Aristophanes, 75
Aristotle, 196, 291
Arkansas, 52
Army. *See* U. S. Army
Arno, Peter, 68
Arnold, Benedict, 171, 172
Arrowsmith (Lewis), 183, 184, 185
Arthur, Chester A., 318
Articles of Confederation, 295, 302
Arts: censorship of, 110, 159-160, 161-163; fine and graphic, 98; as "pastime for women," 72-73; patronage of, 73; revival in South, 35-36
Aryanism, 112
Asheville, North Carolina, 36
Asia: spread of Communism in, 191-192; white colonialism in, 284
Assassinations, 279-281, 285
Assembly, freedom of, 313
Atheists, in America, 81
Athens, ancient, 118, 195-196, 207, 217, 248-249, 268, 278
Atlanta, Georgia, 232
Atlantic Ocean, defense of, 122, 124
Atom bomb, 155-156, 158-159, 189, 190, 259, 260, 262, 321; attack on Hiroshima and Nagasaki, 321-322;

Russia in possession of, 164, 192, 260, 262, 312
Atomic power, 156-159
Attila the Hun, 67
Augustus Caesar, Roman Emperor, 73
Autocracy, 115; colonial America as, 9, 11, 12
Automobile accident deaths, 250-251

Babbitt (Lewis), 183, 185
Babbitt, George F. (fictional character), 18, 73, 117, 183, 184
Bach, Johann Sebastian, 88, 98
Bache, Benjamin F., 185
Bailey, Josiah W., 101
Balance of Power, 327, 332
Baldwin, James, 256-257
Ball, Lucille, 190
Baltimore, First Lord, 81
Baltimore, Maryland, 14-20, 77, 78-79, 80, 81, 83, 172, 199, 221; architecture, 17, 18, 78; race disorders in, 280, 282, 283, 284; race relations in, 282-283
Baltimore *Evening Sun,* 19, 82, 108
Baltimore *Sun,* 15, 107, 108, 110, 200, 201, 221, 256, 259, 262
Bangs, John Kendrick, 32
Banking crisis, early 1930s, 108, 122
Basel, University of, 285, 286
Bay of Pigs invasion of Cuba, 247, 248, 254, 303, 304
Bayard, Pierre Terrail, Seigneur de, 171
Beard, Charles A., 293
Beauregard, General Pierre G. T., 29
Becker, Police Lieutenant, 42
Beethoven, Ludwig van, 89, 118; *Eroica,* 88-89
Ben-Gurion, David, 212
Bennett, James Gordon, 220
Benton, Thomas Hart, 134, 224
Berkeley, Sir William, 171
Berlin airlift, 322-323
Bilbo, Theodore G., 237, 265
Bill of Rights, 100, 104, 313. *See also* Press: freedom of; Speech, freedom of
Birmingham, Alabama, 28; civil rights murders in, 267, 271
Bismarck, Fürst Otto von, 151

Black, Harry C., 201
Black Codes, 234
Black Hundreds, Tsarist Russia, 24
Black Muslims, 256
Black Power, 284
Blacks. *See* Negroes
Blaine, James G., 175
Blease, Coleman L., 237, 265
B'nai B'rith, 6-7
Bolshevism, 100, 103-104, 106, 328
Books, censorship of, 110, 159-160, 161-163
Bootlegging, 42
Borah, William E., 60, 179
Borgia family, 173
Boston, Massachusetts, 9, 16, 172, 279
Boswell, James, 202
Boulanger, General Georges, 88
Bowers, Claude G., 175
Bowles, Samuel, 220
Boyd, James, 27, 29, 36
Bozzaris, Marco, 3
Bradford, Gamaliel, 50
Brancusi, Constantin, 98
Bready, James H., 295
Briand, Aristide, 46
British Empire, 118, 124; fleet, 122
Britton, Nan, 60
Broadway, New York, 28
Broedel, Max, 201
Brogan, D. W., 197, 233, 302
Brothels, police suppression of, 44
Browder, Earl, 119
Brown, John, 46, 174
Brown, Walter, 109
Brown v. Board of Education, 271
Brutus, 3
Bryan, William Jennings, 46, 47, 48, 50, 51, 53, 59, 79, 161, 179, 241, 267, 278, 289, 297; "Cross of Gold" speech, 53
Bryanism, 51
Buddhism, 81, 290-291
Bull Moose Movement, 297
Bunche, Ralph, 234
Bunyan, Paul (mythical hero), 147
Bureau of Standards, 95
Burleson, Albert S., 62, 63
Burr, Aaron, 146-147, 149-150

Business, 151; as employer, 113-114; of 1920s, 67
Butler, Andrew P., 186
Butler, Nicholas Murray, 99
Butler, Samuel, 163

Caesar, Julius, 166, 218, 223, 263, 281, 296
Cagliostro, Count Allesandro di, 46
Caldwell, Erskine, 266
Calhoun, John C., 29, 48, 134, 174, 179, 189-190, 209, 235, 237, 242, 270-271, 275
Calgacus, Caledonian chief, 206
California: annexation, 171; punitive efforts in, 62, 80
Caligula, Roman Emperor, 173, 186
Calvinism, 206
Cambodia, invasion of, 304, 306
Camus, Albert, 302
Cannon, Bishop James, 60
Capitalism, 107, 111, 123-124, 125-126, 279
Capone, Al, 65, 136, 173, 207
Carmack, Edward W., 24, 25
Casca, 274, 277
Castlereagh, Viscount Robert, 327
Castro, Fidel, 260, 261
Catholics: in colonial Maryland, 81; discrimination against, 114; as presidential candidates, 241, 244, 267; parochial schools, 95; Southern bias against, 3, 4, 5, 115
Cato, 171
Cellini, Benvenuto, 27
Censorship, 110, 159-165
Cervantes Saavedra, Miguel de, 75
Chamber of Commerce, 115
Chamberlain, Houston, 265
Chamberlain, Neville, 150, 152, 191
Chaney, James E., 264
Change, resistance to, 166-167, 206-207, 330
Chapman, Gerald, 65
Charlemagne, 319
Charles II, King of England, 171
Charleston, South Carolina, 9, 36
Charles XII, King of Sweden, 145
Charlotte (North Carolina) *Observer,* 14
Chase, Harry Woodburn, 96

Chase, Salmon P., 247
Chateaubriand, François René de, 173
Chaucer, Geoffrey, 259, 261
Chauvinism, 104, 107
Checks and balances, 310
Chesapeake Bay, 275
Chester, Pennsylvania, racial disorders, 268
Chesterton, G. K., 81
Chiang Kai-shek, 191, 225
Chicago, Illinois, 172; racial disorders, 268; police scandals, 42
Child Labor Amendment, 118
Child raising, 84-88
Child's Garden of Verses, A (Stevenson), 183
Childs, Marquis, 329
China: Communist, 249; Communist, Knowland urging war against, 195-197; Communist, Nixon's policy toward, 306; imperial, 208; nationalist, 225; U. S. "loss" of, 191-192
Chinard, Gilbert, 202
Choate, Rufus, 48
Christianity, wars of, 116, 117
Churchill, Sir Winston, 128-129, 314, 329
Cicero, Illinois, 65
Cimabue, Giovanni, 98
Cincinnati, Ohio, 8
Cincinnatus, 303
Cities, 16-17, 145; police scandals in, 41-42, 43-45; political corruption in, 176, 178; race riots, 268, 280, 282, 284
Civil disorders of 1960s, 267-269, 277, 279-280, 282, 283, 284
Civil liberties. *See* Liberty, individual
Civil rights movement, 267-269; murders, 264-266, 267, 271; white backlash, 269
Civil service, purges of "subversives" from, 161-164
Civil War, 29, 30-31, 57, 117, 153, 174-175, 177, 190, 232, 233-234, 236, 257, 275, 299; aftermath, 158; Confederate effort and losses, 30
Civilization, U. S. versus European, 117, 118

Clay, Henry, 29, 48, 134, 174, 186, 235, 236, 289
Clemenceau, Georges, 70
Clendening, Dr. Logan, 74
Cleon, 248, 249
Clergy, in America, 9
Cleveland, Grover, 123, 203
Cleveland, Ohio, police scandals, 42
Coast and Geodetic Survey, 95
Cobb, Frank I., 25
Cohn, Roy, 215
Cold War, 329
Coleridge, S. T., quote from, 256
Collectivism, 126. See also Communism; Fascism; Nazism
Colleges, 94. See also Universities
Collier, Julia, 22
Colonial America, 9, 81, 171, 236
Columbia (South Carolina) Record, 23
Columbia University, 99
Columbus (Georgia) Enquirer-Sun, 22
Communications, changing patterns of, 142, 143, 154, 166, 223, 330
Communism, 100, 106-107, 110-112, 114, 125-126, 163, 167, 312-313; in China, 191; conspiracies blamed for civil disorders of 1960's, 279; in Cuba, 243; in Indo-China, 191-192, 277; McCarthyist attack on, 188, 195, 312; theory of government of, 114, 115. See also Bolshevism; Soviet Russia
Communist Manifesto, 208
Communist Party, U.S., 119, 161; membership statistics, 313
Communist scare. See Communism, McCarthyist attack on; Red scares; Subversion, fear of
Communists, 46, 54, 81, 115, 119, 189, 190, 214, 304, 312-313. See also Bolshevism; Soviet Russia
Compromise of 1850, 174
Concurrent majority, doctrine of, 238
Condon, Edward U., 213
Confederacy, 137, 232, 233, 267; war effort and destruction of, 30
Congressional elections: of 1954, 192-193, 197; of 1970, 297

Conkling, Roscoe, 7, 301
Conscription, 57
Consent of the governed, 115-119
Conservatives, 156, 157; of South, 6, 23-24; at universities, 98-99
Constitution(s). See State constitutions; U. S. Constitution
Constitutional Convention of 1787, 124, 125, 126, 127, 275, 302
Constitutional Limitations (Cooley), quote from, 101
Cooley, Thomas McIntyre, 101
Coolidge, Calvin, 48, 59, 60, 66, 67, 108, 125, 126, 187, 225, 297, 317, 323
Cornell, Ezra, 94
"Corn-field gunboats" policy, 152
Cornford, Francis M., 225, 275
"Corporative state," 117
Corruption, political, 175-177, 305
Cost of living: in 1959, 227; in 1972, 299
Cotton manufacture, in South, 28, 34-35, 36
Cox, James Middleton, 59, 315, 316
Crawford, William H., 224
Credit Mobilier, 175
Cremona, violin makers of, 25
Crèvecoeur, Michel Guillaume Jean de (Hector St. John), 180
Crime, during 1920s, 65
Cromwell, Oliver, 136, 160, 179
Cuba, 260; Bay of Pigs invasion of, 247, 248, 254, 303, 304; Communist takeover, 243; missile crisis, 260, 261
Culture: black versus white, 283-284; democratization of, 158-159, 169-170; technology emphasized over, 208
Czechoslovakia, 191, 324, 329

Dallas, Texas, 271
Dana, Charles A., 24, 25, 220
Daniels, Jonathan, 237
Daniels, Josephus, 23
Danton, Georges J., 235
Darrow, Clarence, 60, 162, 278
Daughters of the American Revolution, 61
David, King of Israel, 261

David Harum (Westcott), 182
Davis, Jefferson, 29, 137, 175
Davis, John William, 59, 267, 315
Dawes, Charles G., 8
"Days" (Mencken), 199
Deak, Francis, 109
Debs, Eugene, 62
Declaration of Independence, 63,
    167, 302, 327, 328
Defense: low U. S. spending for,
    prior to World War II, 122, 131-
    132, 133; naval, 122, 124,
    151-152
De Gaulle, Charles, 225, 245
Delaware, 80
Democracy, 107, 111-112, 115-116,
    117-119, 131, 133, 135, 154, 178,
    179-180, 289, 302-303, 305-306,
    314, 326, 332; defined, 115;
    endangered by arrogation of power
    by politicians, 299-301, 304-308,
    310-311, 318-319; essentials of,
    117-119, 166-170; Jeffersonian,
    143, 145, 153-154, 155, 301, 306;
    majority rule, 87, 179, 314;
    "Second" Republic seen as, 10, 11,
    12; World War II as defense of,
    122-123, 128
Democratic Party, 95, 97, 101, 112,
    116, 133, 134-135, 136-137, 239,
    252, 309, 314-318; coalitions
    across party lines, 161; and
    McGovern nomination, 296, 297;
    need for renewal, in 1960, 242; in
    1924 presidential election, 267; in
    1954 congressional election, 193,
    197; 1956 National Convention,
    24, 203; 1960 presidential can-
    didate, 239-240, 241-242, 316;
    presidential candidates since 1912,
    315-316; Presidents since 1912
    assessed, 316-318; and the South,
    136, 267
Democratization of culture, 158-159,
    169-170
Denby, Edwin, 109
Depression (1930s), 49, 51, 52, 61,
    93, 108, 122, 130, 179, 323;
    recovery from, 131 (*see also*
    New Deal)

Desegregation of universities, 257-
    258
Detroit, Michigan, 168; police
    scandals, 42; racial bias, 235
Dewey, John, 219, 289
Dewey, Thomas E., 239, 259
Diamond, Legs, 65
Dickens, Charles, 229, 277
Dictatorship, 303
Dies Committee, 146
Dill, Clarence C., 101
Disarmament, 13
Doak, William N., 109
Dodd, Thomas J., 256
Dodsworth (Lewis), 183
Domino theory, 276
Donnelly, Ignatius, 297
Dooley, Mr. (fictional character),
    241
Douglas, Helen Gahagan, 227, 292,
    304
Douglas, Stephen A., 146, 186, 242,
    247
Douglass, Frederick, 268
Doyle, James, 240
Drake, Sir Francis, 171
Dred Scott decision, 172, 271
Drew, Daniel, 299
Du Bois, W. E. B., 7, 268
Duffy, Edmund, 201
Duffy, Father Francis P., 267
Dulles, Allen, 254
Dulles, John Foster, 191, 211, 224-
    225, 227, 247, 276-277, 300, 312
Dunkirk, evacuation at, 292
Dunne, Finley Peter, 241
Du Pont de Nemours, Pierre Samuel,
    170, 238
Dwight, Theodore, 185

Early, General Jubal A., 29
Eastern Shore (Maryland), lynchings,
    80
Eastland, James, 237, 238
Economic determinism, theory of, 112
Economics, uncertainty factor in,
    86-87
Economist (London), 139
Economy: of 1970s, 299, 300; post-
    Civil War South, 31, 34-35, 236;
    post-World War I, 160-161, 323;

revival in South, after 1900, 28, 30, 36. *See also* Great Depression
Ecurey, Sir Walter of, 259, 260, 262
Edison, Thomas Alva, 117, 289
Education, 11, 86, 166, 204; elementary schools, private vs. public, 95; graduate schools, 92-95; higher, cost of, 92-95; musical, 84-86, 90-91; preparation for peace as part of, 206, 208; public, 92-95, 166-167; teaching of American history in, 121; of women, 32. *See also* Universities
Edward III, King of England, 256, 261, 262
Edwards, Jonathan, 37
Egypt, 211, 212
Eighteenth Amendment, 4, 19, 82, 274. *See also* Prohibition
Einstein, Albert, 50, 96, 97, 286
Eisenhower, Dwight D., 187, 196, 197-198, 203, 211, 215, 226-227, 242, 243, 247, 322; foreign relations under, 225; information gap under, 252-253; in Little Rock crisis, 230; McCarthy and, 194-195; and Nixon, 192-193, 197-198; and Vietnam, 252-253, 276, 277, 300
Eisenhower, Dr. Milton, 308, 329, 330
Elections. *See* Congressional elections; Presidential elections; Suffrage
Eliot, Charles William, 94, 95
Ellis, Havelock, 74
Elmer Gantry (Lewis), 183
Emancipation Proclamation, 75, 256, 257
Embargo Act of 1808, 124
Energy production, 156-157
Enver Pasha, 3
Equality under the law, 271, 284, 300, 311. *See also* Fourteenth Amendment
Eroica Symphony (Beethoven), 88-89
Euclid, 98
Euripides, 281
Europe, 328; Balance of Power, 327; fear of Americanization, 64; Marshall Plan aid to, 312, 323-324, 329; and NATO, 322-323; police practices and effectiveness in, 44-45; totalitarian regimes of, 100, 103-104, 106, 125-126; universities of, 94; World War II, 122-123, 321
Everett, Edward, 48
Executive privilege, 310
Export trade, U.S., 123
Extremism, 309

Fair Deal, 227
Fall, Albert B., 109, 173, 177, 309
False arrest and charges, 41, 43-44
Farley, James A., 113, 135, 195
Farm Board, 109
Farm subsidies, of 1930s, 113
Fascism, 100, 103-104, 106, 110-112, 115, 118, 126, 177. *See also* Nazism
Faubus, Orville, 238
Faulkner, William, 231, 266
FBI, 165, 225, 264
Federal government, increase in powers of, 77, 123, 124
Federal Reserve System, 66
Federal spending: for defense, 122, 131-132, 133; under FDR, 109-110, 122, 131-132, 133; under Hoover, 109
Federalism, 141, 149-150, 303, 313; new, 303
Federalist, The, 130
Feminism, 75
Fenno, John, 185
Fermi, Enrico, 286
Fess, Simeon D., 109
Fillmore, Millard, 68
Finland, Soviet attack on, 131
First Amendment, 100, 101
First Ladies, 245
Fitzgerald, F. Scott, 294
Flag: salute to, 104; teachings regarding, 106
Florida, 172, 266
Ford, Henry, 35, 68, 113, 289
Foreign policy, U. S., 252-253, 303-304, 312; after World War I, 64, 67; based on fear, 226, 303-304, 312; domino theory in, 276; under Dulles, 191, 211, 225, 227, 276-

277, 300, 312; in Indo-China,
191-192 (*see also* Vietnam);
Marshall Plan aid, 312, 322, 323-
324, 329; of massive retaliation,
227; in Mideast, 211-212; and
morality, 211-212; under Nixon,
304-305, 306, 312; under Truman,
322-324. *See also* International
relations
Forever Amber (Winsor), 161
Forrest, General Nathan B., 29
Fort McHenry, 79
Fosdick, Harry Emerson, 47
Foster, Stephen, 232
Fouché, Joseph, 171, 173
Founding Fathers, 114, 124, 125,
167, 185, 263, 270
Fourteenth Amendment, 230, 271,
300
Fox, George, 46
Foyle, Kitty, 127
France: civil liberties in, 106;
collapse in World War II, 122,
312; departure from Indo-China,
190-191; recovery after wars, 31,
329. *See also* French Revolution
Franchise. *See* Suffrage
Franco, Francisco, 116
Frankfurter, Felix, 97, 99
Franklin, Benjamin, 104, 107, 125,
173, 294
Frederick, Maryland, 82
Free enterprise, 87, 107, 123-124
French Revolution, 152, 221, 288,
303, 327
Freneau, Philip, 185
Freud, Sigmund, 73-74, 75, 294
Fries, Brigadier-General Amos A., 54
Frietchie, Barbara, 82
Froissart, Sir John, 256, 258-259,
260-261, 262
Fulbright, J. William, 188, 300
Fundamentalism, 13

Galen, 287
Galileo, 287
Gallup poll of 1960, 241
Gamaliel, 98
Gambling, 42, 45-46; squads, 42
Gandhi, Mohandas, 47, 268, 279
Garfield, James A., 187

Garibaldi, Giuseppe, 7
Garrison, William Lloyd, 23, 179,
275, 279
Gary, Elbert H., 47
Gastonia, North Carolina, 65
General Motors Corporation, 188
Geneva Conference (1954), 191
Genghis Khan, 67
George III, King of England, 9, 210
Georgia, 22, 174, 237, 283
Georgian architecture, 78
Georgics (Virgil), 33, 237
Germany: background for Hitler's
rise to power, 129-131; demo-
cratic experiment of Weimar, 118;
Enabling Act of 1933, 128;
imperial, 166; Marshall Plan aid
to, 323; Nazi, economic determin-
ism, 112; Nazi, racism, 112, 113,
133, 290; Nazi, rearmament, 131,
146; Nazi, social discipline of,
113; "principle of leadership,"
117, 133; purge of 1934, 136;
recovery after World War I, 31;
totalitarianism, 103-104, 106,
112-114, 117-118 (*see also*
Nazism); in World War I, 54,
123; in World War II, 132, 321.
See also Hitler, Adolf
Gettysburg, Pennsylvania, 257
Giafar, 306
Gibbon, Edward, 332
Gilman, Daniel Coit, 94
Giotto, 98
Girondins, 327
Gladstone, William E., 46
Glasgow, Ellen, 29
Glass, Carter, 101, 116, 146
Gobineau, Comte Joseph Arthur de,
265
Godbey, Earle, 23, 27
Golden Age of America, 10
Goldwater, Barry, 256, 315
Gone With the Wind (Mitchell),
232
Goodman, Andrew, 264
Gordon, Lord George, 46
Government: absolute, 306; and
change, 166-167; checks and
balances in, 310; choice of, in
1787 and in 1940s, 125-127;

Communist theory of, 114, 115; concept of supremacy of the state, 62-63, 104, 106-107, 113, 115; democratic, 107, 111-112, 115-116, 117-119, 143, 145, 153-154, 305-306, 314, 332 (*see also* Democracy); dictatorship and tyranny, 303; function and purpose of, 114, 115, 129-130, 317; Hamiltonian, 114, 142-144; marks of intelligence in, 65-67, 107; phases of, in America, 7-14; provision of public services, 166-169; representative, 306; separation of powers, 310, 311; totalitarian, 87, 103-104, 106, 112-115, 117, 125-126, 332; town-meeting style of, 307

Grady, Henry, 24, 25, 232

Graham, Frank P., 237

Grandfather clauses, in South, 231, 236

Grant, Ulysses S., 8, 47, 173, 175, 177, 232

Great Britain, 82, 118, 306, 329; false arrest consequences in, 44; fleet of, as protection for U. S., 122, 123, 124; and IRA, 284-285; low homicide rate, 44; public education, 166-167; public safety, 166; in World War II, 122, 123, 128, 129, 292

Great Man theory of history, 219, 229

Great Depression. *See Depression* (1930s).

Great Society, 316

Greece, ancient, 169, 196, 248-249. *See also* Athens; Sparta

Greek tragedy, 264, 281

Greeley, Horace, 24, 25, 167, 220

Green, Paul Eliot, 27, 28, 36

Green Pastures, The (Connelly), 41

Greenbackism, 51

Greensboro, North Carolina, 27-28, 268; *News,* 23

Greenville, South Carolina, 165

Grote, George, 195, 248, 249

Guest, Edgar A., 117

Gump, Andrew (fictional character), 5

Haardt, Sara, 200-201

Haiti, 11, 64, 283

Hall, Grover, 22-23, 27, 28, 34

Halsted, Dr. William S., 15

Hamilton, Alexander, 114, 125, 130, 140-148, 185, 275, 309, 313, 315; background of, 144, 146; duel with Burr, 145, 146-147; *Federalist* theory of, 130, 313; versus Jefferson, 140-145, 148-151, 152-155; realist or idealist, 140-148, 153, 154-155; role in 1800 election, 149-150

Hamiltonianism, 114, 140-141, 142-144, 145-155

Hammurabi, 331

Händel, Georg Friedrich, 89

Hanna, Mark, 47

Hanoi, bombing of, 304, 312

Harding, Warren G., 59, 60, 67, 108, 173, 225, 294, 315, 316, 317; scandals in administration of, 60, 173, 305, 311

Harlem, riots in, 268

Harper's Magazine, 69, 171, 174, 222

Harriman, E. H., 47

Harris, Julian, 22, 23, 27, 28, 34

Harrison, Benjamin, 203, 263, 294, 296

Harrison, William Henry, 187

Harun al-Rashid, 306

Harvard, John, 94

Harvard University, 92, 94, 95, 99

Haugen, Gilbert N., 21

Hay, John, 47

Haydn, Franz Joseph, 89

Hayes, Rutherford B., 3, 161, 203, 230, 298

Hazlitt, William, 219, 296

Heflin, J. Thomas, 60, 134, 194-195, 237, 265, 269

Heilbroner, Robert, 326

Hemingway, Ernest, 228

Henry, O. (*pseud.*). *See* Porter, William Sydney

Henry, Patrick, 125, 209

Herodotus, 332

Herrenvolk, 179, 265, 290. *See* also Master race

Herrin, Illinois, 65

Hersey, John, 218
Heyward, DuBose, 27, 28, 29, 36
Hibbard, Addison, 29
Hindemith, Paul, 88, 98
Hinduism, 163
Hiroshima, 155, 156, 322
Hiroshima (Hersey), 218
Hiss, Alger, 254-255
Hitler, Adolf, 88, 100, 104, 106,
    111, 112-113, 114, 135, 136, 137,
    139, 145, 162, 173, 177, 179, 182,
    292; arms spending of, 131, 146;
    background for rise to power, 129-
    131; versus Roosevelt, 128-133,
    138-139.
Ho Chi Minh, 276, 306
Hobbes, Thomas, 326
Holmes, Justice Oliver Wendell, 102-
    103, 104, 105, 106, 255, 302, 303,
    331-332
Hoover, Herbert C., 8, 48, 49, 54, 55,
    59, 60, 67, 107, 108, 109-110,
    112, 125, 225, 238, 315, 317
Hoover, J. Edgar, 313
Hopkins, Johns, 79, 94
Hopkins, Mark, 94, 219
House Un-American Activities
    Committee, 213-214
Hughes, Charles E., 8, 225
Hughes, Rupert, 60
Hugo, Victor, 249, 292
Hull, Cordell, 108
Human Society in Ethics and Politics
    (Russell), 325
Humphrey, Hubert H., 301, 316
Hungary, 1956 uprising in, 205, 208
Hyde, Henry, 201
Hydrogen bomb, 192, 215, 286

Ickes, Harold L., 109
Illinois, 172
Illiteracy, 231, 237
Impeachment, 310-311
Imperialism, 295, 307, 327
Income tax, 54, 66
India, 192, 211, 212; British repres-
    sion in, 118
Indian campaigns (American), 55,
    56, 57

Indo-China: French departure from,
    190-191; U.S. policy in, 191-192.
    See also Vietnam
Indonesia, 276
Industrial Revolution, 124, 130, 288
Industry, in South, 28, 34-35, 36
Inflation, 299, 300
*Influence of Sea Power Upon History,
    The* (Mahan), 151
Ingersoll, Robert, 162
Intellectuals, 51-52, 228; in New
    South, 28-29, 30, 32, 36, 270; as
    political leaders, 46-47, 50, 209
International relations, U.S.: after
    World War I, 63-64, 67; after
    World War II, 211-212, 225, 226,
    311-312, 318, 323-324; Nixon
    policies, 306. *See also* Foreign
    policy
International trade, 123-124
Interposition, doctrine of, 238. *See
    also* Nullification, doctrine of
Irish Free State, 82
Irish Republican Army (IRA), 284-
    285
Isaiah (Prophet), 139
Isolationists, 138, 156
Israel, 211-212, 280
Italy: "corporative state," 117;
    democratic government of 1920s,
    118; totalitarianism, 103-104, 106,
    117, 118. *See also* Fascism
Ivan the Terrible, Tsar, 306

Jackson, Andrew, 10, 12, 29, 115,
    147, 174, 230, 245, 301, 315;
    lack of education, 47; leadership
    quality of, 46, 47-48, 50, 53; and
    Rachel, 38-40; stature of, 146, 147
Jackson, Andrew, Jr., 38
Jackson, Rachel, 38-40
Jackson, General Thomas J.
    ("Stonewall"), 29
Jacksonians, 47
Jacobins, 327
Jaffé, Louis, 27, 28, 34
James, Jesse, 173
Jameson, Sir Leander Starr ("Dr.
    Jameson"), 88
Jamestown, Virginia, 236, 331

Japan, 56, 159, 198, 306, 317, 321; atom bomb attacks on, 158, 321-322; police of, 161
Jaspers, Karl, 285-286, 287, 289-290
Jay, John, 309
Jeans, Sir James, 50
Jefferson, Thomas, 9-10, 29, 94, 125, 130, 145, 146, 148-154, 156, 161, 170, 185, 203, 235, 237, 238, 273, 315; as appeaser, 150; Dolley Madison as official hostess for, 245; election to presidency, 149-150; versus Hamilton, 140-145, 148-151, 152-155; idealist or realist, 140-145, 150-155, 314; personal qualities of, 46-47, 150-151, 301; political philosophy of, 9-10, 103, 145, 153-155, 161, 303, 306, 314; as a politician, 66; as President, 151-152, 301; quoted, 103, 145, 161, 190, 314; and slavery, 275
Jeffersonianism, 114, 141, 143, 145, 153-154, 155, 306
Jenner, William E., 186
Jeremiah (Prophet), 235
Jersey City, New Jersey, ghetto riots, 268
Jesus Christ, 207, 279
Jews: bias of South against, 114; differentiated from Zionists, 299; discrimination against, 114, 162; Nazi persecutions of, 113; religious freedom of, 81
John Birch Society, 249, 309
John Lackland, King of England, 171, 173
John of Austria, 145
John of Gaunt, 261, 262
John of Leiden, 291
Johns Hopkins University, 79, 94, 99, 201; Institute of Law, 92; Medical School, 19-20; Medical School founders, 15
Johnson, Andrew, 194; impeachment of, 311
Johnson, Hiram W., 60
Johnson, General Hugh S., 96
Johnson, John Arthur (Jack), 7
Johnson, Lyndon B., 240, 247, 313, 315, 316, 319; Great Society of,

316; and Vietnam, 275-276, 277, 300, 304
Johnson, Samuel, 240
Johnston, General Albert S., 29
Johnston, General Joseph E., 29
Joinville, Jean de, 259-260
Journalism: function of, 221, 256-262; influence of, 185, 288-289; personal, 21-27, 217-224; pundits of, 259
Julian, Roman Emperor, 135
Julius, Pope, 210

Kaiser, 160
Katanga, 256
Keats, John, 232, 233
Kefauver, Estes, 203
Kelly, Dr. Howard A., 15, 19
Kemble, Fanny, 38
Kennedy, Jacqueline Bouvier, 244-246
Kennedy, John Fitzgerald, 203, 243, 276, 313, 319; assassination of, 262, 279, 281; and Bay of Pigs invasion, 247, 254, 303; as a politician, 247; presidential candidate in 1960, 239-240, 241-242, 243-244, 316; as President, 246-248, 252-253; tragedy and legend of, 262-264; and Vietnam, 252-253, 276, 277, 300
Kennedy, John Pendleton, 232
Kennedy, Joseph Patrick, Sr., 112, 281
Kennedy, Joseph Patrick, Jr., 281
Kennedy, Kathleen, 281
Kennedy, Robert Francis, 279, 280-281, 282, 285
Kent, Frank, 221
Kent, James, 102, 103
Kentucky, Pineville, 65
Ketch, Jack (as eponym of hangmen), 214, 287, 291
Khrushchev, Nikita, 245, 247, 260
Killian, Dr. James R., Jr., 215
King, Martin Luther, Jr., 268, 269, 279-280, 282, 285
King, Rufus, 125
Kipling, Rudyard, 329
Kissinger, Henry, 303, 304-305, 306, 312, 315, 330

Knickerbocker Trust Company, 48
Knights of Columbus, 6-7, 315
Knowland, William, 195-196, 197
Know-Nothingism, 51
Korean War, 165, 252, 279, 322
Kosciusko, Thaddeus, 3
Ku Klux Klan, 3-7, 8, 13, 115, 165,
   267, 315; Baltimore and, 19, 20;
   FDR and, 110; post-Civil War
   years of, 36-37; Southern press
   and, 22, 24

Labor, 164, 175; Plutocrats' attitude
   toward, 11, 113; strikes, 113, 226-
   227; supply, 160
Labor racketeering, 113
Lady Chatterley's Lover (Lawrence),
   134
Lafayette, Marquis de, 79, 245
La Follette, Robert M., 289
LaGuardia, Fiorello, 146
Lancaster, Henry, Earl of, 261
Landon, Alfred M., 107, 109, 112,
   114, 119, 134
Laos, 249; invasion of, 304
Latham, Robert, 27, 28, 34
Law, John, 176
Leadership: defined, 47, 52-53; and
   intellectualism, 46-47, 50, 52, 209,
   324; lack of, 46-50, 67; U.S., 209
"Leadership principle," Nazi
   Germany, 117, 133
League of Nations, 66, 67, 178, 327
Lease, Maryellin, 297
Le Duc Tho, 305
Lee, Euel, 80
Lee, General Robert E., 29, 79, 168,
   174, 177
Leisure, 157, 158
Lenin, Vladimir I., 50, 114, 136,
   145, 182, 288, 328
Leninism, 112
Léon, Ponce de, 166
Leonardo da Vinci, 73
Lewis, Sinclair, 183-185
Lex talionis, 284
Libel, press and, 101
Liberalism, liberals, 46, 52, 188, 203-
   204, 229, 291-292, 313; of Adlai
   Stevenson, 273-274; post-World
   War II, 156-159, 239; Roose-

veltian, 203-204; Wilsonian, 66,
   204, 229
Liberty, individual, 87, 100-107,
   313; during Wilson's presidency,
   61, 62-63; in 1920s, 62, 63. *See
   also* Press, freedom, of; Religion,
   freedom of; Speech, freedom of
Library of Congress, 95
Lincoln, Abraham, 3, 7, 10, 62, 66,
   115, 139, 146, 174, 187, 233, 246,
   248, 263, 273, 275, 296, 315,
   331; Emancipation Proclamation
   of, 75, 256, 257; as a politician,
   66, 247
Lincoln, Mary Todd, 245
Lindbergh, Anne Morrow, 130
Lindbergh, Charles A., 65, 152
Lindsay, Vachel, 210
Lippmann, Walter, 47, 248, 259,
   288-289, 293, 320
Liquor, police control of, 42, 46
Literacy tests, for voter registration,
   231
Literature, 98; censorship, 110, 159-
   160, 161-163; revolt of the 1920s,
   184-185; Southern flowering, 27,
   28-29, 32
Little Rock, Arkansas, 230, 238
Livingston, Cora, 38, 39
Livingston, Edward, 186
Lloyd George, David, 46
Lodge, Henry Cabot, Sr., 47, 60, 178
Long, Huey, 177, 179, 187, 194,
   195
Longstreet, General James, 29
Longworth, Nicholas, 8
Los Angeles, California, 16, 106
Lost Generation, 29
Louis IX (Saint Louis), King of
   France, 259-260
Louis XIV, King of France, 310
Louis XVI, King of France, 221
Louisiana, Black Codes of, 234; Mer
   Rouge, 65
Lowden, Frank, 8
Luther, Martin, 4
Lycurgus, 331
Lynchings, 37, 80. *See also* Ku Klux
   Klan

McAdoo, William G., 267

MacArthur, General Douglas, 292, 322

McCarthy, Joseph R., 186, 189, 194-195, 215, 227, 248, 249, 292, 303, 312

McCarthyism, 188, 195, 241, 249, 312

McClellan, General George B., 79

McCormack-Tydings bill, 101, 103

McCosh, James, 308

Macdonald, Ramsay, 9

Macedon, 196, 249

McGill, Ralph, 237

McGovern, George S., 296, 297, 298, 299, 301, 316

Macintosh, Douglas Clyde, 63

McKinley, William, 187, 241, 278

McNary, Charles L., 21

Mad Mullah (Mohammed Ahmed), 50, 51

Madison Avenue, New York, 204

Madison, Dolley, 244-245

Madison, James, 29, 66, 125, 146, 153, 235, 237, 245, 246, 315, 320

Mafia, 24

Mahan, Admiral Alfred T., 151, 152

Main Street (Lewis), 183, 184, 185

Maine, 242

Majority rule, 87, 179, 314

Malenkov, Georgi, 196

Manet, Edouard, "Olympe" of, 246

Mao Tse Tung, 259, 260

Marcus Aurelius, Roman Emperor, 180

Marcy, William L., 318

Marshall, General George C., 186, 323

Marshall, John, 29, 235

Marshall, Thurgood, 234

Marshall Plan, 295, 312, 322, 323-324, 329

Martial law, 9

Marx, Karl, 163

Mary (Bloody), Queen of England, 177

Maryland, 19, 76-83, 101, 275, 279; architecture, 78; Catholics and Jews in, 81, 114; in colonial era, 9, 81; Court of Appeals, 80; Eastern Shore of, 77, 80; lynchings, 80; place names, 78; Salisbury, 65; State Constitution, 82, 103, 114

Mason, George, 125

Masons, in Mexico, 117

Masrour, 306

Mass production, 117

Massachusetts, 80, 172; in colonial era, 9; non-church members excluded from full citizenship, 114; racial bias, 236

Massive retaliation, 227

"Master race" concept, 133, 290. *See also Herrenvolk*

Materialism, 45, 144

Mather, Cotton, 160

Mayflower, The, 270

Means, Gaston B., 60

Medford, Massachusetts, 236

Medical profession, 43

Medici, Lorenzo de', (the Magnificent), 27, 73, 147

Mellon, Andrew, 8, 12, 35, 108, 109

Mencken, H. L., 16, 19, 43, 60, 107, 108, 172, 199-202, 219, 220, 221, 293

Mencken, Sara Haardt, 200-201

Mendelssohn-Bartholdy, Felix, 113

Mendès-France, Pierre, 191

Mensheviks, 327

Mer Rouge, Louisiana, 65

Meredith, James, 257

Meredith, Owen, 74

Merovingian dynasty, 319

Metternich, Fürst Clemens Nepomuk, 327

Mexican War, 57

Mexico, 57-58, 117, 119

Mill, John Stuart, 210

Millikan, Robert A., 50

Missiles, 215-216, 259-260, 262; Cuban crisis, 260, 261

Mississippi, 242, 257; Black Codes of, 234; civil rights murders in, 264-266, 271

Mississippi Bubble, 176

Mississippi Valley, 168

Missouri Compromise, 143, 153, 189

Mitchell, Broadus, 99

Mitchell, Margaret, 232

Mitchell, Martha, 297

Mommsen, Theodor, 182, 332

346

Monarchy, rejected in 1787, 125, 126
"Monkey laws," 46, 96
Monroe, James, 10, 66, 237, 304
Montgomery, Alabama, streetcar boycott, 268
Montgomery, Alabama, *Advertiser,* 22
Mooney, Tom, 60, 62
Morality, defined, 235
Morals: loosening of, 87; police misplaced as guardians of, 42-45
Morgan, House of, 49
Morgan, John Pierpont (the elder), 47, 48, 297
Morgan, John Pierpont (the younger), 49
Morgenthau, Henry, Jr., 109
Morse, Samuel F. B., 142, 154
Moslems, 81, 117
Mosley, Oswald, 122
Mount Vernon (home of Washington), 275
Mozart, Wolfgang Amadeus, 73, 89
Mulrooney, Edward P., 41, 46
Munich Conference (1938), 191, 212
Murphy, J. Edwin, 201
Murphy, Edgar Gardner, 237, 265, 269
Music, 36, 88-92, 98; amateurs of, 89-92; education, 84-86, 90-91; of Foster, 232; as "pastime for women," 72-73
Mussolini, Benito, 7, 50, 79, 88, 104, 106, 111, 145, 179, 182; Hitler compared to, 112
Myrdal, Gunnar, 234, 282

Nagasaki, 322
Napalm, 287, 291
Napoleon Bonaparte, Emperor, 89, 144, 172, 223, 249, 288, 292, 327, 329
Napoleon III, Emperor, 89
Nashville, Tennessee, 39
National Association for the Advancement of Colored People, 6-7, 267
National Association of Manufacturers, 156
National debt, 113, 122, 160

National Museum, 95
National security, 303, 310
Nationalism, 290-291
NATO, 322-323
Naval unpreparedness, 122, 151-152; World War II, 122, 124, 152
Navy. *See* U. S. Navy
Nazism, 100, 103-104, 106, 112-114, 118, 126, 136, 290. *See also* Fascism
Nearing, Scott, 97
Negroes: alleged inferiority, 234, 265, 283-284; civil rights murders of, 264-266, 267, 271; cultural development, 234, 283-284; discrimination against, in South, 115, 230-231, 234, 236; emancipation of, 75, 256, 257; as "freedmen" versus "freemen," 258, 271-272; first arrival in American colonies, 236, 270; literacy tests for voter registration, 231; lynchings, 80; as noncitizens, 114, 234, 257; partisan voting patterns, 299; progress of, 237, 268, 269-271, 282-283; race riots of, 268-269, 277, 280, 282, 283, 284; racial bias against, 3, 4, 5, 163, 234-236, 265, 283; Southern, assimilation of, 270-272; Southern, civil rights movement, 268-269; Southern, population figure, 268
Nehru, Jawaharlal, 259
Nero, Roman Emperor, 145, 171, 306
New Deal, 77, 108-110, 129, 132-135, 139, 204, 227; constitutionality of measures questioned, 101
New England: town-meeting government, 307; triangular trade, 236
New Jersey, 114, 237
New Market, Virginia, 29, 30, 31, 37
New Orleans, Louisiana, 28, 38, 39, 172; Battle of, 40, 143; racial bias, 236
New Republic, 239
New York City, 15, 16, 168; Brooklyn Bridge, 176; Central Park, 176; as cultural and social center, 16-17, 39; Harlem riots, 268; police scandals, 41, 42, 44, 45;

prostitution, 43-44; Southern playwrights on Broadway, 28; Tweed ring, 175, 176, 178

New York Times, 307

New York *World,* 12, 25

New Yorker, 256

Newark, New Jersey, 16

Newman, Frances, 27

Newspapers: influence of columns versus editorials, 221; personal journalism, 21-27, 217-224; of South, 4, 6, 21-24, 26-27. *See also* Press

Nicaragua, 11, 56, 64

Nicias, 196, 248-249

Nixon, Richard M., 203, 211, 296, 312, 313, 319, 321; abuse of power by, 304-307, 310-311, 330; assessment of, 242; campaigns against Jerry Voorhis and Helen Gahagan Douglas, 227, 292, 304; Eisenhower and, 192-193, 197-198; foreign policy of, 304-305, 306, 312; and Hiss case, 254-255; and impeachment, 310-311; 1972 reelection of, 304-305; as President, 292-293, 296-297, 304-305, 306-307, 310; presidential candidate in 1960, 240, 241-242, 244, 247, 316; presidential candidate in 1968, 304, 316; presidential candidate in 1972, 297, 299, 301, 316; as Vice President, 192, 193, 197, 198, 203, 211, 304; and Vietnam War, 292, 299-300, 304-305, 306, 312; his White House staff, 305, 306, 310

Non-violence, policy of, 268-269

Norfolk, Virginia, 28

North Atlantic Treaty Organization, 322-323

North Carolina, 14, 15, 23, 27, 28, 33, 36, 53, 86, 234, 237, 245, 293; Battle Hymn of, 240; civil rights movement, 257, 268; Civil War effort and destruction, 30; Gastonia, 65; grandfather clause in voting registration, 231; Reconstruction in, 30; University of, 33, 172, 237

North Vietnam, 276, 300, 304

Northcliffe, Viscount Alfred Charles, 25

Notes on Virginia (Jefferson), 142

Nuclear age, 259-260, 262, 286, 290-291. *See also* Atom bomb; Hydrogen bomb

Nullification, doctrine of, 174, 230. *See also* Interposition, doctrine of

O'Bannion, Dion, 60, 65

Obeah, 283

Odum, Howard W., 237, 265, 269

Office of Production Management, 132

Ohio Gang, 11

Oil industry, 156

Oppenheimer, J. Robert, 189-190, 207, 213, 215, 222-223, 286, 292

Oregon, annexation of, 171

Osborn, Henry Fairfield, 47

Osler, Sir William, 15

Over-production, 51

Ovid, 216

Owens, Hamilton, 201

Owens, John, 201

Pacifism, 53-58

Page, Thomas Nelson, 232

Page, Walter H., 30

Painter, Sidney, 173

Palmer, A. Mitchell, 62, 63, 206

Panama, 57

Panics, financial: of 1837, 51; of 1907, 48; of 1929, 49, 51

Parton, James, 38, 39

Patriotism, degeneration of: into chauvinism, 104; into fanaticism, 206; into nationalism, 290

Patterson, Paul, 201

Pavlov, Ivan Petrovich, 97

Peabody, George, 79

Peabody Conservatory of Music, 79

Peace, education of Americans for, 206-209

Pearl, Raymond, 201, 202

Pearson, Drew, 289

Peloponnesian War, 248

Pennsylvania, University of, 92

Pennsylvania State University, 92

Penrose, Boies, 47

Peonage, in South, 24

People, selective constitutional
   definitions, 114-115
People v. Croswell, 102
Pepin the Short, 319
Percy, William Alexander, 36
Peres the Ploughman's Crede
   (Langland), 166
Pericles, 73, 217, 248
Perkins, George W., 297
Pershing, General John, 53
Pétain, Marshal Philippe, 59
Peter the Great, Tsar, 171-172, 329
Peterkin, Julia, 27, 28, 29, 36
Ph.D. degree, 92-93
Phidias, 73
Philadelphia, Mississippi, murders in,
   264, 266, 267, 271
Philadelphia, Pennsylvania, 16;
   Convention, 275
Philippines, 11
Phyfe, Duncan, 219
Pickering, Timothy, 303
Pierce, Franklin, 263
Pinckney, Charles, 236
Pineville, Kentucky, 65
Pioneers, American, 121
Pittsburgh, Pennsylvania, police
   scandals, 42
Plancus, consulship of, 210
Plato, 98, 158, 263
Platt, Thomas Collier, 47
Plessy v. Ferguson, 271
Plutocracy, "Third" Republic seen as,
   10-13
Plutocrats, 10-11; as presidential
   candidates, 7-9, 12
Poincaré, Raymond, 70
Poland, 324, 329; German attack on,
   132; Soviet attack on, 131
Pole, Sir Michael de la, 258-259
Police, 41-46; in England, 44; in
   European countries, 45; false
   arrest and charges by, 41, 43-44;
   function of, 43; scandals, 41, 42,
   44, 45; vice squads, 41-42, 43-44
Political competence, 115-116, 117-
   118
Political parties, U. S., 116, 134-135,
   136-137, 241, 296, 298-299, 314-
   316; arrogation of power by,
   299-301; coalitions across party

lines, 161. *See also* Democratic
   party; Republican party; Two-
   party system
Polk, James, 66
Polyandry, 283, 284
Polygamy, 284
Polytheism, 283
Populism, 50-51, 265
Porter, Sylvia, 227
Porter, William Sydney (O. Henry),
   27-28, 233
Potomac River, 275
Power production, 156-157
Praxiteles, 73, 98
Prejudices (Mencken), 172, 199
President Is Calling, The
   (M. Eisenhower), 329
Presidential candidates, 119; of 1900,
   241; of 1924, 267; of 1928, 315;
   of 1936, 107, 109, 134; of 1940,
   127, 134; of 1948, 239; of 1956,
   187-188; of 1960, 239-240, 241-
   242, 316; of 1972, 296, 299,
   301; Plutocrats as, 7-9, 12
Presidential elections: of 1800
   (Jefferson-Burr tie), 149, 298; of
   1828, 298; of 1860, 298; of 1876
   (Hayes-Tilden dispute), 3, 161,
   298; of 1896, 297; of 1912, 297,
   298; of 1924, 267, 315; of 1928,
   48; of 1932, 298; of 1936, 107,
   135; of 1940, 133; of 1948, 239,
   278; of 1952, 197, 198, 252; of
   1960, 241-242, 244; of 1968,
   285, 304; of 1972, 296-301, 304-
   305; 1972 dirty tricks, 305
Presidents, 314-319, 320; of aristocratic "First Republic," 9-10; of
   democratic "Second Republic," 10;
   education of, 47; from the South,
   29, 237; Virginia dynasty, 9, 174,
   237
Press: freedom of, 100-103, 104-106,
   313; and Watergate, 305. *See also*
   Journalism; Newspapers
Priestley, J. B., 228-229
Princeton University, 92, 95; Institute
   for Advanced Study, 96
"Principle of leadership" (Nazi
   Germany), 117, 133
Prior restraint, 101-102

Private property, 131
Production: agricultural, excess of,
113, 160; New Deal boost to,
108-109, 122
Prohibition, 13, 19, 54, 82, 99,
178, 274, 278, 279; abolished,
110. *See also* Eighteenth Amend-
ment; Volstead Act
Prohibition squads, 42
Proletariat, 112, 115, 145; dictator-
ship of the, 117
Propaganda, 119, 220
Property, private, 131
Property requirement for full citizen-
ship, 114
Prostitution, 41, 42, 43-44, 45, 74
Prussianism, 62
Public health services, 11, 166, 167
Public opinion, informed, tradition
of, 118-119
Public safety, 166, 167, 168
Public services, 166-170
Public transportation, 166, 167
Public utilities, 156
Public welfare, 122, 169. *See also*
Welfare
Public works: graft in, 176; New
Deal programs, 108, 109-110, 131
Pulitzer, Joseph, 25
Pulitzer, Ralph, 25
Pulitzer Prize, 28, 34, 36
Puritanism, 9, 37, 160, 162-164

Quacks, 43
Quarles, Donald A., 208, 209
Quay, Matthew Stanley, 47

Rabelais, François, 73-74, 75
Race riots, 268-269, 277, 280, 282,
283, 284
Racial discrimination, 114, 115, 230-
231, 234; in voter registration in
South, 231, 236
Racial prejudice, 3-7, 234-237, 265,
282-284, 300; of Nazi Germany,
112, 113, 133
Racketeering, 42, 65; labor, 113
Radicalism, at universities, 96-99
Radio, 221; censorship of, 161-163;
and Watergate, 305
Railroads, 142, 156, 175-176

Raleigh News and Observer, 23
Randolph, Edmund, 125
Randolph, John, 48, 186, 236
Ransom, John Crowe, 36
Rascob, John J., 60
Realism, political, defined, 308-309
Reason, defined, 270
Reconstruction Finance Corporation
(RFC), 109
Reconstruction of South, 29-37, 206,
231, 236
Red scares, 46, 54, 100, 110, 162,
163, 164, 304, 312-313
Reed, James A., 60
Reed, Thomas, 47
Reid, Whitelaw, 47
Reign of Terror, 288
Religious discrimination, 81, 114.
See also Catholics; Jews
Religious freedom, 81
Remarque, Erich Maria, 29
Republic: First, 9-10, 11; Second,
10, 11, 12, 13; Third, 10-12
Republican Party, 95, 100, 116, 134-
135, 137, 239, 278, 314-315,
316; coalitions across party lines,
161; 1928 National Convention
of, 7, 9; 1928 presidential hope-
fuls, 8-9, 12, 315; 1936 presidential candidate, 107, 134; 1940
presidential candidate, 127, 134;
in 1952, 252; in 1954 congressional elections, 192, 197; 1960
presidential candidate, 241-242,
316; in 1972 elections, 299-300;
and McCarthy, 194; and Watergate
burglary, 309; weakness of, in
1954-55, 194, 197
Research institutes, 94, 98
Research work, 94, 95, 97-98, 285-
287
Reston, James, 293
Revolution(s), 116, 117, 130, 288,
302-303, 327-328; right of, 327,
328
Reynolds, Robert ("Our Bob"), 237
Rhee, Syngman, 225
Rhett, Robert Barnwell, 174
Richard II, King of England
(Richard of Bordeaux), 258, 261
Richmond, Virginia, 172

Riots: racial, 1960's, 268-269, 277, 280, 282, 283, 284; World War I, 65
Ritchie, Albert Cabell, 82
Robertson, Field Marshal Sir William, 8
Robespierre, Maximilien de, 179, 288
Rochester, New York, ghetto riots, 268
Rockefeller, John D., 121, 175
Rockefeller, Nelson A., 241
Roland, 263
Roland Park, Baltimore, 18
Rolfe, John, 331
Rome, ancient, 171, 175, 274, 303
Roosevelt, Eleanor, 245, 299
Roosevelt, Franklin D., 114, 115, 116, 122, 128-140, 146, 157, 164, 182, 194, 210, 227, 242, 245, 246, 248, 267, 278, 328; absence of corruption under, 135-136; assassination attempt on, 214, 281; assessment of, 316, 317, 318; background for his election, 129-131; bankers and, 214; black support for, 299; called a dictator by critics, 110, 301, 310; vis-à-vis Churchill, 128-129; Common-wealth Club speech of, 139; election margins of, 136-137; "fear of fear itself" quote, 303, 307; federal spending under, 109-110, 122, 131-132, 133, 135; fireside chats of, 253, 310; first administration praised, 107-110, 317; versus Hitler, 128-133, 138; his impact on political system and debate, 133-134, 289; liberalist heritage of, 203-204; 1940 reelection of, 133; personal qualities of, 138-139, 301; revival of Democratic Party by, 267; stature of, 146; Theodore Roosevelt and, 102; and Truman, 321; and UN, 327; war-time support for, 137-138; and war unpreparedness, 131-133
Roosevelt, Theodore, 10, 12, 60, 178, 203, 207, 239, 278, 281, 315; Bryan's influence on, 47, 51; and

F. D. R., 102; as a leader, 47, 48, 49-50, 316-317; as a politician, 66
Rosenwald, Julius, 8
Ruark, Robert, 251
Rubinstein, Anton Gregor, 88
Runnymede, 234
Rush, Richard, 186
Russell, Sir Bertrand, 9, 97, 325
Russia, 329. See also Soviet Russia
Russian Revolution, 288, 302, 327-328

Sacco, Nicola, 60, 62, 80, 99
Saint-Just, Louis Antoine Leon de, 288
Saint Paul, 98, 163, 180, 236, 291
Salem witch-hunts, 171, 206
Salisbury, Maryland, 65
San Francisco, California, 16
Sargant, Dr. William, 274, 277
Sargent, John Singer, 20
Saudi Arabia, 211
Saul, King of Israel, 261
Schachner, Nathan, 185
Schine, David, 215
School integration, 257-258, 271, 283
Schools, public, 166-167; versus private schools, 95
Schopenhauer, Arthur, 220, 294
Schubert, Franz, 89
Schwerner, Michael, 264
Science, 151, 285-287, 290-291
Scopes trial, 45, 96
Scotland, 233, 234
Secession, 233. See also Nullification, doctrine of
Secret societies, 24
Segregation, 235, 267
Senate Watergate Committee, 310
Separation of powers, 310, 311
Serbia, 30
Sévigné, Madame de, 71
Sewall, Samuel, 171
Seward, William H., 247
Sex, 73-75; education, 73
Shakespeare, William, 148, 183, 223
Sharpsburg, 79
Sherman, Roger, 125
Sherman, General William Tecumseh, 172, 175, 232

Shimei, 261
Sibelius, Jean, 73, 88
Sieyès, Abbé, 181
Silver, James W., 271
Simmons, Colonel William Joseph, 3-7
Sinclair, Upton, 106
Sit-ins, civil rights, 268
Slavery, 189, 233-234, 256-257, 275; abolition, 256; earliest trade, 236, 270
Smith, Alfred E., 48, 50, 59, 112, 267, 303, 315
Smith, Lillian, 266
Smithsonian Institution, 95
Smoot, Reed, 134
Smoot-Hawley Tariff, 43
Social conscience, 113
Social discipline, 113-114, 115
Social Forces, 29
Social security, 108
Social services, 179. *See also* Welfare
Socialism, 111, 124; in university faculties, 98-99
Socialist Party, 156, 161
Society women, 71
Socrates, 98, 207, 219, 277, 279, 291
Sodom, 44
Soil Conservation Program, 160
Solon, 181, 331
Sophocles, 281
South, 158, 177-178, 230-238, 266-272; arts in, 35-36; assimilation of blacks, 270-272; Black Codes of, 234; black-to-white population ratio, 268; civil rights movement in, 268-269; civil rights murders in, 264-266, 267, 271; conservatives of, 6, 23-24; cultural lag of, 230; de jure discrimination, 231, 236; desegregation, 257-258, 267; economic revival, after 1900, 28, 30,36; and F. D. R., 136-137; filibustering bloc in Senate, 177; industry, 28, 34-35, 36, 168; intellectual regeneration, 30, 32, 36; the land and the legend, 232-233; literary revival, 27, 28-29, 32; "lost generation" of, 29-37, 237-238; lynchings, 37, 80; news-

papers and journalism in, 4, 6, 21-24, 26-27; in 1924 election, 267; in 1932 election, 136-137; pogroms, 5, 24; political process of, tainted by fraudulence, 231, 236; political thinking, 270-271; post-Civil War economy, 31, 34-35, 236; racial discrimination, 115, 230-231, 234, 236; racial prejudice, 3-7, 234-236, 265, 269; religious prejudice, 3, 4, 5, 81, 115, "Solid," 136, 267; voter registration laws, 231, 236; white attitudes toward civil rights movement, 269. *See also* Reconstruction of South
South Africa, apartheid legislation of, 234
South Carolina, 23, 36, 242; racial bias, 236
South Vietnam, 276-277
Southeast Asia, 276, 300. *See also* Indo-China; Vietnam
Soviet Russia, 158, 168, 196, 208, 312-313, 329; attacks on Finland and Poland, 131-132; and China, 191; detente policy toward, 306; "dictatorship of the proletariat," 117; economic determinism, 112; exports of, 46; Kennedy and, 247; Marshall Plan aid rejected by, 323-324, 329; and Mideast, 211, 212; nuclear capability, 164, 192, 260, 262, 312; totalitarianism, 103-104, 106, 114-115, 117-118; wheat sale to, 306. *See also* Bolshevism; Communism; Russian Revolution
Space exploration, 215-216, 260
Spain, 116; Inquisition, 63
Spanish War, 57
Sparta, 196, 248, 249
Speech, freedom of, 100-101, 102-103, 104-106, 118, 119, 313
Spellman, Cardinal Francis J., 263
Sputnik, 215, 216
Stalin, Joseph, 88, 112, 114, 115, 162, 163-164, 182, 288, 327; Hitler compared to, 112
Stallings, Laurence, 27, 28
Standard of living, 168

State: function and purpose of, 114, 115; idea of supremacy of, 62-63, 104, 106-107, 113, 115; "religion" of the, 103-107
State capitalism, 124
State constitutions, 114; Maryland, 82, 103, 114; Southern, literacy test-grandfather clause, 231
State socialism, 124
State universities, 92-93, 94-96, 98-99
States, sovereignty of, 275
Statute of limitations, 255
Stavisky, Serge Alexandre, 176
Steel industry, 226
Steele, Wilbur Daniel, 27
Stephens, Alexander H., 29, 146
Stephenson, George, 142, 154
Stevens, Thaddeus, 173, 194
Stevenson, Adlai E., 186, 187-188, 203-204, 215, 239-240, 241, 243, 247, 248, 273-274, 289, 294, 316
Stevenson, Robert Louis, 183
Stock market: crash of 1929, 49, 108, 121, 125, 173, 323; in 1959, 227
Stravinsky, Igor, 88
Stribling, T. E., 27
Strikes, labor, 113, 226-227
Stringfield, Lamar, 28, 36
Stuart, General James E. B., 29, 33
Student unrest, 279
Suburbia, 18; women of, 71
Subversion, fear of, 100-107, 162, 249, 303. See also Red scares
Suez Crisis of 1956, 205
Suffrage: grandfather clause in literacy tests, 231, 236; limitations on, 114-115; Southern racial discrimination in, 231, 236; women's, 66
Sukarno, Achmed, 276
Sumner, Charles, 172, 179, 186
Sumner, William Graham, 167
Sunday, Reverend Billy, 15
Surplus tax, 118
Swallow Barn (Kennedy), 232
Swann, W. F. G., 98
Symington, Stuart, 240, 247
Syracuse, ancient, 195-196, 248

Szilard, Leo, 286

Taft, William Howard, 12, 47, 209
Taft-Hartley Act, 226
Talleyrand-Périgord, Charles Maurice de, 140, 173, 245, 327
Talmadge family, of Georgia, 237, 238
Tamerlane, 67
Tammany Hall, 73, 79, 95
Taney, Roger B., 172, 270
Tarheelia, 251
Tariff legislation, 108. See also Smoot-Hawley Tariff; Underwood Tariff
Tariff of Abominations, 141
Tarleton, Colonel Banastre, 152
Taxation, 54, 109, 118, 167; federal 122. See also Income tax
Taylor, Zachary, 263
Teapot Dome oil scandal, 177, 278
Technology, emphasis on, 208, 209, 215, 286, 330, 331
Television, 221; and Watergate, 305, 307
Temple University, 92
Tennessee, 39; monkey law of, 46, 96
Texas, annexation of, 57, 171
Theocracy, 160; colonial America as, 9, 11, 12; philosophy of, 13
Thirteenth Amendment, 256
Thomas, Norman, 64
Thompson, William Hale (Big Bill), 13
Thoreau, Henry David, 220
Thucydides, 248-249, 332
Thyssen, Fritz, 146, 152
Tilden, Samuel J., 161, 298
Times (London), 25
Tojo, Hideki, 182
Tom Sawyer (Twain), 184
Tonkin Gulf Resolution, 300, 304, 318
Totalitarianism, 87, 103-104, 106, 112-115, 117, 125-126, 332
Town meeting, 307
Toynbee, Arnold J., 196, 207, 328, 332
Tragic Era, The (Bowers), 175
Transportation, 142, 154

Triangular trade, 236
Tristan and Isolde (Wagner), 89
Trotsky, Leon, 9-10, 288
Truman, Harry S., 161, 174, 203,
215, 227, 239, 247, 252, 278,
279, 316, 318, 320-324; A-bomb
decision of, 321-322
Tugwell, Rexford G., 109
Tydings, Millard E., 101
Twain, Mark, 228; *Tom Sawyer,* 184
Tweed, William Marcy, 175, 176,
178, 318
Two-party system, 241, 296, 314.
See also Political parties, U.S.
Tyler, John, 48, 66

Underwood Tariff, 66, 67
Unemployment: of Great Depression,
51, 123; in 1959, 227; of 1970s,
299, 300
Union Pacific Railroad, 175
United Nations, 158, 211, 243, 256,
322, 327
Universities: and academic freedom,
95-100; American versus European, 94; desegregation of, 257-
258; income of, 92, 93-94;
private versus public, 92-96, 98-
99; private, justification of, 96-100;
research function of, 94, 95, 97-98
University of Mississippi, 257, 258
University of North Carolina, 29, 33,
96, 237
University of Pennsylvania, 92
University of Virginia, 29
Upshaw, William D. ("Earnest
Willie"), 82
U. S. Army, 55, 56, 101, 120, 121,
160
U. S. Congress, 101, 236; in Eisenhower's presidency, 192-193, 197,
242; and "subversives," 213-214;
and Vietnam War, 300, 304. *See
also* Congressional elections; U. S.
House of Representatives; U. S.
Senate
U. S. Constitution, 9, 82, 101, 102-
103, 114, 124, 129, 132, 236,
270, 295, 302, 303; Bill of
Rights, 100-107, 313; compact
theory of, 238; doctrines of inter-

position and nullification, 174,
230, 238; "high crimes and misdemeanors" phrase of, 311; called
"an experiment" by Holmes, 102-
103; need for overhaul of, 313;
Preamble, 311; separation of
powers, 310, 311; signers of, 328;
war-making powers, 300; "We,
the people" defined, 144
U. S. economy, 156, 160, 176-178;
hunger in, 130
U. S. geography, 171-172
U. S. governing policy, 166
U. S. history, 121, 172, 183
U. S. House of Representatives, 65,
101; impeachment power of, 311;
Un-American Activities Committee,
213-214
U. S. Navy, 54, 55, 56, 101, 152;
post-World War II, 160; weakness,
122, 124, 151-152
U. S. Navy Department, 100, 132
U. S. politics, 160-161
U. S. Senate, 100-101, 103, 134, 310;
Southern filibustering bloc in,
177
U.S.S.R. *See* Soviet Russia
U. S. Supreme Court, 63, 231, 311;
Dred Scott decision, 172, 271;
1954 school desegregation decision
(Brown v. Board of Education),
257, 271, 282; *Plessy v. Ferguson*
(separate but equal) decision, 271
U. S. War Department, 100, 132;
in 1815, 143
U. S. wars, 55, 56, 57; presidents in,
61
U-2 incident, 253

Van Buren, Martin, 66, 301, 315
Vanderbilt, Cornelius, 299
Vanderbilt University, 95
Vanzetti, Bartolomeo, 60, 62, 80, 99
Vere, Robert de, Duke of Ireland,
258-259, 261
Vermont, 242
Vice Squads, 41-42, 43-44
Victoria, Queen, 294
Victorian era, 87
Vietcong, 277
Viet-Minh, 191

Vietnam, 312; early U. S. involvement in, 252-253, 300; War, 276-277, 279, 284, 285, 292, 295, 299-300, 304, 306, 312; withdrawal from, 292-293, 300, 304-305, 306, 312
Violence: during and after World War I, 64-65; of 1960s, 278-285
Virgil, *Georgics,* 33, 237
Virginia, 80, 152, 275; in colonial era, 9, 171, 236; Military Institute, 29; presidential "Dynasty," 9, 174, 237
Virginia Quarterly Review, 29, 266
Volstead Act, 12, 82. *See also* Prohibition
Volunteer army, 57
Von Braun, Wernher, 215-216
Voorhis, Jerry, 292, 304
Vote. *See* Suffrage
Voter registration laws, Southern grandfather clause in, 231, 236

Wagner, Richard, 89; Wagnerian opera, 130
Wake Forest University, 257-258
Walker, James J., 161
Wall Street, 37, 48-49, 156
Wallace, Henry A., 109, 162, 164, 192
Walter family, London *Times,* 25
War, 53-58, 116-117, 205-206, 288; debts, 13; declarations of, 300
War of 1812, 57, 247
War of Jenkins' Ear, 117
Wars, American, 55, 56, 57; presidents in, 61
Warwick, Earl of, 175
Washington, Booker T., 268
Washington, George, 9, 10, 11, 29, 38, 79, 125, 126, 127, 139, 140, 142, 168, 185, 237, 245, 248, 263, 273, 275, 301, 315, 328; Baltimore statue of, 18, 20; decision-making of, as President, 150; and Hamilton, 147, 149, 150; stature of, 146, 147
Washington, D.C., 16, 42, 77-78; race riots in, 280, 284
Washington Post, 307

Watergate affair, 302, 305, 307-308, 309-311, 316, 321
Watson, Albert W., 269
Watson, John B., 50, 97
Watterson, Henry, 24-25, 34, 47, 220
Wealth, distribution of, 108-109
Wealth of Nations, The (Smith), 87
Webster, Daniel, 48, 134, 174; in Benét story, 265
Welch, Dr. William Henry, 15, 166
Welfare: recipients of, 122; state, 174
Wessel, Horst, 174
West, Andrew Fleming, 95
Wheeler, Wayne B., 73
White, Walter, 37
White, William Allen, 47
White House: first ladies, 244-246; Nixon staff, 305, 306, 310
White supremacy, 4-7, 234, 265, 283-284
Whitman, Walt, 289, 305
Whittier, John Greenleaf, 82, 174
Wilbur, Curtis Wright, 109
Wilbur, Ray Lyman, 109
William the Silent (William I, Prince of Orange), 263
Williams, Tennessee, 266
Willkie, Wendell, 134, 137
Wilmington, Delaware, 16
Wilson, Edmund, 161
Wilson, Thomas Woodrow, 12, 23, 29, 59, 115, 139, 161, 173, 187, 210, 237, 239, 294, 314, 315, 316, 317-318, 328; administration of, 61, 62-63, 64, 66, 67-68, 316-317; his administration compared with 1920s policies, 59-68; assessment of, 10, 46-47, 65-66, 182; Bryan and, 51, 79, 161; hate for and criticism of, 52, 60, 62, 172, 194, 195; as a hero, 172; as a leader, 46-47, 50, 67-68, 316-317; and League of Nations, 178, 327; and Mexico, 119; political philosophy of, 66, 204, 229, 317-318, 330-331; at Princeton University, 94, 95; stature of, 146
Wise, Rabbi Stephen Samuel, 47
Witherspoon, John, 94

Woman suffrage amendment, 66
Women: American Womanhood, 69-73; education of, 32; emancipation of, 75; job opportunities, 75, 86; pay, 75; and sex, 73-75; upper versus lower class, 71
Wood, Clement, 27
Woollcott, Alexander, 201
Woollcott, William, 201, 202
World Court, 13
World War I, 29, 30, 53-54, 55, 57, 62, 64, 122, 123, 278; cost of, in casualties and money, 109; World War II seen as continuation of, 126
World War II, 122, 126, 132, 278, 300, 317, 321, 329; U. S. military unpreparedness, 122, 124, 131-133, 152; use of atom bomb, 321-322
Wright, Charlton, 23, 27
Wycliffe, John, 259

Xenophon, 292

Yale, Elihu, 94
Yale Divinity School, 63
Yale University, 94
Yorktown, Battle of, 147
Younger Generation, 68-69

Zangara, Giuseppe, 214
Zionists, 299

AMERICA-WATCHING

Designed by Gerard A. Valerio

Composed by the Service Composition Company, Baltimore, Maryland
in Garamond
Printed by Universal Lithographers, Inc., Timonium, Maryland
on 70 lb. Mohawk Superfine, Eggshell Finish
Bound by the Delmar Company, Charlotte, North Carolina
Frontispiece photograph by C. B. Nieberding
Binding design by Madeline Hebbel of KBH Graphics, Inc., Baltimore, Maryland
inspired by a wrought-iron screen incorporating the initials KJ and GJ,
originally designed by Stephens Berge, executed by Carl Arndt, and mounted on
the terrace at the home of Kathryn and Gerald W. Johnson.